Philip and Athens

Views and Controversies about Classical Antiquity
General Editor: M. I. Finley

Philip and Athens

Selected and introduced by
S. PERLMAN
Tel-Aviv University

HEFFER / *Cambridge*
BARNES & NOBLE BOOKS / *New York*
(division of Harper & Row Publishers, Inc.)

This volume first published in 1973
by W. Heffer & Sons Limited
Cambridge, England

Heffer ISBN 0 85270 076 8
Barnes & Noble ISBN 06 495518 4

[*The pagination of the present
volume is given in square brackets*]

Photographically reprinted in Great Britain
by Lowe & Brydone (Printers) Limited
Thetford, Norfolk

Contents

Acknowledgements

Acknowledgements for permission to use material reproduced i this volume are due to the authors, and as follows:

I   Oxford University Press for the University of Hul for *Koine Eirene*

II   *La Parola del Passato*
Gaetano Macchiaroli Editore, Napoli

III, IV, X   *Classical Quarterly*
Clarendon Press, Oxford

V   *Revue des Études Grecques*
Société d'Édition 'Les Belles Lettres', Paris

VI   *Journal of Hellenic Studies*
© Society for the Promotion of Hellenic Studies London

VII   *Historia*
Franz Steiner Verlag, Wiesbaden

VIII   The Director, University of California Press, Berkeley for *Demosthenes*

IX, XII   *Classical Philology*
Reprinted by permission of The University o Chicago Press. © The University of Chicago Press 1938, 1948

XI   Deutsche Akademie der Wissenschaften zu Berlin

Introduction

In the course of his reign, Philip II (359–336) succeeded in establishing a strong and stable government in Macedon, in acquiring the hegemony over Greece, and in laying the foundations for further expansion and conquest in Asia. These were startling achievements and, already in antiquity, they were regarded as extraordinary and out of proportion in comparison with the history of Macedon until his accession. Typical expressions of this opinion are the famous pronouncement of Theopompus naming Philip the greatest man of Europe[1] and the lavish praise by Diodorus in the opening chapters of his sixteenth book. There may have been some flattery in this praise;[2] but there was certainly an excellent reason for the historian to voice it: the history of Philip's reign, as Diodorus plainly states, provided a clear framework for the history of the whole of Greece, making it feasible to treat this history as a continuous and consistent narrative. The applicability of this methodological principle to the history of Philip's reign should not be taken as an argument in the depreciation of his achievements; it should, however, be borne in mind, especially when Philip's relations with the world of the Greek city-states are under consideration.

The relations between Macedon and Greece during the reign of Philip II, his policies leading to the establishment of his hegemony over Greece, and the reactions of the Greek city-states, especially of Athens and her leading politicians, these are the subject of this collection. Though this is only one approach to the over-all picture of Philip II's achievements, it is, perhaps, the most important one. The main developments permitting an evaluation of Philip's diplomacy and of his policy towards the Greek city-states are: (1) Philip's policy in respect of Chalcidice, Amphipolis and the cities of the Thermaic Gulf; (2) the negotiations leading to the Peace of Philocrates and the basic principles of that peace; (3) the settlement in Greece after the battle of Chaeronea and the establishment of the Corinthian League. All these are directly or indirectly concerned with the relations between Athens and Macedon, and several of the articles have been chosen because they represent an attempt at a new line of evaluation of Athenian policy. The attitudes and basic ideas of the great political leaders of Athens (especially the justification of the Panhellenic ideology in the struggle against Philip) and the main tenets and aims of Philip's settlement in Greece further elucidate the complicated pattern of Macedonian–Greek relations. The limited space of a volume of this kind prevents the inclusion of many other excellent papers and parts of larger works which are still easily available to the reader;

but the bibliographical list will prove, I hope, to be of some help in this respect.

It is the absence of excerpts from the larger works especially that prevents an evaluation of Philip's achievements against the background of Macedonian history and the development of Macedon's policies towards Greece. It may be appropriate, therefore, to add to this introduction a brief account sketching the background, thus helping the reader to assess the achievements of Philip II.

The history of Macedon really begins when this northern kingdom comes into contact with the Greeks during the Persian wars. The earlier Macedonian migrations and conquests are known only in meagre outline.[3] There is still no unanimity among scholars as to the origin of the Macedonians and their ethnic relationship to the Greeks. Though most agree that the Macedonians were a Greek tribe, it is also clear that they remained for a long time outside the main stream of political and cultural developments within the Greek world. Only at the beginning of the fifth century B.C. was a conscious effort made by a Macedonian king to gain recognition as a Greek. Alexander I (c. 494–450 B.C.) was admitted to the Olympic games, probably following upon a vigorous propaganda campaign publicizing his Philhellenic policy during the Persian wars. Nevertheless, the Macedonians were regarded as a non-Greek people ruled by a Greek dynasty.[4] The policy of Hellenization, which Alexander I inaugurated, did not strike deep roots even at the Macedonian court and certainly did not spread widely. The policy of inviting Greek artists and men of letters to reside at the Macedonian court was continued in the fifth and fourth centuries.[5] And while it is true that greater importance was probably attached to (and greater interest shown in) the attainments of material culture and the acquisition of certain technological advances made by the Greeks, especially in warfare, this trend was accompanied by a modicum of spiritual Hellenization at court; it was this combination that singled out the Macedonians from among their northern neighbours. Not only was the Macedonian royal house recognized as a Greek dynasty, thus providing Macedon with a historical past common to all the Greeks, but the policy of Hellenization also served to justify Macedonian claims to a position of influence in the Greek world.

Macedon differed from Greece first and foremost by her lack of urbanization; and it even seems that those cities which developed on Macedonian soil very soon turned against the Macedonian monarchy. But, though Macedon remained a territorial monarchy, t very early adopted one of the most important Greek reforms, establishing an army of hoplites.

Once again, there is no consensus of opinion among modern scholars as to the date of the reform and its scope.[6]   The elevation of the infantry — as πεζέταιροι — only to the status of equality with the aristocratic cavalry was an important step towards the organization of the popular assembly and the development of Macedonian absolutism.   The transformation of the infantry into the hoplite army and the building of strongholds and improved roads were probably a lengthy process.   There can be no doubt that Philip II improved the organization of the phalanx and fostered its tactical use in battle.   It may also be that, because of his conquests, Philip II could attach the hoplites more closely to his own person and to the monarchy.   But it is also certain that the military reform began not long after the Persian wars, and that there was a phalanx in the Macedonian army already in the fifth century.   In this, too, the Macedonians were closer to developments in the Greek world than their northern neighbours.

The success of the Greeks in the wars against the invading Persians also resulted in the liberation of Macedon from Persian suzerainty.   Alexander I Philhellene could now turn his energies and his military power to expansion.   This expansion was directed southward toward the Thermaic Gulf, and eastward to Thrace up to the Strymon; in both cases the expansion was towards the Aegean and the Greek world, and soon brought Macedon into conflict with Athens, which was then emerging as the hegemonical Greek power.[7]   The expansion towards Thrace also brought the silver mines of Dysorus within the Macedonian sphere, thus augmenting the income of the Macedonian king and providing him with the means to strengthen his position both at home and abroad.[8]   Possibly Alexander I had already exploited the rivalry between Athens and Sparta in order to promote Macedonian interests in Thrace.

Thus it was Alexander I who had set the course of Macedonian expansionist policy; and the limits of that expansion were not greatly exceeded before Philip II.   The Macedonian kings were satisfied with the vassal and dependent position of the kingdoms of Orestis, Elymiotis and Lyncestis,[9] which maintained their autonomy and their own princely houses.   Makeshift arrangements, mainly defensive and alternating between war and peace, were all that could be achieved in Macedon's relations with the Illyrians. Macedonian expansion was directed from the first towards the Greek city-states, or towards areas in which the Greek city-states were interested.

Perdiccas II (*c.* 450–413/12), who succeeded his father after an internal struggle for the throne,[10] maintained the integrity and independence of Macedon in the face of the incursions and interference of the leading Greek powers and in spite of the attack by the Odrysian Thracians under Sitalces.[11] This he achieved by a policy of shifting alliances, thus exploiting the rivalry between Athens and Sparta during the Peloponnesian War. Perdiccas' support of Potidaea in her revolt against Athens was a counter measure directed against the establishment of Amphipolis in 437 B.C.[12] His support of the establishment of the Chalcidic League caused Athens to react by conquering Therme and supporting Sitalces' attack on Macedon.[13] The Athenian success at Sphacteria and the appearance of Brasidas in the north brought Perdiccas II even closer to the Spartan side, in the hope that Brasidas would help in subduing Arrhabaeus, prince of Elymiotis.[14] The failure of this policy brought about a change, namely, the agreement with Athens in 422 B.C.;[15] but then again there was a revival of the alliance with Sparta in 418,[16] and finally a joint attack against Amphipolis in 414,[17] Macedon supported Athens.

Perdiccas II certainly attained his goal. Though he did not increase the territory of the kingdom, Macedon remained free and independent in the face of all incursions and attempts to limit Macedonian sovereignty. The great Greek powers were opposed not by arms, but first and foremost by diplomacy. This diplomacy of shifting alliances now became one of the traditional methods employed by the Macedonian kings in order to safeguard their independence from the Greeks.

Archelaus (413/12–399), who ruled Macedon during the second part of the Peloponnesian War, was a great promoter of Greek culture in Macedon; he also built roads and strengthened fortresses in the country. It may very well be that Archelaus wanted to strengthen Macedon both militarily and culturally before embarking on an active foreign policy. However, Archelaus pursued a policy of peace and friendship with Athens during most of his reign. This policy was caused by the weakness of Athens during the second part of the Peloponnesian War and by the priority given to Macedon's military problems. The Athenians were most grateful to Archelaus for his support of democracy in 411, and the policy of friendship between the two states was based on the preservation of the *status quo*: Macedon would not intervene in Thrace or Chalcidice, and Athens would not intervene in the Thermaic Gulf. Archelaus gave support for the building of the Athenian fleet, and the Athenians extended help in subduing the revolt of Pydna.[18] It

,as only after the Peloponnesian War that Archelaus embarked on
, policy of expansion. It was probably not long before 400 B.C.
hat Archelaus intervened in Thessaly in support of the Aleuadae.
Ie chose the moment well: the Greek states were weakened after
he Peloponnesian War; Sparta was preparing for the campaign in
Asia, and Persia was still under the influence of Cyrus the Younger's
evolt. Macedon could now try the policy of expansion again.
t is possible that the Macedonian king now gained the district of
'errhaebia.

The first Macedonian thrust towards Greece proper caused a
trong reaction. Sparta, though busy with her campaign in Asia
Minor, fortified Heraclea at the entrance to central Greece, and
stablished a garrison at Pharsalus. The pamphlet περὶ πολιτείας,
:omposed at about the same time, calls for the expulsion of the
)arbarian Macedonians and the preclusion of any interference on
heir part in the affairs of Greece.

Archelaus' attempt at expansion into Thessaly was cut short by
:he dangers threatening Macedon from the north, especially on the
)art of Lyncestians and Illyria, and by internal unrest; the latter
resulted in the murder of Archelaus in 400/399 B.C. It is interesting
:o note that the policy of expansion in the direction of Thessaly was
later revived by Amyntas III and Alexander II; in both cases, the
international situation in Greece was very similar to that which
prevailed at the first attempt by Archelaus. It was the weakening
of Macedon through the internal struggle for succession, on the one
hand, and the revival and strengthening of a Greek power striving
for hegemony, on the other, which probably prevented the successful continuation and fulfilment of this policy of expansion. But
there can be no doubt that the three Macedonian kings of the fifth
century determined the pattern and the aims of their country's
later foreign policy.

In the fourth century, the Olynthian League and then Thebes
joined the number of strong hegemonical powers which interfered in
the internal affairs of Macedon, hindered Macedonian expansion
and even tried to extend their influence and territories at the
expense of Macedon.[19] Amyntas III not only invoked the help of
Sparta against Olynthus, but later even joined Athens as a counter-
measure directed against the growing power of Sparta. The
Theban intervention after Leuctra increased the internal unrest in
Macedon after the murder of Alexander II. The ascension of
Perdiccas III and the murder of Ptolemy of Alorus were acts of
anti-Theban policy; in order to shake off the oppressive influence
of Thebes, Macedon chose the path of pro-Athenian policy. A

further shift took place, however, after the battle of Mantinea when Macedon conquered Amphipolis, leaving Athens little option but to accept the new state of affairs in the north.[20] Perdiccas II probably saw in Amphipolis a stepping-stone for further expansion To ensure the success of his policy, Perdiccas III felt it imperative first of all to protect his borders to the west and to the north; the battle against the Illyrians put an end to the life of Perdiccas III, and so cut short a successful beginning.

It was in this manner that the Macedonian kings of the fourth century (prior to the accession of Philip II) continued the policy of repeatedly shifting alliances with the leading Greek powers, while at the same time trying to expand their influence towards the Aegean, Thrace and Thessaly. But although the fourth-century Macedonian kings managed to preserve the integrity of their kingdom, as did their predecessors of the fifth, they were not very successful in stabilizing their rule and their achievements, or in preserving Macedonian conquests intact. Although Perdiccas II's death in the fifth century was followed by a struggle for the succession accompanied by considerable unrest, the periods of internal instability and contention for the throne were much longer and more violent in the fourth century. Philip II himself had to defend his throne against pretenders and competitors, and it would seem not unlikely that only his murder prevented a possible renewal of internecine strife.

The internal struggles undoubtedly weakened Macedon in the fourth century. They were often provoked and stirred up by the leading Greek powers. Their impact was not disastrous only because the Greek hegemonical powers and their leagues were weakened at the same time. When Philip II became ruler of Macedon, Sparta was practically isolated in the Peloponnese, the Boeotian League had been dissolved, and the second Athenian League was foundering. The means and the aims of Macedonian foreign policy with respect to the world of the Greek *poleis* had been determined by his predecessors. The changes in inter-*poleis* relations and in the structure of power in the Greek world provided a new opportunity to Philip II.

Notes

1 *F.Gr.H.* 115 F 27.
2 Polyb. 8.9–11.2.
3 Thuc. 2.99.
4 Hdt. 5.20; Isocr. V 107–108. For the Athenian propaganda against the Greekness of the Macedonians and the Philhellenic claims of the royal dynasty, see Dem. XXIII 200; Lyc. *c. Leocr.* 71; cf. Dem. I 5; VI 21, 25; XVIII 66; Ps.-Dem. XII 7.
5 Hippocrates and Melanippides were reported to have stayed at the court of Perdiccas II. It was, however, Archelaus who, more than any other king, endeavoured to imbue the Macedonians with the spirit of Greek culture. In the fourth century Perdiccas III maintained close contacts with the Academy (Euphraeus), and these ties were kept up during the reign of Philip II (Speusippus). Philip had the opportunity to learn about Greeks and their culture as a hostage in Thebes. The invitation to Aristotle to come to Pella was likewise within the tradition of the Macedonian court.
6 *F.Gr.H.* 72 F 4; Thuc. 2.100.2; Diod. 16.3. The reform is variously attributed to Alexander I, Archelaus, Alexander II, and Philip II.
7 Thuc. 1.100–101; Plut. *Cimon* 14–15; cf. Hdt. 9.75; Thuc. 4.102; Diod. 11.70.5; 12.68.2; Paus. 1.29.4; Isocr. VIII 86.
8 Hdt. 5.17; Thuc. 2.99; Head, *H.N.²*, 199–200.
9 Thuc. 2.99.2.
10 For the chronology of the Macedonian kings, see K. J. Beloch, *Griechische Geschichte*, III², 2, 49–72.
11 Diod. 12.50; cf. Thuc. 2.29.
12 Thuc. 4.102.
13 Tod, no. 68; Bengtson, *Staatsverträge*, no. 165; Meiggs–Lewis, no. 65. On the repulsion of the Thracian attack and the agreement with Sitalces and Seuthes: Thuc. 2.101; Diod. 12.51.2.
14 Diod. 12.67–68.
15 Bengtson, *Staatsverträge*, no. 186.
16 Bengtson, *Staatsverträge*, no. 196.
17 Thuc. 7.9.
18 Diod. 13.49.2; Andoc. II 11; Meiggs–Lewis, no. 91.
19 Olynthus: Xen. *Hell.*, 5.2.11 sqq.; Bengtson, *Staatsverträge*, no. 249, 253; Tod, vol. II, p. 33. The attempt at expansion by Alexander II in Thessaly: Diod. 15.61. The intervention of Thebes in Macedonian internal affairs: Bengtson, *Staatsverträge*, no. 265; cf. no. 277; Aesch. II 26 sqq.; Diod. 15.77; 16.2.
20 Aesch. II 30.
21 Diod. 16.2.4.

1

T. T. B. Ryder

The Eclipse of the Leading Powers and Rise of Macedon

VI

The Eclipse of the Leading Powers and Rise of Macedon

THROUGHOUT the period covered by the last three chapters Common Peace was, as it were, a going concern. One at least of the three leading states, and often more, had been at any one time struggling to win the position of protector of the Peace, and there had been some loosening of the old spheres of influence to match the developments and adaptations in the treaties themselves. But, though in some respects the Peace of 362/361 was an improvement on its predecessors, since it was not concluded through the initiative of any one power or through the private compromise of any two powers to further their own policies, but apparently through general weariness, and since it was accompanied by the germs of an idea of defensive unity against external enemies, yet after it the leading states seem no longer interested in a Common Peace policy.

The Spartans remained absorbed in their feud with the Messenians, their diplomacy in Greece directed towards obtaining allies against them and their activities outside Greece towards replenishing the treasury; and when in 353 they canvassed other Greek states about substituting 'possessing their own territory' for 'having what they held' in the terms of the Peace[1] (an interesting indication that the Peace was still thought to be valid in spite of the warfare of the intervening period), their motive was clearly to find recognition and military support for their claim to Messene, and they met with no favourable response.

The Thebans made a desultory attempt in the Peloponnese to assert their own interpretation of the demobilization clause in the treaty soon after its conclusion.[2] But their energies were

[1] Dem. xvi. 16.   [2] Diod. xv. 94. 2.

subsequently taken up in maintaining their power in centra
Greece, where the struggle with the Athenians continued in
directly in Thessaly and then in Euboea. The showdown wit.
the Phocians in 356 was a part of this struggle,[1] but it develope
into a protracted and exhausting war of its own, on whic
Theban efforts were concentrated for a decade. There is n
sign in the sources that the Thebans tried to use championshi
of political liberty as a propaganda weapon in this war alon;
with their avowed support of the god of Delphi.

It is not possible to pass definite judgement on the Atheniar
diplomatic activity recorded on inscriptions from the years 362
361 and 361/360: the making of alliances with four Peloponne
sian states, the Arcadians, Achaeans, Eleans and Phliasians, anc
then with the Thessalians.[2] These moves clearly were directec
against the Thebans, but it is not certain that they should be seer
as a return to a policy of bilateral alliances and as evidence o
loss of faith in the effectiveness of the latest treaty; the treaty
after all in spite of its compulsory guarantee clause providec
no definite machinery for states feeling in need of protection te
obtain it, and it was natural that they should seek the security
of a precise contract with one more powerful, regarding it, as
it were, as within the framework of the Peace. The confederacy
had been formed as such an alliance, but these new allies were
not enrolled into it, though the confederate states were included
in both alliances as the allies of the Athenians,[3] and their council
was consulted before the conclusion of the first,[4] and may well
have been before that of the second also.

Whatever the truth about these alliances, there are other
signs that the Athenians had abandoned their policy of respect
for the principles of Common Peace. Callistratus, its most
powerful advocate, was prosecuted again and this time exiled;[5]
and the Athenians' attitude towards their allies seems to have
become more high-handed. The practice of sending settlements
of Athenian citizens to key places in and around the Aegean,

---

[1] For previous trouble with Phocians—Xen. *Hell.* VII. v. 4; Phocian exiles
honoured at Athens—*IG* ii². 109 (year 363); Athenian alliance with Phocians at
the beginning of the war—Diod. xvi. 27. 5 and 29. 1.

[2] Tod 144 and 147; the first came after the battle of Mantinea, see Tod's commentary, pp. 137 ff.

[3] Tod 144, vv. 18–19; 147, vv. 12–13.   [4] Tod 144, vv. 12–14.

[5] Cf. Sealey, art. cit., *Historia*, v (1956), 197 ff.

which had been one of the most unpopular features of the fifth-century empire and against which the territory of the confederates had been guaranteed in the charter, had been resumed with Samos probably as early as 365; and cleruchies were now sent to the newly captured Potidaea (in 362/361) and Methone.[1] It is true that neither city is known to have been enrolled into the confederacy, and so the letter of the charter was probably not infringed, and that the settlers sent to Potidaea were invited by the pro-Athenian government,[2] but these moves were not likely to allay anxiety. Moreover, the captures of these and other cities round the north-west Aegean were episodes in the unsuccessful campaign against Amphipolis; and this was continued with some vigour even after the Peace might have been expected to put an end to the Theban threat in the area, which could have constituted an excuse for Athenian action in the sixties; and the cities, it seems, became simply dependents of Athens, though probably secured with some assistance from the allies. Efforts to secure the Chersonese also continued, and dangerous succour was sent to rebellious satraps, while the internal security of the Aegean was neglected to the extent that Alexander of Pherae was able to send out his ships on damaging piratical raids.[3]

The prestige of the Athenians was certainly on the wane, for in the summer of 357 their success in Euboea against the Thebans and the re-enrolment of the Euboean cities in the confederacy[4] could not prevent a serious movement of secession among the allies. Though this movement received the outside prompting of Mausolus, ruler of Caria, and seems to have been sparked off by coercive action from the Athenians,[5] its scale and strength suggest that it was based on a deep-seated dissatisfaction with Athenian leadership.

The secession was led by Rhodes, Chios and Cos, who were joined by the independent Byzantines, and perhaps by other cities in the Hellespontine area;[6] but in spite of the devastation

---

[1] Potidaea in 361—Tod 146; Methone—cf. D. M. Robinson, 'Inscriptions from Macedonia 1938', *Trans. Amer. Philol. Assoc.* lxix (1938), 58.

[2] Tod 146, vv. 5 ff.

[3] Amphipolis, Chersonese, and Alexander's raids, see Hammond, *History of Greece*, p. 514; aid to satraps, cf. R. P. Austin, 'Athens and the Satraps' Revolt', *J.H.S.* lxiv (1944), 98 ff.   [4] Tod 153, esp. vv. 8–9.

[5] Cf. Marshall, *Second Athenian Confederacy*, pp. 109 ff.   [6] Cf. ibid., l.c.

of several islands by the rebel fleet of a hundred ships[1] the move
ment did not spread through the Aegean. The Athenians them
selves put a comparable fleet to sea and garrisoned vulnerabl
islands;[2] but all their efforts to defeat the rebels failed, and
when their admiral Chares put himself and his army in th
service of a rebel satrap, Artabazus, to obtain sorely needec
money, the Great King reacted strongly, reasserting his author
ity against Greek interference on the mainland of Asia for th
first time in a decade, and ordered him to withdraw.[3]

Chares complied, and the Athenians now made peace witl
the disaffected allies and recognized their secession from th
confederacy.[4] The terms and wording of this treaty are no
where given by the orators or Diodorus, though an ancien
scholiast wrote of an undertaking by the Athenians to leave *al*
their allies autonomous.[5] The confederacy certainly continued
to exist right down to the Macedonian conquest in 338, but its
charter had included strict guarantees of autonomy and it is
not impossible that there was some renewal of guarantees to the
loyal allies, connected perhaps with the withdrawal of Athenian
officers and garrisons sent out for protection in the war, but
probably not part of the agreement with the rebels, which must
have amounted to something more than a bare guarantee of
autonomy.[6]

The confederacy hereafter continued in existence and the
individual allies continued to be treated more or less in accordance with the terms of the charter. But the military power on
which the Athenians had based their championship of the
Peace between 378 and 366, and more recently their defiance
of the Persians had vanished. Though there was still popular
agitation for a policy of action even against the Persians, political
control at Athens was in the hands of moderates headed by
Eubulus, who eschewed foreign adventures and concentrated

[1] Diod. xvi. 21. 2.
[2] Andros—Tod 156, vv. 10 ff.; Amorgos—Tod 152, v. 10.
[3] Diod. xvi. 22. 1 ff.
[4] Diod. l.c., Isocr. viii. 16.   [5] Schol. Dem. iii. 28.
[6] Accame, *La lega ateniense*, pp. 192 ff., has argued that the treaty was simply
a bilateral agreement between the Athenians and the rebellious allies, rejecting
Schaefer's interpretation of Dem. xv. 26 and of the scholiast (*Demosthenes und seine
Zeit*, i (2nd ed., Leipzig, 1885), 188 ff.). Isocr. viii. 16 would make this point
certain, if there were agreement on the date of Isocrates, viii, *On Peace* (cf. p. 91,
n. 2).

on the conservation of Athenian resources, which were used only to defend the Athenians' most pressing interests.[1]

Athenian policy, then, for the next few years followed a course that was passively consistent with the principles of Common Peace (the latest expression of which, the treaty of 362/361, does seem, as has been seen, to have been regarded still as the normal condition of Greek affairs in spite of recent conflicts), rather than of active support or of exploitation of them. But there were those who counselled a fresh declaration of support for the Peace and a more positive foreign policy aimed at restoring Athenian prestige and power by its protection.

One of these was Isocrates, who published his pamphlet *On Peace* soon after the treaty with the allies in 355.[2] In it his advice to the Athenians was twofold: first, to make peace not only with the rebellious allies, as had been done, but with all men, by re-establishing the King's Peace,[3] and second, to abandon the naval hegemony.[4] Put beside that part of the *Panegyricus* where the original King's Peace was denounced as being not a treaty but an ukase, Isocrates' commendation of the Peace makes strange reading. True, he seems to have in mind the treaty of 375 in particular,[5] a renewal of the King's Peace which many Athenians and probably Isocrates himself had regarded at the time as a triumph for Athens. Yet that treaty too had been concluded through the mediation of the Persians and had recognized their authority in the Asiatic cities. In the *Plataicus* Isocrates had been able to ignore the King's part in this treaty, though using the treaty itself as the basis of his case against the Thebans. Now in *On Peace* he made no bones about the King's connexion with the Peace,[6] even though it was probably open to him to argue that the King had not been concerned in the latest treaty of 362/361. The reason for Isocrates' frankness is not hard to see and demonstrates again the basic realism of his policies. Artaxerxes had recently made

[1] Cf. Hammond, *History of Greece*, pp. 545 ff.
[2] For the date cf. Momigliano, art. cit., *Annali di Pisa*, ser. ii, v (1936), 109 ff.; the work is placed before the end of the war by G. Mathieu, *Les Idées politiques d'Isocrate*, p. 116, F. Kleine-Piening, *Quo tempore Isocratis orationes quae περὶ εἰρήνης et Ἀρεοπαγιτικός inscribuntur compositae sint*, Diss. Münster (Paderborn, 1930), p. 42, and M. L. W. Laistner, 'Isocrates: De Pace and Philippus', *Cornell Stud. in Class. Phil.* xxii (1927), p. 17.
[3] Isocr. viii. 16.
[4] Ibid. 64.
[5] Cf. the reference to the removal of garrisons in c. 16.
[6] viii. 16.

a very real threat to intervene, and the Athenians had hurriedly given way. There was still considerable feeling against the Persians at Athens and soon after the publication of this pamphlet a popular agitation in favour of war with Persia led to a debate, in which Demosthenes spoke effectively for restraint in his speech *On the Symmories*.[1] No responsible public figure could give any encouragement to this anti-Persian hysteria.

More significant than Isocrates' newly expressed attitude to the King is the difference between the way in which he now proposed that the Athenians should support the principles of Common Peace or, as he put it, should 'behave as the common treaty commands'[2] and the way in which he had in the *Plataicus* proposed that they should support them. Then, in the *Plataicus*, the Athenians were to use the principles of Common Peace as a means of justifying the establishment, by force if necessary, of Athenian authority over the Thebans. Now he recommended the Athenians to give up their hegemony, which, he said, had been unjust, impracticable and positively dangerous to the city;[3] Athenian power and prestige should now be built up through peaceful support of the principles of Common Peace, through what might be called moral diplomacy. The best interests of Athens were still Isocrates' first concern, but now they were more akin to the best interests of other and lesser cities.[4]

A Common Peace policy of this sort was probably the only practicable alternative to the negative peace policy of Eubulus and others, but the latter prevailed. The residue of the confederacy was not dissolved, a modicum of naval power was retained, and ships continued to be built on a considerable scale.[5] Isocrates soon realized that the abandonment of the naval

---

[1] For the date of *On the Symmories*, cf. Jaeger, *Demosthenes*, p. 224, n. 6.

[2] C. 20—Isocr. here used the phrase αἱ κοιναὶ συνθῆκαι, the nearest he ever came to κοινὴ εἰρήνη; he often used 'the peace', ἡ εἰρήνη, to mean the King's Peace or a renewal of it.

[3] Isocr. viii. 66.

[4] Only Momigliano, art. cit., *Annali di Pisa*, ser. ii, v. (1936), 112 ff., has discussed *On Peace* in the context of Common Peace, showing that Isocrates was advocating a policy of support for the Peace with an eye to the greater glory of Athens. Those who believe that he was a panhellenic idealist have always found this work hard to fit in—e.g. Laistner, op. cit., *Cornell Stud. in Class. Phil.* xxii (1927), who succeeds in discerning as his real aim here the formation of a Greek alliance against Persia (p. 18).

[5] *IG* ii². 1613, a naval list for 353/352, gives 349 ships, though these were far too many for the Athenians to be able to man or pay for at sea.

hegemony was too much to ask for. A few months later he published his *Areopagiticus*,[1] a pamphlet which had as its chief theme the need for constitutional changes at Athens to restrict the power of the many, but contained some advice on foreign policy; moral diplomacy to protect the Peace was still recommended though now it was to be backed by a naval hegemony that was not oppressive.[2] At about the same time Xenophon published his short pamphlet on the *Revenues*,[3] and in it the historian who in his *Hellenica* ignored the common pattern of the Common Peace treaties recommended a similar foreign policy to that put forward by Isocrates.[4] Here again a new foreign policy was made the result of internal changes, this time economic, favouring the propertied classes. It should be remembered that for trade and agriculture peace is better than war and that diplomacy is cheaper than war and more acceptable to the taxpayers.

It is clear that Isocrates at least now came under strong attacks from his critics, for in 354 or 353 he published his *Antidosis*, the defence of his life and his beliefs; but it is reasonable to see his unpopularity as caused more by the oligarchic views expressed in the *Areopagiticus* than by his advocacy of a Common Peace foreign policy. Backing for such a policy indeed was not at this time limited entirely to those with oligarchic sympathies; the early speeches of Demosthenes show that support of the Peace was one of his principal ideas.

Shortly before Isocrates had published his *Areopagiticus*, Demosthenes had delivered his first political speech, *On the Symmories*. Hitherto he had supported the moderates in the law-courts and he now spoke against popular clamour for a war with the Persians. He was mostly concerned with showing that the King was not threatening Athens, and that to fight him would be exceedingly dangerous; and, though he denounced in principle Persian interference in Greece and hinted at the

---

[1] For the date cf. Momigliano, art. cit., *Annali di Pisa*, ser. ii, v (1936), 122 ff.; for other views cf. F. Miltner, 'Die Datierung des Areopagitikos', *Mitteil. d. Vereins klass. Philol. in Wien*, i (1924), 42 ff., and W. Jaeger, 'The date of Isocrates' *Areopagiticus* and the Athenian opposition', *Harv. Class. Stud.* Suppl. i (1940), 409 ff.   [2] Isocr. vii, esp. 80.
[3] For the date cf. Thiel's edition (Amsterdam, 1922), p. xii, and Momigliano, art. cit., *Annali di Pisa*, ser. ii, v (1936), 120.
[4] C. v. 10.

attitude he was later to take up over Rhodes,[1] he did not mention the King's Peace as the basis of relations between Athens
and Persia (before this audience it would scarcely have been
tactful to do so). As for relations with other Greeks, he bade the
Athenians pursue a just policy and begin no unjustified wars,[2]
but he did not in this context allude to freedom and autonomy
or to *the* Peace. A just policy was, however, not to be one of
complete isolation and non-interference; he urged a reform of
the financial system not only for the defence of Athens, but also,
he hinted, for the protection of others.[3]

War was prevented, but Demosthenes' practical proposals
were not carried out. In 353 he spoke again on foreign affairs
in favour of an alliance with the Megalopolitans against the
Spartans. This alliance, he argued, would contribute towards
the essential object of Athenian foreign policy, which was to
keep both the Spartans and the Thebans as weak as possible,[4]
because the best way to this object was to ensure that the
Athenians should protect the weaker states against the strong,
and be seen to be the guardians of freedom.[5] This freedom is
specifically connected with the conditions of *the* Peace[6] (that of
362/361), but no such stress was laid on the Peace as to suggest
that respect for its principles rather than the propaganda value
of defending freedom was an influential factor in the decisions
of the Athenian people. Demosthenes had also to meet the
objection that the alliance made with the Spartans in 369 had
never been repudiated, and was thus led into the generalization,
familiar in the twentieth century, that in the pursuance of a just
foreign policy there was no room for alliances which bound the
city to support another, right or wrong.[7] His arguments in these
ways seem to develop from the needs of the present situation
into specious generalizations about the implications of a Common Peace policy, principles which were not real starting-
points, but were designed to give a good moral flavour to
measures of expediency.

Isocrates, by contrast, though he did commend his policy
as being beneficial to the city in particular, seems more of
an idealist, because he dealt only in generalizations and was

---

[1] Dem. xiv. 6. [2] Ibid. 3, 35, 37, and 41. [3] Ibid. 13.
[4] Ibid. xvi. 4–5. [5] Ibid. 15 and 32. [6] Ibid. 10.
[7] Ibid. 6.

not arguing any special problems of foreign policy. But the difference was largely superficial; to be the protectors of freedom, as Isocrates urged, the Athenians would constantly have had to declare their own position on individual issues, and in their private debates on the merits of a case could not have been silent on the true interests of their city. On this occasion Demosthenes failed to carry the day, but the policy of those in control was not altogether passive, for they had concluded an alliance with the Messenians in 355, though still themselves allied to their implacable enemies, the Spartans.[1] This move had so far prevented any outbreak of war between the two cities.

Two years later Demosthenes spoke in favour of assisting the Rhodian democrats against the royal house of Caria, who had virtually gained control of the island after the Social War, in which the Rhodians had seceded from the Athenian confederacy. Earlier he had warned the people against provoking the King, but now he claimed that the King was in the wrong, because his vassals had interfered in a city to which he had abandoned any claim 'in the treaty' (the King's Peace).[2] As in the case of the Megalopolitans, Demosthenes made the point that by supporting the Rhodians the Athenians would be defending freedom and thereby win repute.[3] But he did not proceed from there to more theorizing on the implications of a Common Peace policy, eschewing, for instance, the relevant corollary of his previous argument, that a just policy recognizes not only no permanent friends, but also no permanent enemies. Instead he chose to interpret the defence of freedom as the defence of democracy, and was prepared to say that 'I believe it would be better for you that all Hellenic peoples should be democracies and be at war with you than that they should be governed by oligarchies and be your friends'.[4] His argument is a salutary reminder that there were other views of international justice than those of Isocrates and Xenophon; that Athenians especially were likely to believe it no less important that the people within a city should be free from the domination of a few powerful men than that the city itself should be free from the domination of its more powerful neighbours.

Again Demosthenes failed to persuade the Athenians and soon

[1] Paus. iv. 28. 1 ff.; cf. Dem. xvi. 8–9.
[2] Dem. xv. 27.
[3] Ibid. 3–4, 8.
[4] Ibid. 18.

he was completely absorbed in his campaign against Philip of Macedon.[1] Philip's growing power had been encroaching on Athenian interests since 357, and in 352 Eubulus and his colleagues had shown energy rare for them in sending an expedition to block his passage through Thermopylae. Eventually it was their failure against Philip that turned them again to consider the possibility of another Common Peace treaty.

Soon after the fall of Olynthus to Philip in 348 Eubulus and Aeschines had directed a diplomatic campaign to bring the Peloponnesian cities into the war alongside the Athenians, but without success.[2] When a further series of embassies were sent out to these and other Greek cities in the winter of 347/346, peace negotiations with Philip had already begun[3], and the ambassadors were this time given the alternative object of bringing the other Greeks into a peace agreement with him; and, as the Greek cities to be approached were at present neutral, the idea must have been to expand any bilateral agreement with Philip into a Common Peace treaty.[4] But this possibility was clearly not something for which the Athenian leaders were in the last resort ready to sacrifice their chances of ending the war with Philip.

In the final negotiations between the Athenians and Philip's ambassadors in the spring of 346 a Common Peace treaty does seem to have been the object of the Athenians' allies in the confederacy. First they proposed that no debate should take place in the Athenian assembly on the subject of peace with Philip, until the embassies returned from the other Greek states, in order that the Greeks should be able to take part if they wanted;[5] but this proposal was overruled, and Demosthenes saw

---

[1] The First Philippic was delivered probably in 351, but its date is a vexed question—cf. Cawkwell, 'The Defence of Olynthus', *C.Q.* N.S. xii (1962), 122 ff.

[2] Dem. xix. 304 ff.

[3] Aeschines ii. 57, 60–61 (including quotation from the first decree of the allies), iii. 58, 65, and 68, against the denial of Demosthenes (xviii. 23). Schaefer, *Demosthenes und seine Zeit*, ii (2nd ed., Leipzig, 1886), 220, identified these embassies with those referred to in Dem. xix. 304 ff., and assigned them to the earlier period; Cawkwell, 'Aeschines and the Peace of Philocrates', *Rev. d'étud. grec.* lxxiii (1960), 418 ff., also identifies, but thinks the Demosthenes' passage refers to the winter of 347/346.

[4] The Peace alternative is clearly stated by Aesch. ii. 57; Cawkwell, art. cit., *Rev. d'étud. grec.* lxxiii (1960), 426, suggests that his statement is a reading-back from a later date and thinks that, when these embassies were sent, peace was not yet being seriously considered by Aeschines and Eubulus.

[5] Quoted by Aesch. ii. 60–61.

that the dates for the debate were fixed without reference to it.[1] Perhaps the presence of some ambassadors from some of the other Greek states (which may have been the case)[2] encouraged the allies to continue to press for some kind of a Common Peace treaty; at any rate they passed a new motion recommending that the Athenians should discuss and decide on peace terms (as was already their intention), but that any Greek city should be allowed to be included in the Peace within three months.[3]

This motion was one of two before the assembly when the debate began; the other, proposed by Philocrates, was for a bilateral peace between Philip and his allies and the Athenians and their allies with the express exclusion of Halus and of the Phocians[4] (allies of the Athenians, but not members of the confederacy), on whom Philip had fairly evident designs. The allies' motion seems to have won much favour at first,[5] but the Athenian people were chiefly concerned with the fate of Halus and the Phocians, and were provoked by Philocrates' proposal into fresh bellicosity, which Aeschines and his friends had to work hard to assuage.[6] It also became clear that Philip would accept no terms which did not leave him freedom of action over Halus and the Phocians[7] and in the end a bilateral treaty was concluded with no reference to Halus and the Phocians, a treaty which Aeschines and Eubulus, as well as Demosthenes, supported.[8]

[1] Decrees adduced by Aeschines (ii. 61, iii. 68), but not extant.

[2] Cf. Demosthenes' assertion (xix. 16).

[3] Quoted by Aesch. iii. 68 ff., but not mentioned in Aesch. ii; referred to probably by Dem. xix. 15 and 144. Schaefer, *Demosthenes und seine Zeit*, ii. 216 ff., and Accame, *La lega ateniense*, pp. 202 ff., identify this decree with that quoted in Aesch. ii. 60–61. However, that decree does not deal with the debate concerning peace as already arranged, but proposes that it should be deferred until the ambassadors return; this decree is clearly said to have been presented on the first day of the debate and deals with the nature of the Peace being discussed (cf. Cawkwell, art. cit., *Rev. d'étud. grec.* lxxiii (1960), 420, n. 1). The use of the compound προσέγραψαν in Aesch. iii. 69, cannot be regarded as a strong argument for identification. Cawkwell, art. cit., p. 435, agrees that the allies' proposal was for a Common Peace.

[4] Dem. xix. 159; for the two proposals, cf. Hammond, *History of Greece*, p. 552, and A. W. Pickard-Cambridge, *C.A.H.* vi, 236.

[5] Aesch. iii. 71.

[6] Aeschines' speech referred to by himself at ii. 74 and by Dem. xix. 16; cf. Cawkwell, art. cit., *Rev. d'étud. grec.* lxxiii (1960), 437, whose explanation of the purpose of the speech largely agrees with this.　　　　　　[7] Cf. Aesch. iii. 72.

[8] Dem. xix. 159 and 278; the Peace supported by Aeschines—Aesch. ii. 79, &c.; by Eubulus—Dem. xix. 290 ff.; by Demosthenes—Aesch. ii. 68.

It is hard to be certain whether Philip's objection to the express inclusion of Halus and the Phocians in a bilateral treaty would have extended also to a Common Peace treaty, but it seems more likely that they would have. It is true that he would have had precedents (though not very auspicious) for arguing that the Phocians at any rate had put themselves outside the protection of such a treaty, but Common Peace treaties had a general stabilizing effect which he could well have thought undesirable, and were based on a general recognition of autonomy that the destroyer of Olynthus might feel would be embarrassing; and, although there were states, such as the Thebans, likely to support him rather than the Athenians, they could not be relied on, and, though he did three years later profess himself ready to accept an Athenian proposal to expand the bilateral treaty into a Common Peace treaty, he only set about organizing a Common Peace in 338, when the *status quo* was favourable to himself. Further, though he was ready to exploit inter-city rivalries, he does not seem to have indulged in that particular kind of support of autonomy, in championing small cities against larger neighbours and separatist movements within federal states, that characterized a persistent attempt to pose as the champion of peace and freedom; not, that is, until after his victory at Chaeronea, when he broke up Theban control of Boeotia and dissolved the Athenian confederacy.

As for the Athenian leaders, any intentions they may have had of pressing for a general treaty to cover all Greece were frustrated, partly by the fact that public controversy became centred on the position of Halus and the Phocians, partly by the response of the Peloponnesian cities which must have been largely, if not wholly, negative;[1] moreover, if Philip was opposed to the idea, they would certainly have been apprised of his attitude by the Macedonian ambassadors, and, even if he were not, they might well have had second thoughts about its advantages. Demosthenes at any rate, hard though he worked for peace at this juncture, seems to have despaired of the other Greeks at an early stage.[2]

---

[1] The only indication that some states responded is Demosthenes' assertion (xix. 16) that ambassadors were present at the debate in the assembly—cf. Cawkwell, art. cit., *Rev. d'étud. grec.* lxxiii (1960), 438.

[2] Dem. xviii. 23, an inaccurate statement, but one which probably represented

The short period between the conclusion of the Peace of Philocrates, which included on Philip's insistence an alliance between the two parties, and Philip's attack on the Phocians saw the publication of Isocrates' *Philippus*.[1] There in the form of an open letter to Philip Isocrates presented what might have seemed to any Athenians but those few at the top who were aware of Philip's plans—and even to some of them—a practicable and honourable alternative to a policy of continued hostility to Philip and of using the Peace as a breathing-space before renewing the struggle. He urged Philip to lead a pan-hellenic crusade against Persia (as a decade later he set out to do) as the leader of Greece and not as its conqueror as he was to become. He presented the Persian war as an alternative to and not as a consequence of aggrandisement in Greece, and urged Philip to use his influence and not his power to bring peace, preserving for the Athenians a special position as his most valuable allies.[2]

In the proposed pacification of Greece the importance of the four leading cities, the Argives, the Thebans, the Spartans and the Athenians, was stressed; Philip should reconcile each of them with himself and also with one another, and this reconciliation should precede any expedition against the Persians. But Isocrates nowhere went into details about the machinery of reconciliation, and it is not safe to say that he was advising Philip to bring about a new Common Peace settlement,[3] though it would by now have been regarded as the natural framework of a general pacification.

With the advantage of hindsight it can be said that at this stage there was virtually no chance of Philip accepting the role of peacemaker in Greece or of the Athenians accepting him. It is doubtful whether Philip would ever have stopped short of becoming the dominant partner in any alliance, and probable that he always intended to establish some sort of control in

his sentiments, shown also by his haste in fixing the debate before the Greeks had responded.

[1] For the date cf. cc. 7–8, which speak of the Peace as newly made.

[2] For this interpretation cf., against the general view, S. Perlman, 'Isocrates' *Philippus*—a reinterpretation', *Historia*, vi (1957), 306 ff.

[3] C. 69 in particular has been adduced by those who see Isocrates' inspiration behind the settlement of 338/337 (cf. Beloch, *Griechische Geschichte*, iii. i. 575, n. 2), but it amounts to nothing more than a general picture of Philip as the arbiter of Greek quarrels.

Greece; he was in particular already planning the intervention
in Phocis which finally alienated Athenian public opinion. But
it is possible that the *Philippus* did something to prepare the
ground for the Common Peace settlement organized by Philip
in 338/337, different though it was from the pacification
envisaged by Isocrates.

Philip now marched against the Phocians, reduced them to
submission, and then summoned the Amphictyonic Council to
discuss their fate.[1] Diodorus' description of what followed[2] has
led to the belief that the Council proclaimed a new state of
Common Peace in Greece. It might have suited Philip's
purpose better now than a few months earlier to have promoted
a Common Peace treaty, as his immediate objectives had been
secured, but his general objections to such a treaty discussed
above would still have been valid, and in fact there is strong
evidence against this interpretation of what is, by comparison
with its appearances in Diodorus' Book XV, a vague and obscure
use of the phrase κοινὴ εἰρήνη.[3] It can be said with certainty that
there was no generally agreed Common Peace treaty at this
time, and with probability that Philip did not, like the Thebans
in 365, try to make propaganda value out of a unilateral procla-
mation of a state of Common Peace.

Athenian relations with Philip remained nominally peaceful.
But the anti-Macedonian politicians, while they did not by
any means have everything their own way,[4] had sufficient support
to prevent any serious attempt to make the Peace and the
alliance really work;[5] and there was, as far as is known, no
move from elsewhere in Greece to avert a renewal of war that
was likely to affect most of the city-states.

In 343 Philip sent an embassy to Athens to express his goodwill and to offer to amend the treaty;[6] in reply the Athenians
proposed that the treaty be extended into a Common Peace to
cover all Greeks.[7] Philip professed himself ready to accept this
suggestion,[8] though there is no certainty that he would in fact
have done so and he may still have considered a general pacification based on the autonomy principle as against his own

---

[1] Diod. xvi. 59.   [2] Ibid. 60. 3.   [3] See Appendix IX.
[4] e.g. the successful prosecution of Timarchus in 345 and the agitation which led
to Demosthenes' Second Philippic in winter 344/343.
[5] e.g. the rejection of Philip's offer to cut a canal through the Chersonese in 345.
[6] Ps.-Dem. vii. 18.   [7] Ibid. 30.   [8] Ibid. 32.

nterests. But in any case the Athenians, under the influence of he anti-Macedonian politicians, also proposed that the clause of the Peace of Philocrates which gave to each side 'what they held' should be replaced (presumably in the general treaty) by its alternative, that all should possess 'their own territory'.[1] As the Athenians claimed as their own Amphipolis and Potidaea, which Philip had taken over, and Cardia, his ally in the Chersonese, this proposal was totally unacceptable to him, and must have been known to be.[2]

It looks as if Philip's opponents at Athens were anxious to avoid making a Common Peace treaty with him, now that he seemed willing to agree to it, thinking perhaps that in these circumstances (maybe, in any) it would be disadvantageous to the city and damaging to their own political position. Speaking to the Athenians about these negotiations, Hegesippus, while idealizing the Athenian proposal for the extension of the Peace of Philocrates to all Greeks ('. . . thinking it just and humane not that only they and their allies and Philip and his allies should enjoy the Peace, while those who were allies of neither themselves nor Philip should be left in the middle and be at the mercy of the more powerful, but that these also should enjoy security by the Peace'),[3] was at pains to show the Athenians how Philip's practice differed from his professions now about the freedom and autonomy of the Greeks.[4]

Philip does not seem to have persisted in any attempt to make capital out of the Athenian attitude, and nothing is known of any favourable reaction to his plan elsewhere in Greece. At Athens the anti-Macedonian politicians were still not all-powerful,[5] but they carried the people with them on all vital issues directly affecting relations with Philip.[6] When they did finally succeed in forming a block against him, it was an alliance for war and it failed on the field of Chaeronea.

---

[1] Ibid. 18.
[2] The Athenians were also prepared to talk about Olynthus and the other Chalcidian cities—cf. Ps.-Dem. vii. 28.
[3] Ps.-Dem. vii. 30–31.   [4] Ibid. 32.
[5] e.g. the rejection of Persian overtures early in 343 and Aeschines' acquittal in the summer.
[6] e.g. the sending of troops to Acarnania in winter 343/342, support of Diopeithes in 341, abrogation of the Peace in 340, and subsequent rejection of Philip's overtures.

II

F. Carrata Thomes

Il trattato con i Calcidesi nella prima attività diplomatica di Filippo II

IL TRATTATO CON I CALCIDESI NELLA PRIMA
ATTIVITA DIPLOMATICA DI FILIPPO II

I primi anni di governo di Filippo II sono tra quelli che sfug-
gono maggiormente ad un giudizio sicuro, che stringa da vicino la
complessa personalità del re. Senza dubbio, la lotta dei pretendenti al
trono macedone dopo la morte di Perdicca III e l'ondata di sangue che
si abbatté sul paese resero assai fluida la situazione degli anni imme-
diatamente seguenti al 359 a. C. La trasmissione stessa delle notizie a
a noi giunte di quel periodo, risente dell'anormalità delle vicende sto-
riche presentandosi, a sua volta, discontinua e oscura piú del consueto.

Ai fini di una valutazione totale, si devono sollevare numerose
questioni preliminari. La politica di Filippo verso le popolazioni
nordiche riveste un carattere meramente difensivo, oppure persegue
un piano, organicamente concepito, di offesa ad oltranza? La politica
all'interno del paese rivela una ferma e ambiziosa intenzione di
trasformare in senso esclusivo la posizione del sovrano, o non piuttosto
si adegua alla tradizione e al rispetto dell'equilibrio costituzionale?
Le prime interferenze, oltre confine, nel settore meridionale del Mar
Tracico assumono, negli intenti di Filippo, un significato preciso e
suscettibile di sviluppo o piú semplicemente rientrano in una sfera
normale di interessi locali e circoscritti? In altri termini, si può
dire che il problema essenziale consista nello stabilire in quale misura
la politica interna ed esterna di Filippo abbia assunto, sin dall'inizio del regno, quell'aspetto autoritario ed aggressivo che ebbe
indubbiamente nei suoi ulteriori sviluppi. [1]

---

[1] Impostazione ed esami diversi della questione e dei fatti presso V. Co-
STANZI, *Studi di St. Macedon. sino a Filippo* (Pisa, 1915), 88 ss.; J. KAERST,

344   FRANCO CARRATA THOMES

L'atteggiamento di Filippo verso gli altri popoli dal 359 a
357 a. C. si concreta in tre fatti fondamentali : patteggiamento con
Peoni, i Traci e gli Ateniesi ; campagna contro gli Illiri ; riconquista
di Anfipoli e di Pidna. A ben vedere, si tratta di tre mosse che
si uniformano ad un unico indirizzo.

Quando Filippo perviene al trono, la situazione è grave e, tra
pretendenti alla corona e nemici che hanno invaso il territorio macedone, il nuovo re è costretto dagli stessi avvenimenti a scegliere
la difficile via degli espedienti diplomatici. I Peoni e i Traci sono
allontanati dalle frontiere per mezzo del denaro o mercé la forza di
persuasione o con qualche scaramuccia di interesse locale, Atene
viene placata con la cessione di Anfipoli (359-358 a. C.). Filippo
si rivela, sin dall'inizio, un abile negoziatore e comincia ben presto
a mostrare le qualità precipue che lo faranno giustamente giudicare
' blandus pariter et insidiosus ' (Just., IX 8, 8).

Così, la campagna contro gli Illiri del 358 a. C. mira soprattutto al ricupero del territorio macedone perduto in seguito alla grave
sconfitta subìta da Perdicca III. Del resto, una campagna offensiva
oltre le frontiere macedoni non è realmente provata dalle testimonianze in proposito. Il lieve ritocco operato da Filippo al confine
tradizionale sino al lago Licnitide (Ochrida),[1] probabilmente non è
che un semplice mantenimento delle posizioni raggiunte nel teatro
stesso delle operazioni, dato che la battaglia decisiva contro Bardili
è combattuta, dopo un lungo inseguimento, precisamente nella pia-
nura di Bitola (Monastir).[2]

La riconquista di Anfipoli e quella di Pidna, attuate rispettivamente nell'autunno e alla fine del 357 a. C., costituiscono il terzo
passo di Filippo verso il consolidamento della normalità sulle frontiere
dello stato. È noto come la tradizione su questi avvenimenti sia
estremamente confusa e incerta.[3] Per ciò che riguarda Demostene,

Gesch. d. Hell., I[8] (Lipsia, 1927), 206 ss. ; A. MOMIGLIANO, Filippo il Maced.
(Firenze, 1934), 41 ss.; F. GEYER, in R.E., XIX 2 (1938), 2266 ss.; R. PARIBENI,
La Maced. sino ad Aless. Magno (Milano, 1947); 66 ss.; P. CLOCHÉ, Philippe II
roi de Macèd. de 359 à 351 av. J. C., in « Les Étud. Class. », 18, 1950, 386 ss.
    [1] Ciò si desume da Diod., XVI 8,1.   [2] L'esatta localizzazione del teatro
di battaglia oggi non è possibile: cf., da ultimo, CLOCHÉ, l. c., 395 ss.   [3] Si
vedano, ad es., gli esami di J. PAPASTAVRU, Amphipolis. Gesch u. Prosopo-
graphie (Lipsia, 1936), 32 ss. e di CLOCHÉ, l. c., 395 ss.

[22]

l'oratore proietta spesso nel passato, senza alcuna esattezza cronologica, le sue implacabili recriminazioni contro Filippo, citando fatti
e dati che, dopo molti anni, possono assumere facilmente un significato
antiateniese, in rapporto alla tensione del momento in cui scrive.
È certo che vi furono trattative diplomatiche tra Filippo e Atene
sulle due città contese, cosí come è sicuro che il figlio di Aminta
approfittò della situazione particolarmente delicata della Guerra So-
ciale, che tanto impegnava la regina dell'Attica in quel tempo. Ma
ciò non significa che l'occupazione di Anfipoli e di Pidna fosse una
sfida, apertamente indirizzata dal Macedone contro Atene. È vero
invece che si trattò soprattutto di un ritorno al vecchio dispositivo
di confine della Macedonia, nel quadro di una reintegrazione totale
del territorio perduto negli ultimi anni. Praticamente Filippo sembra
obbedire, insomma, a questo intendimento : i nemici esterni debbono
essere ricacciati oltre frontiera, Anfipoli e Pidna, che sono sfuggite
al controllo macedone a partire rispettivamente dal 364 e dal 358
a. C., debbono ritornare, ora, sotto la sua autorità. Certo, il possesso
di tali centri procurerà un cospicuo vantaggio per il re, quando
muoverà guerra ai Traci e svolgerà una politica direttamente antiateniese, ma in quel momento esso non prelude, negli intenti del
sovrano, ad una espansione ai danni della sua grande futura rivale.[1]

Ora, le iniziative diplomatiche di Filippo sin qui elencate con-
fluiscono, nella primavera del 356 a. C., in un patto di alleanza
stretto dal re con i ' Calcidesi '. Come è noto, l'esistenza di questo
patto, provata indirettamente da qualche accenno delle fonti letterarie,[2] è stata suffragata nel 1934 dal ritrovamento presso Olinto
di una stele contenente l' ὅρκος del trattato.[3]

[1] L'intervento diretto di Filippo in Tessaglia, di cui parla Diod., XVI 14, 2
non ebbe luogo nel 358/7 ma piú tardi, nel 354/3 a. C. (CLOCHÉ, l. c., 393-394 ;
la tesi di due operazioni belliche distinte è sostenuta da ultimo, con deboli argo-
menti, da TH. D. AXENIDU, 'Η Μακεδονικὴ ἡγεμονια ἐν Θεσσαλίᾳ καὶ ἡ θέσις
τῆς Λαρίσης ἐν αὐτῇ, Atene, 1949, 9 ss., 12 ss.). Probabilmente i Tessali solleci-
tarono l'aiuto del Macedone già nel 358/7 a. C. (senza ottenerlo), laddove Diodoro, confuso dalla vicinanza cronologica dei due episodi, finisce per duplicare
anche i fatti, aggiungendo un rapido cenno sugli avvenimenti descritti compiu-
tamente piú oltre (XVI 35,1 ss.).   [2] Cf. Diod., 8,2-5 ; Demosth., Olynth. II [II]
7,14 ; Philipp. II [VI] 20 ; Chers. [VIII] 65 ; contra Aristocr. [XXIII] 108. E v. pure
Liban., Arg. ad Demosth. Olynth. 2 ; [Demosth.], contra Neair. [LIX] 4.   [3] L'e.
pigrafe è stata trovata e pubblicata (con nitida riproduzione fotografica) da

346   FRANCO CARRATA THOMES

I problemi solle ati dal nuovo testo per la valutazione della politica di Filippo sono numerosi, ma anzitutto s'impone un pregiudiziale chiarimento terminologico. L' epigrafe nomina chiaramente i ' Calcidesi ' (ll. 3, 4, 8, 11, 12), mentre le testimonianze letterarie al riguardo parlano di ' Olintii '. Il problema non è ozioso, poiché, a seconda che si tratti di un accordo tra Filippo e i Calcidesi o tra Filippo e gli Olintii, si prospetta una diversa valutazione della storia dei Calcidesi e degli Olintii durante il regno del padre di Alessandro. Ciò è tanto piú oggetto di discussione, dopo che un' ardita teoria moderna ha svuotato di ogni significato di autonomia politica il termine οἱ Χαλκιδεῖς, identificandolo con quello οἱ ᾽Ολύνθιοι e negando, di conseguenza, l'esistenza stessa di uno stato calcidese nella storia. [1]

Al di fuori di ogni tesi preconcetta, in un senso o nell'altro, giova esaminare se i documenti letterari ed epigrafici possano concordare in modo soddisfacente. L'ipotesi che i Calcidesi in genere non siano da distinguere dagli Olintii, è giustificata principalmente dal criterio metodico di svalutare i dati epigrafici e numismatici a vantaggio di quelli letterari. [2] Dato, ad esempio, che nel trattato si parla di Calcidesi e gli scrittori, invece, riferendosi a quella circostanza, accennano a compensi territoriali promessi da Filippo agli Olintii, si è pensato di potere legittimamente identificare questi ultimi con i Calcidesi. [3] Ma, pur prescindendo dalla maggiore o minore attendibilità di Demostene e di Diodoro, non si vede alcun motivo plausibile per cui la tradizione epigrafica, di natura inoltre ufficiale, debba essere a priori sacrificata a quella letteraria.

D. M. ROBINSON, *Inscriptions from Olynthus 1934. 1. Treaty between Philip and the Chalcidians 356 B. C.*, in « Trans. Amer. Philol. Assoc. », 65, 1934, 103 ss. Le nuove integrazioni del testo, presentate da M. SEGRE, *Il trattato tra Filippo e i Calcidesi*, in « Riv. di Filol. », 63, 1935, 497 ss. sono in gran parte accolte dall' ultimo editore del trattato M. N. TOD, *Greek Histor. Inscript.*, II (1948), n. 158.   [1] Cf. F. HAMPL, *Olynth u. d. Chalkidische Staat*, in « Hermes », 70, 1935, 176 ss.   [2] Cf. HAMPL, l. c., 181, 184, 190 e n. 3. Non si dimentichi, tuttavia, che non sempre gli autori del sec. IV a. C. sono corretti in fatto di terminologia costituzionale. L'uso del nome, piú noto, del capoluogo o della città egemone di una regione in luogo della denominazione ufficiale dello stato si trova di frequente, ad es., in Senofonte (l' esempio di Θηβαῖοι in luogo di Βοιωτοί è tipico).   [3] HAMPL, l. c., 181.

[24]

Demostene allude diverse volte, tra il 352 e il 341 a, C.,[1] agli
avvenimenti del 356 a. C., ma è naturale che l'oratore insista sulle
vicende di Olinto che, quando egli pronunciava le sue orazioni, era
al centro delle piú infocate passioni politiche. Si può dire che per
l'infaticabile e acerrimo accusatore di Filippo, Olinto diventi, anche
nel ricordo degli avvenimenti piú lontani, il simbolo del pericolo
macedone, il bruciante ricordo di una battaglia diplomatica perduta.
Demostene, d'altra parte, impegnato a fondo nell'immediata realtà
politica, non voleva ricordare il passato in sé ma, nel suo tempe-
ramento di uomo politico, lo rievocava solo come nuovo strumento
polemico nella spietata lotta antimacedone. L'oratore doveva essere al
corrente dell'esistenza di una confederazione calcidese se nel 343 a. C.,
accennando agli anni intorno al 379 a. C., affermava che allora ' i
Calcidesi non erano ancora riuniti in un solo stato '.[2] Dove quel
' non ancora ' (οὔπω) prova che piú tardi, dopo la guerra con Sparta
del 383-379 a. C., la confederazione calcidese fu una realtà di fatto,
mentre al tempo stesso il presentare Olinto come vincitrice del conflitto,[3] dimostra ancor piú la disinvoltura di Demostene nell'alterare
la storia per scopi contingenti ed immediati.

Diodoro, che talvolta parla dei Calcidesi come di una entità
politica a sé stante,[4] nel libro XVI, dedicato a Filippo. menziona
solo gli Olintii. Ciò deriva probabilmente dal fatto che per i libri XII
e XIV Diodoro attinge ad una fonte diversa che per il libro XVI.
Ma la fonte di questo libro è Teopompo, scrittore per varie ragioni
informatissimo,[5] e i cui frammenti dei libri XX-XXV delle *Filip-*

---

[1] I luoghi sono: *contra Aristocr.* [XXIII] 108 (del 352 a. C.); *Olynth.* II [II]
7,14 (del 349 a. C.); *Philipp.* II [VI] 20 (del 344 a. C.); *Chers.* [VIII] 65 (del
341 a. C.)   [2] Cf. Demosth., *de falsa legat.* [XIX] 263: ... οὔπω Χαλκιδέων
πάντων εἰς ἓν συνωκισμένων κ.τ.λ. Per la data del discorso v. G. MATHIEU, *Démosthène* (Parigi, 1948), 87.   [3] Cf. *de falsa legat.* [XIX] 264.   [4] Diod., XII
34,2; 46,7; XIV 82,2-3.   [5] V., su ciò, il mio saggio *Cultura greca e unità
maced. nella politica di Filippo II* (Torino, 1949), 3 ss., spec. 7-8 con note.
L'importanza di Teopompo non viene sminuita dal solo fatto che in Diod., XVI
92,5 egli abbia aggiunto alla realtà storica un particolare atto a lumeggiare maggiormente, nell'episodio dell'assassinio di Filippo, la gloria del padre di Alessandro (una giustificazione del procedimento seguíto dallo scrittore nell'occa-
sione ho dato in op. cit., 30-31; infondate, quindi, mi sembrano le deduzioni
di T. S. BROWN, in « Class. Weekly », 47, 1951-52, 108).

piche [1] contengono alcuni chiari accenni ai Calcidesi, come formazione politica indipendente e sovrana. Teopompo parla dei Calcidesi, distinguendoli dagli Olintii, pur conoscendo l'ordinamento civico di questi ultimi ; [2] accenna alle istituzioni dei Calcidesi [3] e al loro πολίτευμα ; [4] ricorda infine che all'inizio delle ostilità del 349-48 a. C. Filippo accolse senza riguardi una loro ambasceria. [5] Il silenzio di Diodoro sui Calcidesi nel libro XVI si potrebbe quindi imputare alla sua trascuratezza di compilatore, ma forse si può pensare che la fonte da lui adoperata, cioè Teopompo, insistesse sempre piú su Olinto, facendone quasi il centro della narrazione storica dei libri XXIII-XXV delle *Filippiche*, per concluderla con la completa rovina della città.

Una comunità politica denominata di regola οἱ Χαλκιδεῖς al tempo di Filippo, è provata anche indirettamente da altri scrittori contemporanei, come Isocrate [6] e Aristotele, [7] da tre epigrafi, rispettivamente del 362, [8] del 358-57 [9] e del 349 a. C., [10] oltre che da alcune fonti posteriori. [11] Si può ritenere con verosimiglianza che lo stato dei Cal-

---

[1] Erano i libri dedicati ad un *excursus* sulla Calcidica (XX-XXI) e alla guerra di Filippo contro Olinto (XXII-XXV) : cf. JACOBY, *FGrHist*, II BD (1927), 377.

[2] Fr. 143 Jac.   [3] Fr. 139 Jac.   [4] Fr. 144 Jac. : il πολίτευμα τῶν Χαλκιδέων è esteso ad Αἰόλειον, città probabilmente situata nella Bottiea orientale (MERITT-WADE GERY-MCGREGOR, *The Athen. Tribute Lists*, I, [1939], 465) e non nella penisola di Pallene (BUERCHNER, in *R.E.* III 2 [1899], 2075).   [5] Fr. 127 Jac., che è collocato dall'editore nel libro XX delle Filippiche. Dato che la guerra era narrata piú propriamente nei libri XXII-XXV, il fr. cadrebbe meglio nei libri XXII o XXIII, che narravano appunto l'inizio del conflitto. Inoltre, mentre il fr. 147 Jac. appartiene con probabilità al libro XXIV, per affinità di argomento si può collocare tra i libri XX e XXV anche il fr. 266 Jac.   [6] Isocr., *de antid.* [XV] 113 riferito al 364 a. C. e scritto nel 353 a. C.: cf. G. MATHIEU, éd. Isocr., III (Parigi, 1942), 88.   [7] Aristot., *polit.* 1274 b 23.   [8] *IG* II² 110 = *Syll.*⁸ 174 = TOD 143. L'iscrizione ricorda (ll. 8-9) le operazioni belliche di Timoteo contro Anfipoli e i Calcidesi (364/3 a. C.).   [9] Si tratta di un frammento di un patto tra lo stato calcidico e il dinasta illirico Grabo, pubblicato da D. M. ROBINSON, *Inscriptions from Macedonia 1938*, in « Trans. Amer. Philol. Assoc. », 69, 1938, 44 ss. e databile, secondo l'editore, all'incirca nel 358/7 a. C.   [10] *IG* II² 258 + 617 ed. E. SCHWEIGERT, in « Hesperia », 6, 1937, 327 ss., ll. 1,10-11, 13-14,19. È verosimile che si tratti della simmachia che i Calcidesi conclusero con Atene nel 349 a. C. (Philoc., fr. 49 Jac.), simmachia che portò poi nel 348 a. C. ad ulteriori contatti diplomatici tra le due potenze (Philoc., fr. 50-51 Jac.). Mentre HAMPL, l. c., 178 è per il 349 a. C., incerto rimane SCHWEIGERT, l. c., 328 s. (350/40 a. C.).   [11] Esame critico di queste presso E. HARRISON, in «Class. Quart. », 6, 1912, 165 ss.

cidesi, ordinato in una confederazione di città libere e autonome, facenti perno su Olinto, sia fiorito verso il 375 a. C. in un organismo statale di notevole potenza, ricco di molte e industri città, come testimonia un passo famoso di Demostene. [1] Nel 375 a. C., infatti, i Calcidesi concludono una simmachia con Atene, [2] nel 364 a. C. sono sconfitti da Timoteo sul loro stesso territorio, nel 358 57 e nel 356 a. C. stringono alleanza con Grabo illirio e con Filippo e nel 349 48 a. C. partecipano attivamente alla comune guerra contro il re macedone. [3] Lo sfacelo della lega calcidica, provocato da Sparta tra il 383 e il 379 a. C., non ha evidentemente portato a conseguenze irreparabili, rivelando l'intima debolezza della potenza lacedemone.

In sostanza, molte sono le testimonianze convincenti che depongono non solo per l'esistenza, ma anche per l'effettiva vitalità di uno stato calcidese tra il 375 e il 348 a. C. Anzi, i dati letterari e numismatici permetterebbero di fare risalire le origini della confederazione calcidese alla guerra del Peloponneso. [4] L'incremento

---

[1] Demosth., *Philipp.* III [IX] 26. Per l'ordinamento interno della confederazione e l'autonomia delle singole città v. BUSOLT-SWOBODA, *Gr. Staatsk.*, II³ (1926), 1504 s.: per la data della rinascita della lega M. CARY, in *Cambr. Anc. Hist.*, VI (1927), 63.   [2] *IG* II² 36 = *Syll.*³ 143 = TOD 119. L'epigrafe è datata rettamente da A. B. WEST, *The Hist. of the Chalcidic League* (Madison, 1918), 108 e da S. ACCAME, *La Lega Aten. del sec. IV a. C.* (Roma, 1941), 87. Altre datazioni in TOD, op. cit., 53 s. che tuttavia infondatamente identifica i 'Calcidesi' del trattato con i soli abitanti del Monte Athos (67). L'espressione Χαλκιδεῖς ἐπὶ Θρᾴκης, che compare alle ll. 2-3 del trattato (cf. pure *IG*. II² 43 = *Syll.*³ 147 = TOD 123, ll. 101 s., del 377 a. C.) e che subisce leggere modificazioni nelle fonti letterarie (HARRISON, l. c., 171 ss.; D. W. BRADEEN, *The Chalcidians in Thrace*, in « Amer. Journ. of Philol. », 73, 1952, 356 ss.), è adoperata ufficialmente e nell'uso comune dagli Ateniesi per distinguere i Calcidesi della Grecia Settentrionale da quelli d'Eubea (su questi ultimi v., infatti, *IG* II² 44 = *Syll.*³ 148 = TOD 124, l. 24, del 377 a. C.).   [3] Senofonte in alcuni luoghi del libro V delle *Elleniche* (2,11 ss.; 3,20 e 26; 4,54) si occupa degli avvenimenti della Calcidica tra il 382 e il 379 a. C., ma non sorprende il fatto che egli menzioni la sola Olinto, dato il ruolo preminente sostenuto da quella città nella guerra contro Sparta.   [4] Lo stato della questione è esposto da HAMPL, l. c., 177 ss. Alla bibliografia ivi citata, siano solo aggiunti U. KAHRSTEDT, *Chalcidic Studies*, in « Amer. Journ. of Philol. », 57, 1936, 416 ss. e J. PAPASTAVRU, Τὸ κοινὸν τῶν Χαλκιδέων καὶ οἱ Ὀλύνθιοι, in Μνημόσυνον Ν. Γ. Παππαδακι (Salonicco, 1947), 95 ss., spec. 104 ss. In particolare sulle monete v. D. M. ROBINSON, *Excavations at Olynthus*, VI (1933), 14 ss.; IX (1938), 124 ss. e inoltre in *R.E.*, XVIII 1 (1939), 327 s.; HAMPL, l. c., 190 n. 3 ; PAPASTAVRU, l. c., 107 n. 3.

dell'operosità e dell'attività commerciale in tutto il territorio della Calcidica, promosso dalla stessa fine della lunga e sanguinosa guerra oltre che dalla politica spartana di ripopolare città e villaggi, [1] finisce per rinsaldare i legami, già stretti sin dal tempo del conflitto archidamico, tra i diversi centri della regione. La confederazione, sorta praticamente dopo il raggruppamento dei Calcidesi intorno ad Olinto nel 432 a. C. e presentata come operante, durante la guerra peloponnesiaca, dalla correttezza terminologica di Tucidide, [2] appare giuridicamente costituita all'inizio del sec. IV a. C.

Verso il 393 a. C., infatti, Aminta III di Macedonia conclude un trattato con i Calcidesi, che vengono indicati con il vocabolo specifico di κοινόν. [3] Ora, è vero che κοινόν talvolta assume il significato di origine etnica, di comunità politica, di lega sacrale, [4] ma ciò non esclude a priori che esso altrove, anche nelle medesime fonti, [5] indichi un organismo federativo in senso proprio. Ma l'epigrafe in esame riporta un trattato, un testo ufficiale cioè, in cui il termine κοινόν deve possedere un valore preciso, giuridico. Tale valore, in rapporto alle altre testimonianze storiografiche già discusse, non può essere che quello di organo confederale dei Calcidesi. Questa interpretazione potrebbe rendere meno ipotetico l'intervento di κοιναὶ ἀρχαί calcidesi nella stipulazione, del trattato con Filippo. [6]

[1] Cf. Xen., *Hell.* II 2,5 9. Le relazioni di amicizia tra Sparta e Olinto favorirono di certo questa politica: v. M. GUDE, *A Hist. of Olynthus* (Baltimora, 1933), 17 s.   [2] Cf. Thuc., I 57,5 ; 58,1-2 ; 62,3 ; II 29,6 ; 58,1-2 ; 79,1-3-5-6-7 ; 95,1 2-3 ; 99,3 ; 101,1-6 ; IV 7 ; 79,2 ; V 3,4 ; 21,2 ; 31,6 ; 80,2 ; 82,1 ; VI 7,4 ; 10,5.   [3] Cf. *Syll.*[3] 135 = TOD 111, l. 11. Per la cronologia v. BELOCH, *Gr. Gesch.*, III[2] 1, 102.   [4] Testimonianze in LIDDELL SCOTT-JONES, *A Greek-Engl. Lex.*, s. v. κοινόν. Sul significato generale di 'comunità politica' insiste HAMPL, l. c., 179 n. 1, 195 s. (anche in «Klio», 32, 1939, 19 ; e cf. KAHRSTEDT, l. c., 427 n. 52 e ROBINSON, op. cit., IX, 144 n. 18), ma, limitatamente a questo punto, le sue conclusioni sono respinte validamente da PAPASTAVRU, l. c., 97 ss., spec. 99 n. 2. In linea di massima, invece, la teoria di HAMPL, l. c., spec. 182 dell'identificazione totale dei Calcidesi negli Olintii sembra accettata da PAPASTAVRU, l. c., 108-110, il quale conclude che il κοινὸν τῶν Χαλκιδέων non costituisce un συμμαχικὸν κράτος ma che piuttosto, in quanto sinonimo di Olinto, indica l' ἡγεμών di una συμμαχία di Calcidesi. Dove però è agevole osservare che il riconoscimento dell'esistenza di una συμμαχία infirma già a priori l'identificazione tra Olinto e i Calcidesi, su cui poggia tutta l'ipotesi.   [5] V., ad es., Hdt., V 109 ; Thuc., IV 78,3 ; Isocr., *Plat.* [XIV] 21 ; *Syll.*[3] 457, l. 10 ; etc.   [6] L'intervento dei magistrati federali nel trattato (l. 3) è stato intuìto

È notevole, poi, che non solo nel patto con Filippo o in quello con Aminta III, ma anche negli altri trattati conclusi dai Calcidesi nel sec. IV a. C., Olinto non venga mai ricordata. L'espressione di ' Calcidesi ', anzi, potrebbe far pensare al deliberato proposito delle altre città di sottolineare la propria vitalità di fronte al centro maggiore della lega. Tale restrizione dell'influenza di Olinto sembra corrispondere alla politica degli Argeadi nella Calcidica.

Perdicca II nel 432 a. C. accentra intorno ad Olinto i ' Calcidesi ', cioè praticamente gli abitanti delle penisole di Pallene e di Sitonia, piú degli altri esposti al pericolo ateniese. Tucidide allude allo stanziamento intorno ad Olinto di popolazioni che avrebbero dovuto rafforzare questa città, pur essendo estranee originariamente ad essa. [1] Può essere che il provvedimento fosse suggerito, al momento, da esigenze belliche ma, negli ulteriori sviluppi, la potenza macedone conseguiva il vantaggio manifesto di potere controllare, dopo averli raggruppati in alcune zone delimitate, gli abitanti di molte contrade sparse nel selvaggio e inaccessibile territorio calcidico. L'antica aspirazione di Alessandro I, di mirare al controllo delle coste calcidesi, [2] è in tal modo ripresa con successo da Perdicca II. Il re, con la nuova sistemazione dei Calcidesi, [3] nell' atto

con felice congettura da SEGRE, l. c., 498 s., che propone la seguente restituzione delle ll. 2-4: συμμαχήσω κατ|[ὰ τὰ ὡμολογημένα (vac.) Χαλκιδέων] μὲν ὀμνύει[ν] Φιλίπ[πω]ι τά[ς τε ἀρ]χὰς τά⟨σ⟩ ξυνὰς καὶ τοὺ|[ς πρεσβευτὰς (?), τοῖς δὲ Χαλκι]δεῦσι αὐτὸν καὶ οὓς ἄλλους Χαλκιδεῖς κελεύσω|[σι. La situazione storica sopra delineata rende preferibile questa lettura a quella proposta dal primo editore e in parte accettata, a suo tempo, dallo scrivente, op. cit., 12.   [1] Thuc., I 58,2 : il 'sinecismo' di Olinto, privato di ogni significato politico da HAMPL, l. c., 188 s., è invece difeso da PAPASTAVRU, l. c., 104 n. 2; assai prudente A. W. GOMME, A Histor. Comment. on Thucyd., I (Oxford, 1945), 206 s.   [2] Le mire di Alessandro I sulla Calcidica sono ispirate al tentativo di spezzare il blocco che Atene ha stretto intorno alla Macedonia dalla Tessaglia, dalla Tracia e da Metone (F. GEYER, Maked. bis z. Thronbesteigung Philipps II, Monaco-Berlino, 1930,49) e rientrano nell'obbiettivo fondamentale di unificare il territorio macedone. La reale portata delle intenzioni di Alessandro I non è posta in evidenza da J. PAPASTAVRU, Μακεδονικὴ Πολιτικὴ κατὰ τὸν 5ον Αἰώνα . Ἀλέξανδρος I (Salonicco, 1936), 65 ss., 71 ss.   [3] La politica calcidese di Perdicca II non è valutata compiutamente, ad es., da GEYER, op. cit., 56 ss. (anche in R.E., XIX 1 [1937], 594 s.), né da J. PAPASTAVRU, Ὁ Περδίκκας Β΄ εἰς τὰς παραμονὰς τοῦ πελοποννησιακοῦ πολέμου, in Γέρας Ἀντ. Κεραμοπούλλου (Atene, 1953), 133 ss.

stesso di accrescere l'importanza di Olinto, [1] ne annullava praticamente gli effetti, contrapponendo alla città i singoli centri che ora
la circondavano.

Anche Aminta III segue il medesimo indirizzo di trattare con
i Calcidesi, risolvendo in essi la preminenza di Olinto. All'inizio
del regno e in un momento particolarmente difficile per la Macedonia.
il re vincola a sé diplomaticamente la potenza calcidese. La costante
preoccupazione di contenere l'espansione di Olinto si rivela in seguito
nella manovra di sollecitare l'intervento di Sparta contro la metropoli
della Calcidica. [2]

Cinque lustri piú tardi, Filippo promette ai Calcidesi il territorio di Antemunte e la città di Potidea, che bloccava l'accesso della
penisola di Pallene. [3] Le trattative tra le due parti, già iniziate probabilmente verso la fine del 357 a. C., sono concluse con una alleanza nella primavera del 356 a. C., subito dopo il ritorno degli
ambasciatori appositamente inviati a consultare il dio di Delfi. As-
sicurate in tal modo le spalle, lo scopo reale dell'offerta di Filippo
è la distruzione di Potidea, che porterà al controllo macedone sulle
coste circostanti. D'altra parte, l'effettivo compenso ai Calcidesi sarà
in gran parte illusorio, una volta ottenuto, [4] e, nondimeno, esso non
verrà devoluto ad Olinto, ma a tutti i membri della lega calcidese,
entrati in fattivi rapporti con il re macedone.

È quanto Filippo può allora fare. Olinto è tenuta a bada, nel-
l'ambito piú vasto della confederazione calcidese, mentre il controllo
delle coste diviene una realtà operante attraverso la compiacente amicizia dei nuovi alleati. È ovvio che gli stessi Calcidesi sono perfet-
tamente d'accordo con il re macedone nell'intenzione di impedire
qualsiasi ulteriore espansione di Olinto, che potrebbe sminuire le
loro singole prerogative.

In tal modo viene creata da Filippo nella Calcidica una situazione che durerà sino alla politica direttamente offensiva del 349 48

---

[1] Per le vicende di Olinto dal 479 al 432 a. C. cf. GUDE, op. cit., 7 ss.
e, diversamente, HAMPL, l. c., spec. 185 (con le critiche di ROBINSON, op. cit.,
IX, 118-120).   [2] Diod., XV 19,3.   [3] Si vedano le testimonianze di Demostene e di Diodoro cit. supra.   [4] Potidea cadrà nelle mani di Filippo nel
giugno del 356 a. C. (CLOCHÉ, l. c., 407 n. 87) ; si può pensare che anche il
territorio di Antemunte sia stato ceduto ai Calcidesi in quel tempo.

a. C. [1]. Nel trattato con i Calcidesi del 356 a. C. esistono le pre-
messe della distruzione di Olinto e del pacifico assorbimento dei
rimanenti Calcidesi nello stato macedone. Si noti, infine, che pur
toccando direttamente gli interessi di cittadini ateniesi con la rovina
di Potidea, Filippo rivela le sue intenzioni pacifiste, accordando ai
cleruchi di Atene stanziati nella città il libero ritorno in patria. [2] La
realistica valutazione delle forze ateniesi è sempre presente alla mente
di Filippo e, sebbene esse siano in gran parte impegnate in lontani
scacchieri, è evidente che il re non si sente ancora abbastanza forte
e preparato per affrontarle.

In quanto alla consultazione dell'oracolo di Delfi, di cui fa men-
zione il patto (ll. 7 ss., 12 ss.), essa fu sollecitata probabilmente da
Filippo piú ancora che dai Calcidesi. Re non greco di un paese bar-
baro, [3] il padre di Alessandro aveva agio, in tal modo, di ribadire
agli occhi dei Greci le proprie intenzioni di pace e di ossequio alle
tradizioni elleniche. L'appellarsi, infatti, all'oracolo delfico, che negli
ideali di pietà e di saggezza incarnava le piú sublimi espressioni dello
spirito greco, [4] rivela la manovra di Filippo di creare uno sfondo
sacro e religioso alla sua azione diplomatica, di probabile effetto per
i Calcidesi e per i Greci tutti.[5] Naturalmente in pratica, poi, l'intervento dell'oracolo si limita a quel ruolo di legislatore religioso che
Platone attribuiva in larga misura al dio di Delfi. [6] Alla Pizia non
è sottoposta la ratifica delle decisioni prese [7] (ciò che comporterebbe
un'influenza politica nell'azione diplomatica in corso), né ad essa

---

[1] Nel 349 a. C. ha luogo un tentativo di accordo tra Atene e alcune città
calcidesi, come Acanto e Dione (*IG* II² 210 + 259 + Inv. Mus. Epigr. 6874
ed. E. SCHWEIGERT, in « Hesperia », 6, 1937, 329 ss., ll. 8 ss.). Alle ll. 12-13
è detto che le città (calcidesi) possono entrare in alleanza con Atene, purché
καθελόντας τὴν κοινὴν πρὸς Φίλιππον. Il patto di Filippo con i Calcidesi del
356 a. C. è dunque valido sino alla grande offensiva macedone del 349/48
a. C.   [2] In merito a tale episodio Diodoro (XVI 8,5) sviluppa il solito motivo retorico della preminenza morale di Atene.   [3] Rimando qui alla mia valutazione di Filippo come uomo politico, op. cit., spec. 16 ss.   [4] Su ciò v.,
ad es., da ultimo H. BERVE, in *Gestaltende Kräfte d. Antike* (Monaco, 1949),
9 ss.; e cf. R. PETTAZZONI, *La religione nella Grecia antica fino ad Alessan-
dro²* (Torino, 1953), 58, 96, 148.   [5] Diversamente CLOCHÉ, l. c., 406 e TOD,
op. cit., 178, che sopravvalutano la reale portata dell'intervento delfico nel trattato.   [6] Su ciò v. P. AMANDRY, *La Mantique Apollinienne à Delphes* (Parigi,
1950), 188.   [7] SEGRE, l. c., 497.

viene richiesto un parere politico, ma semplicemente un suggeri-
mento in tema di prescrizioni cultuali. [1]

Infine, giova notare che la tattica prudenziale seguita da Filippo
sino alla primavera del 356 a. C. fu anche suggerita al re dalla situazione interna dello stato macedone. Sino dall'avvento al trono, la
sottomissione dei principati semi-autonomi della Macedonia Occiden-
tale al potere centrale è perseguita da Filippo con le armi della di-
plomazia, piú che con la violenza. Il re mira alla coesione delle diverse forze in un saldo organismo statale unitario mentre, in tale
processo, la nobiltà finisce per rivestire nella vita della corte macedone un ruolo di primaria importanza. Le grandi famiglie princi-
pesche partecipano, assai piú che non prima, alle alte cariche dello
stato ma, al tempo stesso, il governo è sempre accentrato intorno ai
tradizionali organismi costituzionali. [2]

L'ipotesi che la nobiltà macedone da principio abbia seguito
e vigilato assai da vicino Filippo, vincolandolo rigidamente alla vec-
chia costituzione del paese, sembra tanto piú probabile, se si con-
sidera che il sovrano sino alla metà del 356 a. C.[3] 'non regem sed
tutorem pupilli egit.' [4] La tutela di Aminta IV da parte di Filippo
metteva il re in una situazione di natura eccezionale, che presumeva
un controllo piú stretto di quello solitamente esercitato sui monarchi
macedoni dall'assemblea degli uomini in armi.

Tale vigilanza fu svolta probabilmente dagli ἑταῖροι di Filippo,
cioè dal gruppo dei consiglieri politici, reclutati nell'aristocrazia, che
assistevano da presso il sovrano nell'opera di governo. Gli ' altri ',
che giurano l' ὅρκος con Filippo nel trattato con i Calcidesi (ll. 4-5)
sono da identificare appunto in questi ' eteri '. [5] Ciò significa, in

---

[1] È interessante notare che anche nella famosa visita di Alessandro all'oasi
di Ammone, al dio fu richiesto soltanto un consiglio di natura sacrale (Arr.,
VII 14,7 con le osservazioni di W. W. TARN, *Alex. the Great*, II, Cambridge,
1948, 347 ss.).   [2] V. il mio studio cit., 12 n. 28 (ove è raccolta della bibliografia). La piú recente trattazione sui fondamenti giuridici dello stato macedone
sino ad Alessandro si trova in P. De FRANCISCI, *Arcana Imperii*, II (Milano,
1948), 359 ss. (da cui deriva A. AYMARD, in « Rev. des Étud. Anc. », 52, 1950,
115 ss.).   [3] La proclamazione dell'effettiva sovranità di Filippo avvenne ' ubi
graviora bella inminebant' (Just., VII 5,10) e cioè verso la metà del 356 a. C.
(in estate scoppierà la guerra illirica e in autunno quella tracica: v. CLOCHÉ,
l. c., 412).   [4] Just. 5,9.   [5] Il TOD, op. cit., 174 non sembra escludere
un'eventuale identificazione con degli ἑταῖροι, peraltro non meglio precisati.

sostanza, che il re non poteva giurare da solo e che quindi le sua volontà personale era mediata dai suoi consiglieri, cosí come la sua libertà d'azione era controllata, in specie nelle azioni conclusive.

Anche in forza di tale situazione, è naturale che la politica di Filippo sino alla primavera del 356 a. C. sia improntata piuttosto ad una direttiva diplomatica, che non alla potenza delle armi. In questo senso, il trattato con i Calcidesi segna il coronamento di un periodo storico e la conclusione di un metodo di governo sperimentato con successo per quattro anni.

FRANCO CARRATA THOMES

RIASSUNTO. L'A. sostiene che la politica di Filippo II dal 359 alla primavera del 356 a. C. è ispirata ad un accorto e prudente equilibrio, che culmina nel patto stipulato con il ϰοινόν dei Calcidesi. Mette quindi in luce il valore particolare del trattato, esaminando i problemi ad esso connessi, e cerca di dimostrare la reale entità storica dello stato calcidese nel sec. IV a. C.

III

G. E. M. de Ste Croix

The Alleged Secret Pact between Athens and
Philip II concerning Amphipolis and Pydna

THE ALLEGED SECRET PACT BETWEEN
ATHENS AND PHILIP II
CONCERNING AMPHIPOLIS AND PYDNA

WHAT is the reality behind the famous phrase, τὸ θρυλούμενόν ποτ' ἀπόρρητον ἐκεῖνο in Demosthenes 2. 6? It is commonly spoken of as a secret *treaty*, *pact*, *agreement*, *bargain*, or *understanding*, or as a secret *clause* or *article* (all these terms have been used in recent times), between Athens and Philip II of Macedon, at some time between 359 and 357, whereby the Athenians promised to hand over their ally, Pydna, to Philip, in return for his promise to hand over Amphipolis to them. Among many modern writers in whom this conception appears, in different forms, it should be sufficient to cite Beloch, Bengtson, Bury, Cloché, Geyer, Glotz and Cohen, Hammond, Holm, Meyer, Pickard-Cambridge, Sandys, and A. Schaefer.[1] These and other scholars have dated the pact (or whatever they have chosen to call it) to one of three different periods within the years 359–357: (1) in 359–358, after Philip's defeat of Argaeus and before his campaign against the Illyrians (Beloch, Bengtson, Geyer, Meyer, Schaefer); (2) in 357, during the siege of Amphipolis (Glotz and Cohen, Holm, Pickard-Cambridge); (3) in 357, soon after the fall of Amphipolis (Cloché, Sandys). Among all those who have dealt with the subject in modern times, only Momigliano seems to have taken up a thoroughly sceptical attitude towards the very existence of this alleged agreement.[2]

The only evidence of any importance consists of two passages, Demosthenes 2. 6–7 and Theopompus F 30, which will be examined in turn.

1. Dem. 2. 6–7 (delivered in 349/8). The sentence is involved and needs to be split up into its component parts. Demosthenes is describing a series of cunning actions by Philip, grouped under three heads:

(A) In the beginning Philip won over (προσαγαγόμενον) the simple minds of the Athenians, when certain men tried to drive away the Olynthians who wanted to address the Assembly; and he did this (i) by saying he would hand over Amphipolis to Athens, and (ii) τῷ ... τὸ θρυλούμενόν ποτ' ἀπόρρητον ἐκεῖνο κατασκευάσαι, by making deceitful use of that once notorious secret.

[1] K. J. Beloch, *Gr. Gesch.* iii². 1. 225–6, 229–30; H. Bengtson, *Gr. Gesch.²*, pp. 300, 301; J. B. Bury, *Hist. of Greece³* (rev. R. Meiggs), p. 686; P. Cloché, in various works, including *La politique étrangère d'Athènes*, pp. 154–5, and *Un fondateur d'empire*, pp. 59–62; F. Geyer, in *R-E.* xix. 2, col. 2267, cf. 2269; G. Glotz and R. Cohen, *Hist. grecque*, iii. 230–1; N. G. L. Hammond, *Hist. of Greece*, pp. 515, 538–9; A. Holm, *Hist. of Greece* (Eng. trans., 1896), iii. 210, and 220–1, n. 3; Ed. Meyer, *Gesch. des Alt.* v. 479, 484; A. W. Pickard-Cambridge, *Demosthenes*, pp. 155–7, and in *Camb. Anc. Hist.* vi. 204, 207; J. E. Sandys, *The First Phil. and the Olynths. of Demosth.* (rev. ed., 1910–54),

pp. xl-xli, 161; A. Schaefer, *Demosth. u. seine Zeit*, ii². 19–20, 21. Of these, Beloch and Bury speak of a 'secret article' in a 'treaty'; Cloché and Hammond of a 'pact'. Hammond (p. 538) even speaks of Athens and Macedon as having 'signed a secret pact'. Most other scholars have preferred to use rather vaguer terms.

[2] A. Momigliano, *Filippo il Macedone*, pp. 45–47. The scepticism is based on general considerations, very sensibly expressed. The discussion is brief and does not extend to the constitutional issue or the alternative interpretations of Theopomp. F 30, to be discussed below.

(B) Next he won the friendship of the Olynthians, by (i) capturing Potidaea (which belonged to Athens), and (ii) doing wrong to his former allies[1] by handing Potidaea over to the Olynthians.

(C) And finally Philip won over the Thessalians, by (i) promising to hand over Magnesia to them, and (ii) taking it upon himself to fight the Phocian war for them.

The clear implication is that the ἀπόρρητον was something invented or cunningly utilized by Philip in order to induce the Athenians not to ally themselves with Olynthus. The verb κατασκευάζω need not necessarily have a pejorative meaning (see, e.g., Ps.-Dem. 50. 36), but it clearly has here: the sense is 'fabricate, trump up' (see L.S.J., s.v. κατασκευάζω, 4), or at least 'utilize with fraudulent intent'. The object of the verb (here τὸ . . . ἀπόρρητον) may either be non-existent altogether, a mere pretence (as in Ps.-Dem. 42. 28, 30), or be real enough but deliberately brought into play with evil intent (as in Dem. 21. 92, 103; 18. 151)—we still have to decide between these alternatives. The expression, τὸ θρυλούμενον . . . ἀπόρρητον, a deliberate oxymoron, has an ironical ring.

It is hard to say what promises, if any, were made by Philip to Athens concerning Amphipolis in 359–357. Demosthenes, as we have seen, alleged in 349/8 that Philip had said he would hand over Amphipolis: the context shows that Philip must have made this promise, if at all, not later than 357, before his alliance with οἱ Χαλκιδεῖς.[2] Some four years earlier[3] Demosthenes had claimed more specifically, in 23. 116, that Philip, while laying siege to Amphipolis (in 357), had said he was besieging it in order to hand it over to Athens. Hegesippus, in Ps.-Dem. 7. 27–28 (delivered in 343/2), speaks of an actual letter sent to Athens by Philip while he was besieging Amphipolis, in which he acknowledged that Amphipolis was the property of Athens and said he would restore it to Athens when he had captured it. (This letter, whether real or

[1] Presumably these allies are the Athenian cleruchs in Potidaea: see Ps.-Dem. 7. 10, where Hegesippus speaks of a sworn συμμαχία between Philip and Ἀθηναίων οἱ ἐν Ποτειδαίᾳ κατοικοῦντες (a technically correct designation of the cleruchs—miscalled ἄποικοι in Dem. 6. 20), . . . τοῖς οἰκοῦσιν ἐν Ποτειδαίᾳ. It may surprise some historians to find an Athenian cleruchy entering into a συμμαχία on its own account, an act for which there seems to be no known parallel. (Cf. Ps.-Arist. Oecon. 2. 2. 5, 1347ᵃ18–24, where the same Potidaean cleruchy levies an eisphora.) But Hegesippus' statement is most explicit; and one of the scholia on Dem. 2. 7 (for what it is worth) identifies the συμμάχους of that passage as 'the Potidaeans'. Many of the manuscripts of Dem. 2. 7 have ὑμᾶς (or ἡμᾶς) after συμμάχους, but it is probably better to delete the word, with Blass and others— unless of course we think Dem. is deliberately committing a characteristic exaggeration. Schaefer (op. cit., p. 20, n. 1), accepting ὑμᾶς, takes Dem. 2. 7 as a proof that in 359– 358 'ein Vertrag zustande kam' between

Philip and Athens, and others have reached the same conclusion, for similar or different reasons. But although Athens was on friendly terms with Philip from the time he released his Athenian prisoners on the suppression of the revolt of Argaeus in 359–358 (Dem. 23. 121; Diod. 16. 4. 1; Just. 7. 6. 6) until war broke out in 356 (see Tod, ii. 157 = I.G. ii². 127, line 41: [- τὸν πόλεμον τ]ὸν πρὸς Φίλιππον), and may even have been persuaded εἰρήνην πρὸς αὐτὸν συνθέσθαι, as alleged by Diod., there was surely no συμμαχία between Athens itself and Philip at any time before 346—if there had been, Athens, by far the stronger party during the earlier years of Philip's reign (see Momigliano, loc. cit.), would surely have insisted on Philip's giving a formal acknowledgement of her claim to Amphipolis; and it is evident, if only from later Athenian propaganda, that this did not happen.

[2] Tod, ii. 158 (and see the notes).

[3] Most probably in the summer of 352; but the date of the speech is not certain and may be earlier.

fictitious, must be distinguished from the letter, whether real or fictitious, mentioned by Demosthenes 23. 121, in which Philip in 359–358, on the defeat of Argaeus, declared his readiness to make an alliance and renew his hereditary friendship with Athens.) On the other hand, Aeschines, according to his own story, made no mention of any such promise by Philip when he was explaining to the king in 346 the legal foundation of Athens's assertion of her right to Amphipolis as against Macedon, but merely claimed that Philip's father, Amyntas III, through his representative at a congress of 'the Spartans and the other Greeks', had joined in voting to help Athens recapture Amphipolis.[1] This casts serious doubt upon the assertions of Demosthenes and Hegesippus, because Aeschines had every reason on this occasion to mention Philip's promises given in 359–357, if they were real. It makes one wonder whether perhaps Philip produced some ambiguous formula which the Athenians at first interpreted as an admission of their right to Amphipolis and later realized was capable of being differently construed.[2] Certainly, historians have been far too ready to accept the prejudiced and unsupported statements of Demosthenes and Hegesippus. The only facts of which we can be confident are those given by Diodorus 16. 3. 3 and 16. 4. 1, and Polyaenus 4. 2. 17: Philip in 359–358, withdrawing his garrison from Amphipolis, allowed it to regain its independence, and made peace with Athens.

So far, there is nothing to tell us what the ἀπόρρητον was. Of the scholia, the only one worth considering reads as follows: διὰ τί δὲ ἐν ἀπορρήτῳ; ἵνα μὴ ἑκάτεροι μαθόντες φυλάξωνται, οἵ τε Ποτιδαιᾶται καὶ οἱ Πυδναῖοι. Θεόπομπος δέ φησιν ὅτι περὶ Πύδνης μόνον καὶ Φιλίππου, ἵνα δῷ αὐτὸς μὲν Ἀθηναίοις Ἀμφίπολιν, δέξηται δὲ παρ' αὐτῶν τὴν Πύδναν αὐτοῦ οὖσαν. καὶ τὸ ἀπόρρητον δέ, ἵνα μὴ μαθόντες οἱ Πυδναῖοι φυλάξωνται· οὐ γὰρ ἐβούλοντο εἶναι ὑπὸ τὸν Φίλιππον.[3] The pointless reference to the Potidaeans may have no better foundation than the allusion to Potidaea in the next clause of Demosthenes' sentence: certainly no one will wish to suppose that the Athenians were prepared to give Philip Potidaea, to which they had sent a cleruchy at its own request in 361.[4] The scholiast's statement about Pydna is derived from the well-known fragment of Theopompus, to which we now turn. We shall see that what Theopompus actually says offers no foundation for the theory of a 'pact' between Athens and Philip.

[1] Aeschin. 2. 25–33, esp. 32–33. See the observations of S. Accame, *La lega ateniese*, pp. 165–6. The spring of 369 is plausibly suggested as the date of this congress by Accame (pp. 155–6, 164–6), and by G. L. Cawkwell, *C.Q.* N.S. xi (1961), 80–81; but some doubt remains.

[2] W. Mitford, *Hist. of Greece*, iv. 270, after misquoting Theopomp. F 30, has some sensible remarks on this subject. No information of any value for our purpose is given by the fragmentary Athenian inscription published by B. D. Meritt, in *Hesp.* xxx (1961), 207–8, no. 2, which may refer to an embassy from Macedon about the beginning of Philip II's reign.

[3] See the edition of Dem. by W. Dindorf, vol. viii (1851), p. 85, lines 19–24. The scholion on p. 84, lines 13–18, which asserts that our phrase refers to Oropus and that

the secrecy was due to the need to conceal the affair from the Thebans, can be ignored: Philip was not nearly strong enough in 359–357, even after his capture of Amphipolis, to be able to make any impression upon Athenian opinion by offering to help Athens get back Oropus from the still powerful Thebans. There may have been some confusion in the scholiast's mind with Philip's later alleged promise to hand over Oropus to Athens, which first appears in Dem. 5. 10 (346); cf. 6. 30; 19. 22, 220, 326. In all these passages Amphipolis is mentioned in the same context.

[4] Tod, ii. 146; cf. Ps.-Dem. 7. 10; Diod. 16. 8. 5 (where the Athenian φρουρά will be the cleruchs). Probably the request for the cleruchs was due to the Potidaeans' fear of falling again under Olynthian control.

2. Theopompus, *F. Gr. Hist.* ii. B. 115 F 30 a (= fr. 165 O.C.T). [1]According to the lexicographers, who are trying to provide an explanation of the mysterious phrase in Dem. 2. 6, Theopompus spoke of Antiphon and Charidemus as being sent to Philip as ambassadors, 'to negotiate also for Philip's friendship'. When they arrived, they tried to persuade him to deal in secret with the Athenians, to the effect that Athens should take Amphipolis, promising him Pydna. The Athenian ambassadors, however, said nothing to the Assembly, wishing to keep Pydna in ignorance, with the intention of betraying it; but they dealt ἐν ἀπορρήτῳ with the Council.

Several comments can be made immediately on this passage. First, Theopompus, by describing Antiphon and Charidemus as sent to Philip πράξοντας καὶ περὶ φιλίας, οἳ παραγενόμενοι συμπείθειν αὐτὸν ἐπεχείρουν κ.τ.λ., seems to be attributing the initiative in regard to the promise of Pydna in exchange for Amphipolis entirely to the ambassadors, and certainly does not suggest that they were acting under secret instructions received from the Council before they set out. Secondly, even if in other respects the account of Theopompus is more or less accurate, it is hard to believe that the ambassadors would have told the Council the whole story on their return. It was only too likely that there would be some objectors among the Five Hundred, and the chance of the whole sordid intrigue's leaking out and coming to the ears of the Pydnaeans would be considerable. And much more important, there was not the least point in divulging the affair to the Council, since the Council, as we shall see, could have had no more power than the ambassadors to bind Athens. Thirdly, it is interesting that the two ambassadors were not, as far as we know, men of any very great political consequence. Antiphon may possibly be the man who was later disfranchised, and subsequently executed on a charge of attempting to burn the dockyards as Philip's agent;[2] but he may well be another Antiphon. There is no clue who Charidemus was: he was certainly not the famous *condottiere*, who was continuously engaged in Thrace on behalf of Cersobleptes in the early 350's.[3] The fact—if it is a fact—that these two men only were sent on the embassy in question may perhaps suggest that it was regarded by the Assembly as an exploratory one and was intended to ascertain Philip's attitude rather than to arrive at any definite terms.[4]

[1] There is a puzzle about the book number of this fragment, which is said by the lexicographers to come from Book λα′, i.e. 31, which apparently deals with the year 346 or thereabouts. Since the embassy referred to cannot of course have been later than the capture of Pydna by Philip in 357–356, Jacoby preferred to treat F 30 as coming from Book 1 (which seems to have dealt with the years 360–359), while offering as an alternative Book 3 (dealing with the years 357–356). But see n. 4 on p. 117 below.

[2] See Dem. 18. 132–3; Deinarch. 1 (c. Dem.). 63; Plut. *Demosth.* 14. 5. In view of the opening words of Dem. 18. 134, the date of the execution of Antiphon cannot be later than 343, the date of the Delos affair.

[3] See Dem. 23. 163–73, with Tod, ii. 151, the treaty referred to in sec. 173, which must have been made near the end of 357.

[4] We cannot of course be certain that the two ambassadors named by Theopompus were the only ones. For important embassies (above all, those sent to negotiate treaties) three, five, or ten was the usual number of Athenian envoys. See F. Poland, *De legationibus Graecorum publicis* (Diss., Leipzig, 1885), pp. 53 ff., esp. 57–63; M. Heyse, *De legationibus Atticis* (Diss., Göttingen, 1882), pp. 30–32, both of whom, after setting out all the evidence available in their day, concluded that the number of ambassadors depended on the importance of their mission. Only two ambassadors are apparently sent in Thuc. 2. 67. 2 (to Sitalces); Xen. *Hell.* 7. 1. 33 (to the Great King); Arr. *Anab.* 3. 6. 2 (to Alexander in 331); and (if Epicrates and Phormisius were the only two) in Plato Com. fr. 119 K, ap. Athen. 6. 229f; but none of these embassies seems to have

Quite apart from the fact that any unsupported statement of this very unreliable historian should be examined with special vigilance, far too much has been read into this passage as it stands. Theopompus may reasonably be thought to imply (although he does not actually assert) that there was some kind of secret *agreement* between Philip and *the ambassadors*; but, as reported,[1] he does not speak, even by implication, of any agreement between Philip and *the Athenians*, nor, for very good constitutional reasons, can Demosthenes' words refer to any such agreement.

The constitutional issue is central. A Greek city—a democracy, at any rate—could bind itself only by a treaty authorized by a decision of its supreme governing body—at Athens, of course, the Assembly.[2] The swearing of oaths by men officially empowered to give them on behalf of the city was the essential element. A secret treaty, or a secret clause in a treaty, was a constitutional impossibility for a democracy; and it makes not the slightest difference if instead of using the word treaty we speak of a pact or agreement or arrangement or bargain or understanding—the fact remains that 'the Athenians' could not enter into any engagement at all except by a decision of the Assembly. No one has even tried to produce a parallel to the alleged 'secret pact' over Amphipolis and Pydna, because of course none exists. According to Aeschines, Cleochares of Chalcis said in 346 that the secret diplomacy of the greater powers alarmed men belonging to small states, like himself: τοὺς ... μικροπολίτας, ὥσπερ αὐτός, φοβεῖν τὰ τῶν μειζόνων ἀπόρρητα.[3] This, however, cannot be taken as evidence that Greek cities, democracies at any rate, could conclude secret treaties, or treaties with secret clauses: it refers to the sort of secret dealings which Demosthenes says Aeschines had, or pretended to have had, with Philip in 346.[4] There seems to be only one passage in any ancient source which asserts the conclusion of a secret treaty between Greek city-states, and this text (Polyb. 4. 16. 5: Sparta and the Aetolian League) does not deserve to be taken seriously—see the Note at the end of this article (pp. 118–19).

There is only one set of circumstances conceivable *a priori* which might justify us in speaking of the affair we are considering as tantamount to a pact between Philip and 'the Athenians'. We should have to suppose that the Assembly itself explicitly authorized the Council not only to negotiate with Philip through ambassadors instructed and received back in secret session (a course of action of which no other example is known), but actually to conclude terms with Philip on behalf of 'the Athenians'. It is difficult to prove that nothing of this sort can possibly have happened, but even Theopompus does not assert it, and no parallel to such a procedure is known from the whole history of Athenian democracy. Anyone familiar with Athenian diplomatic methods will realize that anything of the sort is unlikely in the extreme. The Council could certainly meet ἐν ἀπορρήτῳ to discuss matters which it might not be in

been negotiating a treaty (and see Poland, op. cit., p. 61, with 56).

[1] Since he is being quoted explicitly in elucidation of the mysterious phrase in Dem. 2. 6, it is unlikely that anything relevant has been omitted by the lexicographers.

[2] There seems to be no comprehensive, up-to-date work on this topic to which reference can usefully be made. See, however, Ch. Lécrivain, in Daremberg–Saglio, *Dict. des Ant.* iii. 2. 1025–30; ii. 2. 1197 ff., esp. 1206–8; also E. Bickerman, *R.I.D.A.* i (1952), 199–213; D. J. Mosley, *Proc. Camb. Philol. Soc.* N.S. vii (1961), 59–63. Most of our evidence of course relates to Athens, but the rule was doubtless the same for other democracies: see, e.g., Thuc. 5. 40–41 (esp. 41. 3), Argos.   [3] Aeschin. 2. 119–20.

[4] See the references at the end of n. 3 on p. 112 above.

the public interest to disclose to all the world;[1] and on occasion the Assembly might make the Council αὐτοκράτωρ or κυρία for implementing the provisions of some decree;[2] but the known examples[3] contain nothing remotely comparable to the supposed pact we are considering. The Council is never made αὐτοκράτωρ or κυρία to send out ambassadors or to take any other kind of independent action, or even independent decisions, in any major matter,[4] let alone enter into an engagement on behalf of the people: the usual situation is that a decree of the Assembly authorizes the Council to fill in any details not provided for by the decree.[5]

At this point it is desirable to forestall an objection based upon the appeal to modern analogy. The democratic states of modern times, it will be said, may in general be unable, equally with Greek cities, to bind themselves by treaty without a public decision of their supreme organs of authority; but their governments have often, on their own initiative, negotiated secretly with foreign powers, and entered into engagements by which they have undertaken to be bound, either by the addition of secret clauses to public treaties or independently of such treaties.[6] The simple answer to this is that a Greek

---

[1] The material passages are: Diod. 11. 39. 5; 11. 42. 5; Ar. *Eq.* 647–50; Diod. 13. 2. 6; Andoc. 1.45 (cf. 15); 2. 3, 19–21; Lys. 13. 21; *Hell. Oxy.* 1. 1–2 (but note the Council's disclaimer); Lys. 31. 31; Ps.-Dem. 25. 23; Harp. s.v. ἀπεσχοινισμένος; Diod. 17. 111. 3; perhaps Aeschin. 3. 125.

[2] The three fifth-century examples, in all of which the word used is αὐτοκράτωρ, are: (1) in 450, D 11 in *A.T.L.* ii. 57–60 (= *S.E.G.* x. 14), 86 (= *I.G.* i². 22. 73), fragmentary; (2) in 434, D 1 in *A.T.L.* ii. 46–47 (= *I.G.* i². 91), 7–9 makes the Council αὐτοκράτωρ for convening the Logistai; (3) in 415, Andoc. 1. 15: the Council was made αὐτοκράτωρ for investigating the affair of the Mysteries and the Hermae. In all seven of the fourth-century examples the word used is κυρία: (1) in 377, Tod, ii. 123 (= *I.G.* ii². 43), 31–35: the Council is to be κυρία for destroying stelae prejudicial to the allies; (2) in (probably) 365/4, *I.G.* ii². 216 b. 3–5, as restored by D. M. Lewis in *B.S.A.* xlix (1954), 40–41 (see *S.E.G.* xiv. 47): the Council is to be [κυρία] to decide anything lacking in the decree; (3) in 356, Tod, ii. 157 (= *I.G.* ii². 127), 34–35: the same; (4) in 352, *S.I.G.*³ 204 (= *I.G.* ii². 204), 85–86: the same; (5) Dem. 19. 154 says that in 346 the Assembly had made the Council κυρία regarding the ('second') embassy to Philip (which had already been voted by the Assembly), apparently because the regular Assembly days for that prytany had all been used up; (6) after 336/5, *I.G.* ii². 435. 7–9: the same as nos. 2–4; (7) in 325/4, Tod, ii. 200 (= *I.G.* ii². 1629) 264–9: ἐὰν δέ του προσδέει τόδε τὸ ψήφισμα τῶν περὶ τὸν ἀπόστολον, τὴν βουλὴν κυρίαν εἶναι ψηφίζεσθαι, μὴ λύουσαν μηθὲν τῶν ἐψηφισμένων τῶι δήμωι. In

fact the Council added an extra quadrireme (*I.G.* ii². 1629. 272 ff.—not in Tod). And see Lyc. *c. Leocr.* 37 (338). Cf., outside Athens, Tod, ii. 201 (= *O.G.I.S.* 2), 37–38 (Mytilene, 324). For an admirable brief discussion of the working of the Athenian democracy which brings out very well the role of the Council, see A. H. M. Jones, *Athenian Democracy*, pp. 99–133.

[3] Many of them are discussed by Cloché, *R.É.G.* xxxiv (1921), 233 ff., at pp. 248–54 (secret sessions) and 254–8 (Council αὐτοκράτωρ or κυρία).

[4] The Assembly might go so far as to instruct the Council to elect ambassadors to receive the oaths of another state after the terms of the treaty had been settled (*I.G.* ii². 16 b. 10–13, of 394); but even this is exceptional.

[5] According to Cloché (op. cit., p. 256), there is an insinuation in Tod, ii. 200. 264–9 (see n. 2 above) that the Council might take decisions clearly contrary to votes of the Assembly. Surely not. Of course there was always the possibility that the Council might disobey its instructions, or act carelessly. In this case the Council is simply being given a warning to take special care.

[6] Among the examples involving Great Britain are the two so-called 'Mediterranean Agreements' of 1887 (of the first of which Lord Salisbury wrote to Queen Victoria on 10 Feb. 1887: 'It is as close an alliance as the Parliamentary character of our institutions will permit'); the secret clauses of the Anglo-French entente of 1904; the exchange of letters on 22 Nov. 1912 between the British Foreign Secretary and the French ambassador; the 'secret treaty' of Mar.–Apr. 1915 between Britain, France, and Russia

116   G. E. M. DE SAINTE CROIX

city—a democracy anyway[1]—had nothing like a 'government' in the technical
modern sense, and it is modern 'governments' which have entered into these
secret engagements. It may well be far from clear who precisely is bound by
them, and indeed whether they are really anything more than 'gentlemen's
agreements'—governments may not be able to guarantee that their successors
will regard themselves as bound, but at least they can commit themselves, and
hold out a fair prospect of committing their states as long as they remain in
power. Greek democracies had no 'governments' which could enter into such
engagements, and there is no evidence that they tried to make up for this by
giving special powers ad hoc to their βουλαί, to their generals or other magistrates, or to special envoys.

Even when ambassadors were made αὐτοκράτορες (or τέλος ἔχοντες), their
city was not bound until it ratified any terms they accepted.[2] Ambassadors,
or other politicians acting on their own initiative, might make secret representations of their own to a foreign power, and sometimes these might have a
material effect upon the course of action adopted by that power. An ambassador
reporting back to the Assembly might represent, like Callias in 340, πράξεις
πράττειν δι' ἀπορρήτων,[3] and if his credit with the people were good, they
might be the more influenced by him in making their final decision. Such
representations, however, could be no more than an expression of personal
views, or at most personal engagements to act in a particular way and to try to
persuade others to do so. Demosthenes makes various assertions about what
Aeschines had said in the Assembly when reporting back from the 'second
embassy' to Philip in 346.[4] Whether these assertions were true or false, they
imply that Athenian ambassadors sent to a foreign power might indeed 'arrange

regarding Constantinople and the Straits, later published by the Bolsheviks; the Sykes–Picot agreement between Britain and France of Jan. 1916; and the abortive 'agreement of St. Jean de Maurienne' of Apr.–Aug. 1917 between Britain, France, and Italy. See A. J. P. Taylor, *The Struggle for Mastery in Europe 1848–1918*, pp. 310–13 and 320–2, 415, 480–1, 540–2, 543, 561.

[1] And the position was evidently much the same under many oligarchic constitu-tions. Although it was 'the Four Hundred' (Thuc. 8, chs. 70. 2; 71. 1, 3; 86. 9; 89. 2; 90. 1; 92. 2; Arist. *Ath. Pol.* 32. 3) who sent ambassadors to the Spartans to negotiate for peace in 411, the constitution set up by the oligarchs in the spring had specifically re-served to 'the Five Thousand' the right to make treaties (*Ath. Pol.* 29. 5, reporting the decisions taken at Colonus in a very different spirit from Thuc. 8, chs. 67. 2–3; 68. 1; 69. 1). In 421 the Boeotarchs of the oligarchic (*Hell. Oxy.* 11. 2) Boeotian League agreed to commit the League to a series of alliances, with every expectation that their arrange-ments would be meekly endorsed by the Federal Council, the supreme authority in Boeotia (αἱ τέσσαρες βουλαὶ τῶν Βοιωτῶν, αἵπερ ἅπαν τὸ κῦρος ἔχουσιν—clearly the four constituent panels of the Federal Council

since they are referred to in the same con-text in the singular, τὴν βουλήν: Thuc. 5. 38. 2–3; cf. *Hell. Oxy.* 11. 2–4); but the Council refused to ratify the alliances. In a close oligarchy like Sparta, however, the ephors, who had considerable powers in dealing with foreign affairs, might take it upon themselves to do things which the magistrates of a democracy would never have dared to do: see, e.g., Diod. 14. 21. 1–2.

[2] See Xen. *Hell.* 2. 2. 17–22; cf. Thuc. 5. 40. 3–41. 3 (Argos. The envoys appear to have been αὐτοκράτορες, although they are not explicitly said to be). In 392/1 the terms arranged at Sparta by Andocides and his colleagues, who were αὐτοκράτορες (Andoc. 3. 33–34), were rejected by the Assembly and the ambassadors exiled: Philoch., *F. Gr. Hist.* iii B 328 F 149. We must not assume from what Andoc. says, in his attempt to gain credit for the forty days for consideration, that the ambassadors could have accepted the Spartan terms *and bound Athens* thereby—the Assembly could still have repudiated their action.

[3] Aeschin. 3. 96. Cf. Dem. 19. 22.

[4] Dem. 19. 19–23 (esp. 22–23), 35–39, 42–43.

ALLEGED SECRET PACT BETWEEN ATHENS AND PHILIP II 117

things'—or at least try to do so, and claim to have done so—which were not actually included in the formal treaty. (The ambassadors on the occasion in question had been instructed to 'accomplish any good thing within their power'.)[1] But it is worth noticing that all the claims Demosthenes puts into Aeschines' mouth are about what *Philip* will do for the benefit of Athens.[2] If any ambassador undertook that *Athens* would do something going beyond his instructions (normally contained in writing, in pursuance of the decree sending out the embassy),[3] he did so at his peril,[4] and the foreign power he had been sent to would know perfectly well that all he meant was that he would use his best endeavours at Athens to bring it about. Even if Theopompus F 30 is substantially true, the most we can read into it is that Antiphon and Charidemus, anxious for friendship between Philip and Athens, said that if he would affirm, or formally reaffirm,[5] Athens's right to Amphipolis, or perhaps actually hand that city over to Athens, *they and their political associates* would use all their influence with the Athenians to stop relief being sent to Pydna, should Philip attack it, and perhaps even assist Philip more effectively by taking measures to betray Pydna to him; and that when they returned to Athens, they told the Council something of what had passed—but probably without mentioning Pydna.[6]

What, then, is Demosthenes' ἀπόρρητον? Does it necessarily refer to the events described in Theopompus F 30?

Among the large number of historians who have accepted the fragment of Theopompus as true and have used it to interpret Dem. 2. 6, only Thirlwall[7] and Grote[8] have entirely avoided the blunder of speaking of a treaty or pact, or at any rate an arrangement or understanding, between Philip and 'Athens' or 'the Athenians'. Grote declared that Antiphon and Charidemus not only reported to the Council (as Theopompus says) but 'took their instructions from it'. This, as we have seen, is not the natural interpretation of the Theopompus

---

[1] Aeschin. 2. 104, 120. Cf. Tod, ii. 123 (= *I.G.* ii². 43), 72–77.

[2] Cf. the alleged promise of Philip to give Athens Euboea and Oropus (in return, apparently, for her abandoning her claims to Amphipolis), mentioned by Dem.—see n. 3 on p. 112 above.

[3] See, e.g., Andoc. 3. 35; Dem. 19. 278.

[4] If the ambassador Antiphon is indeed the man who was later disfranchised (see p. 113 above), and if he and Charidemus did negotiate with Philip about Pydna, as Theopompus says, one might be tempted to wonder whether the disfranchisement was due to the story's becoming public knowledge after Philip's capture of Pydna in 357/356. But this is highly speculative: the διαψήφισις of 346 would be an obvious occasion for the disfranchisement, which of course need not have had anything to do with the embassy of 359–357. Mr. G. W. Bowersock has suggested to me that if the lexicographers are right in attributing F 30 of Theopomp. to Book 31 of his *Philippica* (see p. 113, n. 1, above), then the whole story of the promise to surrender Pydna may

have been introduced for the first time in 346 (to which Book 31 presumably referred), in an attempt to blacken the character of Antiphon, now regarded as an agent of Philip, and procure his disfranchisement at the διαψήφισις.

[5] The question is: had Philip acknowledged Athens's claim to Amphipolis (see pp. 111–12 above) before receiving the embassy? And if he had, why was it necessary for the ambassadors to offer him Pydna? Several scholars (notably Grote, Cloché, and Sandys) have thought of the embassy as being sent to Philip after the fall of Amphipolis. Perhaps in that case a treaty of peace had in fact been concluded, as Diod. (16. 4. 1) says, but without the express mention of Amphipolis which he records, and the ambassadors were now seeking an unequivocal renunciation by Philip, or even the actual delivery of the city to Athens?

[6] See p. 113 above.

[7] C. Thirlwall, *Hist. of Greece*, v. 192–4, cf., however, 196–7: 'the secret compact'.

[8] G. Grote, *Hist. of Greece* (new ed., 1888), ix. 231–2.

fragment, which is worded in such a way as to attribute the initiative to the ambassadors. It would certainly provide a subject (the Council) for Theopompus' singular verb πέμπει, but this could also be explained as referring to the Athenian δῆμος, or (although this usage is far less common in ancient writers than it is today) to the mover of the decree sending out the ambassadors. Realizing, no doubt, that the mere complicity of the Council would not by itself be of the slightest help in explaining Dem. 2. 6 (where the ἀπόρρητον is represented as being *used by Philip as a means of inducing the Assembly to refuse the alliance offered by Olynthus*), Grote stated it as a fact that the Assembly was influenced by the knowledge that 'negotiations, unavoidably secret, were proceeding, to ensure the acquisition of Amphipolis'—which, on Grote's chronology, had already fallen to Philip at the time of the embassy of Antiphon and Charidemus. Although this account goes far beyond the evidence we have, it is the best explanation that can be given by those who want to interpret Demosthenes in the light of Theopompus. Nevertheless, this is not at all a satisfactory solution, because it does not really fit Demosthenes' words, unless we assume he was speaking in a very slovenly manner. The ἀπόρρητον, if interpreted in the light of Theopompus F 30, was the exchange of Amphipolis for Pydna, and Philip's side of the bargain was the surrender of Amphipolis. Demosthenes will then be saying that Philip successfully influenced the Athenians against helping Olynthus (1) by saying he would hand over Amphipolis to Athens, and (2) by (making deceitful use of that once notorious secret, that is) promising to hand over Amphipolis to Athens!

The only alternative, which should be seriously considered, is to reject the connexion between the two passages and admit that we just do not know what Demosthenes' ἀπόρρητον was: it need not have been concerned with Pydna, or even Amphipolis. If we turn back to the analysis of Dem. 2. 6–7 on pp. 110–11 above, we can see that the second part of the sentence, viz. clause (B), describes two successive stages of Philip's activity in relation to Potidaea, and that the third part, clause (C), deals with two entirely different and unrelated actions by Philip. Why should the ἀπόρρητον necessarily have had anything to do with Amphipolis?[1] Why could it not have been something *invented* by Philip?[2]

A NOTE ON POLYB. 4. 16. 5

The only text which speaks of what we should call a 'secret treaty' between Greek city-states is Polyb. 4. 16. 5: the Spartans in 220 διαπεμψάμενοι λάθρᾳ πρὸς τοὺς Αἰτωλοὺς φιλίαν δι' ἀπορρήτων ἔθεντο καὶ συμμαχίαν. Polybius was particularly hostile to both the Aetolians and the Spartans, and anything he says to their discredit needs to be scrutinized with special care. In his *Hist. Comm. on Polyb.* F. W. Walbank rightly observes that 'φιλίαν . . . καὶ συμμαχίαν (even δι' ἀπορρήτων) seems an exaggeration at this date'. The existence on this occasion of anything more than a purely informal engagement between certain leading men among the Spartans and Aetolians is indeed more than doubtful, for the following reasons (the references are all to Polyb. Book 4):

[1] Philip might have pretended, for example, that he would grant the Athenians special privileges in connexion with timber which grew in areas he controlled, but that he could not afford to enter into a public treaty for the time being, as it might prejudice his relations with other states to which he was already committed.

[2] As Momigliano (loc. cit., p. 110, n. 2 above) was inclined to think. See the discussion of the meaning of κατασκευάσαι, p. 111 above.

1. The Aetolians, who in the summer of 220 had taken an official vote merely to εἰρήνην ἄγειν towards the Spartans (15. 8), were, as is well known, constitutionally incapable of entering into a treaty of alliance except by a decree of their primary assembly: even the ἀπόκλητοι had no power to bind the League in such a way (see 26. 6, etc.). On the Aetolian side, therefore, the reality behind 16. 5 can be no more than a personal undertaking by Scopas and his friends.

2. At the time of the alleged secret alliance with the Aetolians, and thereafter, Sparta was still officially a member of the alliance set up in the time of Doson (see 24. 4, 6, 8). Even in 22. 5 (220 still) all we hear is that three of the five Spartan ephors (of 221/20) ἐκοινώνουν τοῖς Αἰτωλοῖς τῶν πραγμάτων, and Adeimantus in 22. 10 can speak of τοὺς Αἰτωλοὺς πολεμίους ὄντας. The next board of ephors at Sparta (of 220/19) simply διεπέμποντο πρὸς τοὺς Αἰτωλούς, ἐπισπώμενοι πρεσβευτήν (34. 3); and when Machatas arrives and addresses the Spartan assembly (34. 4–10) there is no indication that a συμμαχία already existed, and indeed συντίθεσθαι in 34. 8 shows that in Polybius' mind it did not, whatever he may have said in 16. 5. It is only in 35. 5 (220/19), after the ephors have been killed, that the Spartans, now dominated by the pro-Aetolian faction, συνέθεντο . . . πρὸς τοὺς Αἰτωλοὺς τὴν συμμαχίαν. Although it was certainly possible for the Spartan assembly to meet in secret, it looks as if 16. 5 can refer at most to private unofficial promises given personally by the three pro-Aetolian ephors of 221/20 (22. 5) to the chief men of the Aetolian League (see Walbank, *Philip V of Macedon*, p. 30).

Similarly, we must not take seriously the statement in Diod. 12. 73. 1 that the reason for which the Athenians ejected the Delians (in 422) was ὅτι λάθρᾳ πρὸς Λακεδαιμονίους συντίθενται συμμαχίαν. At the most, there could have been no more than secret negotiations between some leading Delians and the Spartan ephors. But Diodorus' statement is probably devoid of all foundation: contrast Thuc. 5. 1 (with 3. 104. 1–2); 5. 32. 1.

New College, Oxford   G. E. M. DE SAINTE CROIX

IV

G. L. Cawkwell

The Defence of Olynthus

THE DEFENCE OF OLYNTHUS

DEMOSTHENES prophesied[1] that, unless Athens stopped Philip in the north, she would have to deal with him in Greece itself, and the events of 346 proved him right. Right in this much, he has been presumed right in general, and the policies of those he opposed have received only scant consideration before being dismissed as the selfish pursuit of peace by the rich, who were so blinded by their material interests that they could not see the real issues involved.[2] It is the purpose of this article to question, from a purely military standpoint, the soundness of Demosthenes' policy.

First, however, as always with Demosthenic questions, it is necessary to answer some questions of fact.

I. THE FIRST PHILIPPIC

Ever since 1893, when Schwartz[3] delivered his attack on the dating of the first Philippic by Dionysius of Halicarnassus,[4] scholars have been divided on the question, and Schwartz has had a considerable following.[5] His attack was twofold; first, a destructive criticism of Dionysius' methods and limitations, and then an attempt to date the speech in 349 after Philip had begun the war which ended in the destruction of Olynthus.

Whatever may be said of Dionysius' dating, it should be clear that the speech does not belong where Schwartz sought to put it. First, Demosthenes alludes only once to Olynthus, and in a casual fashion at that (ταύτας ἀπὸ τῆς οἰκείας χώρας αὐτοῦ στρατείας εἰς Πύλας καὶ Χερρόνησον καὶ Ὄλινθον καὶ ὅποι βούλεται § 17). If the occasion of the speech had been Philip's attack on

I wish to thank Mr. P. A. Brunt, Mr. G. E. M. de Ste Croix, and Mr. A. R. W. Harrison for helpful criticism. They should not be supposed, however, necessarily to accept any of the views expressed.

For convenience, whenever I have named a month of the Athenian calendar I have inserted in Roman numerals which month of the year it is.

[1] 1. 25, 3. 8, 4. 50.
[2] Schaefer, *Demosthenes und seine Zeit*, ii², speaks of a 'wretched peace-party and bribed orators' (p. 51) and 'der selbstsüchtigen Partei, welche unter Eubulus Leitung den Staat beherrschte'. Schwarz, 'Demosthenes erste Philippika' in *Festschrift Theodor Mommsen*, speaks of 'die Partei des Besitzes und die Besitzenden' (cf. pp. 13, 35, 39, 49) and of 'die Friedenspartei'. Cf. Cloché, *La politique extérieure*, p. 219, and Jaeger, *Demosthenes*, p. 142 ('the same rich politicians of the peace party'). The double accusation of pacificism for personal profit is almost *communis opinio*. The alleged pacificism is, by implication, called in question by this article. What is the ground for supposing that Eubulus and his supporters were rich and the 'patriots' poor? Demosthenes likes to talk about the riches of his opponents (e.g. 3. 29) but we do not have their replies. Demosthenes was a rich man

himself, and indeed most of οἱ πολιτευόμενοι must have been fairly well off.
[3] Op. cit.
[4] *Ad Amm.*, pp. 725 and 736.
[5] Amongst those who commit themselves Kahrstedt, *Forschungen*, p. 121, n. 211, Pokorny, *Studien*, pp. 125 f., and Momigliano, *Filippo il Macedone*, pp. 110 and 112, n. 1, follow Schwartz. Pickard-Cambridge, *Demosthenes*, p. 184, Cloché, op. cit., p. 203 (cf. *Un fondateur d'empire*, p. 111), and Jacoby, Commentary on Philochorus frag. 47, favour the early date. Jaeger, *Demosthenes*, pp. 120 f., believes in the early date and a later (and so misleading) edition (cf. p. 123, n. 5 below). Focke, *Demosthenesstudien*, pp. 21 f., dates the speech in October 350. Sealey, *R.É.G.* lxviii (1955), 77 f., attempts a general defence of the accuracy of Dionysius' dates for Demosthenes.

Olynthus, surely that fact would have dominated the speech just as it dominates the Olynthiacs, and Demosthenes could not have treated it as just another incident. Indeed once Olynthus was attacked the city had every reason to seek Athenian alliance to which earlier it had professed itself not disinclined,[1] but neither does the speech contain any hint of an appeal from Olynthus, nor, more seriously, does Demosthenes suggest that Athens should now send an embassy to make an alliance, although it is clear from the Olynthiacs that there was a strong body of opinion at Athens in favour of alliance before Olynthus offered it.[2] The explanation must be that the war had not yet begun. Secondly, the emphasis of the speech is on preparation: the proposals are designed to enable Athens to act in time whenever a major crisis arises, and in the meantime to harry Philip with a small force which can admittedly do no more than make piratical raids (οὐκ ἔνι νῦν ἡμῖν πορίσασθαι δύναμιν τὴν ἐκείνῳ παραταξομένην ἀλλὰ λῃστεύειν ἀνάγκη § 23). But if Philip had already attacked Olynthus, there was already a major crisis, and one far more serious than Methone, Pagasae, or Potidaea, calling not for preparation against possible future dangers, but action in the present. The whole nature of Demosthenes' proposals shows that the attack on Olynthus had not yet begun. Thirdly, Demosthenes is very vague about how his standing light force is to act. Apart from the general commission to pillage just mentioned, there is nothing at all specific. Ποῖ οὖν προσορμιούμεθ'; ἤρετό τις. εὑρήσει τὰ σαθρά, ὦ ἄνδρες Ἀθηναῖοι, τῶν ἐκείνου πραγμάτων αὐτὸς ὁ πόλεμος, ἂν ἐπιχειρῶμεν (§44). After the war between Olynthus and Macedon had begun, such vagueness is inconceivable. The most important thing would have been the defence of Olynthus and the maintenance of its port, Mecyberna, and the next thing would have been the distraction of Philip by co-operating with Olynthian forces in attacking Macedonian territory. Demosthenes had sufficient strategic sense not to furnish silly answers to silly questions. The strategic situation he is discussing is not war between Olynthus and Philip. Finally, the attack on Olynthus in 349 was precisely what Athens had hoped for:[3] it gave her an ally of great value both in military power and as a base of operations and the news of that attack could hardly have produced despondency in Athens. Yet it is with an attack on a mood of despondency that Demosthenes begins his speech. Πρῶτον μὲν οὖν οὐκ ἀθυμητέον, ὦ ἄνδρες Ἀθηναῖοι, τοῖς παροῦσι πράγμασι, οὐδ' εἰ πάνυ φαύλως ἔχειν δοκεῖ.[4] For these reasons Schwartz's attribution of the speech to 349 should be abandoned. The attack on Olynthus, to which the speech alludes, cannot be that which began the war, and, despite all the words that have been spent on the silence of our sources, there must have been an earlier attack.[5]

There is one point which Schwartz thought confirmed his dating and which must be reconsidered. In § 34 Demosthenes speaks of attacks on Lemnos and Imbros, and on shipping off the southern end of Euboea, and finally of a raid at Marathon as a result of which the Sacred Trireme was captured. These

---

[1] Dem. 23. 109.
[2] 1. 7, 3. 7.
[3] Ibid.
[4] § 2.
[5] Jaeger, op. cit., pp. 120 f., admirably set out reasons for dissociating the speech from the attack on Olynthus in 349 but, believing that the reference to a sudden attack on Olynthus in § 17 must concern the events of 349, explained it as the insertion of a later edition. His promised special study (p. 238, n. 35) has never, as far as I know, appeared. If it is merely a question of choosing between the hypothesis of a later edition and that of an otherwise unattested attack on Olynthus, in view of the nature of the sources the latter is far preferable.

124   G. L. CAWKWELL

operations Schwartz referred to the very situation described by Aeschines (2. 72 f.) and alluded to by the speaker in [Demosthenes] 59. 3; and from this latter passage he inferred that Aeschines was talking about events of 349/8. Thus he found confirmation for his date for the first Philippic. This argument rests on a misunderstanding of the passage in [Demosthenes]. The speaker there is contrasting the two alternatives before Athens at the time when she was debating whether to intervene πανδημεί, as he claimed, in Euboea and Olynthus (§ 4): either she could gain victory, recover τὰ ὑμέτερα (i.e. Amphipolis, etc.), wholly defeat Philip, and become the greatest power in Greece, or she could be too late to save Olynthus, abandon her allies to destruction, gain the reputation of faithlessness, and run the risk of losing what remained of her possessions, Lemnos, Imbros, Scyros, and the Chersonese. Clearly the speaker means that the danger of losing these places was consequent on the failure to save Olynthus, and the natural interpretation is that, once Philip had dealt with Olynthus, he turned to other matters which touched Athens more directly. That is, he is speaking of the period between the fall of Olynthus and the Peace of Philocrates, the period which Aeschines was discussing.[1] So, unless one is prepared to accept Dionysius' ascription of the second half of the first Philippic to 347/6, there is no reason to identify the raids of § 34 of that speech with the dangers spoken of by Aeschines, and certainly under no conditions is there reason for referring them to 349/8. Indeed there is some positive evidence that they belong earlier. Both Philochorus[2] and Androtion[3] appear to have recounted the incident concerning the Sacred Trireme, and, although there is no precise indication of date in the case of Philochorus, Androtion is of some help: he dealt with this incident in his sixth book, and the seventh covered 350/49 and possibly even 353/2. So this Marathon incident[4] at least has nothing to do with the period to which Schwartz assigned it, and, if he could land at Marathon, he could certainly manage the other raids listed in § 34 in the earlier period. So Schwartz's identification and dating of the events of § 34 is singularly unfounded and should neither detain us nor deter us from rejecting his date for the first Philippic.[5]

It is easy to reject Schwartz's date, but to find the true date is at least difficult. One minor obstacle may be removed. Schwartz remarked:[6] 'I will leave to the supporters of the so-called tradition the unenviable task of giving a consistent account of how the speech On the Liberty of the Rhodians which is set by the tradition in the archonship of Theellus (351/0) can be later than

[1] Cf. Justin 3. 8. 11 f. who recounts the fall of Olynthus, then Philip's activities in Thessaly and Thrace, and ends 'et ne quod ius vel fas inviolatum praetermitteret, piraticam quoque exercere instituit'. It is also to be noted that the decree which Aeschines went on to describe in 2. 73 suits the period of Philip's campaign against Cersobleptes in 346, when Chares was in command at the Hellespont (Aesch. 2. 90).

[2] F.G.H. 328 F 47.

[3] F.G.H. 324 F 24.

[4] Although the landing at Marathon is cited last by Demosthenes in § 34 and prefaced by τὰ τελευταῖα it is not clear that it was the latest in time of the events mentioned.

As Jacoby pointed out (Commentary on Androt. frag. 24), the order is perhaps deliberately geographical and τὰ τελευταῖα may simply denote 'the crowning instance of Philip's privateering'. What is clear from Androtion is that Philip was active with piratical raids earlier than the Olynthian war.

[5] Schwartz, op. cit., p. 34, also related the reference in § 37 to the troubles in Euboea in 349/8. However, Philip does not appear to have been involved in these troubles (cf. section II of this article) and the letters cannot be dated.

[6] Op. cit., p. 31.

the first Philippic.' In the course of that speech, while belittling the menace of Persia, Demosthenes remarked ὁρῶ δ' ὑμῶν ἐνίους Φιλίππου μὲν ὡς ἄρ' οὐδενὸς ἀξίου πολλάκις ὀλιγωροῦντας, βασιλέα δ' ὡς ἰσχυρὸν ἐχθρὸν οἷς ἂν προέληται φοβουμένους (§ 24), and Schwartz implied that after the first Philippic, in which 'the Macedonian appears for the first time as the national menace' and which 'opened the long series of classic attacks by the great orator who reached the height of his art and powers only when he had found his great opponent',[1] it is not possible that Demosthenes could refer to Philip in so casual a fashion. This is no real difficulty. Schwartz himself unwittingly supplies the answer in his next sentence: 'Demosthenes was much too good an orator to adopt this tone against Philip, if he had not been sure that he was echoing popular opinion.' By the date of the Rhodian appeal in winter 351/0[2] fourteen months[3] had passed without a new move by Philip, whereas the danger of Persia had begun to make itself felt once more. Not only had Artaxerxes, shortly before the campaign to Egypt, sent money to Thebes[4] wherewith to continue the Sacred War, but the prospect of a Persian victory in Egypt was truly alarming. For if he restored his own house, the King, whose threat had ended the Social War to Athens's disadvantage,[5] and whose preparations three years earlier had caused great uneasiness in Athens,[6] would be free to reassert himself as patron of a new King's Peace. These were the real fears in winter 351/0 against which Demosthenes had to argue; a tirade against Philip would by no means have served his purpose. It is in any case naïve to suppose that once Demosthenes had begun to attack Philip he could never relax. After all, after the first Philippic and the Olynthiacs he undertook the defence of Philocrates who was prosecuted for his proposal to negotiate with Philip for peace in mid 348,[7] and presumably on that occasion he tempered his abuse. The politician who could in 346 propose a decree about special seats for the Macedonian embassy at the Dionysia[8] knew how to trim the sails of his oratory before the winds of his own passion, if indeed they blew constantly.

Unless the dating of Dionysius for the first Philippic is accepted, no solution of the problem is likely to command universal assent; there is no overwhelming case against a date in 350. Yet there are grounds for associating the speech, as Focke suggested,[9] with the expedition of Charidemus in October 351. The latest event mentioned in the speech that can be dated is Philip's march to

---

[1] Op. cit., p. 30.
[2] The speech On the Liberty of the Rhodians is dated to 351/0 by Dionysius of Halicarnassus, ad Amm. p. 726, under which year Diodorus (16. 40) set the Persian attack on Egypt alluded to in § 11 of the speech. Since the date of the Persian attack must have been readily available in what Dionysius calls the κοιναὶ ἱστορίαι (ad Amm. pp. 724 and 740), 351/0 is commonly accepted as the date of the speech. Focke, op. cit., pp. 18 f., tried to upset this largely with regard to the dates of the dynasty of Caria (cf. §§ 11 and 27 of the speech), but see Kahrstedt, op. cit., pp. 22 f.
[3] For date of Philip's attack on Heraeum Teichos cf. Hammond, J.H.S. lvii (1937), 57.
[4] Diod. 16. 40. 1.

[5] Cf. Histoire grecque, iii. 200.
[6] Demosthenes' speech, On the Symmories, dated to 354/3 by Dionysius (ad Amm. pp. 724–5), dealt with the danger of Persian attack. Beloch's rejection of this date (Gr. Gesch. iii. 2. 261) rests on his dating of Pammenes' mission to 354 and is not justified (cf. Hammond, op. cit., pp. 58 f.). The Persian preparations, the rumour of which occasioned Demosthenes' speech, may well have been the first step towards invading Egypt. The Persian force which wrested from Sparta the supremacy of the sea at Cnidus in 394 was being collected in 397/6 (Xen. Hell. 3. 4. 1).
[7] Aesch. 2. 14.
[8] Aesch. 2. 55, and 110 f.
[9] Op. cit., pp. 21 ff., esp. p. 25.

Heraeum Teichos in November 352,[1] but some time has evidently elapsed since
that crisis and Demosthenes is speaking at a time when there is no question
either of urgent aid to any particular danger-point[2] or of alliance and when
Athens seems to be doing very little about the war in the north. The lull
between the decree of November 352 and the departure of Charidemus ten
months later seems a suitable context for the speech. A force is, however, to be
sent out (τῇ νυνὶ βοηθείᾳ § 14). Is this Charidemus' expedition? He sailed out
with ten triremes for which he had to find his own crews without the help of the
state,[3] and the demand for service in person is central to the speech. Although
it cannot be proved, it seems reasonable to suppose that Demosthenes is
attacking a proposal to send out a force with 'empty' ships. In §§ 43 f. he says : καὶ
τριήρεις κενὰς καὶ τὰς παρὰ τοῦ δεῖνος ἐλπίδας ἂν ἀποστείλητε, πάντ᾽ ἔχειν οἴεσθε
καλῶς; οὐκ ἐμβησόμεθα; οὐκ ἔξιμεν αὐτοὶ μέρει γέ τινι στρατιωτῶν οἰκείων νῦν,
εἰ καὶ μὴ πρότερον; In § 45 he speaks of sending out στρατηγὸν καὶ ψήφισμα
κενόν. That is, he is opposing the ψήφισμα κενόν which would send out a general
but no citizens, and he has accordingly to defend himself against the charge of
delaying the expedition. Such was the interpretation of Focke, and it seems
reasonable if not sure. The speech concerns an expedition sent out when nothing
much appeared to be happening, and this could well be the expedition of
Charidemus.

If the speech is to be related to Charidemus' expedition of 351/0, how does
this affect the credit of Dionysius? He describes[4] the speech as ἐν τῷ δήμῳ, περὶ
τῆς ἀποστολῆς τοῦ ξενικοῦ στρατεύματος καὶ τῶν δέκα φυγαδικῶν[5] τριηρῶν εἰς
Μακεδονίαν. Although this appears to refer to Demosthenes' own proposals, it
would also be a suitable description of Charidemus' expedition and, in case
Dionysius did know what he was talking about, it is to be noted that the relating of the speech to Charidemus does not conflict with Dionysius' description.
The difficulty is in the dating. Charidemus went out in the third month of
351/0,[6] whereas Dionysius dates the speech in 352/1. Despite what has recently
been said in defence of Dionysius' date,[7] few will feel sufficient confidence in the
Dionysian datings to say that the speech cannot be concerned with the expedition of Charidemus and that the credit of Dionysius must prevail. Yet there is
a way out of the difficulty. Demosthenes says that the Athenians actually sent
Charidemus out in Boedromion (III)[8] but it may be safely presumed that this
was the date of departure and not necessarily of the decree. For the first part of
the Attic year the Etesian winds effectively prevented ships sailing northwards ;
the length of time that they blew varied and the figures given by ancient sources
range from twenty-three to sixty days, but the commonest is forty days.[9] If

---

[1] § 17. Cf. Dem. 3. 4 f. The date is probable, if not certain.
[2] Cf. § 1. Of course, Demosthenes would
be speaking in relation to a προβούλευμα concerning ἡ νυνὶ βοήθεια (§ 14), but what he
means is that the situation has not been
changed by some new development.
[3] Presumably this is the meaning of κενάς
in Dem. 3. 5. By the law of Periander
trierarchs ceased to be responsible for finding
their own crews (Dem. 21. 155), but the
δῆμος must on occasion have provided no
citizens ἐκ καταλόγου and thus left the general
to find his own crews entirely. Cf. the con-

trast in Philochorus, F.G.H. 328 F 49 between
the ships of Chares and ἃς συνεπλήρωσαν.
[4] Ad Amm., p. 725.
[5] Three manuscripts have φυγαδικῶν and
two γαδικῶν and the emendation of Boehneck,
ταχικῶν, changed by Morell to ταχειῶν, has
found general acceptance.
[6] Dem. 3. 5.
[7] Cf. Sealey, R.É.G. lxviii (1955), 77 f.
[8] See n. 6 above.
[9] Cf. P.–W. vi. 1. 714. Focke, op. cit.,
p. 10, suggested that the date of Charidemus' expedition was related to the Etesians.

Charidemus' expedition was voted late in Scirophorion (XII) 352/1, he then had to find crews and he may well have been unable to leave Athens until the Etesians stopped blowing; if no new trouble had threatened in the meantime, there would be no great reason for haste.[1] Thus the first Philippic might both have been delivered in 352/1 and have concerned the expedition of Charidemus. Whether Dionysius (or his sources) could have gathered such precise information from the general histories, which he professed to use,[2] it is hard to say and his misdating of the second half of the speech is very suggestive. On the other hand, it should not be assumed that the general histories left him in as great ignorance as our own.

For the present purpose it is not necessary either to salvage or to abandon Dionysius. What is reasonably clear is that the first Philippic was not concerned with the effort to save Olynthus, but was a criticism of the conduct of the long-standing war against Philip, and so the proposals it contains are to be judged in relation to that war.

II. Euboea 349/8

The history of the Athenian intervention in Euboea needs reconsideration. The view developed by Parke[3] that there were two expeditions, the second of which was πανδημεί, has found its way into some accounts of the period.[4] As a result Athens is represented as having spent six months or more in fruitless operations, part of the time with all the strength she could send out, while the really important business of the defence of Olynthus was ruinously neglected. The Athenian part in the war in the north itself needs consideration, but it is necessary first to deal with Euboea.

The principal source for the Athenian intervention in Euboea is Plutarch's *Life of Phocion*, chh. 12–14. His account is as follows. When Plutarch of Eretria called on the Athenians to help him, Phocion was sent ἔχων δύναμιν οὐ πολλήν, since the Athenians expected that there would be ample support for him from the island itself. When he got there he found that this was not so and all he could do was to occupy a position at Tamynae where he held together the best part of his force; the rest slipped back to Athens. In due course he was attacked, Plutarch deserted him, and he was in a position of considerable danger, but when his troops broke out of their camp and attacked, the enemy were routed. After this Phocion expelled Plutarch from Eretria, took possession of a fortress, Zaretra, and sailed home. His successor, Molossus, was less successful and was actually taken captive. Thus by this account there was only one expedition to Euboea during Phocion's period of command.

Parke, however, has argued for two expeditions. In his view three passages

---

[1] The Great Mysteries ended on 22 Boedromion (Deubner, *Att. Feste*, p. 72), and the Etesians would have ceased earlier, but, if Philip had not acted under cover of the season, there would have no longer been need for haste. If the debate to which the first Philippic belongs was held not long before the Etesians, there was good reason for the haste of οἱ "ταχύ" καὶ "τήμερον" εἰπόντες (§ 14). It should be added, however, that Demosthenes' allusion to the Etesians (§ 31)

does not suggest that Philip may shortly exploit the seasons.

[2] *Ad Amm.*, pp. 724 and 740.

[3] *J.H.S.* xlix (1929), 246 f. Parke follows Kahrstedt, op. cit., pp. 56 f., in postulating two expeditions, although he differs in detail.

[4] e.g. Momigliano, *Filippo il Macedone*, p. 111, n. 1, and Cloché, *Un fondateur d'Empire*, pp. 131 f.

128 G. L. CAWKWELL

combine to show that Athens sent out a large force to relieve the small force under Phocion marooned at Tamynae.

(a) Dem. 39. 16, where the speaker says that the defendant was left in Athens for the Choes, ὅτ᾿ εἰς Ταμύνας παρῆλθον οἱ ἄλλοι. 'The use of οἱ ἄλλοι', according to Parke, 'implies that this was an expedition of all the citizens'.

(b) [Dem.] 59. 4, where in talking about the crisis in which Apollodorus brought forward his financial proposal the speaker says it happened μελλόντων στρατεύεσθαι ὑμῶν πανδημεὶ εἴς τε Εὔβοιαν καὶ "Ολυνθον. This shows that an expedition πανδημεί was under consideration.

(c) Dem. 21. 162, where speaking of the Athenian reaction to the news that Phocion was in danger Demosthenes says that the Council promptly decided to recommend to the People that all the remaining cavalry should go out (πάντας ἐξιέναι τοὺς ὑπολοίπους ἱππέας). Parke takes this to confirm that an expedition πανδημεί actually took place.

It is melancholy that a theory based on evidence so handled should find acceptance. Not one of the three passages justifies Parke's use of it. First, Dem. 39. 16. The inference from οἱ ἄλλοι is weak; the speaker may mean no more than 'the others who were called on to go'. It neither proves nor disproves. What is interesting in the passage is the word παρῆλθον. This is commonly used to describe the march of an army along a coast,[1] and it is used by Aeschines,[2] who distinguished himself in the campaign,[3] to describe the advance of the infantry in Phocion's force along the coast from where they landed to Tamynae. So this passage may well refer to the original expedition (and, incidentally, provide the date for it). Secondly, Dem. 21. 162. One has only to read the whole of §§ 162 and 163 to see that what the Council proposed was never ratified by the People. When the meeting of the Assembly began, the situation was still felt to be serious as is seen from the action of Midias in volunteering to equip a trireme, but οὐκ ἐδόκει, προϊούσης τῆς ἐκκλησίας καὶ λόγων γιγνομένων, τῆς τῶν ἱππέων βοηθείας ἤδη δεῖν, ἀλλ᾿ ἀνεπεπτώκει τὰ τῆς ἐξόδου. So how could the Council's proposal show that there was a second expedition to Euboea? Thirdly, [Dem.] 59. 4. This does, indeed, show that an expedition πανδημεί was under consideration in 349/8, but the passage as a whole also suggests that the expedition never went. In this passage, already discussed above, the speaker is seeking to show that Apollodorus was wrongly prosecuted and punished for his proposal concerning the use of the Theoric Fund; his method is to describe the situation at the time the proposal was made and to suggest that the collapse of Athenian plans to save Olynthus was due to the prosecution of Apollodorus. He says that

(i) Athens was in the position where
  (a) she could *either* save Olynthus *or* come to disaster, δι᾿ ἀπορίαν χρημάτων καταλυθέντος τοῦ στρατοπέδου § 3, and
  (b) she was actually on the point of sending out a large expedition to Olynthus (μελλόντων στρατεύεσθαι ὑμῶν πανδημεὶ εἴς τε Εὔβοιαν καὶ "Ολυνθον),
(ii) Apollodorus proposed the measure that would have financed the expedition (§ 4).

[1] Cf. Thuc. 8. 16, 22, 32, Xen. *Hell.* 2. 1. 18, 4. 5. 19. [2] 3. 86. [3] Aesch. 2. 169.

[54]

We are left to infer that the reason for the breaking-up of the armament was the prosecution. Probably this was mere pleading and the expedition was abandoned for the good reason that it was no longer needed at Tamynae,[1] but in any case it seems that one of the facts which the speaker was distorting was that this expedition πανδημεί never went out. That is, the passage confirms the very opposite of what Parke maintained.

Of course it is clear that some of those from the original expedition who had been allowed to return to Athens when no hostile force at first appeared, like Midias and Demosthenes himself,[2] were recalled by Phocion; there were notably the knights who had never gone farther than Argura but who were needed to relieve those who were being sent on to Olynthus.[3] But that was all, and the dating is quite plain.[4] The expedition to help Plutarch went out, as Dem. 39. 16 shows, just before the festival of the Choes on 12 Anthesterion (VIII), the battle of Tamynae was fought about a month later shortly before the Dionysia[5] (which began on 9 Elaphebolion (IX)), and presumably the cavalry that crossed from Chalcis to Olynthus went not long after the battle, perhaps late in Elaphebolion (IX).

Despite the arguments of Pokorny,[6] modern writers[7] continue to treat the trouble in Euboea as a distraction for the Athenians arranged by Philip. This view is based on the statement in our manuscripts of Aeschines (3. 87) that Callias of Chalcis sent to Philip for help (παρὰ Φιλίππου δύναμιν μεταπεμψάμενος). This reading, as Pokorny pointed out, is doubtful. The scholiast on § 86 gives a short account of the trouble in Euboea and includes the statement that for his campaign against Plutarch Cleitarchus took παρὰ Φαλαίκου τοῦ Φωκέων τυράννου δύναμιν but has nothing whatever to say about Philip. Further, a few lines later Aeschines himself speaks of Callias' brother transporting τοὺς Φωκικοὺς ξένους. On these grounds alone the case for changing Φιλίππου to Φαλαίκου is fairly strong, but, considered from a more general standpoint, it becomes very strong indeed. For it would be difficult to say why, if Philip had been involved in any way in the trouble in Euboea in 349/8, Demosthenes was both opposed to the expedition and proud of having been so,[8] and still more difficult to understand why, in the charges and counter-charges with which the speeches of the period are filled, his policy is never attacked or defended. Nor do the passages which might be used to support the manuscript reading of Aeschines afford any real help. The letters of Philip to the Euboeans alluded to in the first Philippic[9] belong to 351 or earlier, and hardly provide evidence of an appeal in 348. Again, the words with which Plutarch in his life of Phocion introduces his account of the war (παραδυομένου δὲ εἰς τὴν Εὔβοιαν τοῦ Φιλίππου καὶ δύναμιν ἐκ Μακεδονίας διαβιβάζοντος κτλ.) may be no more than a retrojection of later events.[10] Certainly the references of Demosthenes to Philip's

---

[1] Schaefer, op. cit. ii². 82, is probably right in supposing that the news about Tamynae arrived in the course of the ἐκκλησία.

[2] Plut. Phoc. 12. 3, Dem. 21. 132, 133.

[3] Dem. 21. 164 (cf. 132) and 197.

[4] Cf. Beloch, Gr. Gesch. iii. 2. 278 f.

[5] So Demosthenes stayed to produce his chorus and was subsequently charged by Midias with desertion (Dem. 21. 110).

[6] Op. cit., pp. 132 f.

[7] e.g. Pickard-Cambridge, op. cit., pp. 208

f.; Beloch, Gr. Gesch. iii. 1. 495 n. 1, Histoire grecque, iii. 135; Cloché, op. cit., p. 135.

[8] Dem. 5. 5.

[9] Dem. 4. 37.

[10] Beloch, loc. cit., regards Plutarch's introduction here as decisive confirmation of the manuscripts' reading in Aesch. 3. 87, but in view of the later connexion of Cleitarchus and Philip (Dem. 9. 58, etc.) it is not surprising that Plutarch should write inaccurately.

intervention in Euboea[1] give no hint of any Macedonian troops being there before 343 and Plutarch must be at least exaggerating. More probably he is merely borrowing from the later period a suitably dramatic background for Phocion's expedition. The Euboeans certainly were in diplomatic communication in 348 with Philip, as the message they delivered to Athens in the middle of the year testifies,[2] but this is far from proving that the movement against Plutarch of Eretria was initiated by Philip, or that Philip was seriously involved in Euboea so early. All in all, it seems better to emend the text of Aeschines than to suppose that Demosthenes could pride himself on opposing an expedition against troops sent by Philip. Yet, even if Aeschines did write παρὰ Φιλίππου, there is little reason to think that he was telling the truth, and it will be assumed in what follows that the Euboean war was not part of the war against Philip but an isolated local struggle.

III. THE ATHENIAN AID TO OLYNTHUS IN 349/8

Under the archonship of Callimachus (349/8) Philochorus[3] recorded the three Athenian expeditions to Olynthus. The first was of 2,000 peltasts, 'the 30 triremes with Chares and the 8 ἃς συνεπλήρωσαν'; the second was of 4,000 peltasts, 150 knights, and 18 triremes under the command of Charidemus, 'the general at the Hellespont'; the third was of a further 17 triremes, 2,000 hoplites, and 300 knights with Chares in command of the whole force.

These three expeditions can be dated fairly precisely. The first is the least satisfactory. Olynthus fell during the Macedonian Olympia[4] which were held shortly after the end of the third month of the Attic year,[5] and Demosthenes[6] says that all the Chalcidian cities were taken in a year. So this would mean that the war began early in 349/8, and since it is unlikely that Olynthus delayed appealing to Athens, the first expedition, which, as Philochorus[7] shows, followed closely on the alliance, must have left Athens early in 349/8 also. This date is confirmed, if Jacoby[8] is correct in his theory that of citations from Philochorus those that begin, like this one, with an archon's name followed by ἐπὶ τούτου ... concern the first entry in the Atthis for the year; the alliance and the first expedition would thus be the first events mentioned in 349/8. So if the first expedition of Chares is put in early Boedromion (III), i.e. shortly after the Etesian winds, that will not be far wrong.

The third expedition is presumably the one that was too late to save Olyn-

---

[1] 9. 57 f., 19. 83, 87, 204. Cf. Schaefer, op. cit. ii². 81, n. 2, who rejects the possibility of Philip actually sending help but keeps the manuscript reading in Aesch. 3. 87, and dismisses Aeschines' account as 'lügenhaft'.

[2] Aesch. 2. 12.

[3] F.G.H. 328 F 49–51.

[4] Diod. 16. 55, Dem. 19. 192 ('Ολύμπι' ἐποίει).

[5] Cf. the narrative of Arrian, Anab. 1. 10 and 11. 1. For the Macedonian Olympia see P.–W. xviii. 1. 46. The usual view is that Olynthus fell during the Greek Olympia (cf. Beloch, Gr. Gesch. iii. 2. 280), but neither does this allow sufficient time for the events of Aesch. 2. 12 f. nor is there any reason to sup-

pose that the Greek Olympia were celebrated in Macedon also. Cf. R.É.G. lxxiii (1960), 417, n. 2.

[6] 19. 266, presumably more or less correct if not exact. The fact that Diodorus (see p. 132, n. 7) splits the war into two archon years does not affect the question of the accuracy of Demosthenes' statement as to the duration of the war.

[7] F.G.H. 328 F 49 συμμαχίαν τε ἐποιήσαντο ... καὶ βοήθειαν ἔπεμψαν. (The lacuna of about eighteen letters does not affect the close connexion between the making of alliance and the dispatch of the expedition.)

[8] Cf. Commentary to Philochorus, p. 532, lines 9 f.

thus. There were at any rate only three expeditions recorded in Philochorus[1] and it is most unlikely that he omitted a further expedition. Olynthus fell shortly after Boedromion (III) 348/7 and it seems likely that the bad weather which delayed Chares[2] was caused by the Etesian winds. So the final Olynthian appeal and the voting of this last expedition, both of which were put by Philochorus under 349/8, should be set as late in 349/8 as possible, i.e. in Scirophorion (XII). As to the second expedition, that of Charidemus,[3] the cavalry that went from Euboea to Olynthus[4] about the time of the Dionysia of 348 must have gone under him. So his expedition should be put in spring 348.[5]

The citations from Philochorus concerning the expeditions are suggestive. In the first there is a distinction between the thirty ships with Chares (τὰς μετὰ Χάρητος) and eight for which the Athenians helped to provide crews (ἃς συνεπλήρωσαν).[6] The latter are presumably the triremes which, Demosthenes[7] says, were equipped by volunteer trierarchs, but the former are spoken of as a force already in existence. One may infer that the response to the Olynthian appeal was to send the regular squadron in the north supplemented by what patriotic citizens cared to add. That was all that happened in autumn 349. As to the second force, that of spring 348, Charidemus is spoken of as τὸν ἐν Ἑλλησπόντωι στρατηγόν as if this was a regular appointment, and it may be suggested that the eighteen ships of his force were the ten he sailed out with in 351 together with the eight volunteered triremes that had sailed north the previous autumn. That is, once again the response to the Olynthian appeal was to use the force already out on active service. Of the third expedition Philochorus says that they sent out τριήρεις ἑτέρας ἑπτακαίδεκα. Why ἑτέρας? The word does not occur with reference to Charidemus' ships, and the explanation is that apart from ἃς συνεπλήρωσαν ὀκτώ these are the only ships Athens specially sent out during the war (and they were too late). They must have been added to the forces already operating, and the description of Chares as general τοῦ παντὸς στόλου suits this: he was to take command of both Charidemus' ships and the reinforcements as well as having his own ships, τὰς μετὰ Χάρητος.[8]

Thus the city appears to have sent out very little special help to Olynthus. Nor was what was available constantly employed around Olynthus, if we may judge by the mysterious inscription, *I.G.* ii². 207. This consists of four fragments of which the first, containing the name of the archon for 349/8, is lost. The matters referred to in the second large fragment appear to be concerned with current affairs,[9] and it is necessary to reckon with the decree in dealing with

---

[1] Cf. Scholiast to Dem. 2. 1 (Dindorf, viii. 74, line 10), quoted by Jacoby, *F.G.H.* iii B, p. 113 (i.e. beneath F 49 and 50).

[2] 'Suidas', s.v. Κάρανος: βοηθοὺς ἔπεμψαν Ἀθηναῖοι ναῦς μ´ καὶ Χάρητα στρατηγόν· οὗ χειμῶνι ἀποληφθέντος, προδόντων δὲ τὴν *Ὄλυνθον Εὐθυκράτους καὶ Λασθένους, τὴν μὲν ἀνάστατον ἐποίησε (Φίλιππος) . . . .

[3] *F.G.H.* 328 F 50.

[4] Dem. 21. 197.

[5] Those who, like Kahrstedt, op. cit., p. 61, place the third expedition in spring 348 do so because they suppose that Olynthus fell at the time of the Greek Olympia. For the whole question of the dating of the expeditions cf. Schaefer, op. cit. ii². 118 f.

[6] Cf. Schaefer, op. cit. ii². 76 n. 4.

[7] 21. 161.

[8] It is not clear whether Chares was in Athens to go with these reinforcements. The explanation commonly given of the haste with which he sought to render account of his conduct of the Olynthian war (Dion. Hal. *ad Amm.*, p. 734, and Ar. *Rhet.* 1411ᵃ) is that he was hurrying to get off with the last expedition. Cf. Schaefer, op. cit. ii². 143.

[9] Accame, *La lega ateniese*, p. 196, took the mention of syntaxeis in line 13 of fragment b (τῶν συντάξεων τῶν ἐλ Λέσβωι) to refer to an earlier period, because Mytilene was not in the Athenian Confederacy in 349/8, but the phrase could well refer to the other cities of

349/8. It appears that in the month of Thargelion (XI) Chares, Charidemus, and Phocion were all in some way involved with Orontes, satrap of Mysia, and were drawing on the συντάξεις of Lesbos for whatever they were doing. Nor is it likely that some minor affair like the purchase of corn for the fleet is in hand. For, while Chares and Charidemus might have been seeking provisions from Orontes, the presence of Phocion is suggestive. He had been in command in Euboea in Elaphebolion (IX) and must have been called away from that war for this business in the north-east.[1] So the three generals must have been engaged on something which we do not know about but which was far removed from Olynthus.

Athens and her generals appear to have done little to save Olynthus, but, before attempting explanations, it is important to consider what militarily speaking the situation of Olynthus was.[2] The evidence is scanty but two points do emerge. First, the actual siege of the city did not begin until late in 349/8. In spring 348, when Charidemus arrived to help, the Olynthians joined with him in an attack on Pallene and Bottiaea and ravaged the land.[3] This implies that the Macedonians controlled much of the territory of the Chalcidic League, but that Olynthus itself was still open. The siege began after the capture of Torone and Mecyberna (διὰ προδοσίας) had stopped easy access to the sea and the Olynthians had been twice defeated in battle.[4] Presumably these were the events that occasioned the last appeal to Athens, that of Scirophorion (XII) 349/8 (μὴ περιιδεῖν αὐτοὺς καταπολεμηθέντας).[5] Till then the city had been free and open. Secondly, the war was in two distinct phases as regards Philip's expressed intentions. Before the final pressure on Olynthus, he was thought to be aiming at reducing the city to terms, not at destroying it.[6] That is, Athens was led to fear that Olynthus might return to the position she was in before she made peace with Athens in 352, but no worse than that. In the earlier stage Philip picked off Chalcidic cities one by one[7] but, serious as things were, perhaps there was no likelihood of a sudden collapse. The betrayal of Torone and Mecyberna transformed the situation.[8] In this way, Philip, by good luck

the island that remained in the Confederacy in that year, and although the inscription is too fragmentary to allow of certainty, the various matters touched on in fragment b appear to be concerned with operations in progress. Until fragment a is rediscovered, doubt will remain as to whether fragments b, c, and d really belong to it, but the considerations advanced in the editio minor of *I.G.* seem sufficient.

[1] The troubles in Euboea continued almost until the Olympic truce of 348 (Aesch. 2. 12). Presumably the recall of Phocion (Plut. *Phoc.* 14. 1) was connected with the subject of *I.G.* ii². 207.

[2] Cf. Focke, op. cit., p. 23 n. 38.

[3] Philochorus, frag. 50.

[4] Diod. 16. 53.

[5] Philochorus, frag. 51.

[6] Cf. Dem. 1. 4 ... τὰς καταλλαγάς, ἃς ἂν ἐκεῖνος ποιήσαιτ' ἄσμενος πρὸς 'Ολυνθίους. Also 9. 11, 8. 59, and 2. 1.

[7] The account of Diodorus gives the attack on Olynthus in two stages. In 16. 52. 9 under

349/8 he records the destruction of Γεῖρα (probably a corruption of Σταγεῖρα) and the subjection of other places. In 16. 53 under 348/7 Philip μετὰ πολλῆς δυνάμεως attacks and captures Torone, Mecyberna, and Olynthus. Thus Diodorus' account is perhaps chronologically correct, is consistent with the situation in the first Olynthiac (cf. § 17, where the aim is said to be 'to save the cities for the Olynthians'), confirms that Olynthus was not immediately besieged, and reflects the two stages of Philip's expressed intentions.

The attempt of Focke (op. cit., pp. 10 f.) to date the attack on Γεῖρα in 350 (to which he supposes that Dem. 4. 17 refers) has nothing positive to recommend it. Cf. Momigliano, op. cit., p. 112, n. 1. The notice about Γεῖρα is not inevitably linked with the notice about Pherae (probably a repetition of the notice at Diod. 16. 37. 3 and 38. 1).

[8] It is not clear where the treachery of Lasthenes and Euthycrates (Dem. 9. 56 and 19. 265 f.) fits in. One would expect that it

or by good generalship, grabbed the city before the Athenians could save it.

It remains to date the third Olynthiac in relation to these events. About the first two speeches, which both clearly belong to the first appeal from Olynthus,[1] there is no debate, but opinions have differed as to the third. Kahrstedt[2] maintained that it must have been spoken before Athens intervened in Euboea; Pokorny[3] denied this and argued for a date late in 349/8; and in considering Athens' conduct of the war in the north it is important to determine which view is right. The main point urged by Pokorny for the late date is that the cautious manner in which Demosthenes made his proposal for the change of the law about the Theoric Fund suggests that Apollodorus had already come to disaster in proposing the same change.[4] This is not as strong as it might at first sight seem. In the first Olynthiac also Demosthenes touched on the Theoric Fund and with equal caution declined to initiate any change,[5] and, if Pokorny's point were valid for the third oration, it would be equally so for the first, to which it clearly cannot apply. It might happen to be true that Demosthenes used such words after Apollodorus was prosecuted, but they do not require the late dating of the speech.[6] On the other hand, Kahrstedt's argument about the complete silence of Demosthenes with regard to Euboea is of the greatest weight. Once Athens had sent a citizen army to Euboea, which operated to such poor effect, Demosthenes could hardly have maintained silence as to the contrast between what Athens was prepared to do for the worthless Plutarch and what she was doing to fight Philip in Chalcidice. In particular, one should attend to his detailed attack on Eubulus and his supporters in §§ 21 and ff. In §§ 27 and 28 they are blamed for neglecting the war in the north and in § 29 he goes on to pour scorn on the public works which were an important part of their home policy, but of the intervention in Euboea, in which Eubulus' supporters played so prominent a part, there is not a word. Is it really possible that Demosthenes kept silence because, as Pokorny argued,[7] he did not want to exacerbate feelings? He had said enough, and that most directly, to give great offence. Why should he have foregone his most telling point? The only proper answer is that he was speaking before the troubles in Euboea had begun.

This much has been widely accepted, but opinion has divided as to whether the third Olynthiac followed the two earlier speeches at a long enough interval for the situation to have changed considerably.[8] In support it has been urged that Thessalian affairs are touched on in the first two[9] but not in the third. In itself this proves little; news from Thessaly within a short time could have rendered Demosthenes' proposal of an embassy pointless. Nor does the supposed allusion to a victory of a force of mercenaries[10] necessarily indicate that

---

belonged to the period of the two battles (Diod. 16. 53) before the siege began, but Diodorus says that it was the cause of the fall of the city. Perhaps the Greek sources grossly exaggerated or even misrepresented the act of Lasthenes and Euthycrates in surrendering.

[1] Cf. 1. 2 and 2. 11.
[2] Op. cit., p. 61.
[3] Op. cit., pp. 119 f.
[4] Cf. Dem. 3. 10 f. and [Dem.] 59. 3 f.
[5] § 19. "Τί οὖν;" ἄν τις εἴποι, "σὺ γράφεις ταῦτ' εἶναι στρατιωτικά;" μὰ Δί' οὐκ ἔγωγε.

[6] Focke, op. cit., pp. 27 f., errs in the other direction in claiming that, because Demosthenes does not mention Apollodorus, the speech must have been before the latter's proposal.
[7] Op. cit., pp. 123 f.
[8] The arguments in favour of a long interval between the second and third Olynthiacs have been mustered by Pokorny, op. cit., pp. 119 f.
[9] 1. 21 f., 2. 11.
[10] § 35.

the first of Philochorus' expeditions is in the field; mercenary forces had been fighting the war against Philip for years. Again it has been alleged that the third speech is markedly different in tone,[1] but even in the first speech Demosthenes took the extreme view of what was at issue,[2] and in any case it would not be surprising that, if Athens was proposing to answer the Olynthian appeal with no more than a mercenary force, Demosthenes should adopt a more gloomy tone as he contemplated the preparation of a mere eight 'volunteer' triremes.[3] So nothing compels a considerably later date for the third speech, while there is positive evidence for associating it with the first Olynthian appeal. In § 6 he says νῦν δ' ἑτέρου πολέμου καιρὸς ἥκει τις, and in § 7 ἐκπολεμῶσαι δεῖν ᾠόμεθα τοὺς ἀνθρώπους ἐκ παντὸς τρόπου, καὶ ὃ πάντες ἐθρύλουν, πέπρακται νυνὶ τοῦθ' ὁπωσδήποτε. These passages are closely akin to the first two speeches and appropriate only to the early stages of the Olynthian war.[4] Thus there is a strong case for dating the third speech close to the other two.[5] In any case, since the speech was delivered before the Euboean affair and since Demosthenes was recommending a full-scale citizen expedition, he presumably spoke within the navigating season of 349, and that is all that is necessary for the present discussion.[6]

IV. THE ALTERNATIVE STRATEGIES

In the war against Philip there were two strategic necessities for Athens. First, she had to keep Philip from breaking into Greece and co-operating with Thebes in an attack on Attica itself, and the second matter, of equal or even greater importance, was to protect her lifeline through the Hellespont and the Bosporus, clearly in constant danger through Macedonian expansion eastward.[7] The war in the north was in itself far less important and it acquired interest for serious Athenian statesmen in so far as it became a possible means of preventing Philip from ruining Athens by attack or by starvation. Demosthenes saw all

[1] Cf. esp. §§ 1 and 9.

[2] Cf. § 25.

[3] This would also explain why in the third Olynthiac he has ceased to demand mere εἰσφοραί: he now saw that only a regular war-fund would make possible an expedition of the sort he demanded, and that the difficulty of getting an εἰσφορά voted was a brake on sustained major efforts against Philip.

[4] Cf. Blass, *Attische Beredsamkeit*, iii. 1. 320.

[5] Momigliano (op. cit., p. 112, n. 1) is a supporter of this view. Its most extreme form is to be found in H. Erbse, *Rh. Mus.* xcix (1956), 379 f., who supposes that all three Olynthiacs were delivered at one and the same ἐκκλησία! This both argues an importance of Demosthenes which he probably did not possess, and is a strange notion of Athenian assemblies. (Are there any clear cases known where the same man made two set speeches on the one day on the one subject?) But Erbse's analysis of the speeches effectively shows their close connexion.

[6] As noted above, the first appeal of Olynthus came very early in 349/8, and it was the first matter recorded in Philochorus for that year (cf. p. 130, n. 8), but in view of uncer-

tainty about the procedure of νομοθεσία it would be unsafe to argue from Demosthenes' demand for the appointment of nomothets (§§ 10 f.) that the third Olynthiac belongs in the first prytany of 349/8.

[7] How important was the possession of the Chersonese for the safety of the Athenian corn supply? Athens had managed her supply despite the hostility of Byzantium since 364 (cf. Accame, *La lega*, p. 179, n. 3) and down to 352 the Chersonese was not entirely under her control. So it might be argued that the Chersonese was only of value to Philip if he could use his fleet which in 349/8 was still much too weak. This is in some degree true, but ports were necessary; Sestos was a regular stopping place (cf. [Dem.] 50. 20 and Ar. *Rhet.* 1411ᵃ14, where Sestos is described as the corn-table—τηλία—of the Peiraeus) and indeed from 365 it was in Athens's possession (Nep. *Tim.* i. 3). If Philip took Sestos and persuaded or obliged the Byzantines to act against Athenian ships at Hieros ([Dem.] 50. 17, Philochorus F 162—for its site, on the Asiatic side of the Bosporus, see P.-W. iii. 752), the corn supply would have been at least seriously affected.

this clearly.[1] The question to be discussed is whether the strategy he advocated was the best possible for attaining the two main aims.

First, it must be confessed that it is not certain how Demosthenes thought Olynthus was to be defended. The precise proposals of the first Philippic were made with no thought of alliance with Olynthus but sought merely a more effective prosecution of the long struggle for Amphipolis. Nor is there any reason to suppose that the two later expeditions to save Olynthus satisfied Demosthenes any more than the first had done.[2] He was very much in a minority in opposing intervention in Euboea, by his own account the only dissentient voice,[3] and it is unlikely that the man who had demanded an expedition παντὶ cθένει κατὰ τὸ δυνατόν[4] approved of the raiding force of Charidemus or the final expedition of Chares. Indeed, although Demosthenes had been eminent in the courts in the 350's, he appears to have had practically no success whatever in initiating policy[5] until under cover of having defended Philocrates in 348 he rose to eminence in 346 first as champion of the peace in concert with Philocrates and then as its and his embittered opponent. Until then he probably counted for very little, and the speeches of 349/8 survive because of his reputation as an orator, and not because of his power and influence as a statesman. Thus what Athens actually did is no guide to what Demosthenes demanded and his ideas on strategy in 349/8 must remain to some degree conjectural.

There is, however, in the first Olynthiac, one statement that is sufficiently close to Demosthenes' concrete proposals of 351 to suggest that the entry of Olynthus into the war did not seem to him to call for more than the prompt application of his earlier proposals. In §§ 17 f. he says that two forces are necessary, one to ravage Macedonian territory, the other to save the cities of the Olynthians, and this recalls the two forces proposed in 351, the one of 10 ships, 2,000 foot, and 500 horse, the other of 50 ships manned by the Athenians

---

[1] Cf. 1. 25.

[2] It is sometimes asserted that Dionysius of Halicarnassus related the three Olynthiac speeches to the three expeditions, but, though he may well have done so, this is not a necessary inference from the Letter to Ammaeus X (μετὰ γὰρ ἄρχοντα Καλλίμαχον, ἐφ' οὗ τὰς εἰς Ὄλυνθον βοηθείας ἀπέστειλαν Ἀθηναῖοι πεισθέντες ὑπὸ Δημοσθένους . . .). Cf. Sealey, R.É.G. lxviii (1955), 85. It is a more serious question whether Philochorus did so; for in the Scholiast's introduction to the second Olynthiac (Dindorf, viii. 74, line 10) occur the words ἰστέον δὲ ὅτι φησὶν ὁ Φιλόχορος ὅτι τρεῖς βοήθειαι ἐπέμφθησαν, καθ' ἕκαστον λόγον μιᾶς πεμπομένης, ὡς τῆς πρώτης μὴ οὔσης ἱκανῆς. Did Philochorus record speeches of Demosthenes and assign them so precisely? It would be most surprising if he did and the words καθ' ἕκαστον κτλ. may well be added by the Scholiast. In any case this is a matter affecting the credit of Philochorus, not the importance of Demosthenes.

It is true that Demosthenes' defence of Philocrates on trial for proposing to negotiate with Philip came early in 348/7 (i.e. before

Olynthus fell, cf. Aesch. 2. 14 and R.É.G. lxxiii [1960], 417, n. 2) and the debate that led to the dispatch of the third expedition belonged to 349/8 (cf. Philochorus F 51); so it may have been the delay of this expedition that led him to despair, and we cannot be sure that he had not spoken in support of the last expedition. Yet in general it would seem that it was Eubulus and his supporters who were in power in 349 (v.i.) and it is notable that neither Aeschines (3. 54 and 58 f.) nor Demosthenes (18. 17 f.) in discussing the latter's career has anything to say about Demosthenes' political record before 346. The theory of Glotz (Rev. Hist. clxx [1932]) that Demosthenes succeeded in establishing a war-fund, τὰ στρατιωτικά, in 349/8 has been widely accepted, but it is extremely ill founded, as I hope to show elsewhere. Rather, the failure of Apollodorus ([Dem.] 59. 5) shows that Demosthenes and his supporters were not in a position of power in 348.

[3] 5. 5.

[4] 3. 6.

[5] See n. 2 above.

136   G. L. CAWKWELL

themselves (αὐτοῖς ἐμβᾶσιν).[1] The emphasis of 349/8 was still on citizen service, but he may have wished to send even larger numbers (εἰ γὰρ μὴ βοηθήσετε
παντὶ σθένει κατὰ τὸ δυνατόν, θεάσασθ᾽ ὃν τρόπον ὑμεῖς ἐστρατηγηκότες πάντ᾽
ἔσεσθ᾽ ὑπὲρ Φιλίππου[2]). However, it is sure that he would not have wanted to do
less than he had earlier proposed.

The raiding force is hardly serious. It was too small to do much real damage
and Philip would hardly abandon the assault on Olynthus to deal with it
when he had sufficient numbers of infantry and cavalry to afford a reserve
which could make raiding a dangerous and unprofitable occupation. For if
Demosthenes was still, militarily speaking, in the fifth century, Philip was not,
nor should it be assumed that the failure of Demosthenes' opponents to agree
with him on this point was due to other than common sense. However, the
real point of difference in his proposals, viz. that large numbers of citizens
should be sent to save the cities of the Chalcidic League, is most important
and there are certain considerations which perhaps did not escape his opponents.

First of all, how reliable were the Olynthians? The history of their relations
with Athens gave little cause for confidence. They had defected from the
Athenian Confederacy, presumably about the time that Athens persuaded the
Hellenes and Amyntas to recognize her claim to Amphipolis,[3] and faced by
the threat of a resumption of power by Athens in the north of the Aegean they
had struggled on until Philip came to their aid, his first act being to deprive
the Athenians of Potidaea by which Olynthus was threatened.[4] As Philip's
power grew the Olynthians were not able to agree whether Macedon was more
formidable than Athens. The peace they made with Athens in defiance of the
terms of their treaty with Philip[5] indicated no more than a temporary success
of the phil-Athenian party: even this may have been due not to agreement
about Philip but rather to exhaustion by nearly two decades of naval war;
unlike Philip, Olynthus shared fully in the trade of the Aegean.[6] Shortly after
the peace with Athens, perhaps not long after the 'sudden campaign' alluded
to in the first Philippic (§ 17), the leader of the phil-Athenians, Apollonides,
was exiled[7] and it is notable that that speech gives no hint that Olynthus might
be brought into alliance. By the time that Philip attacked Olynthus in 349 the
situation had changed again. The city was sheltering the pretender to the
Macedonian throne,[8] and there was a general demand in Athens that it should
be drawn into the war.[9] How far, then, could the Olynthians be trusted? If
Athens committed a large number of her citizens to the defence of the Chalcidic
cities, what guarantee was there that their very presence would not stimulate
those who feared Athens so greatly to seek a fresh agreement with Philip and
so to endanger a large proportion of the Athenian citizen body? And what, if in
seeking such an agreement treachery played a part? Such questions must have
occurred to Athens's statesmen. Torone and Mecyberna fell, if Diodorus[10] is to
be trusted, by treachery, and the action of Lasthenes and Euthycrates, whatever it was, played a decisive part in the fall of Olynthus.[11] Would these things

[1] 4. 16 f.
[2] 3. 6.
[3] Accame, op. cit., p. 178.
[4] Cf. P.–W. xviii. 328.
[5] Dem. 23. 109, and § 2 of Libanius'
Hypothesis to Ol. 1.
[6] Xen. Hell. 5. 2. 16. Cf. [Dem.] 35. 35.
[7] Dem. 9. 56.
[8] Justin. 8. 3. 10.
[9] Dem. 3. 7.
[10] 16. 53.
[11] Dem. 8. 40, 9. 66, and Diod. 16. 53. 2.

not have happened if Athens had intervened in large numbers? In the first Olynthiac[1] Demosthenes was at pains to say that Olynthus could be trusted to fight is out with Philip. The course of the next twelve months was to prove him too optimistic. Perhaps his opponents had clearer vision and harder political heads.

Secondly, if there was a danger of arriving too late, there was a danger of committing large forces too early. The discussion of the course of operations above has shown that the early stages of Philip's attack on Olynthus were in a sense non-committal; the siege of the city itself did not begin until it could be so quickly carried through that Athens could not possibly send adequate help in time. The truth is that the choice of a time for attack lay with Philip. His earlier 'sudden campaign'[2] had been followed by two or more years of waiting. Was Athens in 349 to commit a large force to Olynthus and keep it there summer and winter for a similar period until the attack came? If so, the cost would have been heavy.[3] Five thousand men could not have been kept content in Olynthus for any length of time with the mere allowance for buying food that Demosthenes had proposed in 351 for the small active force. Now it is true that Athens's failure to provide adequately for her armies in the fourth century was a serious factor in the decline of her power, and it may be true that Eubulus and his supporters were unduly concerned with saving money, but there certainly could be no question at this period of spending as much money as a long garrisoning of Chalcidic cities would require.[4]

Thirdly, if Athens committed herself heavily to the defence of Olynthus, it was by no means clear that Philip would be confined to Macedon. Geography was on his side; he could have been well on his way to the Chersonese before Athens could act. In 346 the Athenian ambassadors left Philip in Pella barely more than two weeks before the Dionysia began on 9 Elaphebolion (IX),[5] but by the 24th day of that month Philip had wrested from Cersobleptes his kingdom, and captured the Holy Mount near the shores of the Propontis.[6] Such lightning movement no doubt surprised all Athenians, but that Philip could and would move quickly must have been realized. To stop such an attack on the Chersonese, even as large a force as 5,000 hoplites in Olynthus would have been ineffective, for they would have been too few to invade Macedonia; presumably Philip no more committed all his forces in these years than Alexander did against Persia. So another large force was needed for the Chersonese. Yet if Athens was to rush out large bodies of citizens every time an attack was feared, her strength would be dissipated, even if not endangered, with serious consequences for Greece itself. What would happen if Philip again tried to force the Gates?

All in all, there were strategic considerations which counselled against intervening with a large body of citizens to save Olynthus, and if Demosthenes' opponents declined to take his advice, their attitude was not entirely unreasonable. Nor would it be just to suppose that the help sent by Athens was

[1] § 5.
[2] i.e. the attack mentioned in Dem. 4. 17.
[3] The Potidaea campaign seriously affected Athens in the Archidamian war. Even if pay was only half what it had been then, Athens could hardly afford such large sums.
[4] The small force of ten ships proposed in 351 was to cost 92 T a year (Dem. 4. 28); a

larger force would have cost, perhaps, four times as much. Such expenditure would have assisted Philip in itself, for Athens could not keep it up indefinitely.
[5] Cf. Cloché, *Étude chronologique*, etc., pp. 122 f.
[6] Aesch. 2. 90.

sent in cynical neglect of the city's real interests. Indeed, but for treachery, Mecyberna might have been kept open and the second expedition of Chares might have saved Olynthus, if only temporarily. Statesmen are not necessarily at fault whenever their country's forces are defeated. Basically the control of Olynthus was a difficult military problem, which a united and powerful Macedon was likely to solve to its own satisfaction. Philip was able to operate on short lines of communication with the advantages of the seasons and with a specialized national army against the outmoded military conceptions of the city-state.[1] In war chance always plays a part, but it is at least doubtful whether Demosthenes would have succeeded where others failed. He saw clearly the menace of Philip, but his powers as a strategist did not match his oratory.

By contrast there is much to be said in favour of what Athens actually did do. First, when there was any question of Philip coming into Greece, energetic measures were taken. Not only in 352 did Athens send a substantial force to support the Phocians,[2] but also in 347/6 Eubulus and Aeschines reacted with great vigour to the possibility of Philip intervening in the Sacred War[3] and Athens was prepared to send out a fleet of fifty ships and a large proportion of the citizen body;[4] Philip might have been excluded by force of arms had not the shifting policy of Phocis forced the Athenians to seek peace.[5] The expedition to Euboea was perhaps part of this policy. Philip had not yet intervened, but, if the island had fallen completely under the control of Athens's enemies, the result might have been that either Philip or the Thebans could have used the island as a base and the chances of stopping Philip at the Gates been considerably weakened. The strategic importance of Euboea was shown when the Macedonians fixed one of the fetters of Greece at Chalcis, and, despite Demosthenes' dissent, the Athenians probably did right to intervene in 348. Although the campaign miscarried to some extent,[6] it is to be noted that the island did not come under Philip or Thebes before the Peace of 346. Secondly, the Athenian attitude to Philip's threatening advance to Heraeum Teichos in 352 was sensible enough despite the scorn of Demosthenes.[7] As long as the Chersonese

---

[1] How far did Demosthenes understand the change in the conditions of warfare? From 9. 47 it is clear that he was aware, at least by 341, that warfare had become professional and specialized, but his own proposals in the First Philippic and elsewhere hardly suggest that he fully appreciated the change in both tactics and strategy. In the fifth century when Macedon was weak and Athens strong, it had proved hard to guarantee the security of the Macedonian sea-board (cf. *S.E.G.* x. 66 = *A.T.L.* D. 3; [Dem.] 7. 12 is not to be taken too seriously), and in the fourth, when the balance of power had so greatly shifted, the difficulties of fighting Philip close to his base at the farthest stretch of Athens' communications were probably too great for Athens.

[2] The Athenian success in stopping Philip in 352 was greater than has been generally realized. Diodorus 16. 37 records the Phocian recovery after the battle of the Crocus Field, including the assembly of a large allied force

of which the 5,400 Athenians under Nausicles was barely more than half, but at the end of chapter 37 he leaves his narration of the Sacred War and returns to Philip. Chapter 38 recounts the check to Philip at Thermopylae κωλυσάντων τῶν Ἀθηναίων with 10 mention of the Spartans, etc. The reasonable explanation is that only the Athenians got there in time. This is confirmed by Dem. 19. 319 where in speaking of the check to Philip Demosthenes says τότε τῶν ὄντων ἀνθρώπων ἁπάντων οὐδενός, οὔθ' Ἕλληνος οὔτε βαρβάρου, Φωκεῦσι βοηθήσαντος πλὴν ὑμῶν. Cf. Justin 8. 2. 8. That Athens saved Phocis so easily must have had a grave effect on the ideas of Athenian statesmen: Philip learnt his lesson.

[3] Dem. 19. 9 f. and 303 f. Cf. *R.É.G.* lxxiii (1960), 418 f.

[4] Aesch. 2. 133, Dem. 19. 52, 322.

[5] Cf. art. cited in n. 3 above.

[6] Plut. *Phoc.* 14. 1.

[7] 3. 4 f.

was directly threatened, the Athenians prepared to intervene with a large armament, but, when Philip was found to be unable to press on with his attack, the expedition was dropped, reasonably enough. What point would there have been in sending out a large proportion of the citizen body to meet an attack that might never develop, but leaving Athens less able to apply herself to the defence of the Gates? The fact that the Chersonese remained safe justified the policy adopted. Nor should we let Demosthenes mislead us with his lists of scandalous failures.[1] How could Athens have saved Methone indefinitely against a strong Macedon? Even in the fifth century when the Macedonian kingdom was weak and the power of Athens enormous, the condition of Methone was highly insecure. To have committed large numbers of Athenians to the salvation of this city in the 350's would have been madness.[2] And what was really to be done for Pagasae, the port of Pherae? All Thessaly had joined with Philip in destroying the Pheraean power, and if Athens had got large forces involved over such a trifle, disaster might have come upon her very much more quickly than it did. After all, the war for Amphipolis was an absurdity, both militarily and politically, which had to be maintained since public opinion at Athens would not suffer the only sensible solution, viz. to abandon the quest. After a decade of fruitless and debilitating struggle followed by the reverses of the Social War Athens was not likely to win and the sane alternative was adopted of virtually leaving the war to take care of itself. If chance took a hand with an assassination or treacherous betrayal of the city, all might be well, but the mistake was not made of becoming ruinously involved in the vain struggle. Chares appears to have been out almost constantly from 353 to 346 on operations in the north[3] and after the operations of Iphicrates, Timotheus, and lesser men like Timomachus had produced no real gain these activities of Chares were probably as much as any sensible man could justify. Ampler forces were sent to help the Olynthians and they might have saved the city had the port of Olynthus not been handed over to Philip; the objections to committing more were at least in part strategic.

Although Eubulus is rather a shadowy figure, he and his supporters were probably responsible for Athenian policy between the Social War and the Peace of Philocrates. This is certain with regard to the Euboean expedition,[4] and the direction of affairs in 347/6 was clearly the work of Eubulus and Aeschines. Possibly this is true of the expeditions of 352; the general who commanded at Thermopylae, Nausicles, may be the man who was later

[1] 4. 35, 1. 9.
[2] Cf. p. 138, n. 1.
[3] Theopompus, F.G.H. 115 F 249 (of 353 cf. Schaefer, op. cit. i². 443, n. 3); Polyaenus 4. 2. 22, Diod. 16. 34. 3 and 35. 5 (all of 352); Philochorus, F.G.H. 328 F 49 (of 349— 'the thirty ships under Chares', i.e. he was already provided with a force); I.G. ii². 207, line 12 (of early 348). One might guess that just as Charidemus was in 348 and probably earlier ὁ ἐν Ἑλλησπόντωι στρατηγός, Chares was throughout the period 353 to 348, and perhaps to 346 (cf. Aesch. 2. 73 and 90 but note I.G. ii². 1620, line 19), the general in command of the war for Amphipolis, ὁ

στρατηγὸς ἐπ' Ἀμφίπολιν (Aesch. 2. 27), and that the thirty ships of 349 were the size of fleet he normally had (in Polyaenus, loc. cit., he has only twenty ships).

[4] Midias, who as ξένος καὶ φίλος of Plutarch of Eretria played a leading part in the dispatch of the expedition (Dem. 21. 110, 200), was a close associate of Eubulus (Dem. 21. 205-7). Phocion appears with Eubulus in support of Aeschines in 343 (Aesch. 2. 184). Hegesileos, who mysteriously ἐπεστρατήγησεν in Euboea (Schol. Dem. 19. 290 = Dind. p. 443 l. 24) was a cousin of Eubulus (Dem. 19. 290).

associated with Aeschines.[1] There is less precise information about the war in the north, but we may still be fairly confident that Eubulus was ultimately responsible. For, when Demosthenes was inveighing in the third Olynthiac[2] against those who had influence over the δῆμος, he specially alludes to the public works programme which played a large part in Eubulus' financial schemes,[3] and goes on to attribute what he regards as lack of enterprise to the domination of those who control the city's finances, clearly Eubulus and his group. So in the sense that Eubulus prevented the sending out of large forces of citizens by keeping a tight rein on the city's finances, he was responsible for what was not done in the north.

Why Eubulus followed this policy is largely a matter for conjecture. The one thing that is clear is that in early 346 he was prepared to make a serious attempt to unite Greece against Philip;[4] there is no direct evidence of what he thought about the defence of Olynthus. He may have simply failed to perceive what Demosthenes perceived so clearly, viz. that Philip was a real danger to Greece. It is equally possible that he was aware of the danger of Philip,[5] but was aware also of the strategic considerations that counselled against risking a second Sicilian disaster and neglecting Athens' primary concerns. We do not know enough about him to say. The argument of this article is in brief this, that in so far as Eubulus opposed Demosthenes' proposals for the conduct of the Olynthian war, whether for the right reason or the wrong, Eubulus happened to be, strategically speaking, right.

University College, Oxford   G. L. CAWKWELL

[1] For Nausicles, Diod. 16. 37. 3. There are several bearers of the name (cf. *Pros. Att.*), but there are two main candidates for the generalship of 352. First, Nausicles, son of Clearchos, who appears in the period after Chaeronea (*I.G.* ii². 1496 col. ii *l.* 40 f., 1628 *l.* 71, 1629 *l.* 707) and who is the associate of Demosthenes (Aesch. 3. 159, Plut. *Dem.* 21, Dem. 18. 114, Plut. *Mor.* 844 f). Secondly, the Nausicles who supported Aeschines in 343 (Aesch. 2. 184), presumably the man who had proposed Aeschines for the embassy in 346 (Aesch. 2. 18) and who was himself one of the ambassadors (§ 4 of 2nd Hyp. to Dem. 19). Since the former only appears after 338, the latter, the associate of Aeschines, called in 343 because he was an important man, is to be preferred.

Confirmation of Eubulus' connexion with the defence of Thermopylae is perhaps pro-vided by Diophantus of Sphettus, who proposed the decree of thanksgiving in 352 (Dem. 19. 86 and schol.). He was an associate of Aeschines (Dem. 19. 198, where Demosthenes says he will compel him to give evidence against Aeschines) and also associated with the financial administration (Aesch. 3. 24 and 25 and schol.).

[2] §§ 28–32.

[3] Aesch. 3. 25, Dinarchus 1. 96, *I.G.* ii². 505, 1668.

[4] See p. 138, n. 3.

[5] As Jaeger, op. cit., p. 108, insisted, the march of Philip to Heraeum Teichos made Demosthenes aware of the real danger. Considering that Athens was at war with Philip and that she depended so much on the safety of the corn supply, it would be surprising if Demosthenes was the only person to regard Philip seriously in 349/8.

V

G. L. Cawkwell

Aeschines and the Peace of Philocrates

AESCHINES AND THE PEACE
OF PHILOCRATES *

The decision to seek peace with Philip was taken early in 346 and
an embassy of ten men including Aeschines, Philocrates and
Demosthenes together with a representative of the Second Athenian
Confederacy, set off for Macedon about a month before the City
Dionysia. They were successful with Philip and returned to
Athens shortly before the Dionysia with the news than Macedonian
ambassadors were on their way, and could be expected at Athens
before the festival began. In fact, they did not arrive in time to
do business and on 8 Elaphebolion the people made preparations
for prompt action as soon after the Dionysia as possible. A decree
was passed to the effect that there should be two meetings of the
people, on 18 and 19 Elaphebolion: on the 18th the Athenians were
to deliberate and on the 19th to decide. On the 19th the decision
was for peace with Philip and the decree embodying the decision
was the decree proposed by Philocrates, amended in certain respects,
and known as the decree of Philocrates. The second meeting did
not, however, go according to plan. Originally the people had
ordered that on the second day there should be no debate, but on
the 18th it was decided to call the Macedonian ambassadors, and,
when early in the proceedings of the following morning Antipater
made clear what Philip would not accept, a new debate was
necessary in which Aeschines took part and supported Philo-

* This article was read to the Oxford Philological Society in Hilary Term 1956.
I wish to thank Professor Andrewes, Mr. C. Hignett, Mr. R. Meiggs, and
Mr. B. R. I. Sealey for generous help. They should not, however, be supposed
necessarily to share all or any of the views here expressed.

crates (1). It is the purpose of this article to consider the conduct of Aeschines, who has suffered from Demosthenes' accusations. Even if one declines to believe everything, or even anything, that Demosthenes says about him, one retains the impression that he was pursuing a short-sighted policy of pacifism, and regards his support for Philocrates on 19 Elaphebolion as typical of the attitude Demosthenes later denounced. This is far from just to Aeschines. His policy in 346 changed as the situation changed but it was neither short-sighted nor pacifist.

After the Athenians had failed to take adequate measures to save Olynthus although they had been prepared to do everything to save Euboea, Demosthenes, realising that the Athenian refusal to fight the war in the North meant that Athens would have to deal with Philip in Greece, began to support those who advocated a peace with Philip. At some time near the fall of Olynthus, perhaps just before, he had successfully defended Philocrates in the courts, when attacked for his proposal to negotiate (2). When Olynthus fell, the Greek world was horrified at the fate of the survivors, and the peace movement in Athens came to a stop. Demosthenes retired into silence. The next important move was made not by Demosthenes, but by Eubulus and Aeschines. It was of a very different sort, and merits more attention than it has received.

---

(1) Cp. Chapters VII and VIII of Pickard-Cambridge *Demosthenes*.

(2) Aesch. 2.12-15. The view is commonly held that the order of Aeschines' narrative must not be considered exact. Cp. Pokorny, *Studien*, p. 134f. Since the events narrated began with the capture of an Athenian during the Olympic truce of 348 and Philip celebrated the Olympia after the capture of Olynthus (Diod. 16.55, Dem. 19.192), Pokorny held that there was not enough time to fit in all that Aeschines narrated, including the trial and acquittal of Philocrates, before the fall of Olynthus, and he accordingly placed Demosthenes' defence of Philocrates later — in which case the acquittal is nothing less than astonishing. However, Pokorny argues on the false assumption that the Macedonian Olympia were held at the same time as the Greek Olympia. That they were not is clear from Arr. *Anab.* I, 10 and 11. The news of the fate of Thebes reached Athens in 335 in the middle of the Great Mysteries (i.e. mid-Boedromion) and the Athenians interrupted the festival to send an embassy to Alexander. After receiving this embassy, Alexander returned to Macedonia and celebrated the Olympia. So the Macedonian Olympia were in late autumn, not in mid-summer, and there is room before the fall of Olynthus for all of Aeschines' narrative. For the Macedonian Olympia cp. P. W. XVIII. 1. Col. 46.

418   G. L. CAWKWELL

Eubulus proposed in the assembly and the people decreed that
ambassadors should be sent throughout the Greek world to summon
the Greeks to Athens to deliberate about the war against Philip (1).
A prominent part was taken by Aeschines. He it was who, τὸ
κατ᾽ ἀρχάς, brought Ischander son of Neoptolemus (2) before the
Council, and then before the people, with some startling information,
whatever it was. On the day that Eubulus' decree was proposed
to the people, Aeschines made an important speech: in it he accused
Philip of plotting against Greece, and called on the Athenians to
act; he had the secretary read out first the decrees of Miltiades
and Themistocles, monuments of Athenian resistance to barbarian
invasion, and then the ephebic oath, which required every man to
defend his country; and with these appeals to Athens' pride he
persuaded the Athenians to ratify the decree of Eubulus and
summon the Hellenes. Subsequently Aeschines went on an
embassy to Arcadia and appeared before the Ten Thousand. He
called on the Arcadians not to endanger themselves and Greece
by following the policies of Hieronymus, the leader of the pro-
Macedonian party in Arcadia (3). Despite the satisfaction which
his embassy afforded to the phil-Athenian party, he does not appear
to have effected any real change. For, when he returned to Athens,
he reported to the Athenians that something might be done if
Athens followed up with a further embassy (4). After this, the
next thing heard of Aeschines is that he was chosen to go to Macedon
on the first embassy to Philip.

To what period does this activity of Aeschines belong? There
are clear indications in Demosthenes and Aeschines that some of the
embassies sent out by the decree of Eubulus were either present
or expected on 19 Elaphebolion 346. Demosthenes (5) had said
that Aeschines made his speech on the 19th ἐφεστηκότων τῶν πρέσβεων καὶ ἀκουόντων, οὓς ἀπὸ τῶν Ἑλλήνων μετεπέμψασθε ὑπὸ

(1) Dem. 19.10, and 303f.
(2) Neoptolemus was the well-known actor. Cp. Dem. 19.315, 5.7, and
P. W. XVI. 2 col. 2470. Demosthenes sneers at the son as τὸν δευτεραγωνιστήν
(19.10).
(3) Dem. 19.11 and 305. For Hieronymos cp. Dem. 18.295 and Polyb. XVIII.
14.
(4) Dem. 19.306.
(5) 19.16.

τούτου πεισθέντες. To this Aeschines made his reply (1) : Τοὺς γὰρ λόγους τούτους ἐναντίον φησὶ τῶν πρέσβεων λέγεσθαι, οὓς ἔπεμψαν πρὸς ὑμᾶς οἱ Ἕλληνες μεταπεμφθέντες ὑπὸ τοῦ δήμου, ἵνα κοινῇ καὶ πολεμοῖεν, εἰ δέοι, Φιλίππῳ μετὰ ᾿Αθηναίων, καὶ τῆς εἰρήνης, εἰ τοῦτο εἶναι δοκοίη συμφέρον, μετέχοιεν. Σκέψασθε δὴ πράγματος μεγάλου κλοπὴν καὶ δεινὴν ἀναισχυντίαν ἀνθρώπου. Τῶν γὰρ πρεσβε-ιῶν, ἃς ἐξεπέμψατε εἰς τὴν Ἑλλάδα, ἔτι τοῦ πολέμου τοῦ πρὸς Φίλιππον ὑμῖν ἐνεστηκότος, οἱ μὲν χρόνοι τῆς αἱρέσεως, ὅτε ἐξεπέμφθησαν, καὶ τὰ τῶν πρεσβευσάντων ὀνόματα ἐν τοῖς δημοσίοις ἀναγέγραπται γράμ-μασι, τὰ δὲ σώματά ἐστιν αὐτῶν οὐκ ἐν Μακεδονίᾳ ἀλλ᾿ ᾿Αθήνησι · ταῖς δὲ ξενικαῖς πρεσβείαις ἡ βουλὴ τὰς εἰς τὸν δῆμον προσόδους προβουλεύ-ει· οὗτος δ᾿ ἐφεστάναι τὰς ἀπὸ τῶν Ἑλλήνων φησὶ πρεσβείας. Παρελθὼν τοίνυν, Δημόσθενες, ἐπὶ τὸ βῆμα τοῦτο ἐν τῷ ἐμῷ λόγῳ, εἰπὲ πόλεως ἥστινος βούλει τῶν Ἑλληνίδων τοὔνομα, ἐξ ἧς ἀφῖχθαι τότε φῂς τοὺς πρέσβεις · καὶ τὰ προβουλεύματα αὐτῶν ἐκ τοῦ βουλευτηρίου δὸς ἀναγνῶναι, καὶ τοὺς ᾿Αθηναίων κάλει πρέσβεις, οὓς ἐξέπεμψαν ἐπὶ τὰς πόλεις, μάρτυρας. Κἂν παρεῖναι καὶ μὴ ἀποδημεῖν, ὅτε ἡ πόλις τὴν εἰρήνην ἐποιεῖτο, μαρτυρήσωσιν, ἢ τὰς πρὸς τὴν βουλὴν αὐτῶν προσόδους καὶ τὰ ψηφίσματα ἂν παράσχῃ ἐν ᾧ σὺ φῂς ὄντα χρόνῳ, καταβαίνω καὶ θανάτου τιμῶμαι. This exchange between Demosthenes and Aeschines within three years of the events under discussion would seem to show that the attempt to summon the Hellenes for a congress of some sort at Athens had been be-gun at no very great interval before the crucial discussions of Ela-phebolion 346.

This dating is confirmed by the decree of the Allied Synedrion which Aeschines (2) goes on to cite in support of his statements about these ambassadors. According to Aeschines, this decree ran as follows : ἐπειδὴ βουλεύεται ὁ δῆμος ὁ ᾿Αθηναίων ὑπὲρ εἰρήνης πρὸς Φίλιππον, οἱ δὲ πρέσβεις οὔπω πάρεισιν, οὓς ἐξέπεμψεν ὁ δῆμος εἰς τὴν Ἑλλάδα παρακαλῶν τὰς πόλεις ὑπὲρ τῆς ἐλευθερίας τῶν Ἑλ-λήνων, δεδόχθαι τοῖς συμμάχοις, ἐπειδὰν ἐπιδημήσωσιν οἱ πρέσβεις καὶ τὰς πρεσβείας ἀπαγγείλωσιν ᾿Αθηναίοις καὶ τοῖς συμμάχοις, προ-γράψαι τοὺς πρυτάνεις ἐκκλησίας δύο κατὰ τὸν νόμον, ἐν δὲ ταύταις βουλεύσασθαι περὶ τῆς εἰρήνης ᾿Αθηναίους · ὅ τι δ᾿ ἂν βουλεύσηται ὁ

(1) 2.57-59.
(2) 2.60.

δῆμος, τοῦτ' εἶναι κοινὸν δόγμα τῶν συμμάχων. Aeschines claims to quote word for word (ἐν ᾧ διαρρήδην γέγραπται) and immediately after quoting the decree, he has it read out; it seems unlikely that he is misrepresenting it. So by 8 Elaphebolion, the likely date of the decree (1), the ambassadors sent out by Athens had not returned. Presumably they had but recently been sent out.

Schaefer long ago denied this, and assigned the sending of the embassies to the period just after the fall of Olynthus, i.e. late 348. His argument seems to be this (2). References of Aeschines suggest that Aeschines' attempt to unite the Greeks was made before the peace negotiations began. Aeschines (3) says the embassies were sent out ἔτι τοῦ πολέμου τοῦ πρὸς Φίλιππον ὑμῖν ἐνεστηκότος. Again, in defence of his δημηγορία καὶ πρεσβεία ἐν τοῖς μυρίοις, he says (4) ἐγὼ δ' ἐν μὲν τῷ πολέμῳ συνίστην, καθ' ὅσον ἦν δυνατός, 'Αρκάδας καὶ τοὺς ἄλλους "Ελληνας ἐπὶ Φίλιππον · οὐδενὸς δ' ἀνθρώπων ἐπικουροῦντος τῇ πόλει, ἀλλὰ τῶν μὲν περιορώντων ὅ τι συμβήσεται, τῶν δὲ συνεπιστρατευόντων, τῶν δ' ἐν τῇ πόλει ῥητόρων χορηγὸν ταῖς καθ' ἡμέραν δαπάναις τὸν πόλεμον ποιουμένων, ὁμολογῶ συμβουλεῦσαι τῷ δήμῳ διαλύσασθαι πρὸς Φίλιππον καὶ τὴν εἰρήνην συνθέσθαι. These passages Schaefer took to show that the whole affair was over before the peace negotiations began, and he found confirmation in Demosthenes' speech On the Crown. In that speech (5) Demosthenes replies to the charge

(1) Pace Schaefer II², p. 216f., this decree of the Allies is not the same decree as that cited by Aeschines at 3.70. The latter was presented to the people on 18 Elaphebolion, as Aeschines says (3.69), and it is the decree which both Aeschines and Demosthenes claimed to have supported in the course of the two days' debate, but this decree of the Allies (2.60) provides for the holding of the two days' debate and presumably belongs to the same period as the decree of Demosthenes, which also provided for that debate, and which Aeschines proceeds to cite in 2.61. The decree of the Allies and the decree of Demosthenes are compared by Aeschines to show that Demosthenes sought more than the Allies intended. It seems reasonable to suppose that the two decrees were presented to the people on the same day and that this is an instance of the Second Athenian Confederacy at work; the Allies proposed a two-day debate and Demosthenes specified which days. Since Demosthenes' decree was presented on 8 Elaphebolion, that is the likely date of the proposal of the decree of the Allies.

(2) II², p. 167f.

(3) 2.58.

(4) 2.79.

(5) 18.23, 24.

made by Aeschines (1) that he had forced through the peace in such a hurry that he did not even wait for the ambassadors sent out to summon the Greeks, and his reply is : οὔτε γὰρ ἦν πρεσβεία πρὸς οὐδέν᾽ ἀποσταλμένη τότε τῶν Ἑλλήνων, ἀλλὰ πάλαι πάντες ἦσαν ἐξεληλεγμένοι. So Schaefer concluded that whatever one made of Aeschines' challenge in the speech On the False Legation, the truth was that the whole business of Eubulus and Aeschines was over and done with before the peace negotiations began, and he assigned it to the period just after the fall of Olynthus, because Aeschines, in reporting his embassy to the People, spoke (2) of meeting Atrestidas coming from Philip with a gift of Olynthian prisoners of war. Of course, this meeting with Atrestidas proves nothing: Philip could have made the gift one or eighteen months after the fall of Olynthus. Yet the main argument of Schaefer does need an answer.

First, the passage of the De Corona. If the late dating of the embassies is correct, and they had not in fact returned by 18 Elaphebolion, Aeschines' charge was just; Demosthenes had not waited for the Greeks to arrive, and it was a difficult point for Demosthenes to deal with. He may have thought that, 16 years after the event, his easiest course was a flat denial. The charge had been made at some length by Aeschines (3); if Demosthenes had a good reply, it is surprising that he should furnish it, unattested and in two lines of text. But why should this sentence of the de Corona, uttered at so great an interval after the events referred to, be supposed to reveal the truth that the ample arguments of both Aeschines and Demosthenes within 3 years of the peace are supposed to dissemble ? In 343 Aeschines was accused by Demosthenes of betraying Greece in the very presence of the Greeks whom Aeschines had summoned: Aeschines answered that the Greeks he had summoned had not yet arrived. In 330 Aeschines (4), consistent with what he had said before, accused Demosthenes of not waiting for the Greeks who had been summoned; Demosthenes changed his line, and, despite what he had himself

(1) 3.65.
(2) Dem. 19.306.
(3) 3. 64-74.
(4) See especially 3.68.

said in 343, issued his brief denial. Why should Demosthenes
in 330 receive a credit denied him in 343?

Next, the passages of Aeschines cited by Schaefer. Of course,
the embassies were sent out during the war, but it does not follow
that they had returned with word that their appeals had been
turned down, before the Athenians decided to negotiate for peace.
Ἐν τῷ πολέμῳ (1) and ἔτι τοῦ πολέμου τοῦ πρὸς Φίλιππον ὑμῖν ἐνεστηκότος (2) would be proper for any time up till the decision to
seek peace with Philip, i.e. early in Anthesterion (3). The
passage in which Aeschines answers the charge that he changed
his policy for corrupt reasons, is consistent with Schaefer's interpretation, but does not necessitate it. It has to be considered
in relation to the passage in Demosthenes which it answers (4).
Demosthenes' point is that between 18 and 19 Elaphebolion
Aeschines changed from opposing Philocrates to supporting him;
at that point, Demosthenes argues, Aeschines showed that he had
been corrupted. So it was with the speech on 19 Elaphebolion
that Aeschines had especially to deal. If, as is suggested, the
embassies were summoned at such a time that they could have
arrived by the Dionysia, and did not in fact arrive, then Aeschines'
words were a perfectly proper account of why, of the two alternatives posed by the Macedonian envoys on 19 Elaphebolion, he
preferred the alternative of peace, οὐδενὸς ἀνθρώπων ἐπικουροῦντος
τῇ πόλει, ἀλλὰ τῶν μὲν περιορώντων ὅ τι συμβήσεται, τῶν δὲ κ. τ. λ.

The passages in which Schaefer trusted are neither so plain
nor so trustworthy as he supposed. Their value is little compared
to the exchange between Demosthenes and Aeschines in 343.
To Demosthenes' serious charge, Aeschines simply replied that the
Hellenes had not yet arrived. If this reply was false, why did he
make it? If the summons had gone out long before and had
gone unheeded, Aeschines had only to show from the dating of
Eubulus' decree that it was so long ago that nothing either had or
could come of it, and he would have proved Demosthenes a liar.

(1) Aesch. 2.79.
(2) Aesch. 2.58.
(3) See below and Cloché, *Étude chronologique sur la troisième guerre Sacrée*,
p. 122f.
(4) Dem. 19.10-16 esp. 14f.

But he did not answer in that way, for the truth is that the ambassadors had been sent out only shortly before Elaphebolion, and the Greeks were still to be expected at the Dionysia 346. According to Schaefer, he answered a lie with a bigger lie, and when he had no need to do so misused a document to back up his lie. Thus Schaefer makes Aeschines not just a liar, but a fool. Neither of the principals in 343 was exactly that.

Pickard-Cambridge (1) decided that « it is difficult to avoid concluding that there must have been some Athenian envoys out on a mission » at the time of the negotiations in Athens, and he thought that probably « some of the envoys sent in the winter had not yet returned ». But if some of the envoys had returned, why did Aeschines issue his challenge ? That would have been to present Demosthenes with the opportunity to ruin him. Demosthenes did not accept the challenge, and the reason must be that none of the envoys had returned and Aeschines was safe to issue his challenge. Nor is the value of the challenge to be impugned by asking « Why, if no one else was back, since Aeschines was, did Demosthenes not name him ? » Whether Aeschines' embassy was recent or long past, Aeschines was back, and, if he could be named, why did he issue the challenge? The solution must be that he could not be named, that his embassy to Arcadia was of a different sort from the others; Aeschines had been sent out to expostulate with the Arcadians, and report back to Athens promptly, which he did; the others had been sent out, each one to many cities, to summon the Greeks for the Dionysia, and it is of these that Aeschines issued his challenge.

It might be argued that the evidence of the *De Corona* and in particular the word πάλαι deserves more respect and that it points to two sets of embassies, one shortly before Elaphebolion and one much earlier, and that the decree of Eubulus and the embassy of Aeschines to the Peloponnese belong to the earlier period (2). The evidence will not allow this. Both the main passages of Demosthenes, which speak of the embassies (3), make Aeschines

(1) *Op. cit.*, p. 260f. Cp. Pokorny, *op. cit.*, p. 143-4.
(2) Cf. Kahrstedt, *Forschungen*, p. 64f, followed by Pokorny, *op. cit.*, p. 139f. and Wüst, *Philipp II*, p. 21, n. 2.
(3) See *supra*, p. 418.

really responsible for the summoning of the Greeks, and his charge against Aeschines is that on 19 Elaphebolion he betrayed the Greeks whom the Athenians summoned ὑπὸ τούτου πεισθέντες. There is no escape. Eubulus' decree must have been recent. There might have been an earlier attempt to organise the Greeks, but unless one invokes the doubtful aid of Diodorus (1) Demosthenes' remark in the *De Corona* would be the only evidence for it, and anyone who rereads all the passages in the two speeches on the subject of these embassies will find it hard to avoid believing that only one set of embassies occurred.

The decree of Eubulus was recent. How recent? The *terminus ante quem* is provided by the dating of the first embassy to Philip. That embassy, to judge by various indications of time in Demosthenes, left Athens about a month before its return shortly before 8 Elaphebolion (2); that is, they must have left about 6 Anthesterion. Some time must be allowed between the decree and their departure, and if one supposes that the decision to negotiate with Philip was taken in the Council, discussed by the Allied Synedrion, and ratified by the people in the very last days of Gamelion and the early days of Anthesterion, one cannot be far wrong. Aeschines was back from his embassy to the Peloponnese in time to be elected to the Embassy, and so his departure for the Peloponnese must be pushed back into Gamelion at the latest. Presumably he allowed no great lapse of time between the decree of Eubulus and his departure, but, if one allows for some delay, the middle of Gamelion is the *terminus ante quem*. A *terminus post quem* is harder to establish. On the one hand, the Decree of the Allied Synedrion (3) presented to the People on 8 Elaphebolion suggests that, although the ambassadors sent out by the Athenians had not

---

(1) Between Diodorus' notice of the capture of Olynthus (16.53) and the ending of the Sacred War there is practically nothing about Greek affairs save the final operations of that war. There is no notice of the Peace of Philocrates and Diodorus' notice about the Athenian hostility led by Demosthenes, which includes the remark about the embassies (16.54), is of the most general kind, and although Diodorus puts it all under 348/7, it is highly doubtful whether his date is of any importance. Furthermore, he appears to attribute the sending of the embassies to Demosthenes, which, in view of the other evidence, is certainly wrong.

(2) Cp. Cloché, *op. cit.*, p. 122f.

(3) Aesch. 2.60.

yet in fact returned, they might havè done so: therefore the decree
of Eubulus must be pushed back sufficiently far to make a Congress
of Greeks in Athens at the Dionysia just physically possible.
On the other hand, since Aeschines could challenge Demosthenes
to name one single ambassador who had in fact returned to Athens
by 19 Elaphebolion, the decree despatching the ambassadors cannot
be placed very long before that date.   Short of an epigraphic
miracle, there is no means of knowing how many ambassadors had
been sent out, what had to be done in each city, and how many
cities had to be visited by the ambassador who could be expected
to return to Athens first.   Pericles' Congress Decree (1), the
Coinage Decree (2), and the Assessment Decree of 425 (3) suggest
only that procedure varied. So precise calculation is impossible.
Yet it is hard to imagine that if the ambassadors had set out as
much as three months before Elaphebolion 19, nòt one would have
got back to Athens. In the Allied Decree presented to the People
on 19 Elaphebolion (4) three months is the period allowed for the
Greeks to join in the peace. If that was sufficient for the Greeks
in general, presumably one of the ambassadors sent by Eubulus'
decree, no matter how much they had to do in each city he visited,
could if he had been sent out by 19 Poseideion, have been back
by 19 Elaphebolion.   It seems therefore a not unreasonable
conjecture that Eubulus' decree was passed after, say, 19 Posideion,
and before mid Gamelion, and, despite ignorance of the ambassadors' tasks and itineraries, one would prefer the latter rather
than the former half of that period.

What was the object of Eubulus' decree which Aeschines
supported?   There appears to have been no mention of peace
with Philip in the invitations to the Greek states. In Demosthenes' words (5) they were to deliberate περὶ τοῦ πρὸς Φίλιππον
πολέμου. Aeschines (6) describes his part in this way : πρότερον
παρεκάλουν ἐπ' ἐκεῖνον τοὺς "Ελληνας. Aeschines' speech to the

(1) Plut., *Per.* 17.
(2) *A. T. L.* D. 14.
(3) *A. T. L.* A. 9.
(4) Aesch. 3.70.
(5) 19.10.
(6) 2.164. Cp. 2.79.

426   G. L. CAWKWELL

people, when he first brought Ischander before them, the start of
the whole affair, was clearly a call to action against Philip (1).
The purpose of the embassies was to rouse the Hellenes for war.
There is only one passage (2) which suggests that Eubulus' decree
envisaged the possibility of peace, but Aeschines, naturally enough
in the context, suggested as much only because once Athens had
decided to seek peace, the purpose of consulting the allies changed.
All the other evidence shows clearly enough that Eubulus and
Aeschines aimed at organising the defence of Greece against the
threat of Philip. That is why Demosthenes sneers at Aeschines (3)
as « the first and only one to see that Philip is the common enemy
of all the Greeks ». Had no one even listened to the *First Philippic*
and the *Olynthiacs*?

What caused Eubulus and Aeschines to begin this movement?
It was mid winter. What was new in the situation of Philip that
occasioned such alarm ? In both the passages (4) in which Demosthenes enlarges on Aeschines' part in the sending of the embassies
he mentions the part played by Ischander. Aeschines brought
him before the People τὸ κατ' ἀρχάς, and said that he had come
from the phil-Athenian party in Arcadia. So the information
came from Arcadia. What it was exactly must remain a matter
for conjecture, but it was presumably concerned with Arcadian
politics. Word might have reached Greece of some new design
of Philip, but it would be surprising if it came by way of Arcadia.
Rather should one look for an explanation in Arcadian affairs.
Nothing more is heard after 352 of Arcadian efforts to keep themselves free of the Spartans, but, no doubt, this anxiety, which later
led Arcadia to rest its hopes in Philip and kept it out of the defence
of Greece (5), was as lively in 347/6 as it had been in 353/2. Sparta
remained intransigent about the recovery of lost ground in the
Peloponnese, and in 347/6 Thebes, the guarantor of Arcadian
independence, was not in any position to help. In that year
Coronea, Corsiae, and Orchomenus were all under Phocian control,

(1) Dem. 19.303.
(2) Aesch. 2.57.
(3) 19.302 and 10.
(4) See *supra*, p. 418.
(5) Dem. 18.304, etc.

and Boeotia itself was being ravaged (1). Such was the plight
of Boeotia that she had herself to appeal to Philip for aid, and if
Thebes had to seek salvation outside Greece, Arcadia could hope
for no immediate help in case of Spartan invasion, and might well
be looking to the same source for her own comfort. It may be
suggested that what caused the decree of Eubulus was some proposal
in the Ten Thousand to seek alliance with Philip of Macedon.
Certainly, something was afoot between Philip and Arcadia :
Aeschines, according to Demosthenes (2) spoke of Philip as δια-
φθείρων τινας τῶν ἐν Ἀρκαδίᾳ προεστηκότων.

Why did Athens, instead of waiting for the Hellenes and presenting
a united front to Philip, turn round and seek peace? The date
of this change of policy is fairly closely fixed: in Gamelion the
Athenians were still bent on war, in the first days of Anthesterion
they decided to seek peace. What was it that produced the volte
face?

Phocian affairs may provide the answer. In early summer 347
the Phocians deprived Phalaecus of the generalship (3) and continued the war that summer without his aid, but not without success.
The Boeotians appealed to Philip (4) and in early 346 (5) it became
known in Greece that Philip intended to campaign that year against
Phocis. The Phocians then sent an embassy to Athens to ask for
Athenian aid. That it was the news of Philip's intention which
led them to do so is suggested by a passage of Aeschines (6). In
speaking of Phocian affairs he says: ἡ μὲν γὰρ Θετταλῶν καὶ Φιλίππου στρατεία πρόδηλος ἦν, οὐ πολλῷ δὲ χρόνῳ πρότερον ἢ τὴν πρὸς
ὑμᾶς εἰρήνην γενέσθαι, πρέσβεις πρὸς ὑμᾶς ἦλθον ἐκ Φωκέων, βοηθεῖν
αὐτοῖς κελεύοντες ... κ.τ.λ. He does not say explicitly that the appeal
was the immediate consequence of the news about Macedon, but
that it was seems a fair inference from the juxtaposition of the two
statements. Aeschines goes on to say that, on receipt of this
appeal, the Athenians passed a decree that the Phocians should

(1) Diod. 16.58 f.
(2) 19.10.
(3) Diod. 16.56.2 and 3.
(4) Diod. 16.58.2.
(5) Aesch. 2.132.
(6) Ibid.

hand over the strong points which controlled the Gates to the general Proxenus, and that an expedition of 50 triremes and the best part of the Athenian army should go out to defend the pass. By the time these ambassadors got back to Phocis (they would have been away about 13 days) (1) Phalaecus was general again. He arrested the ambassadors, and refused to make the customary truce for the Eleusinian Mysteries with the σπονδοφόροι from Athens (2). Proxenus then discovered that the Phocians would not hand over the strong points, and sent a letter to Athens announcing that he had been rebuffed. On the day that Proxenus' letter was read to the people, the σπονδοφόροι in person reported that the Phocians had even refused the truce for the Mysteries. On that same day the people was deliberating about the Peace (3).

From this narrative it is clear that there were two pieces of news of great significance for Athens. The first was that Philip intended to invade Phocis; the danger of Philip's intervention became much more real. The second was that the Phocians would not allow Athens to share in the defence of Thermopylae as she had in 352. The first could only confirm Athens in the policy recently embarked on: Greece was in direct peril, and the defence must be organised,

(1) Cp. Dem. 19.59.

(2) It is here presumed that Cloché's demonstration (op. cit., p. 119f.) that the Mysteries in question are the Lesser Mysteries is correct. To Cloché's arguments might be added that the reference to the 50 ships, ' ἢ μέγα φρονεῖς ' ἔφη 'ἐπὶ ταῖς ἐψηφισμέναις μὲν πεντήκοντα ναυσίν, οὐδέποτε δὲ πληρωθησομέναις ;' (Aesch. 2.37), made by Aeschines at Pella suggests the latter alternative : the ships probably went (Dem. 19.322). Cp. Sealey Wiener Studien, LXVIII, 1955, p. 148f.

(3) 'Ἀλλ' ἐν τῇ αὐτῇ ἡμέρᾳ περί τε τῆς εἰρήνης ἐβουλεύεσθε, καὶ τῆς ἐπιστολῆς ἠκούετε τῆς Προξένου, ὅτι Φωκεῖς οὐ παραδεδώκασιν αὐτῷ τὰ χωρία, καὶ οἱ τὰ μυστήρια ἐπαγγέλλοντες μόνους τῶν ἄλλων Ἑλλήνων ἀπέφηναν Φωκέας οὐ δεδεγμένους τὰς σπονδάς. The hypothesis of Sealey (l. c.), that the news of the changed situation in Phocis explains why there was a change of opinion at Athens on 19 Elaphebolion, cannot be right. The 55 day truce for the Mysteries ended on 10 Elaphebolion (I.G. I².6) and the σπονδοφόροι must have known about the situation in Phocis long before 18 Elaphebolion. It is inconceivable that they did not make their report long before 18 Elaphebolion. Sealey points to τῆς εἰρήνης in the passage quoted above and takes it to mean that the Athenians were debating not just peace, but the specific proposals of Philocrates. Yet it would be sensible enough for Aeschines, when talking of the peace three years later, to use these words about any of the debates which led to the making of the peace.

but it was not hopeless; as in 352 Philip could be stopped at the
Gates. But the second piece of news entirely changed the situation.
Not just Greece, but Athens faced the worst. How could she defend
herself by land against Macedon and Boeotia? It was impossible
and the only thing to do would be to avoid any possibility of war.
The change in Phocis made all the difference to Athens and it is
here suggested (1) that it was precisely for this reason that Athens,
having summoned the Hellenes for war, began to seek peace, that
Aeschines was sent to lend his ability to the plea; his policy was
not discredited; there was an entirely new situation, demanding a
new policy.

It is necessary to consider whether this is consistent with what
we know of the chronology of the period. The embassy to Philip
was voted in the first days of Anthesterion. When did Proxenus'
letter and the σπονδοφόροι reach Athens? According to Cloché (2),
the news must have reached Athens about 15 Gamelion. His
argument is as follows: since the truce for the Lesser Mysteries
ran from 15 Gamelion to 10 Elaphebolion (3), the σπονδοφόροι must
have reached Phocis and been rebuffed by Phalaecus before 15
Gamelion. If this is correct, and the news that Phocis refused to
be defended by Athenian forces reached Athens about 15 Gamelion,
and if it took Athens two to three weeks to react, the suggestion
that it was just this news that led Athens to change her policy is
considerably weakened. If the Gates were not to be securely
held, and if Philip might that summer pass into Boeotia, not a day
was to be lost. Negotiating a peace and then getting it sworn to
was bound to be a lengthy business — so lengthy that some must
have wondered whether it could be done at all before the campaign began — and the urgency of the situation is indicated by
the haste with which the first embassy made its way to Macedon (4).

(1) Schaefer, o. c., p. 188f. saw that the news from Phocis was very important. « Von diesem Tage an wurden alle ferneren Rüstungen ausgesetzt... ».
But in his account it simply reinforced the peace movement already begun.
However, the proper dating of the embassies of Eubulus' decree shows that as
late as Gamelion Athens was still bent on war and the sudden change to a
policy of peace demands an explanation, and the Phocian revolution provides it.
(2) O. c., p. 119f.
(3) I.G. I² 6.
(4) Dem. 19.163.

So a full two to three weeks delay between the receipt of the news from Phocis and the decision to send the first embassy would be most surprising. However, perhaps Cloché is not correct in supposing that the σπονδαί must have been declined before 15 Gamelion.

The dates of the Lesser Mysteries are not precisely known (1), but it seems likely that, as the 55 days of truce ran from the middle of one month to the 10th day of the second month following both for the Lesser and for the Greater Mysteries, the Lesser Mysteries fell in Anthesterion in much the same part of the month as the Greater Mysteries in Boedromion; that is, they fell in the middle of the 55 day period. Such an arrangement of the truce would allow people from many of the distant parts of Greece time to get to Athens, attend the celebrations and return home before the truce was ended. However, 55 days were necessary only for more distant places. A place like Phocis which could be reached within a week need not make the truce until, say, the first days of the month in which the Mysteries were celebrated. It cannot be proved that this is what did in fact happen, but probabilities seem to favour so, and there is possibly some confirmation. In an Athenian decree, published in 1939 (2), Athens protested to the Aetolian κοινόν that, although the κοινόν had accepted the truce for the Mysteries, the people of Trichonium had arrested and held captive the σπονδοφόροι. The decree is dated to the third prytany of the year, that is after 14 Boedromion in that year (3), at the earliest just after the Greater Mysteries (4). Since the rescue of these unfortunate σπονδοφόροι was an urgent matter, it seems unlikely that the news of what had happened had reached Athens much before the Greater Mysteries were held, if indeed before at all. Although it may have taken some time for the news to leak out,

(1) Cp. Deubner, *Attische Feste*, p. 70. Plut., *Demetrius* 26.1 shows that they occurred in Anthesterion; apart from that, there is no precise evidence.

(2) Tod *Greek Historical Inscriptions*, no. 137.   Cp. Sealey, *l. c.*, who has pointed out the significance of this document for dating the movements of the σπονδοφόροι.

(3) Cp. Dinsmoor, *The Archons of Athens*, p. 427.

(4) Indeed the decree may belong to the ἐκκλησία held at the end of the Mysteries, similar in time and purpose to that at the end of the City Dionysia. Cp. Andoc I. 111 and Foucart, *Les Mystères d'Éleusis*, p. 358.

it is not likely that the σπονδοφόροι had been in Aetolia a full month or more, before the Athenians heard of what had happened. Trichonium was not the most distant part of the Greek world, and the incident perhaps occurred well within the period of the truce.

That is the only evidence that can be produced with any confidence (1), but the probabilities favour the hypothesis that Phocis was not offered the truce until some time after the truce had begun. Evidence about the σπονδοφόροι is scarce, but the mention of σπονδοφόροι ἐπὶ νήσων in some accounts of 329/8 (2) suggests that they acted in groups, perhaps much in the manner of the envoys sent out by Pericles' Congress Decree. In that decree one group of five men was to issue the people's invitation to Boeotia, Phocis, the Peloponnese, and then through Locris to Acarnania and Ambracia. On such a trip the greatest economy of time would

(1) Perhaps further evidence can be found in *I. G.* II² 1672, the accounts of the Superintendent of Eleusis for the year 329/8. In the first prytany there is a payment of 250 dr. σ]πο[ν]δοφόροις ἐπὶ νή[σ]ων εἰς μυστήρια τὰ μεγάλα (l. 4); in the fourth prytany a payment of an unpreserved amount σπονδοφόροις εἰς μυστήρια [τ]ὰ με[γάλα - - - -] (l. 106); and in the tenth prytany e further payment of something to σπο]νδοφόροις εἰς μυστήρια [- - - - (l. 227). Unfortunately prytanies 7, 8 and 9 are not preserved (and the tenth prytany badly), and it is not clear whether the third payment is for the Greater or Lesser Mysteries. Remembering that in Pericles Congress Decree five envoys were sent to the Islands, one is tempted to suggest that 250dr is the pay of 5 σπονδοφόροι at a drachma a day for 50 days, and that, since the entry is early in the record of the first prytany, they were expected to be out until about the start of Boedromion, i.e. they might still be offering the Truce after the period of the Truce had begun. Similarly payment in the tenth prytany may be for other σπονδοφόροι setting out in the middle of Scirophorion 328 to announce the Mysteries of Boedromion 328, taking a month longer than the σπονδοφόροι ἐπὶ νήσων in view of the longer journeys involved, so that they could be back at much the same time. But the interpretation of these two entries is so conjectural that they could lend support to practically any hypothesis. There is no way of knowing how many σπονδοφόροι ἐπὶ νήσων there were, whether σπονδοφόροι might not be careless about when they drew their pay, whether the position of an entry inside the record of a particular prytany need reflect the time within the prytany when the payment was made, etc. The entry for the fourth prytany (in 329/8 Pyanepsion 15 to Maimakterion 20) should give pause. Pace Cloché (*o. c.*, p. 119, n. 1) the σπονδοφόροι are certainly concerned with the Greater Mysteries (εἰς μυστήρια [τ]ὰ με[γάλα - - - -] Had they only just returned to Athens between 21 and 56 days after the Mysteries, or had they been slow to draw their pay? The payment in the 10th prytany of 329/8 may be pay overdue for the announcement of the Lesser Mysteries.

(2) See n. 1 above.

be effected by going first to the most distant places, and then working homewards : in this way the envoys of those places furthest from Athens would be on their way soonest, and the Congress least delayed. Such an economy of time would be less important in the case of the announcement of the truce for the Mysteries, but if the σπονδοφόροι performed their task in this way, the distant places could receive the truce at the time by which they had to have it if anyone was to get to Athens for the Mysteries, and the closer places would be allowed sufficient time for their citizens. Phocis certainly was one of the last places in the Greek world to be visited by the σπονδοφόροι in 346. The σπονδοφόροι, themselves brought the news to Athens that the Phocians were the only Greeks to have declined the truce. If Phocis was visited last on one occasion, and Trichonium within the truce on another, it may well be true that the cities near Athens were not visited by the σπονδοφόροι until the period of the truce had begun.

At any rate, there is no compulsive reason for supposing that the truce must have been offered to Phocis before 15 Gamelion, and if the Lesser Mysteries were held after the middle of Anthesterion, Phocis may have been visited by the σπονδοφόροι at the end of Gamelion, and news of the Phocian refusal have reached Athens in the very early days of Anthesterion, that is, in the very period that the Council recommended to the people that the first embassy be sent to Philip.

Against this suggestion there are two points to be considered. First, Aeschines said that on the same day the Athenians were deliberating about the Peace and heard Proxenus' letter; perhaps Athens had already begun to think of peace before the letter arrived, and the suggestion might be made that into an ἐκκλησία soberly considering the making of peace this all-important news was brought by a letter-carrier — a scene with something of the drama of the reception of the news about Elatea. Yet even in that tense moment the news had been put first before the Council (1), and such would surely be the case with the letter of Proxenus. Indeed, the synchronism of deliberations about the peace and the news from Phocis powerfully suggests that it was just this news

(1) Dem. 18.169.

which made the difference. The ἐκκλησία which received the
letter and the report of the σπονδοφόροι, had the decree ordering
the first Embassy to Philip proposed to it as being the Council's
decision as to what should be done about the news: the letter and
the report of the σπονδοφόροι were the cause of the Council's προβούλευμα and the explanation of it. The second objection is more
difficult. Aeschines in his survey of the events leading up to the
appointment of the first embassy (1) does not provide an account
of this change in Phocis to explain why Democrates finally went
before the Council and persuaded it to call Aristodemus and get
on with making peace. Yet in this survey Aeschines omits his
own activity, and this is quite as surprising as the fact that he does
not say how his efforts came to nothing. Indeed there is no
explanation in Demosthenes or Aeschines of why Athens changed
hed policy: the reason, which everyone at Athens knew, is left for
us to guess.

To sum up the position so far reached, it is maintained that
between about 19 Posideion and mid-Gamelion Athens led by
Eubulus and Aeschines set out to organise the defence of Greece
against Philip, and envoys were summoned to Athens to consolidate
a general συμμαχία, but that late in Gamelion Phocian policy
suddenly changed and Athens, seeing that she could not be sure
of the Gates, suddenly changed her policy too, and sent off the
first embassy to negotiate for peace. The envoys of Greece had,
however, been summoned, and were still to be expected. When
and if they arrived, they would find a different situation to what
they had been led to expect. With this in mind it is necessary
to examine the part played by Aeschines in the crucial debates
of 18 and 19 Elaphebolion.

Philocrates' decree as presented to the people with the sanction
of the Council was amended on the 19th Elaphebolion in an important respect. Demosthenes says (2) that Philocrates was not able
to write in the peace, although he tried to do so, the words πλὴν
Ἀλέων καὶ Φωκέων, but was compelled by the people ταῦτ᾽ ἀπα-
λεῖψαι, γράψαι δ᾽ἀντικρυς Ἀθηναίους καὶ τοὺς Ἀθηναίων συμμάχους.

---

(1) 2.12-18.
(2) 19.159. Cp. Pokorny, o. c., p. 154, in answer to Kahrstedt, o. c., p. 133.

Although this is hardly likely to be wholly fictitious (for Aeschines would surely have seized on it if it were), it is misleading in two respects. First, if the amendment had merely removed the words πλὴν Ἁλέων καὶ Φωκέων, the effect would have been to allow Phocis to share in the Peace, and it was precisely this which Philip would in no circumstances accept (1). Secondly, the Peace of Philocrates, the terms of which were those of the amended decree of 19 Elaphebolion, concerned none of Athens' allies save the members of the Second Athenian Confederacy (2) and the mere excision of words πλὴν Ἁλέων καὶ Φωκέων would not suffice to change a peace which concerned all of Athens' allies into one that concerned only a special group of them. There must have more to the amendment than Demosthenes lets us know.

If this is correct, the original clause may not have concerned simply Athens and allies of Athens, and it might be suggested that Philocrates had sought to include all the states of Greece except Phocis and Halos, by offering alliance with Athens in a Common Peace. There is no sure way of deciding, but on the whole this is unlikely. If Philocrates' decree had envisaged a Common Peace, that would inevitably have involved what Demosthenes is said to have termed τὰ τῶν Ἑλλήνων μελλήματα (3), and if in opposing such delays (4) he had been opposing the clause in Philocrates' decree about the parties to the Peace, he could have claimed the credit for the amendment. This he never did, though, if he could, he would have done. So probably Philocrates aimed not at a peace that was open to all except Phocis and Halos, but rather one less comprehensive and more readily negotiated, and in this his proposal must have differed sharply from that of the Allies.

Now for the part played by Aeschines on the two days. In the debate of the 18th these two views of the Peace were opposed.

(1) Cp. the second Argument to Dem. 19, § 7.   When Philip swore to keep the peace, he said ‚σπένδομαι ’Αθηναίοις καὶ τοῖς ’Αθηναίων συμμάχοις χωρὶς ‘Αλέων καὶ Φωκέων’.

(2) This is clear from the decree passed on 25 Elaphebolion (Aesch. 3.74) ordering the σύνεδροι of the Allies to swear the oath to Philip. Only members of the Confederacy were represented in the συνέδριον and Phocis and Halos were not members and never had been as far as is known.

(3) Aesch. 3.72.

(4) Ibid.

The first, the proposal of Philocratès, was the Council's προβούλευμα
and was, comparatively, exclusive of the Greeks. The second was
represented by the decree of the Allied Synedrion (1), whereby
any Greek state, i.e. including Phocis and Halos, could share in the
Peace. This decree left the terms of the Peace to the people, but
recommended that it should be possible for any of the Greeks who
wished, to be inscribed in the course of the next three months on
the list of those participating in the Peace, and so to participate.
This would be a κοινὴ εἰρήνη, and the Greeks, summoned by Eubulus
and Aeschines, would be able to play their part. That this was
the intention of the Allied Decree is confirmed by that other Allied
Decree of 8 Elaphebolion (2), which had made the holding of the
two Assemblies dependent on the reports of Eubulus' ambassadors.

Aeschines opposed Philocrates and supported the decree of the
Allies. Demosthenes records his speech as follows (3) : ἀναστὰς
τῇ προτέρᾳ τῶν ἐκκλησιῶν ἐν αἷς περὶ τῆς εἰρήνης ἐβουλεύεσθε,
ἤρξατ' ἀρχήν, ἣν ἐγὼ καὶ τοῖς ῥήμασιν οἶμαι τοῖς αὐτοῖς οἷσπερ οὗτος
εἶπεν ἐν ὑμῖν ἀπομνημονεύσειν. ' Εἰ πάνυ πολὺν' ἔφη 'χρόνον ἐσκόπει
Φιλοκράτης, ὦ ἄνδρες Ἀθηναῖοι, πῶς ἂν ἄριστ' ἐναντιωθείη τῇ
εἰρήνῃ, οὐκ ἂν αὐτὸν ἄμεινον εὑρεῖν οἶμαι ἢ τοιαῦτα γράφοντα.
Ἐγὼ δὲ ταύτην μὲν τὴν εἰρήνην, ἕως ἂν εἷς Ἀθηναίων λείπηται,
οὐδέποτ' ἂν συμβουλεύσαιμι ποιήσασθαι τῇ πόλει, εἰρήνην μέντοι
φημὶ δεῖν ποιεῖσθαι.' This account agrees with Aeschines' statement (4) : Τούτῳ τῷ δόγματι (i. e. τὸ δόγμα συμμάχων) συνειπεῖν
ὁμολογῶ, καὶ πάντες οἱ ἐν τῇ προτέρᾳ τῶν ἐκκλησιῶν δημηγοροῦντες.
By supporting the Allied Decree Aeschines was opposing the exclusion of Phocis, but, more than that, he was basing the peace on a
general Hellenic settlement, which would include the states which
he and Eubulus had summoned. He was transforming his policy
of Posideion, viz. the union of Greece for war, into a policy of
uniting for peace.

The δημηγορία of Demosthenes on that first day is less obvious.
If, as Aeschines says (5), everyone, who spoke on the 18th, supported

(1) *Ibid.*, 3.69.
(2) *Ibid.*, 2.60, 61.
(3) 19.13, 14.
(4) 3.71.
(5) *Ibid.*

the decree of the Allies, Demosthenes must have done so too. In fact, that is what he, himself, says in a general way (1), but, like Philocrates, he regarded the decree of the Allies as an idle dream. Just as Philocrates had known enough to include in his decree the two things which Philip would require — the exclusion of Phocis, and the making of a συμμαχία — so too Demosthenes knew enough to press the people on the 18th to summon the Macedonian envoys before that day was done (2). He knew what Antipater would say; the sooner he said it the better. Aeschines realised the danger. He persuaded the people not to hear the envoys until the following morning. He may have hoped against hope that the united resolve of the Assembly might, if the Macedonians had a night to consider, have its effect. If the envoys saw that the Athenians would only make a peace that was a κοινὴ εἰρήνη, they might, since Philip wanted peace, accept the Athenian version.

According to Aeschines (3) the people went away from the debate on the 18th of the opinion, that there would be a peace, a peace shared by all the Greeks but that the question of συμμαχία with Philip had better wait διὰ τὴν τῶν Ἑλλήνων παράκλησιν. Demosthenes had proposed on 8 Elaphebolion that the people deliberate καὶ περὶ συμμαχίας (4); Philocrates had included the clause in his decree (5). Aeschines prevailed and the issue was postponed on the 18th. He must have gone home feeling that he had had a not unsuccessful day. He might yet be able, by means of the Congress he had summoned, to save Greece from Macedonian intervention.

Next morning, the 19th, his hopes were finished. Although the decree ordering the two assemblies had not so provided, Demosthenes got up immedietäly (6) and told the people that the general agreement of the previous day was of no use now, that Philip's ambassadors insisted on alliance as well as peace, and refused to

(1) 19.15.
(2) Dem. 19.144.
(3) 3.71.
(4) Aesch. 2.61.
(5) Dion. Hal., *Ep. ad Amm.*, 1.11, p. 740.
(6) Aesch. 3.71, 72.

grant peace with mere prospects of alliance to come when the
Hellenes had met and made up their minds: the Athenians, he said,
could not ἀπορρῆξαι τῆς εἰρήνης τὴν συμμαχίαν οὐδὲ τὰ τῶν Ἑλλήνων
ἀναμένειν μελλήματα. He then called Antipater to the βῆμα to verify
his statements. The whole of Aeschines' policy was finished.
Now he had to decide between a peace of the sort proposed by
Philocrates, and having no peace at all, between the delays of the
Greeks and war on the one hand, and, on the other, peace but not
the sort of peace he had advocated the previous day. It was not
a real choice: war meant fighting Philip in Greece. This was the
moment for Eubulus. He indicated Athens' danger by declaring (1)
that if the people rejected the peace, his whole financial policy
would have to be reversed. Nothing since his rise to power had
induced him to change his policy. That he now judged the situation so serious was decisive, and Philocrates' decree carried the day.

This second day's debate was centred not on the issue of the
18th, viz. what sort of peace Athens should make, but on the
new issue of whether she would make peace at all; the sort of peace
she was no longer free to choose. In this new situation Aeschines
was for peace, as his words the previous day foreshadowed, εἰρήνην
μέντοι φημὶ δεῖν ποιεῖσθαι (2), and this meant supporting Philocrates
against the advocates of war. Demosthenes (3) gives the burden
of his speech : ἀναστὰς ἐδημηγόρει καὶ συνηγόρει 'κείνῳ πολλῶν
ἀξίους, ὦ Ζεῦ καὶ πάντες θεοί, θανάτων λόγους, ὡς οὔτε τῶν προγόνων
ὑμᾶς μεμνῆσθαι δέοι οὔτε τῶν τὰ τρόπαια καὶ τὰς ναυμαχίας λεγόντων
ἀνέχεσθαι, νόμον τε θήσειν καὶ γράψειν μηδενὶ τῶν Ἑλλήνων ὑμᾶς
βοηθεῖν, ὃς ἂν μὴ πρότερος βεβοηθηκὼς ὑμῖν ᾖ. This had nothing
to do with the Greeks whom he had summoned. Demosthenes
would have it thought that Aeschines had betrayed them, and three
years after the event play could be made of the contrast between
Aeschines' two speeches, but in truth Aeschines' behaviour was the
natural consequence of the Macedonian intervention. A κοινὴ
εἰρήνη and συμμαχία of all the Hellenes was now out of the question.
When he spoke against military aid for those who had not previously

(1) Dem. 19. 291. For the second day's debate see esp. Pokorny, o. c.,
p. 159.
(2) Dem. 19.14.
(3) 19.16.

given it to Athens, he was referring to Phocis, and opposing those who were prepared to continue the war and make the best of the Phocian alliance: such a course might well end in the complete military defeat of Athens. If Phocis was to be saved, it would have to be by diplomacy. The amendment of Philocrates' decree (1) was perhaps the expression of that hope.

So, after all, the movement begun in Posideion had come to nothing. What Eubulus and Aeschines might have achieved was prevented perhaps by ἄγνοια or κακία or both (2), but, above all, by the policy of Phocis. Did any states send representatives to the Congress that never happened? Demosthenes' charge (3) suggests that some did, although Aeschines shows that none had arrived soon enough to go before the Council in time for the Assembly of 18 Elaphebolion. Perhaps that was how Critobulus of Lampsacus was in Athens shortly after, representing Cersobleptes (4). Beyond that there is no indication. The silence of the sources reflects the fruitlessness of a policy which, but for Phalaecus, might have kept Philip out of Greece in 346.

G. L. CAWKWELL,

University College, Oxford.

(1) Neither Demosthenes nor Aeschines can have proposed the amendment. If either of them had done so, he could hardly have refrained from mentioning the fact.
(2) Dem. 18.20.
(3) 19.16.
(4) Aesch. 2.83.

VI

G. T. Griffith

The So-called Koine Eirene of 346 B.C.

THE SO-CALLED KOINE EIRENE OF 346 B.C.[1]

IT was inevitable that somebody should suggest a *Koine Eirene* in the year 346 B.C. True, no ancient document or author records one. But these two words were much in the mouths of Greek statesmen in the 4th century, and much valuable work has been done on the subject in recent years.[2] Indeed it is an interesting comment on the history of our own times that it has been reserved for the present generation of historical writers to reconstruct and understand the chapter in Greek experience which these words represent. It is probably true to say that few Greeks in the 5th century (or even earlier) regarded war as anything but a bad thing; but on the Greeks of the 4th century the greatest war of their history had left its mark without leaving an immunity from further visitations of the same disease, and as a result responsible statesmen (and not merely ordinary men and women) were now agreed that war was a *very* bad thing, to be preferred, in fact, only to a worse thing still, namely (for small states) to loss of autonomy, and (for the great states) to a fatal loss of prestige. The visible outcome of these feelings was a new kind of peace, *Koine Eirene*. Its main characteristics, distinguishing it from the ordinary type of ' peace ' established by belligerent states when they finished a war, were that it should aim at being permanent, should include most (if not all) of the Greek cities not subject to Persia, and should guarantee the autonomy of every city: and there was provision for collective action to be taken in the event of the Peace being broken. That three such Peaces were established in the forty years immediately preceding 346, and a fourth in 338–7, is certain; but it is by no means so certain that there was also a *Koine Eirene* established in 346 itself, as Wüst is the latest to assert.

The words *Koine Eirene* do occur in the text of Diodorus describing the end of the Sacred War in this year, so that it may appear at first sight that the onus of disproof is on the sceptics, especially when there seems no reason, *a priori*, why there should not have been a *Koine Eirene* here.[3] The year itself is a fitting one, since it marks the end of two long wars which, running concurrently, had brought little but disaster to any single Greek state. The idea itself seems perfectly in tune with the spirit of the age and

---

[1] See most recently, Fritz R. Wüst, *Philipp II von Makedonien und Griechenland in den Jahren von 346 bis 338*. I received this book for review, and perhaps owe the author an apology for concentrating on this one topic, where I disagree with his views; but he himself (p. v) regards this same topic as the most important single issue of all those that he considers in his book. I must take this opportunity of saying that the book as a whole is an interesting and useful addition to the literature relating to this period.
[2] For the whole literature, see Wüst, especially pp. 20 and 177. For the present question (the Peace of 346) the most important works are F. Täger, *Der Friede von 362–1* (reviewed by H. Berve in *Gnomon*, 1933, pp. 301 *sqq.*): A. Momigliano in *Riv. Fil. Class.* xii, 1934, pp. 482 *sqq.*, and *Filippo il Macedone*, p. 122: G. de Sanctis, *Riv. Fil. Class.* xii, 1934, especially p. 150: F. Hampl, *Die griechischen Staatsverträge des 4 Jahrhunderts*, especially pp. 56 *sqq.*
[3] Diod. xvi, 60, 3 (quoted below).

71

the ultimate desires (realised in the Corinthian League) of Philip, the chief gainer from these wars. Athens was not averse from it.[4] In short, scepticism here runs the risk of seeming reactionary and pedantic as well as (at the moment) unfashionable. Nevertheless, a notable sceptic has recently appeared. F. Hampl in his detailed and penetrating examination of the whole problem of *Koine Eirene* in the 4th century has given his reasons for excluding the Peace of 346 from the list of genuine *Koinai Eirenai*, a list which embraces the King's Peace of 386 (in fact though not in name), and (in name as well as in fact) the Peaces of 375–4, 371, 362–1, and 338–7; but these reasons have not convinced Wüst.[5] I venture, therefore, to submit further evidence which seems to me to support Hampl's view, for though it is certainly important to realise that the ideas underlying these *Koinai Eirenai* are a new and significant development in Greek history, it is also important not to abandon oneself to the seduction of the new idea, to present an accurate rather than a schematic picture of the period as a whole.

Hampl gave four reasons for rejecting the Peace of 346 from his list of genuine *Koinai Eirenai*: (1) The passage Diodorus xvi. 60, 3, though it contains the words κοινὴ εἰρήνη in connexion with this peace, nevertheless applies them in a loose and non-technical sense: ἀκολούθως δὲ τούτοις διέταξαν οἱ Ἀμφικτύονες τὰ περὶ τὴν ἐπιμέλειαν τοῦ μαντείου καὶ τἆλλα πάντα τὰ πρὸς εὐσέβειαν καὶ κοινὴν εἰρήνην καὶ ὁμόνοιαν τοῖς Ἕλλησιν ἀνήκοντα. (2) The Amphictyonic Council was not a body competent to establish a *Koine Eirene*. (3) *Argumentum ex silentio*, in this case relatively strong, because the speeches of Demosthenes and other orators after 346 ought to disclose a *Koine Eirene* if it existed; nevertheless, in Hampl's view, their silence on the subject is complete. (4) Remarks of Hegesippus in 343 exclude the possibility of a *Koine Eirene* in existence at the time.[6]

Wüst's reply is as follows. In reply to (2) he argues that the Amphictyonic Council *was* competent, and I think he may well be right; but I am not here concerned with the question of whether the Council *could*, ever, establish a *Koine Eirene*, I merely want to show that in 346 it did not establish one. Wüst replies to (3) by taking up Hampl's challenge and producing evidence which he takes to refer to a *Koine Eirene* in existence after 346.[7] Wüst's reply to (4) seems to me to miss the point completely and to leave Hampl's position unshaken.[8] To (1) he makes no reply, perhaps because

[4] This has been well shown by Wüst, pp. 21 *sq.*: see especially Aeschines iii, 69 *sqq.*; Demosth. xviii, 22.

[5] Hampl, *op. cit.* pp. 64 *sq.*; Wüst pp. 177 *sq.* (a reply to Hampl).

[6] [Demosth.] vii, 30 *sqq.*

[7] *Syll.*³ 224 (request by Messene and Megalopolis to be granted membership of the Amphictyony); [Demosth.] xii, 6, *cf.* Philochorus *apud* Didymum viii. 5 *sqq.*, and Diod. xvi. 441. These points are cleverly made by Wüst (pp. 25 *sq.* and 29 *sqq.*), but in my view, though the passages make sense by his interpretation, they present, equally, not the slightest difficulty to an interpretation assuming no K.E. in existence.

[8] [Demosth.] vii. 30 *sq.* shows Athens still, in 343, trying to 'improve' the Peace of 346 by expanding it into a K.E.: this Hampl recognises as a decisive argument against there being a K.E. already in existence. Wüst, however (pp. 76 *sq.* and 178), seems to argue that Athens is now in 343 proposing an alternative K.E. to one already existing, the object being to achieve a K.E. under Athenian auspices or leadership, and not under Philip's (the Amphictyony). This argument seems to me to show a misunderstanding both of the nature of K.E. in general and of the political situation in the years 346–3.

he thinks the matter unimportant: if so I cannot agree. Hampl's criticism of the Diodorus passage was just, and was not the whole criticism that can be made. The truth, surely, is that, though Diodorus is a bad historian, he is still perfectly capable of recording a *Koine Eirene* when he believes there is one to record, and his method of doing this is to write ' The Greeks made a *Koine Eirene*' in words direct and unambiguous. A comparison of these simple statements with the vague and pompous allusions of this passage referring to the Peace of 346 suggests very strongly that Diodorus is not here trying to record another *Koine Eirene*, but is merely recording that the Amphictyons now set their affairs thoroughly in order, and in doing so probably used a number of the fine and large phrases to which human frailty is so susceptible in moments when it is conscious of embarking on a new era which is to be far, far better than what has gone before.[9]

Diodorus, then, in my view creates a presumption that this Peace was not a *Koine Eirene*; but in order to change this presumption into certainty I recommend a study of the oration of Demosthenes which is entitled ' *Concerning the Peace*,' because it was composed within a very few weeks (perhaps, even, days) of the events to which Diodorus has alluded, and because ' the Peace ' in question must be the *Koine Eirene*, if that *Koine Eirene* existed.[10] Wüst himself (p. 28) finds it surprising that his *Koine Eirene* has left no impression on the literature of the years following 346, and especially that it is never mentioned by Demosthenes and Aeschines in their speeches about ' the Crown.' Surprising it is indeed, and it will be more surprising still if Demosthenes speaking about ' the Peace ' indicates that *his* ' Peace ' is by no means the same thing as Wüst's Peace (his recently concluded *Koine Eirene*). Nevertheless, this is the conclusion to which the evidence of this speech does point, as I hope to show.

First, the occasion of the speech. It represents the advice of Demos-

---

[9] Cf. Diod. xv. 38. 1 *sq.* (375-4 B.C.)—ὁ τῶν Περσῶν βασιλεύς . . . πρέσβεις ἐξέπεμψεν εἰς τὴν ῾Ελλαδα τοὺς παρακαλέσοντας τὰς πόλεις κοινὴν εἰρήνην συνθέσθαι. τῶν δ᾽ ῾Ελλήνων . . . συνέθεντο πάντες τὴν εἰρήνην.

Cf. Diod. xv. 50. 4 (371)—συνέθεντο κοινὴν εἰρήνην αἱ πόλεις πᾶσαι πλὴν Θηβαίων (cf. 51. 1).

Cf. Diod. xv. 70. 2 (369)—παρακαλῶν τοὺς ῾Ελληνας διαλύσασθαι μὲν τοὺς πολέμους, εἰρήνην δὲ κοινὴν συνθέσθαι (the K.E. did not materialise).

Cf. Diod. xv. 76. 3 (366)—ἔπεισε τοὺς ῾Ελληνας τοὺς μὲν πολέμους καταλύσασθαι καὶ κοινὴν εἰρήνην συνθέσθαι πρὸς ἀλλήλους (for criticism, see Hampl pp. 62 *sqq.*)

Cf. Diod. xv. 89. 1 (362-1)—οἱ δ᾽ ῾Ελληνες . . διελύσαντο πρὸς ἀλλήλους . . . συνθέμενοι δὲ κοινὴν εἰρήνην καὶ συμμαχίαν. . . . It is, surely, impossible not to see a difference between these passages and the passage referring to the settlement of 346, and in the circumstances Wüst's treatment of the matter seems to me a trifle disingenuous—' Leider ist der Bericht über dieselbe bei Diodor sehr knapp wie übrigens auch die übrigen Berichte Diodors vom Abschluss einer κοινὴ εἰρήνη' (p. 22). Diodorus says nothing at all of the establishment of the K.E. of 338–7, but that is because he loses it in the more spectacular συμμαχία

directed against Persia which was concluded very soon afterwards (if not simultaneously): cf. Diod. xvi. 89. 1 *sqq.*, and (especially) U. Wilcken in *S.B. Berlin* 1927, and W. Schwahn, *Heeresmatrikel und Landfriede* pp. 36 *sqq.*

[10] The Amphictyons were probably still in session at Delphi when the speech was delivered (Demosth. v. 14). That it *was* delivered, nobody now doubts, though Libanius doubted it (Demosth. v. ὑπόθεσις), on the ground that in a later speech (xix. 111) Demosthenes accused Aeschines of having been on this occasion the only speaker to speak in favour of agreeing to Philip's election to the Amphictyony. The contradiction is more apparent than real, because Demosthenes in his speech ' on the Peace ' never says a word in favour of electing Philip, he merely shows himself clearly in favour of avoiding war. The *implication*, of course, is that the Athenians must agree to the election; but it remains an implication throughout, most probably because Demosthenes was already collecting stones to throw at his adversaries and had no intention of preparing a house of glass for himself.

thenes to the Athenians on the occasion of their receiving a demand from the Amphictyonic Council that Athens should formally subscribe to Philip's recent election as a member of the Amphictyony and his taking over of the two votes which had previously belonged to the Phocians: these motions had been carried at a meeting of the Council from which, for reasons of policy, Athens had abstained.[11] Notice that none of our sources here mentions anything besides this question of Philip and the Amphictyony. Yet if the Council in reality (as Wüst contends) had been concerning itself with establishing a *Koine Eirene*, this meeting is the very meeting at which its resolution on the subject must have been passed, and from this meeting Athens had abstained. It would follow from this that the communication of the Council to the Athenians which provides the occasion for Demosthenes' speech would have contained also an invitation to Athens to join in the *Koine Eirene*, with the gravest implication of the possible consequences of her remaining excluded from it.[12] This is the vital question on which our sources are perfectly silent;[13] but far more important, clearly, than the silence of Libanius, or of Demosthenes speaking some years later, is the silence of Demosthenes speaking in the very moment of the alleged crisis itself, and this brings us to the internal evidence of the Speech ' *Concerning the Peace.*'

The advice of Demosthenes to the Athenians is (in brief) as follows (see especially *op. cit.* 13):—' The Peace is, for us, a bad peace. Thanks to Philocrates and Aeschines and others ' (though he does not name them here) ' we have been out-manoeuvred by Philip, who is now, moreover, in a better position to do us harm if we give free play to our resentment: for this reason we must make the best of it for the moment, and, above all, we must not court the risk of being the object of a general war '—δεύτερον δ' (*sc.* φημὶ δεῖν ὁρᾶν) ὅπως μὴ προαξόμεθα .... τοὺς συνεληλυθότας τούτους καὶ φάσκοντας Ἀμφικτύονας νῦν εἶναι εἰς ἀνάγκην καὶ πρόφασιν κοινοῦ πολέμου πρὸς ἡμᾶς : and later, φοβοῦμαι μὴ πάντες περὶ τῶν ἰδίων ἕκαστος ὀργιζόμενος

---

[11] Libanius, ὑπόθεσις to Demosth. v; Demosth. xix. 132, etc.; cf. Dion. Hal. *Epist. ad Amm.* i. 10, 737.

[12] It seems clearly implied in the ὑπόθεσις that Athens was not represented at this meeting: had she been represented, there would have been no occasion for the Council to send its own representatives to Athens with this request. The intervention of Aeschines on behalf of the Phocians does not convince me that he was a member of an Athenian embassy accredited to the Council (see Wüst, p. 15). On these events Wüst's chronological table (p. 181) is far from satisfactory: he has ' telescoped ' too many things into this summer of 346, perhaps owing to his mistaken belief that the month Hecatombaeon is June–July (sic.), and therefore, presumably, that the month Skirophorion, in which we have several fixed dates, is May–June. There is, in reality, not much time for the arrangement and ratification of a K.E., which was not as simple a matter as Wüst seems to suppose (he allows it a bare month). The date of Philip's entry into Phocis is certainly mid-July (Demosth. xix. 59 *sq.*), and one

may suppose that the Amphictyonic Council would begin its sessions by the end of July (Diod. xvi. 59. 4—the Council had to be summoned). Demosthenes ' *Concerning the Peace* ' cannot be dated with accuracy. My own impression is that it was delivered in August, before the Pythian Festival in which Athens took no part, an omission which cannot have pleased Philip and might well have been mentioned, if it had already occurred, by Demosthenes in this speech (*e.g.*, at §19); but I am aware that this argument is not a very strong one. But even if it was delivered as late as the end of September (so Wüst), two months is not a generous allowance for the arrangement and ratification of a K.E. My own position, however, is not altered if one argues that the K.E. might be under discussion but not yet ratified when this speech was delivered: my contention is, that in this speech we must expect Demosthenes to refer intelligibly to the project of a K.E., whether completed or not, if it existed at all.

[13] Libanius and Demosthenes: see note 11.

κοινὸν ἐφ' ἡμᾶς ἀγάγωσι τὸν πόλεμον, τὰ 'Αμφικτυόνων δόγματα προστησάμενοι.[14]
These sentences in themselves rather support the possibility of there being
in existence a *Koine Eirene* in which Athens was already included, especially
if one assumes with Momigliano and Wüst that it was sponsored by the
Amphictyonic Council. But this possibility vanishes if we examine the advice
of Demosthenes more closely, and when we realise that, though the speaker is
afraid of a general war he is perfectly prepared to see Athens fight a *local*
war in which none but the protagonists in the quarrel (whatever it may be)
will be involved. The sentence which best illustrates this idea is:—
οὐδέ γ' εἰ πάλιν πρὸς τοὺς Θηβαίους πολεμήσαιμεν δι' 'Ωρωπὸν ἤ τι τῶν ἰδίων,
οὐδὲν ἂν ἡμᾶς παθεῖν ἡγοῦμαι : καὶ γὰρ ἡμῖν κἀκείνοις τοὺς βοηθοῦντας
ἂν οἶμαι, εἰς τὴν οἰκείαν εἴ τις ἐμβάλοι, βοηθεῖν, οὐ συνεπιστρατεύειν οὐδετέροις.[15]
The importance of this remark is self-evident. Demosthenes here
can envisage the possibility of a war against Thebes, and even of a war in
which Athens might be the aggressor (δι' 'Ωρωπὸν—a war having Oropus
as *casus belli* must inevitably begin with an act of aggression, or at least a
policy of aggression, on the part of Athens) ; but yet a war in which Athens
would be able to count on the (limited) support of her own allies, and would
have to fear the intervention (again, to a limited extent) only of the allies
of Thebes. It would be, in fact, merely an ordinary Greek war. The
seizure of Oropus (for example) would *not* involve Athens in a κοινὸς
πόλεμος (see above) : and the Amphictyons would *not* be concerned in the
matter. It follows from this, not indeed that there can have been no
Koine Eirene in existence or contemplated at the moment when Demosthenes
spoke these words, but that there can have been no *Koine Eirene having a
sanctions-clause which bound all participating states to come to the help of victims
of aggression.* This conclusion in itself carries great weight, because there
must always be a strong presumption in favour of such a clause as an
instrument to support a *Koine Eirene*, as is proved by the examples of the
years 386 (probably), 375-4, 371 (after Leuctra), 362-1, and 338-7 B.C.[16]
But it does not yet prove for certain that there can have been no *Koine
Eirene* at all in 346.
     Let us suppose, in fact, that there *was* a *Koine Eirene*, one with a limited
sanctions-clause on the model of the abortive *Koine Eirene* of 371 (before
Leuctra), the clause in this case running—εἰ δέ τις παρὰ ταῦτα ποιοίη,
τὸν μὲν βουλόμενον βοηθεῖν ταῖς ἀδικουμέναις πόλεσι, τῷ δὲ μὴ βουλομένῳ μὴ
εἶναι ἔνορκον συμμαχεῖν τοῖς ἀδικουμένοις.[17] At first sight, again, this seems to
provide the loophole required by those who believe in a *Koine Eirene* in 346 :
it is this limited sanctions-clause, they may say, which permits Demosthenes

[14] *Concerning the Peace*, 14 and 19.
[15] *Id.* 16; *cf.* 14 *sq.* for another hypothetical
case of the same kind, that of a war between Athens
and Philip.
[16] Momigliano and Wüst assume the existence of
such a clause.
    386 B.C. (' King's Peace ')—there is no
    evidence for the obligations of Greek cities,
    but the King of Persia guarantees the Peace
    by implication (see Hampl. pp. 8 *sqq.*).

375-4—the clause has been deduced, with
    certainty as it seems to me, by Hampl p. 17.
371—Xen. *Hell.* vi. 5. 1 *sqq.*
362-1—implied in *Syll.*³ 182 (hypothetical
    case of aggression by Persia).
338-7—*Syll.*³ 260.
Add [Demosth.] vii. 30, for this clause in the
    abortive Athenian proposals of 343.
[17] Xen. *Hell.* vi. 3. 18; *cf.* Hampl, p. 17.

to talk so airily of hypothetical wars with a limited scope, even though Athens might begin such a war as an aggressor. But, again, a closer reading of this speech reveals the fallacy. For Demosthenes is at pains to emphasise that there are only too many states in Greece which at this time ' for private grievances might seize the opportunity of waging against us a collective war' :[18] in a case like this, τὸν μὲν βουλόμενον βοηθεῖν is as good (or, for Demosthenes' purpose, as bad !) as ἅπαντας βοηθεῖν, and in fact Demosthenes is arguing that a local or limited war for Athens is a possibility only in cases where outsiders have no good pretext for intervention. But a *Koine Eirene*, for those who *want* to intervene, provides the best possible pretext, even if its sanctions-clause does not *bind* anyone to intervene. Finally, the idea of a *Koine Eirene* with no sanctions-clause of any kind is not only unsupported by any evidence either before or after 346, but is so clearly absurd as to be out of the question: the Greeks would have thought it a waste of time to swear the oath that bound them to keep it, and a waste of time it most certainly would have been.

No sane politician could have made these remarks which Demosthenes made in the speech ' *Concerning the Peace*,' if there had been in existence at the time a *Koine Eirene* to which Athens had subscribed, still less a *Koine Eirene* from which Athens stood in danger of being excluded.[19] One may cite also, with a view to the picturesque, the arresting phrase with which he concluded the speech—οὐκοῦν εὔηθες καὶ κομιδῇ σχέτλιον, πρὸς ἑκάστους καθ' ἕν' οὕτω προσενηνεγμένους περὶ τῶν οἰκείων καὶ ἀναγκαιοτάτων, πρὸς πάντας περὶ τῆς ἐν Δελφοῖς σκιᾶς νυνὶ πολεμῆσαι.[20] ' The shadow in Delphi ' is the sneer of an ostentatiously ' practical' politician at something which he considers, or affects to consider, of no practical consequence. Would any sane man, however short-sighted, have jeered thus at a *Koine Eirene*, an institution which, whatever its deficiencies, had always been perfectly ' practical' in its intent and its application, and which at this moment (had it existed) would have contained a very serious threat to an aggressive or recalcitrant Athens? On the other hand, ' the shadow in Delphi ' is an exactly appropriate jibe for a practical (and disgruntled) man to make at the expense of a piece of religious chicanery or bunkum: ' by all means, let Philip play at being an Amphictyon, barbarian though he is, and let's hope it keeps fine for him '—this I take to be the implication of ' the shadow in Delphi,' reduced to common speech. The orator who flung out this phrase is very clearly the same Demosthenes who, more than twenty years after, sneered again ' Let him be son of Zeus, and Poseidon as well, if it amuses him ' ![21] Philip's intrusion into the archaic hierarchy of the Amphictyons, like the deification of Alexander, was a piece of vulgar pomposity besides being a political manoeuvre: in both cases, Demosthenes was presumably aware of the political implications and prepared to accept them for the time being as inevitable, but not without a sneer at the vulgarity. Neither Philip nor Alexander grudged him these small satisfactions.

[18] *Op. cit.* 19: he enumerates Argos, Messene, galopolis and ' some of the other Peloponnesians '; ebes, Thessaly, and Philip.

[19] See above, note 12.
[20] *Id.* 25.
[21] Hyperides v. col. 31.

The danger to Athens of refusing this demand of the Amphictyons was the danger merely of a 'Sacred' war directed against herself. I say 'merely,' because a 'Sacred' war, though it might be just as formidable to an isolated Athens as a war directed against her as a breaker of a *Koine Eirene*, was by far the less likely to happen, since it could begin only on a 'sacred' pretext: it would be difficult, for example, for even the Thebans to maintain that an attack on Oropus injured the god at Delphi. Such a pretext could, however, be found (at a pinch) in a refusal by the Athenians to associate themselves with the action of the Amphictyonic Council in electing Philip to fill the place of the Phocians. It seems to me to be a poor pretext, but it was probably good enough, if the situation had arisen. But I hope that at least I have shown that it has nothing whatever to do with a *Koine Eirene*, and I will reinforce this positive evidence with an appeal to what I believe to be plain common sense. Ignoring for the moment the words which I have put forward as directly contradicting the possibility, is it likely that Demosthenes could have spoken '*Concerning the Peace*' without mentioning that 'the Peace' was a *Koine Eirene* or was about to become one? Is it likely that in his speeches delivered in the years after 346 he should never have mentioned directly the institution which (had it existed) would have been the governing factor in Greek politics and diplomacy during those years? Cicero did not leave *concordia ordinum* to be fumbled for and guessed at by modern scholars, and in general politicians in their speeches are not in the habit of relying on oblique and subtle references to events or institutions of the highest contemporary importance: on the contrary, they call a spade a spade unless there is some good reason for calling it something else or for pretending that spades do not exist, and here there is no such reason. I am convinced that if a *Koine Eirene* had existed Demosthenes would not have been too shy to mention it, and to call it *Koine Eirene*.

If this question were a mere matter of words and a name, it would be folly to pursue it farther (or, indeed, so far). Its importance lies most of all in the fact that it contains a clue to the policy and aims of Philip at this time. Wüst has made an excellent point when he emphasises that Athens wanted a *Koine Eirene*; the 'Peace of Philocrates' would have been expanded into a *Koine Eirene* if the Athenian negotiators had had their way.[22] It was due to Philip, evidently, that the Peace of Philocrates was no more than a conventional Greek peace-treaty between Athens and her allies and Philip and his allies. The Phocians were expressly excluded from it, so that it was not concerned with the settlement of Central and Northern Greece. This settlement was effected by a separate instrument, in which Athens was interested only by virtue of her membership of the Amphictyony; and which, also, was no *Koine Eirene*.[23] Finally, the

---

[22] Wüst, pp. 21 *sq.* Athens was still anxious for a K.E. in 343 ([Demosth.] vii. 30 *sqq.*). I have already mentioned (note 8) that Wüst's interpretation of this passage does not convince me in the least. For a correct interpretation, see Hampl, p. 65.

[23] Hampl, p. 65, note 1, believes that it was not even, technically, a 'Peace' at all: 'die amphikt-

yonischen Kriege nur Strafexpeditionen waren und dementsprechend nur durch ein Strafgericht, nicht durch einen "Friedensschluss" beendet wurden.' This view seems to me legalistic almost to the point of being ridiculous. To call the Phocian War, a major war lasting ten years, a punitive expedition, or even a series of punitive expeditions, is worthy

Peloponnese was not directly affected by either of these two settlements, and still presented a fresh field for Philip's diplomacy. It is this separation of Greek affairs into compartments that provides, in my view, the key to Philip's intentions. Generally speaking, a *Koine Eirene* was a stabilising influence: it was a device valuable to a power acting on the defensive or anxious to perpetuate a good defensive position.[24] But there is not the least reason to think that Philip wished to stabilise the situation of 346 in Greece, for though it is true that he had gained much in achieving this present position, it is very clear that he could still hope to gain more if the situation were allowed to develop. Greek affairs at this time represented to Philip a rising market, and he was certainly not the man to tie up his capital in securities yielding a safe but small return. He had most to gain if the situation in Greece remained fluid, and this is why he rejected the idea of a *Koine Eirene*, an idea which was not displeasing to the Athenians, who had now made up their minds to cut their losses but were anxious to insure against losing anything more.

Perhaps the most interesting question of all is, What were Philip's views about a Persian War, and how far was his behaviour in Greece already governed by his plans in this direction? It seems almost certain that the statement of Diodorus, that already at Delphi in 346 Philip had made up his mind to become στρατηγὸς αὐτοκράτωρ of the Greeks in a war against Persia, derives from a source well aware of the settlement of 338–7 by which this aspiration was realised.[25] The statement is, in fact, suspect. On the other hand, nothing is more certain than that the *possibility* of a Persian War must have occurred to Philip, even if no positive and definite plans for it had taken shape as yet in his mind; [26] and he was too good a realist not to know that if he became involved in a war in Asia, the bulk of the Greek states must be either for him or against him. It would, indeed, be the purest folly to think of invading Asia unless he could count on the support of most of the Greeks; not because he would need them in Asia but because he would need peace in Greece itself. And to suppose that most of the Greeks were prepared already in 346 to give him this support is, surely, a misinterpretation which ignores the years of Philip's ' peaceful penetration ' of Greece after 346, to say nothing of its ignoring the battle of Chaeronea and the display of overwhelming military strength which alone could introduce the Corinthian League as a piece of practical politics. That is not to say that Philip in 346 was already intending to fight the battle of Chaeronea. He may have hoped to gain control of Greece purely by

---

of certain modern schools of diplomats. There can be no doubt that everybody in Greece called the settlement of 346 at Delphi εἰρήνη, just as ordinary people in the near future will call the settlement that ends the present war in China ' Peace,' whatever Japanese politicians may call it.

[24] *E.g.*, the ' King's Peace ' of 386, which worked in favour of Sparta, but was a hindrance limiting the revival of Athens as a ' great power,' as her well-known Treaty with Chios shows (*Syll.*[3] 142; especially lines 20 ff.). Similarly, the K.E. of 371 after Leuctra was clearly designed to prevent the

' landslide ' in the Peloponnese which did take place when the Theban invasion took place: I hope to be able to throw more light on this question in a future article.

[25] Diod. xvi. 60. 5, probably from Theopompus; but the name of Theopompus does not make the statement immune from criticism, since Theopompus is no less liable than another to a judgment *post eventum*.

[26] Isocrates v, *passim*: and the ideas expressed here are new only in their application to Philip.

' peaceful penetration '; but the point is that he must have realised that he was very far from being in control of Greece already, and that in Athens, especially, a radical change of heart was needed before any lasting co-opera-tion could be possible.[27]   In short, to attribute either to Philip or to the Greeks in 346 the feelings and experience that were theirs in 337 is nearly as inconsequent as supposing that a man who has a white beard to-day had already a white beard in the year 1900.   It is not impossible that it should have been so; but one requires good evidence that it was so before one will believe it, and in this case the evidence is lacking.[28]

G. T. GRIFFITH.

Gonville and Caius College, Cambridge.

---

[27] See Demosth. xix, 132 for a good summary of Athenian dissatisfaction with the settlement of 346 and hostility to Philip at this time.

[28] My thanks are due to Mr. N. G. L. Hammond for reading this article in proof and making some very helpful suggestions.

VII

S. Perlman

Isocrates' 'Philippus'—a Reinterpretation

ISOCRATES' "PHILIPPUS" – A REINTERPRETATION*

The major part of the pamphlet addressed to Philip and bearing his name was written, and the whole was completed, by Isocrates a short time after the conclusion of the peace of Philocrates.[1] The moment was undoubtedly of crucial importance in the history of Greece and especially in the history of Athens. In spite of the long negotiations which preceded the peace, the most important differences in northern Greece were not finally settled. The state of central Greece was very uncertain. This and Athens' failure to secure the help of a Greek coalition forced the war-party to accept and even co-operate in the conclusion of peace. The peace was, therefore, more of the nature of a respite, or truce, with both sides suspiciously watching each other and preparing for the next trial of strength.[2]

The "Philippus" – probably the last great political writing of Isocrates – published at such a moment is undoubtedly of great importance for the understanding of the Greek political scene at the time.[3] It is therefore not surprising that it has attracted much attention and has been carefully studied and interpreted, probably since its publication.[4] But there is still no great measure of agreement as to its aims. The attitude of modern scholars in this respect has varied as much as their attitude to Isocrates in general.[5]

*I wish to express my gratitude to Prof. A. Andrewes, Mr. G. E. M. de Ste. Croix and Mr. D. M. Lewis of Oxford for their advice and criticism.

[1] For the date of "Philippus", see F. Blass, Die attische Beredsamkeit² II, p. 314 and G. Mathieu, Les idées politiques d'Isocrate, Paris 1925, 155—156. The pamphlet was completed between April and June 346.

[2] Though the "Philippus" was written before Philip's intervention in the Sacred War, Isocrates clearly foresees such a possibility and the threat to peace which might result (§ 74). Moreover, he seems also to consider the possibility that Philip will support the Thebans in their struggle against the Phocians (§§ 50; 54—55). The possibility of an imminent renewal of war was very real, see Demosthenes' speech "On the Peace" and cf. K. J. Beloch, Griechische Geschichte² III, 1, pp. 510—511.

[3] Beloch, ibid. p. 527 n. 1, calls it "die politisch bedeutendste aller seiner Schriften."

[4] The letter of Speusippus (cf. E. Bickermann — J. Sykutris, Speusippus Brief an König Philipp, SB. Sächs. Akad., 1928, 3. Heft) contains the earliest written criticism we have. Dionysius Hal. Ars Rhet. II, p. 347 (Us.-Rad.) calls the pamphlet a disguised encomium of Philip; cf. Blass, op. cit. pp. 120ff.

[5] Compare the two diametrically opposite views on conclusions reached by modern scholarship: C. D. Adams, Recent views of the political influence of Isocrates, C. Ph. (7) 1912, pp. 343—350, which notes the tendency to underline the depth of Isocrates' political understanding and judgment, with H. Ll. Hudson-Williams in Fifty years of Classical

The main point of controversy is, of course, the measure of political insight and foresight shown by Isocrates: to what extent did Isocrates present an original plan for the solution of the political problems of the day, and to what extent was it really implemented. P. Wendland[6] sees in Isocrates the propagator of the Pan-hellenic ideal of a confederated Greek state, later realized by Philip under his own leadership. Athens had failed to achieve this aim and therefore the solution to Greek political instability could come from an outside power only. This line of thought was already foreshadowed by R. von Scala[7] and was further continued by J. Kessler,[8] H. Kramer,[9] and M. Mühl,[10] who see in Isocrates a politician possessing a farreaching, realistic and clear outlook. G. Mathieu[11] continues the list of historians sympathetic to Isocrates. Though he points to a certain discrepancy between the Panhellenic ideals of Isocrates and the final turn of Philip's and especially Alexander's policy, he tries to prove the consistency of the ideas, which Isocrates preached throughout his life; Isocrates, in his view, is rather a Greek, a European and a pacifist, than an Athenian. This basic contradiction between Isocrates' Panhellenism (which stresses the sanctity of the autonomy of the Greek city-state) and the quest for a single power or monarch to fulfil this Panhellenic ideal is the main subject of A. Momigliano's discussion.[12] A. Rostagni,[13] who saw the discrepancy, explained the "Panathenaicus" as a sign of protest against Philip's policy, which took a different course from that suggested in the "Philippus", in which the proposal was made for the diversion of Macedonian

Scholarship ed. M. Platnauer, Oxford 1954, p. 197: "Modern scholars tend to be out of sympathy with Isocrates and his ideals ..." This opinion is fully confirmed by the conclusions of N. H. Baynes, Byzantine Studies and other Essays, London 1955, ch. 8: Isocrates, and by P. Cloché, Un fondateur d'empire, Paris 1956, pp. 159—163; 189—191. Cf. H. Bengtson, Griech. Gesch. (Hdb. d. A. III, 4), 1950, p. 280.

[6] P. Wendland, Beiträge zur athenischen Politik und Publizistik, Gött. Nachr. 1910, I. König Philippos und Isokrates, pp. 123—182; II. Isokrates und Demosthenes pp. 289—323.

[7] R. von Scala, Isokrates und die Geschichtsschreibung; Verhandlungen der 41. Versammlung Deutscher Philologen und Schulmänner in München, Leipzig 1892, pp. 102—121.

[8] J. Kessler, Isokrates und die panhellenische Idee, 1911.

[9] H. Kramer, Quod valeat ὁμόνοια in litteris Graecis, Diss. Göttingen 1915, esp. pp. 38—48.

[10] M. Mühl, Die politischen Ideen des Isokrates und die Geschichtsschreibung, Diss. Würzburg 1917.

[11] G. Mathieu, Philippe et lettres à Philippe, à Alexandre et à Antipatros, Paris 1924. G. Mathieu, Les idées politiques d'Isocrate, Paris, 1925.

[12] A. Momigliano, Filippo il Macedone, Firenze, 1934, esp. chpts. 5 and 6. This is actually the consequence of his conception of the aims of Philip's policy, which according to him are entirely personal and not Macedonian or Greek and which resulted in the establishment of a basis for the supra-national state of Alexander.

[13] A. Rostagni, Isocrate e Filippo, Entaphia in memoria di Emilio Pozzi, Torino 1913, pp. 129—156.

21*

power from Greece. U. Wilcken,[14] after a careful examination of the evidence, came to the conclusion that the principles of the League of Corinth were completely different from the realization of Isocrates' Panhellenism. Isocrates is therefore a dreamer devoid of any political insight or just a tool of Macedonian propaganda. On the other hand, W. Jaeger's[15] great admiration for Isocrates as a pioneer of the ideal of universal culture, educator and thinker is combined with a great amount of praise for the Panhellenism of the orator.

The views are thus divided. On the one hand there is admiration for the political sagacity of Isocrates, his Panhellenism and for his programme of farreaching solutions of the Greek problems, which finds final fulfilment in the establishment of a stable Greek confederacy. On the other hand, there is contempt for the traitor to the Greek city-state, who is blind to the political and military developments around him and a willing tool of propaganda for the arch-enemy of Greece.

This diversity of opinion justifies, perhaps, yet another reconsideration of the problem. It seems to me that a more thorough interpretation of the speech itself and a fuller examination of contemporary evidence is still possible.

From the point of view of composition, Isocrates himself clearly divides his speech into two parts: the first (§§ 1–80) deals with the problems of Greece, the second (§§ 81–147) with the war against Persia. In reality the two problems are inseparable.[16] In § 83 Isocrates clearly states that he sees the Persian expedition at the moment as purely the affair of Philip. The Greek cities may later be consulted and even their co-operation secured, but first and foremost it is the course of future Macedonian policy which has to be decided; Philip, therefore, is the person to be persuaded first of all. But by implication[17] and because of the nature of other problems raised in the speech, it is obvious that the pamphlet is addressed not to Philip alone.[18] The purpose of retaining the prologue on Amphipolis (§§ 1–16) is to stress that it is also Athens (and other Greek states in the second place cf. §§ 8; 23) whom Isocrates addresses.

There is another even more important argument which is brought up by the discussion of the problem of Amphipolis.[19] Isocrates rightly sees the political situation as one in which both parties regard the peace as a truce before

[14] U. Wilcken, Philipp II von Makedonien und die panhellenische Idee, Sitzber. Preuss. Akad. 1929, pp. 291—318.

[15] W. Jaeger, Demosthenes, Berkeley, 1937, esp. pp. 151—155. W. Jaeger, Paideia III, Oxford 1945.   [16] Cf. §§ 86—89.   [17] Cf. § 83;

[18] Cf. §§ 1—2; and see § 155 ὑμῶν τῶν ἀκουόντων in contrast with σοι.

[19] In contrast to Speusippus (§§ 5—8), who wrote the letter to Philip in 344 directly supporting Macedonian policy and attacking the "Philippus", Isocrates does not justify the conquest of Amphipolis or any other Greek city by Philip; it is true that he tries at the same time to persuade the Athenians that a policy of peace and alliance with Philip are of greater benefit to Athens than the recovery of Amphipolis. Speusippus (§§ 2; 4; 8) constantly criticises Isocrates as a bad propagandist of Philip's interests in Greece.

renewing hostilities (§§ 3; 8). Not only does he set out to prevent the renewal of hostilities, but he also indicates the way to an alliance with Athens. Such an alliance will be possible and durable if Philip starts a policy of peace in Greece and expansion in Persia. The objective is not a twofold policy, or presented as cause and effect, but carefully formulated so as to point out not only the close connection between them but actually their identity.

Though Isocrates maintains that the war against Persia is an old idea of his,[20] he also shows that he is conscious of the great change which he is making in the plan (§§ 12–13). There are two reasons for his choice of Philip: he is in a better constitutional position to decide and act than the Greek states;[21] he has got the means for the enterprise (§§ 14–15). Philip's power is to be used for peace in Greece and for war against Persia (πείθειν-βιάζεσθαι), both goals serving but one purpose. This, he quite rightly says, is the gist of his speech. The rest of the pamphlet serves to amplify these two points and to explain how the policy advocated fits into the pattern of Greek politics.

In the second part of the prologue, Isocrates again indicates that he is well aware of the attitude of both sides and of the fact that he is swimming against the current. The plan he is proposing is completely different from the course Philip has chosen so far[22] and which had obviously included expansion in Greece itself. He knows that the continuation of this policy will probably be urged upon the king by his advisers. Public opinion in Athens itself – as personified by Isocrates' friends – seems to expect that. Philip's success has been so magnificent and unexpected, his power has grown so greatly, that his influence in Greece has increased enormously.[23] By pointing to the change of opinion on the part of his friends, Isocrates wishes to indicate that his pamphlet will probably influence Athenian opinion; he therefore expects a careful examination of his proposals by Philip himself.

Isocrates now (§§ 30ff.) enters upon the elaboration of the first part of his basic proposals: Philip should become προστάτης τῆς τῶν Ἑλλήνων ὁμονοίας

---

[20] Cf. § 9. Isocrates refers here to his Panegyricus (cf. also § 84). But there is one important difference. Whereas in the Panegyricus (17) he speaks of hegemony over the Greeks, he never speaks (and does not even mention the word) of Philip's hegemony in Greece in the "Philippus"; cf. Wilcken op. cit. p. 312. The word ἐπιστατέω (§§ 45; 50; 97; 151) is never used to express rule or mastership in Greece, but either initiative in making and establishing peace, or military leadership of Macedonian forces in war against Persia. Cf. also §§ 107; 154.

[21] Cf. § 127. It is worth while to compare here Dem. XIX 184—186.

[22] Cf. § 17: ἀλλὰ πειρασόμενόν σε προτρέπειν ἐπὶ πράξεις οἰκειοτέρας καὶ μᾶλλον συμφερούσας ὧν νῦν τυγχάνεις προηρημένος.

[23] Cf. § 19: οὐκ ἐλάττω τὴν βασιλείαν πεποίηκεν ἀλλ᾿ εὐχῆς ἄξια διαπέπρακται· τί γὰρ ἐλλέλοιπεν;
  Cf. § 30: φημὶ γὰρ χρῆναί σε τῶν μὲν ἰδίων μηδενὸς ἀμελῆσαι, πειραθῆναι δὲ διαλλάξειν τὴν πόλιν ...
His proposals are not contrary to the king's interests.

(§ 16). Philip should try to bring together and reconcile[24] the four great city-states of Greece: Argos, Lacedaemon, Thebes, and Athens; this will bring peace and concord to the whole of Greece (§§ 30–31).

What is ὁμόνοια? Isocrates himself explains the term and the idea (§§ 39–40). It is ἰσομοιρῆσαι πρὸς ἀλλήλους and is the opposite of πλεονεξία, i. e. ὁμόνοια implies stopping the wars of expansion at the expense of each other's interests and preserving peace among the Greek states.[25] There are actually four alliances or confederations and the problem is how to preserve peace among them. The traditional policy pursued by Athens had been a policy of mere expediency (§§ 42–45), which had greatly contributed to the continuity of wars in Greece and resulted in the exhaustion of the four Greek powers;[26] Philip, who is now a great power in Greece, ought to be able to preserve internal peace.[27] And particularly so, since it is now mainly the growth of his own power which threatens the peace of Greece. Philip will be successful if he refrains from further conquests and does not let his πλεονεξία cause another outbreak of warfare in Greece. Isocrates, therefore, stresses the principle that there is to be no infringement of the liberty of the Greek states (§§ 69–70).[28] Philip ought from now on to refrain from power politics in Greece and desist from forming alliances directed against a Greek state (§§ 73–80).[29] All this and the condition of the Greek states at the moment (§§ 35–40; 47–56) point to the success of the scheme.[30] Thus ὁμόνοια is actually not more than the preservation of peace together with the unimpaired autonomy of Greek states.[31]

[24] Διαλλάξαι is reconciliation of Greek states among themselves (cf. §§ 9; 111) and not of the Greek states and Philip. There is no suggestion of any unification. The same applies to ὁμόνοια which is conceived as a problem of the Greek states and not as an alliance of the Greek states with Philip. Peace and equilibrium in Greece will encourage the expedition against Persia.

[25] Cf. Panegyr. 17; 173–4, though the conditions are quite different as we shall see.

[26] Cf. Dem. VIII 42 = X 14. Cf. also Dem. XVI passim; Isocr. IV, 53; Andoc. III, 28.

[27] Cf. § 45: ἄλλως τε καὶ σοῦ ἐπιστατοῦντος ταῖς διαλλαγαῖς...

[28] Cf. n. 20. Cf. §§ 16; 73—75; 80; 86—87; 107—108; 154; Isocrates is probably aware that the picture he draws is very much like that of the Persian king interfering in the affairs of Greece. But cf. §§ 75—76 in which the distinction between the Persian king and Philip is drawn, in order to stress the danger of any further conquest or subjugation of the Greek states. Cf. n. 41.

[29] This is probably directed at Philip's policy in the Peloponnese. Cf. Dem. V. 18.

[30] The whole argument is directed towards the Greeks as well. They can only better their position if they do not prevent Philip from starting on an expedition into Asia. Jaeger, Demosthenes p. 151, unnecessarily sees here a contradiction in terms. Isocrates never thought in terms of Greek unity overriding the city-state (for the Panegyricus cf. Wilcken op. cit. p. 313). Expansion in Persia is in the self-interest of the Greek states (cf. Panegyr. 17) and even more so now when the threat of Philip has increased.

[31] Demosthenes uses ὁμόνοια in the same manner without any implication of a unified Greek state (cf. Dem. XIV 36—37); he, of course, insists that the Greek states make a common effort against any foreign enemy.

Philip freed from the problems of Greece will be able to turn his energies against Persia; an arrangement which will benefit both parties. In all these considerations there is no hint of unification in any form whatsoever, or of any other form of Macedonian rule in Greece.[32] What Isocrates really wants to achieve is the diversion of Macedonian expansion to Persia, thus providing a solution both to the problems of Greece and to the problems of Macedon. He does not urge the Greeks to keep peace unconditionally or to submit to Macedonian hegemony; it is for Philip to lead the way in gaining the goodwill of the Greeks by peaceful diplomatic means.[33]

What will be the position of Athens in this new scheme? It was Athens who had been waging a long war against Philip, which had just been concluded by the peace of Philocrates. And even this peace is very shaky and highly uncertain. Isocrates who judges the political situation correctly, realizes that the relations between Philip and Athens will decide between war and peace in Greece. It is, therefore, not surprising that in his review of the four principal states of Greece (§§ 47–56)[34] the treatment of Athens should be quite different from that of the others. There is a clear implication that whereas Philip may be master of the situation as far as Sparta, Argos and Thebes are concerned, and may be able by political intrigue to get the better of them, it is not so with Athens. Though Athens has made peace with Philip, she will keep it and even become his ally in Greece,[35] if she is satisfied that Philip now aims at an expedition against Persia and not against Greece. Athens should be Philip's partner in Greece and her naval power should complement his land army. The historical examples Isocrates now gives (§§ 57–67) to prove the ease of Philip's task in bringing the Greek cities together seem at first sight to be most curious and inappropriate.[36] There seem to be no common points between the ac-

---

[32] Cf. §§ 114—116 and n. 53.   [33] Cf. §§ 36; 37; 68; 76; 80; Ep. II, 21.

[34] The political pattern of Greece in the fourth century is adhered to; from among the two states in central Greece he is hostile to Thebes and in the Peloponnesus to Sparta, the old rival of Athens. Thus Athens remains the only power in Greece with which Philip should treat.

[35] συναγωνιεῖσθαι cf. Ep. II, 17; 20. Jaeger, Demosthenes, p. 247 n. 5, who seems not to have noticed the passages quoted above from the second letter says that "the word is used merely as a polite way of expressing the subordination of Athens." It may be that Isocrates did not intend to represent the two states as completely equal powers; but he undoubtedly wanted to point out to Philip that a settlement with Athens and her cooperation were of the greatest importance. Cf. Dem. XVIII 63 who, of course, exaggerates the point on the lines of his argument.

[36] It is in cases like these that Isocrates expects his readers to read his speech carefully (cf. ἀκριβῶς λέγειν Panathen. 246; cf. Philippus 29). Baynes op. cit. p. 148, says, "In reading the work of Isocrates one must always be on one's guard — the art of reading between the lines was never more necessary." Cf. E. Meyer, Gesch. d. Alt. V, p. 372. F. Blass, op. cit. p. 92 rightly remarks that Isocrates' Philippus contains certain suspicions and expressions of anxiety on the part of the author which are well masked in the text.

complishments of Conon or Alcibiades and the task set for Philip. But the
author states that the examples are directed against the arguments of his
opponents and those who make propaganda for Philip in Greece.[37] And ʼn
closer scrutiny, the examples appear to have been very carefully chosen; their
common denominator is dominion of the sea[38]. They become even more sensible
if we bear in mind that what is implied are really the relations between Athens
and Macedon. Alcibiades – the obscurity of whose achievements is striking –
is censured chiefly because he persuaded the Spartans to embark on a policy
of naval expansion; a policy which brought turmoil and disaster to the whole
of Greece. Conon,[39] on the other hand, (§ 62 ἀντίστροφα), is described as the
man who revived Athenian naval strength and with the help of Persia began
the restoration of Athenian hegemony. The aim is quite clear: Macedon is a
land power like Sparta. Athens, the maritime power of Greece, will supply her
needs as a partner; this will save Greece from disaster similar to that which
befell her at the end of the Peloponnesian war. Conon is the example of Athen's
strength, even when defeated, and a quite obvious hint at the possibility of an
alliance between Athens and Persia in case of a war between Athens and
Philip.[40] The picture of the resulting power and influence drawn by Isocrates
(§§ 68–71) is there to show that Philip's concessions to the Greeks and his
withdrawal from the policy of conquest in Greece will not be to his
disadvantage or in any way diminish his strength.[41]

Moreover, Isocrates' description of the anti-Macedonian body of opinion
in Athens (§§ 72–80)[42] clearly confirms the aim of the speech as outlined above.
There is the hard core of the anti-Macedonian party, the politicians who
maintain that Philip's political schemes are aimed directly at the conquest and

[37] Cf. § 57 (... τί λοιπὸν ἔσται τοῖς ἀντιλέγουσιν ...). Speusippus (9—10) is surprised
at the example of Alcibiades and suggests that more appropriate examples could have
been brought forward by Isocrates.

[38] Isocrates does not fail to hint in § 53 that one of the causes of Thebes' downfall was
the attempt to conquer the sea. Naval power was regarded a conditio sine qua non of
hegemony in Greece. Cf. Arist. Pol. 1327b 3—6, 1327a 23; Diod. XI .50.

[39] Cf. Dem. XX 68—70. Isocr. IV, 142.

[40] That this possibility of Persian help against Philip is not quite a phantasy, and that
Athenian statesmen seriously considered it, is borne out by Dem. X 33—34; IX, 71.

[41] It has been pointed out by Wilcken op. cit. p. 311–2 that the picture drawn there is
not that of a confederation of states under the command of Philip, but rather that of the
Persian king's court. Cf. Baynes op. cit. p. 145. But Aesch. II 104; 112; 136 describes the
presence in Pella of envoys from many Greek states during the negotiations for the peace
of Philocrates. These things were very well known in Athens, and Isocrates might have
thought of the existing state of affairs and trying to preserve it. Cf. also Dem. XIX 11;
139. Philip probably saw the importance and the value of an understanding with Athens
at the time; cf. Ps. Dem. VII 21.

[42] The elaborate introduction in § 72 shows that Isocrates is not altogether easy in his
mind about Philip's future plans. He clearly describes rumours of an alliance forming under
Philip for the conquest of Greece.

the subjugation of Greece. They influence three more groups of which the third is the most interesting (§ 75). These are the people who admit that Philip is plotting against Greece, but for a worthy cause. It is against these that Isocrates turns his anger (§ 76). For him, no cause, however worthy, can justify the conquest of Greece. The passage seems to be a covert thrust at the Pro-Macedonian party.[43] Isocrates is afraid that Philip might rely on them and take their line of propaganda and policy. He therefore portrays them as Philip's enemies in contrast to Philip's friends (§ 78). With one more warning not to aim at the conquest of Greece, but respect the opinions of her peoples,[44] Isocrates closes the first part of his speech.

After a short introduction (§§ 83–85) in which, as already indicated, it is pointed out that the war against Persia is a matter of decision on Macedonian policy only,[45] Isocrates proceeds to explain and expound the import of that war in terms of Greek politics. Wars against Persia were undertaken before, but did not lead to peace or stability in Greece. They were waged by Greek powers for their imperialistic ends in Greece itself. Such a war would run directly counter to Isocrates' aims. The Greeks will neither take part in it, nor agree to keep quiet at home. Philip's war against Persia must not be based on the pattern of that led by Agesilaus. It must be a real war genuinely directed *against* Persia and not a subterfuge for the ultimate expansion in Greece through the conquest of Asia Minor (§§ 86–88).[46] It is only on this condition that peace in Greece will be preserved and the campaign against Persia will be successful.

Isocrates continues by pointing out to Philip that even in Asia Minor not a policy of subjection, but a policy of freedom, will facilitate his task (§ 104); it will bring over the King's satraps to his side as well as the Greeks who opposed Cyrus[47] because of their fear of subjection (§ 95). Here again Isocrates does not fail to mention the Lacedaemonian decarchies, and to warn Philip against a policy which would bring the Greeks to the side of Persia.[48]

---

[43] Cf. n. 19.   [44] Cf. also §§ 114; 116—118.

[45] Isocrates clearly indicates (§§ 85; 105) that he is mainly concerned with the political aspects of the plan and is not going to give a detailed elaboration of military matters.

[46] Asia Minor should be the area of settlement of the needy Greeks from the mainland and the Greek cities there should be free from any interference on the part of the king (§§ 120; 123). Cf. Wilcken op. cit. p. 292 n. 1 and Isocr. Ep. IX, 11—14. Kessler op. cit. p. 57, says, "Ohne gemeinsamen Kampf gegen den Erbfeind keine dauernde Einheit!" But even Paneg. 173 to which he refers, does not bear out this statement of his. See also the irony in Dem. VIII 27.

[47] The paradeigma of the expedition of Cyrus gives Isocrates an opportunity to praise Philip as a military leader and at the same time to give a short account of the state of the Persian empire. Blass op. cit. p. 316 n. 5, has pointed out that though the same episode was treated in Paneg. 145—149 the treatment in "Philippus" is new to a great extent.

[48] At the beginning of the campaign in Asia Minor both Philip and Alexander reversed the Persian policy of support to tyrants (or oligarchies) and helped in establishing demo-

The rest of the pamphlet (§§ 105ff.) is mostly a variation or variations on the theme already discussed.[49] First comes a number of historical examples (§§ 105–120). These are – apart from the brief mention of Jason of Pherae (§§ 119–120)[50] – actually confined to Philip's royal ancestry. In these again two aims are closely linked: on the one hand, pointed hints and allusions to the Hellenic origin of Philip's family, and on the other, a new formulation of the old warning: the king of Macedon should be content with royal power in his country, but should not try to become king of Greece, for it is contrary to the spirit of the Greeks to be subjected to a royal power. The greatness of the founder of the royal Macedonian house lies in the fact that he did not try to impose his power on Greeks, a thing which would have led to strife and eventually his own downfall (§§ 107–108).[51] Heracles is the example of the Greek leader who reconciled the Greeks among themselves and stopped the wars among them by an expedition to Asia (§§ 109ff.).[52] His φιλανθρωπία, εὔνοια, εὐεργεσίαι and πραότης (§§ 114–116) towards the Greeks are particularly praised.[53] The four characteristics of Heracles and especially his title of εὐεργέτης[54] are very important for the understanding of the propaganda slogans current at the time in Athens and Greece.[55] Though the aims of Isocrates' propaganda were very well defined, viz. to prove the legitimity of the recognition of Philip as a Greek power, the term εὐεργετεῖν is not a substitute for βασιλεύειν or ἄρχειν; Isocrates wanted Philip to be nothing else but εὐεργέτης as far as Greece was concerned.[56] That this is so and that Isocrates certainly did not intend to compromise on the question of Greek independence is confirmed by a comparison with Speusippus. In his letter Speusippus (2–4) accuses Isocrates of not showing to advantage the εὐεργεσίαι of the Macedonian kings towards Greece. Thus Isocrates failed to mention the behaviour of Alexander and the Macedonians during the Persian wars. The omission is

cracies. Cf. Diod. XVI 91, 2; Arrian Anab. I 17, 10; SIG³ 284 and Th. Lenschau, Alexander der Große und Chios, Klio (33) 1940, pp. 201—202.   [49] Cf. Blass op. cit. p. 316.

[50] Cf. Xen. Hel. VI. 1, 12. The question whether Isocrates tried to enlist Jason for a war against Persia is irrelevant for our present enquiry.

[51] This should be enough to prove that Isocrates did not suggest a Panhellenic monarchy. Neither is there any proof of Rostagni's (op. cit. p. 138, n. 5) statement, that Isocrates had changed his attitude towards the idea of monarchical rule in Greece. He refers to Paneg. 125; 151, which fully bear out the statement made in our passage. Isocrates continually points out the difference in the forms of government applicable to the Greeks in contrast to barbarians and Macedonians, cf. §§ 16; 130; 140; 154; cf. XII, 45.

[52] Wendland op. cit. p. 147 and Wilcken op. cit. p. 298 point out that Panath. 72—89 (Agamemnon) is addressed to Philip with the same ideas in mind as the example of Heracles.

[53] §§ 114—116 again show some anxiety on the part of Isocrates as to the king's and his advisers' future plans. (cf. Dem. IX, 21).   [54] Cf. §§ 76; 116; 140; Ep. II, 15.

[55] Cf. Eiliv Skard, Zwei religiös-politische Begriffe, Euergetes-Concordia. Avhandlinger det Norske Videnskaps-Akademi i Oslo, Hist.-filos. Kl. 1931, No. 2, Oslo 1932.

[56] Skard, ibid., p. 58.

undoubtedly surprising,[57] but it is probably deliberate because Isocrates was anxious to define the reciprocal relations between Philip and the Greeks. He confined himself to the example of Heracles and the Heraclidae, because the Greek cities were the εὐεργέται of those ancestors of the royal Macedonian house.[58] Philip's duty is now not only to emulate his ancestor's attitude towards the Greeks, but first of all to repay the debt of help and goodwill due to the Greek cities. The balance between the two parties is preserved. Philip ought to win the co-operation of the Greeks by peaceful diplomatic means.

There is one more point which Isocrates introduces in this part of his speech (§§ 120–123).[59] It is primarily addressed towards the Greeks and is meant to be an additional argument for the advantages of preserving the existing peace, thus enabling Philip to start on his expedition to Persia. For there is the problem of the impoverished Greeks who as roaming bands of mercenaries are a menace to the existing social and economic structure of Greece. This, Isocrates reminds the Greeks, will be solved by their settlement in Asia. Thus Philip's expansion in Asia will add to Greece's safety not only militarily but also economically and socially.[60] He then repeats his warning to both sides, to Philip, that there is a possibility of a Greek-Persian alliance; to the Greeks, that an alliance with Persia will bring a renewal of war inside Greece (§§ 123–126).[61]

Isocrates goes on hinting and warning Philip: he has got enough power in Greece and Europe.[62] An attempt to increase it might be disastrous; a war against Persia will bring in addition glory and immortal fame.[63] It will also prove that he is a statesman and general. After another warning against the king's advisers (§ 143) and additional mythological and historical examples (§§ 144–148) Isocrates advises Philip to preserve freedom in Greece, maintain his royal power in Macedon, and gain tyranny over barbarians (§ 154).

[57] Cf. Skard, op. cit. p. 57, n. 3.   [58] Cf. "Philippus" §§ 32—37.
[59] Cf. § 96 and Paneg. 34—37.
[60] Cf. Isocr. IV 168; VIII 24; 44 ff. Isocrates is not the only one to point to the social and economic tensions in Greece. Cf. Dem. XIV 31; XXIII 139; Xen. Anab. III 2, 26; V, 6, 15; VI, 4, 7—8.
[61] § 127 contains what might be regarded as the strongest expression of Panhellenism in the "Philippus". Cf. Kessler op. cit. p. 53. But what it really comes to is the hope that Philip will not enter the narrow path of Greek politics; cf. §§ 14—15 and Paneg. 81. The argument is completely in agreement with the general aim of the pamphlet, advising the end of Philip's intervention in Greece.
[62] A. Momigliano, L'Europa come concetto politico presso Isocrate e gli Isocratei, Riv. d. Fil. 1933 pp. 477—478, points out that Isocrates is the representative of the conception of European (sc. Greek) expansion to Asia in opposition to the concept of Ephoros who advocates an expansion in Europe, i. e. to the west of Greece. For our purposes his discussion is important so far as it shows that the problem was discussed and was perhaps even of some topical importance.   [63] Cf. §§ 119—120.

From what has been said it is clear that:

1) The pamphlet is directed for consideration by both sides at a time when, as the result of the peace of Philocrates, their policies were not yet completely formulated, but the outbreak of another war was a very real threat.

2) The preservation of peace can be achieved (a) by the cessation of Philip's conquests and interference in Greece and by the diversion of his power to the conquest of Persia;[64] (b) by the acceptance on the part of the Greeks of the conditions created by the peace of Philocrates, and the cessation of their wars of expansion inside Greece.

3) Athens, the maritime power of Greece, will thus preserve her influence in Greece and will co-operate with Philip.

4) There will be no change whatsoever in the existing status of the Greek city-states.

It is obvious that some problems touched upon affect the whole of Greece and not Athens only; these problems concern the peace in Greece, the Greek "refugees" and the treatment of Greeks in Asia Minor. There is certainly no suggestion of any Panhellenic league and even less of a unified Greek state. The nearest to it is the suggestion of an alliance with Athens on the basis of the peace of Philocrates in which the Athenian navy will co-operate with Philip in his enterprise.

That this is really the essence of Isocrates' advice, is further confirmed by Isocrates' letter to Philip.[65] After a rather long introduction (§§ 1–9) in which he speaks of Philip's wound, which is the pretext for sending the letter, Isocrates states his thesis (§§ 10–11). He advises Philip to stop the war he is waging against the barbarians on the northern outskirts of Greece and turn his power against another barbarian, the king of Persia. A. Rostagni[66] has rightly pointed out that this war against the Illyrians could still be considered to prove the attachment of Philip to an expansionist policy within Greece itself.[67] Isocrates, therefore, again puts forward

---

[64] As this is clearly an expansionist Macedonian war and the decision about it lies within the sphere of Macedonian policy, vengeance as a justification of war against Persia is very closely hidden and only slightly implied in the Philippus. Cf. 125 ἡμεῖς δ'οὐδ' ὑπὲρ ὧν ἐπάθομεν ἀμύνεσαι τολμῶμεν αὐτούς. Cf. Thuc. I, 96, 1 and F. Schehl, Gnomon 1932, p. 491. But cf. Paneg. 155; 185. Thus the difference between a Greek war against Persia and a Macedonian expansionist war becomes obvious. Isocrates clearly distinguishes between Macedonians and Greeks as two different nations cf. §§ 19 and esp. 107—108.

[65] Isocr. Ep. II, written in 344. For its date, the political situation in which it was written and its bearing on negotiations which were at that time being conducted between Athens and Philip, cf. E. Meyer, Isokrates' zweiter Brief und Demosthenes' zweite Philippika, Sitzber. Preuß. Akad. 1909 pp. 758—779. The letter preserved as the third in the collection of Isocratean letters is spurious on chronological grounds.

[66] Op. cit. p. 141.

[67] For the very strained relations between Philip and Athens at that time, cf. §§ 19—21 of the letter and Dem. VI, 12.

his plan of diverting the Macedonian power from Greece to Asia. He even hints (§ 12) that he considers it a political mistake on the part of Philip that he had started that war at all, and says that Philip should go on with it only as far as it is important for the security of the borders of his kingdom, but not further (§ 10). Philip should, of course, establish friendly relations with Athens (§ 14 ff.). It is in his interest to secure Athens' alliance or at least her neutrality (§ 17). It is obvious that Isocrates is trying to prevent the outbreak of war. Though he attacks the war party (§ 15) he also points out that Athens is not alone to blame (§ 16).[68] Again he tries to persuade the king against a policy of conquest in Greece (§§ 20–21) and advises him to build his power on the goodwill of Greece (§ 24). Thus at another critical moment, which is very similar to that immediately after the peace of Philocrates, Isocrates for the second time puts forward the same suggestions as those made in the "Philippus".

It now seems clear that Isocrates' "Philippus" deals with a real political situation and should not be looked upon as an all-round plan for the reorganization of Greece on completely new lines, or judged by its influence on the policies of Philip or Alexander. U. Wilcken has clearly shown how little this pamphlet did influence the arrangements made by Philip at Corinth.[69] But he is wrong in calling it a phantasy.[70] In 346 and perhaps even in 344 it was still a very advantageous plan for both sides; the hazards and results of a future war in Greece could not be foreseen with complete certainty by either side. The sooner it is realised, therefore, that Isocrates deals with Greek politics as did other politicians, that he is not the political leader of Panhellenism or the spiritual father of the conception of a cultural brotherhood of men,[71] but first and foremost an Athenian, the better both his pamphlets and the different trends and conflicting ideas on foreign policy at that time in Athens will be understood. One thing stands out clearly; Isocrates was not a tool in the hands of Philip and was not a member of the pro-Macedonian party. He was prepared to accept Macedonian power in Greece to a certain extent and not more. He never subscribed to the ideas of Macedonian conquest of Greece or Macedonian monarchy over Greeks. He put forward a plan which would preserve the existing limit of Macedonian influence and at the same time satisfy both Philip's aspirations for expansion and the love of independence and political freedom of the Greeks.

Oxford   S. PERLMAN

[68] Cf. E. Meyer, op. cit. p. 768.

[69] That the pamphlet and the views put forward in it were discussed in Athens — though we cannot define exactly to what extent — is obvious. The references in Demosthenes cannot be exactly assessed. But cf. Dem. VII 61—63 and XIX 187. On the other hand, Speusippus' letter is a direct attack against Isocrates. Perhaps the scarcity of references to "Philippus" may be rather taken as an indication of the fact that it was not the basis of pro-Macedonian propaganda in Athens.   [70] Cf. Wilcken, op. cit. pp. 296—297.

[71] See J. Jüthner, Isokrates und die Menschheitsidee, Wiener Studien 1929, pp. 26—31.

VIII

W. Jaeger

The Political Recovery of Athens: Introductory

CHAPTER ONE

THE POLITICAL RECOVERY OF ATHENS

INTRODUCTORY

THE MAN with whom these pages are concerned can no longer be counted among those figures of antiquity whose high reputation in the learned world remains undisputed; it may even seem that I ought to give some excuse for selecting him as my subject. No one who hopes for the unanimous applause of his readers ever does well to take a politician for his hero, especially a politician uncrowned with victory. History is always ready to acknowledge the greatness of a poet or philosopher, no matter how awkwardly he may have fitted his times; but it habitually judges the practicing statesman by his success, not by his intentions. The task of history is to understand the accomplished facts that confront it; and this understanding can all too easily take the form of an apology for those facts, with only a shrug of the shoulders for the side that loses.

But Demosthenes, we may object, was no mere stepchild of *Tyche* stirring our deeper sympathy by his undeserved fate alone. Nevertheless, the classicism of earlier centuries, which venerated him as the unhappy last champion of Greek liberty, has given way to a new type of historical thought arising with the nineteenth century, the effect of which has been sobering. We have now learned that in the time of Demosthenes there was an underlying law of development leading the Greeks away from the old limited city-state to the world empire of Alexander and the world culture of Hellenism. Seen in this vast new perspective, the figure of Demosthenes dwindles to a tiny obstacle in the path of an irresistible historical process. It now seems purely accidental that the tradition preserved so many of his admired speeches while allowing the systematic historical works of the period

[1]

to disappear, thus giving posterity a permanently distorted picture of this epoch, with the true proportions quite upset. But this very calamity has been made a virtue. What Herodotus and Thucydides did for the fifth century, the modern historian has had to do for the fourth. And has he not shown true historical discernment in unmasking Demosthenes' eloquence as empty verbosity despite its two-thousand-year renown, and in making himself pleader for the actual historical forces that overcame Demosthenes' resistance to the march of events?

This has been pretty nearly the *communis opinio* of nineteenth-century historians. It was, of course, natural enough that Johann Gustav Droysen, the discoverer of the post-Alexandrian Hellenism, should have been little interested in Demosthenes; for his enthusiasm for Alexander as the true hero and pioneer of the new age made everything else lapse into insignificance. The situation is different when we come to the great historical works of the positivistic period at the close of the century, especially the *Griechische Geschichte* of Karl Julius Beloch.[1]* Beloch may be regarded as the most consistent representative of this group, not only because his work is rich in the virtues of matter-of-factness, as is well known, but also because his description of Greek development is dominated by the same theoretical bias by which the entire historical thinking of our times has been determined more or less consciously. We have all grown up in this way of looking at things. The fact that Greek political life took the form of a number of autonomous city-states, was, for the national unitarianism of the nineteenth century, a historical scandal. There was a strong feeling that in the end, at any rate, this "particularism" must somehow have terminated in a larger national unity, as in the small states of Germany and Italy in the nineteenth century. The rôle of unifier which had there fallen to the military powers of Prussia

---

* Superior figures refer to notes which will be found on pp. 207-211.

and Savoy, seemed to have been played in Hellas by the kingdom of Macedonia. On this false analogy the whole of Greek history was now boldly reconstructed as a necessary process of development leading quite naturally to a single goal: unification of the Greek nation under Macedonian leadership. That which Demosthenes and most of his contemporaries had looked upon as the death of Greek political liberty, was now all at once regarded as the fulfillment of all the promises with which Fate had blessed the cradle of the Greek people. As a matter of fact, this amounted to judging Greek history by an altogether alien standard; and Demosthenes fell a victim to this misunderstanding. Indeed, a complete revaluation of all historical facts and personages now set in. In general, positivistic scholars have a better developed sense for political, military, and economic factors than they have for the human personality, and this was here operative. Otherwise how could it have happened that just at the time when Demosthenes' stock went down, that of men like Isocrates and Aeschines went up?—a situation which even the most rudimentary sensibility would find psychologically false! Perhaps it is now no longer so difficult to recognize the unhistoricity of the standard that Beloch and others of the same school applied to the events of Demosthenes' period. But when a man has made it his endeavor to obtain a general view of this sort and has at last succeeded, he will find infinite difficulty in escaping its spell when he comes to deal with particulars. For the distortion will extend to the very minutiae of historical judgment. If the standard of measurement is artificial, the findings must likewise be artificial, especially if, as with Beloch, they involve an emotional overtone; in this way the historian becomes little better than a writer of *Tendenzliteratur*, pursuing his prey in every nook and cranny with all the inherent pertinacity and obstinacy of the scholar.

Naturally there have still been defenders of Demosthenes

even after this great reversal of historical opinion. Arnold Schaefer's work, the first volume of which appeared in 1856, was prepared with the utmost philological care and is still of fundamental importance for all special problems. It was virtually untouched by Droysen's novel views; the very title, *Demosthenes und seine Zeit*, indicated that Demosthenes would here be made the point of orientation for the history of the entire fourth century. In this work Schaefer attempted to create a detailed historical picture suffused with that hero worship which classicism had devoted to the great orator of liberty, so as to keep the ideal well fortified against the latest onslaughts. But unfortunately this lovable German scholar was the son of a land not yet politically conscious; he had no eye for the dynamics of political life. Accordingly his enormous zeal remained ineffectual when he came to the critical point of judging Demosthenes' politics, and, to tell the truth, his moralizing orthodoxy is often rather hard to endure. George Grote's version is another thing altogether. But Grote was a banker and a member of Parliament; he views the struggle of the Athenian democracy against the Macedonian empire too much from the standpoint natural to a man of his strong liberal principles, and therefore fails to do full justice either to the opposition party or even to Demosthenes himself.[2] For, as we shall try to prove, Demosthenes' political development was much too complex, and its center of gravity too peculiarly situated, for it to be branded with any partisan label.

If I feel that the time has come for a new evaluation of Demosthenes, that does not mean that we should go back to Schaefer and Grote. Mere reaction is never right, and this would be no more than reaction. Demosthenes can never again be made the focal point of a whole century during which the pendulum swung violently from the sturdy regionalism of a long-established folk to a universalism sweeping away all national barriers. But the fact that history decided against Demosthenes does not diminish our interest in the spirit which made him resist the forces of his time. And what man of understanding would esteem him the less because he was not an Alexander? Thus the history of Demosthenes becomes something more than the biography of any mere party man. For it embodies vicariously a destiny of universal significance: the downfall of the polis or city-state, which had been the typical form of the Greek state throughout its classical period. It had now become inevitable that the old highly developed unity of Greek life as manifested in the polis should be dissolved in the cosmopolitanism of the world empire. The fruit was ripe and ready to fall. This process may seem quite "organic" to the modern historian; but for those to whom it was part and parcel of their daily life—those in whom the spirit of Greek history was still alive—it was an act of unheard-of violence against the moral and spiritual nature of the older Greek civilization. Of this fearful crisis Demosthenes' struggle is one aspect; Plato's attempt to renew the state is another. To overlook the importance of Plato's endeavor as a factor in history on the mere ground that his ideal state could not be realized, is certainly no more false than to deny the historical greatness of Demosthenes' death struggle to maintain the actual polis, simply because sober reason shows us that it was hopeless.

In our effort to approach Demosthenes anew, we must not expect to understand him entirely in terms of modern politics. Demosthenes is only one man; but his history needs the context of the whole intellectual and emotional history of the Greek state from the end of the Peloponnesian War onward. Perhaps there is no respect in which we have so far advanced in our understanding of the fourth century since Droysen discovered the later Hellenism, as in learning to see how indissolubly the inner development of the Greek spirit in the age of Plato is connected with those outward processes of political history from which we once did our best to keep it immaculately aloof.[3] I shall begin by sketching this inner history up to the time when Demosthenes first appears, and shall then follow its development through his orations. It is, of course, true that a politician's thinking and willing are at every moment bound up with the actualities of the outward situation that confronts him; and anyone who would judge him in his rôle must keep an eye on those actual events in which he actively takes part. Therefore we cannot confine ourselves to the picture which Demosthenes' speeches will give us. Our appraisal of these must be corrected in the light of the facts as far as we are in a position to ascertain them. Unfortunately there are narrow limits to what we can know; for the thing that leaves an impress on our tradition is always the intellectual personality, which gives to events the form of its own thought and experience, whether it is the personality of one who describes, like Thucydides, or of one who participates, like Demosthenes. We can never reconstruct the actual course of events. No matter how hard we may try to free ourselves, we shall always see the fifth century with the eyes of Thucydides and the fourth with those of Demosthenes. Let us therefore *reread Demosthenes' speeches*, but this time for that which they *really* contain—that is, *as sources for our understanding of the inner process by which his political thought develops*. It is not enough to select a few surface facts, throwing away all the rest, as is too often the way of the historian; nor is it enough to limit our study to the art of Demosthenes' rhetoric, as Friedrich Blass has done in his excellent history of Attic oratory.[4] Whichever of these two latter methods we follow, the real intellectual substance of the speeches—that which gives them their life and determines their form—will slip through our fingers. For in the end neither historical nor philological analysis will give us the true Demosthenes. Such a "division of labor," it seems to me, hardly advances our knowledge. Let us try, then, for once to understand Demosthenes himself.

NOTES TO CHAPTER I

[1] Karl Julius Beloch, *Griechische Geschichte* III 1, 2d ed., §§ xiii-xiv. Naturally I have no intention of discussing the entire body of literature on Demosthenes.

[2] A fairer and more understanding estimate of Demosthenes is given by Pickard-Cambridge in *The Cambridge Ancient History* VI (1927), pp. 221 ff.

[3] In the historical works of E. Curtius, K. J. Beloch, and Eduard Meyer, and in *The Cambridge Ancient History*, which deal primarily with political history, this realization forces its way to the surface, and a number of paragraphs are inserted to give a cross-sectional survey of the intellectual and spiritual development. But whereas the famous chapters on cultural history in Mommsen's history of Rome well serve their purpose, it is quite impossible to treat culture as a mere appendix when we are dealing with Greek history. The inner development of the Greek spirit is substantially one with the political fate of the nation. This is never more true than in the fourth century, though this is the very period when politics strives hardest for specialization. But this only makes the close interconnection more evident.

[4] Friedrich Blass, *Die attische Beredsamkeit* III 1 ("Demosthenes"), 2d ed. (Leipzig 1893). This work is of fundamental importance for all questions of rhetorical form. If it fails to touch the problem of form in the deeper sense of the word, the reason is that it too much judges Demosthenes by a later school rhetoric already rigidly schematized, and measures his speeches by standards of that sort.

[5] This, and no mere striving for material completeness or supplementing of previous literature (e.g., Hellanicus), is the deeper reason for the insertion of the so-called *Pentecontaetia* in Thuc. I 89-118.

[6] Thuc. I 73-78.

[7] Thuc. I 75, 3: ἐξ αὐτοῦ δὲ τοῦ ἔργου κατηναγκάσθημεν τὸ πρῶτον προαγαγεῖν αὐτὴν ἐς τόδε, μάλιστα μὲν ὑπὸ δέους, ἔπειτα καὶ τιμῆς, ὕστερον καὶ ὠφελίας. This is emphasized in what follows. Isocrates gives a plausible simplification of the thought of this Thucydidean passage in *Areop.* 6: διὰ τὸ δεδιέναι . . . ἐπρώτευσαν τῶν Ἑλλήνων. His thought is full of Thucydidean ideas in spite of being so far removed from Thucydides on the whole.

[8] Thuc. I 77, 6.

IX

H. B. Dunkel

Was Demosthenes a Panhellenist?

WAS DEMOSTHENES A PANHELLENIST?

WHETHER or not the political viewpoint of Demosthenes was Panhellenic is not a new question. Because the decision made on this point greatly influences one's final judgment of Demosthenes' purpose as a statesman and his sincerity as an orator, nearly every attempt to treat the history of Greece during the fourth century B.C. has considered, at least in passing, that orator's attitude in this regard.[1] The decisions handed down have been far from unanimous. Grote's famous dictum[2] has been followed in more recent

[1] The number of works containing discussions which bear more or less directly on this subject is very large. Without attempting to give a complete bibliography, I add here, for the convenience of the reader, those volumes or articles which I have particularly consulted and to which I most frequently refer in the following pages. K. Beloch, *Griechische Geschichte* (2d ed.; Berlin and Leipzig, 1922), Vol. III, Part I; *Cambridge Ancient History* (New York, 1927), Vol. VI; P. Cloché, *La Politique étrangère d'Athènes* (Paris, 1934), and "La Politique de Démosthènes de 354 à 346 avant J.-C.," *BCH*, XLVII (1923), 97–162; M. Croiset, *Démosthène, Harangues* (Paris, 1924), Vols. I and II; E. Drerup, *Aus einer alten Advokatenrepublik* (Paderborn, 1916); G. Grote, *A History of Greece* (12 vols. ed.; London, 1869), Vols. XI and XII; J. Kaerst, *Geschichte des Hellenismus* (3d ed.; Leipzig, 1927), Vol. I; U. Kahrstedt, *Forschungen zur Geschichte des ausgehenden fünften und des vierten Jahrhunderts* (Berlin, 1910); J. Kessler, *Isokrates und die panhellenische Idee* (Paderborn, 1911); A. Pickard-Cambridge, *Demosthenes and the Last Days of Greek Freedom* (New York and London, 1914); R. v. Pöhlmann, *Isokrates und das Problem der Demokratie* ("Sitzb. der k. bayer. Akad. der Wiss., Philos. Philol. u. Histor. Klasse " [Munich, 1913]), pp. 1–169; E. Pokorny, *Studien zur griechischen Geschichte im sechsten und fünften Jahrzent des vierten Jahrhunderts v. Chr.* (Greifswald, 1913); P. Wendland, "Beiträge zu athenischer Politik und Publicistik des vierten Jahrhunderts; II. Isokrates und Demosthenes," *Nachrichten d. k. Gesellsch. der Wiss. zu Göttingen* (Berlin, 1910), pp. 289–323.

In the interim between the acceptance of this article and its publication, P. Cloché's *Démosthènes et la fin de la démocratie athénienne* and W. Jaeger's *Demosthenes: The Origin and Growth of His Policy* have both appeared. Cloché (pp. 312 ff.) tends to follow the old view ascribing a general Panhellenic policy to Demosthenes. I cannot agree. Jaeger, abandoning the old attempt to see Demosthenes as everywhere the paladin of Panhellenism, traces much the same course as I should. He believes, however, that the orator's change to a Panhellenic viewpoint about the period of the *Third Philippic* is a true development of his policy and is sincere. I note the same change but question the sincerity.

[2] *Op. cit.*, XII, 151: "But what invests the purpose and policy of Demosthenes with peculiar grandeur, is, that they were not simply Athenian, but in an eminent degree Panhellenic also. It was not Athens alone which he sought to defend against Philip, but

[CLASSICAL PHILOLOGY, XXXIII, July, 1938]   291

K   [129]

years by others, such as Pickard-Cambridge,[3] who have seen in Demosthenes an advocate of Panhellenism. On the other side, Drerup[4] and Kaerst[5] have denied that he had any true Panhellenic feeling.

Some of the reasons for this difference of opinion are not far to seek. The struggle between Demosthenes and Philip (or the contrast between the political views of Demosthenes and Isocrates), typifying for many the conflict between the democratic and monarchial types of government, has been carried on, in part, by the modern adherents to those systems. Enthusiastic democrats have attempted to add to the glory of Demosthenes the Athenian patriot by proclaiming him also as the champion of Panhellenic freedom; the opposing party, on the other hand, has found the hopes of Isocrates and the deeds of Philip more praiseworthy. Furthermore, this influence of contemporary political affairs particularly affected the German scholars of the early twentieth century, who have done much of the work in this field. The obvious advantages of the amalgamation of the small warring German states under the Prussian Empire greatly impressed them and inclined them to favor national union under a monarchy rather than the autonomy of small districts. As a result, these writers[6] have tended, in general, to exalt Isocrates as one who attempted to teach this valuable lesson to the Greek states,[7] and, in a measure, to belittle Demosthenes as the defender of the independent city-state.

---

the whole Hellenic world. In this he towers above the greatest of his predecessors for half a century before his birth—Perikles, Archidamus, Agesilaus, Epaminondas, whose policy was Athenian, Spartan, Theban, rather than Hellenic."

[3] *Op. cit.*, p. 23: "He [Isocrates] expressed, as Demosthenes did (particularly in middle and later life), the strongest Panhellenic feeling."

[4] *Op. cit.*, p. 111: "Aber dieser panhellenische Eifer des Demosthenes ist, im Gegensatze zu Isokrates, insofern unecht, als er nur als Mittel zu dem Zwecke dient, die athenischen Verbündeten gegen Makedonien aufzustacheln; für die eigentlichen Ziele des Demosthenes ist der Panhellenismus, der von ihm nur hier [i.e., the *Third Philippic*] als eine hohe, nationale Aufgabe gewertet wird, nichts als eine Pose." And see also his entire discussion of the *Third Philippic*, pp. 111–13.

[5] *Op. cit.*, I, 223: "Nur sollte man seine Auffassung nicht eine nationale nennen und in ihm den Repräsentaten eines hellenischen oder panhellenischen Patriotismus sehen. Die panhellenischen Gefühle bilden nur den schmükkenden Hintergrund, vor dem sich der spezifisch athenische Patriotismus des grossen Redners abhebt."

[6] Beloch, Drerup, Kaerst, Kahrstedt, Kessler, Pöhlmann, and Wendland, with varying degrees of correctness in each individual case, may fairly be named in such a list, especially as regards their defense of Isocrates.

[7] Undoubtedly, these studies have compelled us to give a fairer estimate of Isocrates and his work. Whether they have carried their admiration too far is another question.

Then too, the World War, in which democracy and autocracy were at
least nominally concerned, aggravated this effect.[8]

In the second place, the evidence offered by Demosthenes' speeches
is not wholly consistent, as the following pages will show; some of his
statements seem to indicate that he was a wholehearted Panhellenist,
others that he was a narrow Athenian patriot. The opposing "schools"
have been prone to emphasize that set of quotations which seems best
to prove their own contentions; but, so far as I know, no previous attempt has been made to study as a whole these apparently conflicting
expressions of opinion on the part of the orator. The present study is,
consequently, a consideration of this aspect of Demosthenes' political
activity through an examination of the extant speeches,[9] omitting
as far as possible, the many vexed problems which do not properly
fall within the scope of the present subject.[10] Panhellenism was "in
the air."[11] Was Demosthenes influenced by this sentiment, or was he
only an Athenian patriot, desirous of local independence for his own
city?

If we follow the orations in their chronological order, the speech
On the Symmories, concerned as it is with the suspected invasion of
Greece by Persia, offers the first statements pertinent to the present
discussion. In part, Demosthenes' attitude here is severely realistic.
He mentions several times that the relations of the Greek states, especially those of Athens with the other cities, are not of the best. Only
too many of them would be led by grudges or self-interest to betray
to the barbarian the cause of Greece.[12] For that reason, Athens should

[8] Drerup very obviously wrote under war influence.

[9] Although I consider the orations more as "speeches" than "pamphlets," the question is not important here. So Drerup, *op. cit.*, p. 61. See also C. Adams, "Are the
Political 'Speeches' of Demosthenes To Be Regarded as Political Pamphlets?" *TAPA*,
XLIII (1912), 5–22. For the position Demosthenes as a practical statesman would be
forced to take as compared with Isocrates, a pamphleteer, see below, n. 89.

[10] Discussion of whether Macedonian hegemony was better for Greece than her con-
tinual civil war, whether the Greeks of the period were capable of the proper use of
freedom or of making the effort which Demosthenes demanded, and even whether the
orator himself was a sincere patriot will be avoided. Our purpose is only to determine
whether Demosthenes' views and policies, as expressed, were Panhellenic. A decision
on this question will bring more light to the study of those problems than they to this.

[11] Beloch (*op. cit.*, III, Part I, 515–25) gives a good brief summary of the evidence
for Panhellenic sentiment in the fifth century. For the fourth century, in addition to
the works on Isocrates cited above (especially Kessler), see Kaerst, *op. cit.*, I, 138–53.

[12] xiv. 3–5, 12, 36–38. References are to the text of Butcher in the Oxford Classical
Library.

not stir up a war scare now but should make her own preparations and wait for Persia to take the initiative. Demosthenes professes to feel that under those circumstances Athens could be sure of Greek support. To be sure, part of this co-operation would be secured through the desire of the other cities for Athenian arms and aid.[13] But at the same time, the orator does not base his hopes completely on this self-interest. Although the Great King might gather a large force of Greek mercenaries for action in Egypt or Asia Minor, he could not persuade a Greek to fight against Greece:

For where would he retire afterwards? Will he go to Phrygia and be a slave? For the objects at stake in a war against the barbarian are nothing less than our country, our life, our habits, our freedom, and all such blessings. Who, then, is so desperate that he will sacrifice himself, his ancestors, his sepulchres, and his native land, all for the sake of paltry profit?[14]

Even Thebes, who failed Greece in the former invasion, is likely to fight on the right side.[15] In short, that Greeks fighting in the hire of Persia should assist in the invasion of Greece is unthinkable; and the basis for this hope is reliance on Panhellenic spirit. This recognition of ethnic unity was not uncommon among the Greeks; but it had failed to prevent mutual hatred and jealousy and to unite the Greeks in any active way. Consequently, the orator does not stop with merely the idealistic recognition of Greek unity: he shows that this co-operation conferred practical benefits. Greece as a whole profited from the former instance of united effort against Persia.[16] Of Athens this fact was particularly true since her activities then on behalf of Greece had been the beginnings of her supremacy.[17] In the present crisis too, unselfish action may, secondarily, bring her private gain. But, primarily, Athens must take thought for Greece because it is her Panhellenic duty to preserve the freedom of the Greeks:

For indeed, as regards your policy towards the King, I see that you are by no means on the same footing as the other Greeks; for many of them it is, I suppose, possible to pursue their private interests and abandon the cause of

[13] xiv. 13.

[14] xiv. 31–32. And cf. xiv. 40. This translation and all those following are taken from the volumes of the Loeb Classical Library; orations i–xvii and xx are translated by J. H. Vince; orations xviii and xix, by C. A. and J. H. Vince.

[15] xiv. 33–34.   [16] xiv. 35–36.   [17] xiv. 40.

their fellow-countrymen, but for you, even when wronged by them, it would not be honourable to exact such a penalty from the wrong-doers as to leave any of them under the heel of the barbarian.[18]

Demosthenes, in this speech, has two different points in regard to Panhellenism. First, if Persia attacks, Greece will unite in defense of the fatherland,[19] impelled by Panhellenic feeling.[20] Second, under these circumstances, Athens must, as her Panhellenic duty, protect Greece. Yet both of these sentiments have one point in common: they are pious hopes for the future. Although rumor had it that the king was making preparations against Greece, the invasion was still only a rumor. Hence, the orator's Panhellenic sentiment is not directed toward a present fact. For the immediate need he offers his navy bill, a reform which would primarily strengthen Athens. Although this new power might be used on behalf of the other Greeks, it might well be turned against them if they misbehave.[21] As a result, from this speech we cannot determine whether Demosthenes does have a sincere regard for the Greek states as a whole or whether his remarks are only bombast.

The next speech, that *On Behalf of the Megalopolitans*, does not exhibit even this ambiguous Panhellenic attitude, but is openly Athenian in tone. The Megalopolitans, allies of Thebes, had appealed to Athens for protection against the threatened encroachment of her ally, Sparta. That Demosthenes has the interest of Athens chiefly in mind is clearly stated by the speaker himself at the beginning of his address.[22] He then sets forth exactly what, in his opinion, this interest demands.

Now no one would deny that our city is benefited by the weakness of the Lacedemonians and of the Thebans yonder. The position of affairs, then, if one may judge from statements repeatedly made in your Assembly, is such

[18] xiv. 6.

[19] He chooses here to ignore those sundering hates and hopes which he has himself mentioned (see above, n. 12).

[20] Since Demosthenes asserts that operations against Persia would unite the Greeks, the interesting question arises of how much the youthful Demosthenes may have been influenced by the writings of Isocrates (cf. Wendland, *op. cit.*, *passim*; Beloch, *op. cit.*, p. 525). One striking difference, however, has already been pointed out (C. D. Adams, *CP* VII [1912], 319): Isocrates planned an offensive war against Persia; Demosthenes seems to have felt that only the necessity of defense would unite the Greeks.

[21] xiv. 5, 10–11, 41.   [22] xvi. 1–4.

that the Thebans will be weakened by the refounding of Orchomenos, Thespiae, and Plataea, but the Lacedemonians will regain their power, if they get Arcadia into their hands and destroy Megalopolis. Our duty, then, is to take care lest the Lacedemonians grow strong and formidable before the Thebans are weaker, and lest their increase in power should, unperceived by us, outbalance the diminution of the power of Thebes, which our interests demand. For this at least we should never admit, that we would sooner have the Lacedemonians for our rivals than the Thebans, nor is that our serious aim, but rather to put it out of the power of either to do us harm, for in that way we shall enjoy the most complete security.[23]

In other words, while Sparta must be prevented from making capital out of Thebes' embarrassment with the Sacred War, on the other hand, Thebes too should be weakened further by the restoration of Thespiae and the other Boeotian towns, with Athens taking due care that this strength taken from Thebes is not given to Sparta.[24] In short, Demosthenes is not urging a policy of "balance of power"[25] but hopes so to weaken both Thebes and Sparta that Athens may be supreme in Greece. Although a decision as to whether this advice was best for Greece under the circumstances does not lie within the province of this study,[26] we must note that the orator's argument is distinctly not Panhellenic. Thebes and Sparta are not considered as parts of the Hellenic aggregate; they are merely cities whose power restricts or menaces the complete independence of the speaker's city. The Arcadians, or the Thespians and Plataeans, are not fellow-Greeks whose aspirations and liberties are considered; they are simply pawns in the game of inter-Hellenic politics. Here Demosthenes is not a Hellenic, but an Athenian patriot.

In the *First Philippic* about a year later, the orator adopts much the same tone. When he laments that a Macedonian is settling the affairs of Greece, his prior concern is that this Macedonian is triumphing over Athens.[27] Pydna, Potidaea, and Methone are not considered

[23] xvi. 4–5. This same point is stated even more clearly in xxiii. 102.

[24] xvi. 24–26, 30–31.

[25] So Cloché (*La Politique étrangère*, p. 183) rightly. A policy of balance of power would mean the recognition of equal Theban and Spartan power of admitted superiority, with Athens shifting to keep the balance even. Or at best, if Athens is not to be a mere make-weight, the phrase would denote a tripart division of power. In my opinion, neither of these is the orator's plan.

[26] See Grote's admission, however, *op. cit.*, XI, 94–95.

[27] iv. 10: Μακεδὼν ἀνὴρ Ἀθηναίους καταπολεμῶν καὶ τὰ τῶν Ἑλλήνων διοικῶν.

as Greek cities whose freedom has been threatened or destroyed. They are spoken of almost as property which the Athenians once possessed but lost through neglect.[28] Such an attitude as this bespeaks Athenian imperialism, not Panhellenism.

Speaking *On the Liberty of the Rhodians*,[29] Demosthenes again uses strong language against the other Greeks.[30] At the same time, he does appeal to Panhellenic sentiment. If the Great King does lay claim to Rhodes, Athens must take counsel not for Rhodes alone but for herself and for all the Greeks.[31] Athens must then seek to be recognized as the champion of general Hellenic freedom.[32] But what kind of champion will Athens be? That the actual results may not be so idealistic as the phrase implies, Demosthenes himself seems to hint:

> For I notice that all men have their rights conceded to them in proportion to the power at their disposal. . . . . Of private rights within a state, the laws of that state grant an equal and impartial share to all, weak and strong alike; but the international rights of Greek states are defined by the strong for the weak.[33]

Holding these views, the orator would hardly have Athens be an idealistic champion of Greece. This attitude points more toward another Athenian empire, a scheme which had already twice met resistance and failure.

Passing over the speech *On Organization*,[34] we come to the three *Olynthiacs*, which may well be treated as a unit. Here the orator includes a few touches which might be called Panhellenism. Philip is a barbarian[35] and as such should be ruled by Greeks, not be their ruler.[36] The Athenians should be ashamed to allow Philip to enslave

[28] iv. 4–6. This "objective" manner of regarding fellow-Greeks is similar to that of the preceding speech.

[29] For convenience I have followed the traditional date, 351 B.C.

[30] xv. 14–16.

[31] xv. 13. οὐ γὰρ ὑπὲρ ʼΡοδίων βουλευτέον . . . . ἀλλʼ ὑπὲρ ἡμῶν αὐτῶν καὶ τῶν πάντων Ἑλλήνων.

[32] xv. 30.

[33] xv. 29.

[34] Although its authenticity is now more generally accepted, it offers nothing particularly pertinent to the present question.

[35] iii. 16.

[36] iii. 24. For this thought, deeply rooted in the Greek mind, see Euripides *And.* 663–66; *I.A.* 1400–1401; *Tro.* 971–74; frag. (Nauck) 719.

Greek cities.[37] But the same breath which brands Philip as a barbarian labels the Greek cities which he holds not distressed brethren
but lost or stolen property.[38] The seizure and trading of cities, a game
at which Philip bested Athens, is censured because the Athenians
were not clever enough to win or did not play the game with sufficient zeal.[39] In these *Olynthiacs*, delivered to arouse Athens to the
defense of a city attacked by Philip, Demosthenes had a fine opportunity to stress Panhellenism. Even if the "imperialistic" attitude
which he adopts may have seemed more practical, it is little short of
surprising that more of his appeal does not rest on Panhellenism.

In his discussion *On the Peace*, Demosthenes still has little hope of
Greek unity. Far from striving to be accepted as the champion of
Greek freedom,[40] Athens must now seek to avoid an Amphictyonic
war in which the various cities might merge their private grudges.[41]
And in the *Second Philippic*, which follows shortly, his opinion of the
other Greek states is no higher. Thebes, Argos, and Messene are all
willing, partially out of cupidity, partially out of stupidity, to sacrifice
Greece to Philip if only they may gain some concession to their own
interests.[42] The speaker spares no words in denouncing them. But
what has he to say of Athens? Philip is hostile to her because

he rightly saw that to our city and our national character he could offer
nothing, he could do nothing, that would tempt you from selfish motives to
sacrifice to him any of the other Greek states, but that you, reverencing justice, shrinking from the discredit involved in such transactions, and exercising
a due and proper forethought, would resist any such attempt on his part.
. . . . For by those very acts you stand judged the one and only power in the
world incapable of abandoning the common rights of the Greeks at any price,
incapable of bartering your devotion to their cause for any favour or profit.[43]

In other words, Athens is and will be, Demosthenes says, the champion of Greek liberty; she cannot be tempted from this position by
the wiles of the enemy or driven from it by the unwillingness or in-
gratitude of the Greeks.[44] Is the orator serious here? Aside from a

[37] iii. 20.

[38] iii. 16 (see above, n. 28).

[39] i. 8–9; ii. 6–7. Cf. xix. 22; viii. 15–16.

[40] This had been his suggestion in an earlier speech (xv. 30).

[41] v. 14–19 particularly. [42] vi. 9–12, 19. [43] vi. 7–10.

[44] The second point he made in an earlier speech (xiv. 6).

certain playing upon the vanity of the Athenians, does Demosthenes really feel that they have anything but a selfish interest in the affairs of Greece? Or is this statement mere flattery of the same order as references to Marathon and Salamis? One is inclined to believe the latter. In this same speech, referring to the surrender of the Phocians and Thermopylae to Philip, Demosthenes says that his objections were of no avail because the Athenians believed that Philip was hostile to Thebes and that by restoring Plataea and Thespiae he would further weaken this rival of Athens.[45] This admission certainly shows that, in regard to Thebes at least, Athenian Panhellenism was not fervid. Nor does Demosthenes state expressly here that he objected because the policy implied in the promises of the other envoys was un-Panhellenic: he finds fault because the results endangered Athens.[46] If these two expressions show Athenian feeling and the orator's personal attitude, his eloquent exposition of Athens' championship of Greek liberty rings slightly hollow.

Our doubts as to Demosthenes' Panhellenic feelings are increased by the oration *On the Chersonese*. Philip's subjugation of Greek cities is again represented only as the theft of Athenian property.[47] But even worse, in another speech[48] in which the orator attempts to gain Athenian aid for Greek communities, he does not base his appeal on Panhellenic motive at all. Athens must rescue these people, even though they have been foolish—but not for their sakes or for Greek freedom but in the interest of Athens.[49]

After this unabashed expression of self-interest, the *Third Philippic* presents a surprising change of front. Demosthenes still realizes that the mutual relations of the Greek states are far from happy.[50] He even admits that perhaps the earlier supremacies of Athens, Sparta, and Thebes did commit some offenses against the subject states.[51] Be that as it may, however, the time has now come for Athens to act on behalf of all Greece.[52] So had their ancestors, of glorious memory, concerned

---

[45] vi. 29–30. The same point is made in ix. 11 and xix. 20–21.

[46] Cf. above, n. 39.

[47] viii. 6. Cf., also, iv. 4–6; iii. 16; xix. 22.

[48] The same general situation existed in regard to the *Olynthiacs* too.

[49] viii. 15–16.

[50] ix. 21, 28–29.   [51] ix. 22–25.   [52] ix. 19–20.

themselves with Greek affairs.[53] Now again Athens must assume the leadership. Not only must she send embassies to arouse and organize the other cities but she must herself take action to show that she will do her full share in protecting her own interests and those of Greece.[54] This Panhellenic emphasis of the much admired *Third Philippic* has probably influenced greatly those who would ascribe to Demosthenes a Panhellenic viewpoint. In the speech itself nothing contradicts these expressions or shows that the speaker was not sincere. Only the abrupt change in tone from that of the preceding speeches would lead us to believe that here Demosthenes' Panhellenic sentiment was but a veil for local Athenian patriotism and that he sought to save the Greek cities only because by protecting them could he preserve Athens. As a result, the sentiment of this speech can best be considered in the examination of his entire policy[55] when we have completed our chronological survey of his extant public orations.[56]

The next oration, that *On the Embassy*, also has its Panhellenic touches. Demosthenes refers at some length to the patriotic oratory of Aeschines, who felt that he was the first to see the peril of Greece.[57] Then he gives equal emphasis to the changed and un-Hellenic attitude later adopted by this same orator.[58] At the same time Demosthenes himself delivers a patriotic harangue filled with memories of Marathon

[53] ix. 45, 74.   [54] ix. 70–74.   [55] Cf. below, p. 305.

[56] Although chronologically the *Fourth Philippic* should be considered next, its doubtful authenticity (cf. F. Blass, *Die attische Beredsamkeit* [2d ed.; Leipzig, 1893], III, Part I, 384–92; Croiset, *op. cit.*, II, 112–19) makes it perhaps unfair to include this speech in the main body of the evidence. On the other hand, for most of the points which concern us here this speech affords not so much new evidence as confirmation of statements already made. The affairs of Greece are in disorder (x. 50–51). Athens shares in this mutual jealousy and distrust (x. 52–54). This state of affairs has come about because Athens has deserted the post of guardian of Greece, a trust left to her by the Athenians of old, and has sought her own ease and interest (x. 25, 46–48). One critical point is, however, the orator's advocacy of an alliance with Persia (x. 31–34; he had already suggested an embassy in the "longer version" of the *Third Philippic*, ix. 71). This attempt to win the support of the traditional enemy of Greece has been censured as un-Hellenic and unpatriotic (e.g., Beloch, *op. cit.*, III, Part I, 551) and has furnished material for those who wish to make Demosthenes a Persian agent (e.g., Drerup, *op. cit.*, p. 147). One cannot, however, thus categorically denounce the orator for this suggestion. That Greece was in less danger from Persia than from Macedonia was probably true. If Demosthenes was simply playing one enemy off against a stronger, his attempt to win Persian support does not necessarily convict him of being un-Hellenic (see Cloché, *BCH*, XLIV [1920], p. 146 and n. 2; *ibid.*, XLVI [1922], p. 161).

[57] xix. 10–12, 302–6.   [58] xix. 16, 307–8, 311.

and Salamis,[59] and stating Athens' position as champion of Greece.[60] From this fanfare one might be convinced that the emphasis of the speech was to be upon the Panhellenic duty of Athens toward the Phocians, whose betrayal forms the basis of Demosthenes' charges. He begins his statement of the Phocian question by reporting the speech which Aeschines is supposed to have delivered on his return from the embassy. This address contained the promises dear to Athenian hearts: that Thespiae and Plataea would be restored to weaken Thebes,[61] which would be humbled further by having the guilt of the Sacred War fastened on her, that Amphipolis would be traded to Philip for Euboea,[62] and that perhaps some lost property[63] (i.e., Oropos) would be recovered.[64] Now although these projects were not Panhellenic, they pleased the Athenians, who refused to hear contradictions, even from Demosthenes.[65] But many of these propositions were also quite in line with the policy of Demosthenes. Weakening Thebes, restoring the Boeotian towns (not for their own sakes but to injure Thebes), trading Amphipolis, and recovering property, all these hopes, even if they did run counter to ideal Panhellenic policy, had been cherished by Demosthenes.[66] His action against Aeschines was not apparently motivated by the fact that he opposed the nature of the promises, but by the fact that he thought Philip would fail to keep them.[67] In regard to these measures which were open to consideration on Panhellenic grounds, Demosthenes seems to have acted only as an Athenian.

In regard to the Phocians themselves, he waxes particularly warm.[68] One is almost led to believe that part, at least, of his indig-

---

[59] xix. 271–72, 312–13.

[60] xix. 64.

[61] Cf. above, n. 45.

[62] Cf. above, n. 39.

[63] Cf. above, n. 47.

[64] xix. 20–22.

[65] xix. 24, 35, 74, 111–12.

[66] Cf. above, nn. 45, 39, and 47.

[67] xix. 17, 24, 29, and cf. above, n. 39.

[68] xix. 47, 51, 66. The question of whether we can accept Demosthenes' statements in regard to his efforts to prevent the exclusion of the Phocians from the Peace concerns us only indirectly; however, cf. *CAH*, VI, 248. Even Grote (*op. cit.*, XI, 204–5) is forced to admissions. Furthermore, it is noteworthy that in this speech of defense Demosthenes does not employ any Panhellenic argument for their inclusion in the treaty.

nation at their fate is due to a feeling for them as fellow-Greeks. But
the orator clearly states his point of view:

Yet no man could point out two places in the whole world of more importance to the commonwealth [πόλει] than Thermopylae by land and the Hellespont by sea; and both of them these men have infamously sold and delivered
into the hands of Philip.[69]

You all know that the prowess of the Phocians, and their control of the
pass of Thermopylae, gave us security against the Thebans, and ensured that
neither Philip nor the Thebans would invade either the Peloponnesus, or
Euboea, or Attica.[70]

You saved the Lacedaemonians in old time, and those accursed Euboeans
lately, and many other people, not because they were virtuous, but because
their safety profited Athens, as that of the Phocians would today.[71]

Our orator is apparently no more worried about the Phocians as
Greeks than he is about "those accursed Euboeans." They are to be
saved not because they are Greeks who should be free but because
their safety benefits Athens. Although Demosthenes may at one moment shout about the Panhellenic duty of Athens toward the other
states of Greece, his other remarks frequently force us to admit that
he preserved, or sought to preserve, Greek cities, not so much as free
states for Greece as buffer states for Athens.

Much this same attitude appears in the account of his political
life, the speech *On the Crown*. Here again Demosthenes stresses his
Panhellenic policy. Beginning his career, he took Hellenic affairs as
his province.[72] For one in that position, when Philip began his advance upon Greece, only one course of action, in Demosthenes'
opinion, was open. The rest of Greece was split into factions with
many of the leading states eager to betray the Hellenic cause in the
hope of selfish profit.[73] In this situation, Athens alone could stand
forth as the champion of Greece.[74] Nor did this Panhellenic zeal of

[69] xix. 179–80.

[70] xix. 83.

[71] xix. 75. With the "accursed Euboeans" [καταράτους Εὐβοέας] of this speech may be
compared the "vile Thessalians" and "ill-conditioned Thebans" (xviii. 43: κατάπτυστοι
Θετταλοὶ καὶ ἀναίσθητοι Θηβαῖοι).

[72] xviii. 58–59.   [73] xviii. 43–44, 61–64. Cf. xiv. 3–5, 12, 36–38.   [74] xviii. 64, 71–72.

Athens spring only from the counsels of Demosthenes.[75] The city from her earliest history had sought to defend the freedom of Greece as well as her own power and renown.[76] Neither in the earlier days nor under the orator's sway did Athens scruple to lend aid. That the other cities could not or would not do their full share[77] or that Athens had some grievance against those who sought her help[78] never deterred the city from her duty. This traditional policy of Athens Demosthenes maintained in a manner worthy both of the city and of himself.[79] Those cities which followed the advice of Demosthenes were saved;[80] and, had every city produced one such patriot, they would have preserved their independence.[81]

Although the activity which Demosthenes sets forth[82] may be termed Panhellenic in the sense that it was an effort to protect Greek communities, one wonders, as in regard to the preceding speech, whether they were saved for their own sakes or for Athens'. Certainly, the orator claims much credit for the benefits which his policy conferred upon the city. He protected the Attic frontier both on land and on sea, he insured the delivery of grain, secured places already under Athenian control, made alliances with new strategic points, won allies, and, finally, brought it about that the invasion of Greece ended in a battle not on Attic soil.[83]

I did not fortify Athens with masonry and brickwork: they are not the works on which I chiefly pride myself. Regard my fortifications as you ought, and you will find armies and cities and outposts, seaports and ships and horses, and a multitude ready to fight for their defense. These were the bastions I planted for the protection of Attica so far as it was possible to human forethought; and therewith I fortified, not the ring-fence of our port and citadel, but the whole country.[84]

From this chronological summary of Demosthenes' Panhellenic utterances, one easily sees why opinions on this phase of the orator's policy have been divided. Some of his statements seem to show that he was moved by Panhellenic sentiment; at the same time, other ex-

[75] xviii. 293.
[76] xviii. 66, 100–101, 203–5, 208.
[77] xviii. 237–38.
[78] xviii. 96–101.
[79] xviii. 108–9.
[80] xviii. 80.
[81] xviii. 304–5.
[82] xviii. 79, 237–38.
[83] xviii. 229–30, 300–303.
[84] xviii. 299–300.

pressions offer a basis for the contrary decision. Admitting this apparent contradiction, we can, nevertheless, arrive at certain conclusions in regard to Demosthenes' Panhellenic attitude. First, in Demosthenes we miss that broad sympathy with the points of view taken by other Greek cities and individuals which we should expect in one whose professed policy was the championship of Hellas.[85] Instead of understanding and respect, he expresses distrust and even contempt for them and their policies.[86] Second, he surprises us in that on several occasions when he could have used Panhellenic appeal very pertinently and effectively, he either almost omits any mention of such claims,[87] or, in spite of some Panhellenic touches, he appears to adopt an attitude more appropriate to an Athenian imperialist.[88] In the latter case, the fact that he does make some use of Panhellenic sentiment shows that he was not simply taking a more "practical" rather than an idealistic view for the purpose of carrying his point.[89] Third, many of his Panhellenic expressions refer either to Panhellenic activity in the glorious past,[90] or else to a future, and sometimes hypothetical, position which Athens might take.[91] But when it is a question

[85] E.g., the tolerance implied by Aristophanes in *Acharnians* 509–22.

[86] xiv. 3–5, 12, 36–38, 41; v. 14–19; vi. 9–12, 19; viii. 15–16; xix. 75; xviii. 43.

[87] E.g., in the speech *On Behalf of the Megalopolitans*.

[88] E.g., the *First Philippic*, *On the Liberty of the Rhodians*, *Second Philippic*, and the three *Olynthiacs*.

[89] As has already been stated (p. 293), this study attempts to limit itself to the evidence offered by the extant public orations. One additional point, however, deserves consideration, even though its treatment must be brief. Some defense of the orator's lack of Panhellenism might be made to this effect. Demosthenes was not (particularly if we accept the "speeches" as speeches) writing a commentary on the political events of his day. He was a man of affairs endeavoring to get measures, often unpopular ones, through a legislative body against opposition. As a result, although his personal beliefs may have been of higher or more idealistic type, he used more "realistic" arguments to win the support of those whom expediency and self-interest would convince more than ideals. (The *locus classicus* for this technique is, of course, the speech of Diodotus [Thuc. iii. 42–48].) Being in this position, then, Demosthenes would be less able to express Panhellenic sentiment than Aristophanes was in his plays or Isocrates in his pamphlets. This argument might partially explain a total lack of this sentiment in the speeches; but the reality is, of course, that Demosthenes does use some Panhellenic appeal. It is the fact that he employs this sentiment inconsistently, sporadically, and sometimes not at all which leads us to believe that he was not a Panhellenist whose position prevented his fully expressing his opinions but an Athenian patriot who sometimes found appeal to Panhellenic sentiment useful.

[90] ix. 19–20, 45, 74; xiv. 35–36, 40; xviii. 66, 96–101, 203–5, 208, 237–38.

[91] xiv. 6; xv. 13, 30.

of some immediate action toward which a Panhellenic attitude might be adopted, our orator either makes but little use of Panhellenic appeal or else goes on a completely different tack and pleads Athenian interest.

This constant emphasis on Athenian interests is what impresses us most. In the speech *On the Symmories*, Athens, whatever her future action, will have new strength. By the policy urged on behalf of the Megalopolitans Athens will weaken her rivals. In the case of the Rhodians Athenian democracy must have its interest guarded,[92] and in this speech as well as several of the following orations[93] Athenian imperialism seems implied. Demosthenes, in the *Embassy* and the *Crown*, claims that he did much to unite Greece; but apparently he did it to save Athens. Even the Panhellenism of the *Third Philippic* appears inspired by Athenian patriotism. In short, Demosthenes did use Panhellenic appeal. But he did not, in my opinion, have a true Panhellenic feeling. Athens was his *patris*, and he sought to save it as a city-state. If he attempted to unite Greece or appealed to Panhellenic sentiment, he did so only because he felt that thereby he could save Athens. Demosthenes was an Athenian, not a Panhellenist.

UNIVERSITY OF CHICAGO

[92] Cf. also xiii. 7–9.

[93] The six orations cited (see above, n. 88).

X

G. L. Cawkwell

Demosthenes' Policy after the Peace of
Philocrates

DEMOSTHENES' POLICY AFTER THE PEACE
OF PHILOCRATES. I[1]

IN 346 the Athenians were sadly deceived by Philip. The long war for Amphipolis had taken its toll and the people wanted relief, but the real motive of those
who wanted peace in 346, both Philocrates with his principal abettor Demosthenes, and Eubulus and Aeschines, was to try to keep Philip out of Greece
itself.[2] In Elaphebolion the only debate was about means, whether, as Aeschines
wanted, to try to get Phocis included in a Common Peace, or, as Demosthenes
with a clearer view of what Philip would accept urged, to make a separate
peace and alliance and leave the salvation of Phocis to the future:[3] he probably
thought that, if Philip should afterwards attack Phocis, Athens could choose
between her allies and, as in 352, rush to the aid of Phocis. Philip was too skilful
for that. He detained the second embassy until there was no chance of Athens'
going to the salvation of Phocis before Philip and his allies got the state at his
mercy. In 343 Demosthenes pretended that Aeschines had on the 16th of
Scirophorion misled the Athenians into abandoning Phocis, but it is clear that
Philip left nothing to chance.[4] Phocis was caught in a pincer attack of Macedonians and Thessalians at the Gates and of Thebans from the rear. The Peace
of Philocrates had failed. Philip was established in Greece.

No matter what Philip did or did not do, his control of the Gates was a
disaster of the first magnitude for Greek freedom. By denying him the use of
the sea and the land routes into Central Greece Athens might have united
the city-states of Greece and matched the power of the new national state, but
Macedonian control of the Gates was ruinous. Nor was the seeming benevolence
of the new master much consolation. The abuse of Demosthenes and Theopompus[5] does nothing to lessen the obscurity surrounding the person of Philip:
he may have been a calculating, malignant seeker after power whom the high
phrases of the Panhellenist Isocrates merely amused; he may have been in
fact an admirer of Greek civilization, Ἑλληνικώτατος ἄνθρωπος as Demosthenes
sneered (19. 308), with no desire to destroy what had stirred his ancestors to
their dubious claims of Hellenic origin or to a taste for the friendship of eminent
Greeks.[6] But we simply do not know enough about Philip to say, and speculation[7] whether Isocrates influenced him in any way other than by pointing
out the way to win favour in the Greek cities is useless. The evidence does not
afford us an answer. Nor were the Athenians themselves in a very much
better position. Individuals had met Philip and lived in Pella, but the intimate
acquaintance necessary for a knowledge of Philip's intentions was probably
denied them, and when Philip in 346 acted with more lenience and restraint
than the Athenians expected no one at Athens could be sure that this was

---

[1] I wish to thank Mr. G. T. Griffith and
Mr. A. R. W. Harrison for their helpful
criticisms of a first draft of this article.

[2] Cf. Aesch. 2. 36 (τὸν δῆμον καταπεπονη-
μένον καὶ σφόδρα ἐπιθυμοῦντα εἰρήνης) and
37 (defence of the Gates).

[3] Cf. Cawkwell, R.É.G. lxxiii (1960),
416 f.

[4] Cf. ibid. lxxv (1962), 453 f.

[5] F.G.H. 115 T 19 and F 27, 162, 224.

[6] Cf. Hdt. 5. 22 and see Geyer, Makedonien bis zur Thronbesteigung Philipps, ii. 32 f.,
47 f., 97 f., and Cloché, Histoire de la Macédoine, pp. 97–102.

[7] e.g. Wilcken, Philipp II von Makedonien
und die panhellenische Idee, pp. 7 f.

benevolence and not cunning. So it was right for statesmen to distrust. Indeed, even if Philip were to prove truly benevolent and not despotic, the very fact of Macedonian power overshadowing Greece was a menace to her freedom; the more men are conscious of weakness the more prone they are to accept servitude. So on this ground the sooner the Macedonians were thrown out of Greece the better.

In his distrust of Philip Demosthenes was essentially right and no one who believes in liberty will question it. What does requires discussion is whether the means he chose to secure his end were the right ones. This article argues that in 344/3 he chose the wrong means and that the cause of Greek freedom was not best served by its most famous champion. First, however, there are some matters of fact that require discussion.

1. The Persian Appeal of 344/3

It is received opinion, and rightly so, that the Persian appeal to Athens for φιλία and συμμαχία recorded by Philochorus under 344/3 in a fragment[1] quoted by Didymus in his comment on Demosthenes 10. 34 is the same as that recorded by Diodorus (16. 44) as part of the preparation for the final attack on Egypt; and that the Athenian reply, which in Diodorus is a mere refusal of military aid but which Didymus described as ὑπεροπτικώτερον ἢ ἐχρῆν was furnished in a decree to which Philip referred in his ultimatum of 340 ([Dem.] 12. 6). Furthermore, v 'th the publication of Wüst's *Philipp II von Makedonien und Griechenland* in 1938 the chronology seemed stabilized at last. The Persian appeal was to be set in early 343; the Theban and Argive mercenaries joined the Persian army after the sack of Sidon (Diod. 16. 46. 4), ready for the attack on Egypt in late 343 as the waters of the Nile receded.[2] Thus Mazaeus was left in control of his satrapy and recommenced his coinage in the sixteenth year of Ochus,[3] which began in March 343,[4] and Nektanebo was still free in July 343 to dream of coming disaster,[5] but by spring 342 the Persian reconquest of Egypt had dislocated the supply of papyrus to Greece, as Speusippus remarked in writing to Philip.[6] A long debate seemed at an end.

The publication of Jacoby's Commentary on Philochorus has, however, reopened the question. Jacoby pointed out[7] that the fragment of Philochorus was one of those which begin with an archon's name followed by ἐπὶ τούτου, that this showed that it was the first entry in the Atthis for that year and that therefore the Persian appeal should be set not long after the beginning of the archon year 344/3. That these ἐπὶ τούτου entries were what Jacoby claimed has long been recognized,[8] and surely established by Jacoby himself in his *Atthis* (Oxford, 1949).[9] So far only Jacoby has considered the implications for the events of 344/3 and 343/2. He has rejected the evidence for 343/2 as the date of the Persian reconquest and returned to 344/3, the dating of Beloch,[10] but kept the Macedonian embassy of Python, so long synchronized with the Persian appeal, in early 343.[11] In neither of these points is his case satisfactory,

[1] *F.G.H.* 328 F 157.

[2] The annual rise and fall of the Nile at Cairo averages about 14 feet between the minimum in late May and the maximum in mid-September.

[3] Babelon, *Traité des monnaies*, ii. 2, p. 583.

[4] Cf. Roland G. Kent, *Old Persian Grammar*, p. 161.

[5] For the Dream of Nektanebo *vide infra*.

[6] *Vide infra*.

[7] *Commentary*, p. 532.

[8] Cf. Foucart, *Étude sur Didyme*, p. 162.

[9] pp. 94 f.

[10] *G.G.* iii². 2, pp. 284–7.

[11] Loc. cit. in note 7.

and I wish to argue that the right answer is that there was an interval of about eighteen months between the appeal in early 344/3 and the reconquest of Egypt and that Python's embassy should be dated to 344.

(i) *The reconquest of Egypt.* The evidence for dating this in 343/2 is not to be lightly dismissed. The key-piece is the so-called Dream of Nektanebo[1] which represents the king as being at Memphis on the night of 5/6 July 343 and being shown in a dream τὰ ἐνεστηκότα. There is no way of testing the author's standards of accuracy or his concern for historical probability for the background of his story, but it is hard to see why he should have been so precise if the precise date was not of some importance to the story, and if it was so, then he was probably concerned with an incident that was in some degree historical. So it does not get rid of this evidence, as Sordi supposes,[2] to say that Nektanebo may still have been regarded as king after the Persian reconquest, for it seems unlikely that he would be represented as being in Memphis then. It is a teasing bit, but it would need uncommonly cogent arguments for disregarding it, especially when it is supported as it is. The varied figures of the Manethonic tradition have been made to serve all theories[3] and give no real help here. But the letter of Speusippus[4] does help. It is now generally accepted as genuine and dated to 342 by the allusion to Ambracia in § 7. Since it speaks of a shortage of papyrus in Athens due to the Persian reconquest of Egypt (§ 14), the reconquest must be very recent:[5] it is unlikely that trade in papyrus which grew abundantly all along the Nile in ancient times was seriously disrupted for more than the period of the campaign, a matter of a mere two or three months; within a few navigable months after the invasion supplies in Athens would be back to normal. Thus the letter strongly supports the 343/2 dating. Likewise the fall of Hermias of Atarneus. In the Fourth *Philippic* (§ 31), which is to be dated in 341/0,[6] Demosthenes alluded to the arrest: he did not know about his death.[7] So the arrest, which seems in Diodorus' account (16. 52) to follow fairly closely on the reconquest of Egypt, should be put not long before Demosthenes' speech but not long after the reconquest.[8] There would be too long interval between these two events, if the reconquest were earlier than 343/2.

Secondly, the Great King could not have contemplated an attack on Egypt in 344/3. Diodorus and the Letter of Philip ([Dem.] 12) combine to show that the Persian appeal to Athens preceded the attack on Sidon. Philip was explicit (§ 6)—πρὸ μὲν γὰρ τοῦ λαβεῖν αὐτὸν Αἴγυπτον καὶ Φοινίκην ἐψηφίσασθε . . . κ.τ.λ. Diodorus in 16. 44 put the appeal before the king's advance against Sidon (cf. § 3 πρὸ δὲ τῆς τούτων παρουσίας ὁ μὲν βασιλεὺς διεληλυθὼς τὴν Συρίαν . . . κ.τ.λ.). How could he know that the city would fall so easily? When the Persian ambassadors left for Greece in mid-344, he must have expected a longish campaign in subduing Phoenicia, and his request for Greek soldiers would

[1] Text in Wilcken, *Urkunden der Ptolemäerzeit* i, no. 81, English translation in Olmstead, *History of the Persian Empire*, pp. 438 f.

[2] 'La cronologia delle vittorie persiane e la caduta di Ermia di Atarneo, in Diodoro Siculo', *Κώκαλος* v (1959), 109. For a discussion of this attempt to rearrange the whole chronology see Appendix II.

[3] Cf. Kahrstedt, *Forschungen*, pp. 7 f., Beloch, loc. cit., and Sordi, art. cit., pp. 107 f.

[4] The full text is most conveniently found

in Bickermann–Sykutris, *Speusipps Brief an König Philipp* (Sitzungsberichte der Sächsischen Akademie, Phil.-hist. Klasse, 1928). Most of the text is to be found in *F.G.H.* ii A 69, pp. 35–37.

[5] Note 18 to the *Commentary* on F. 157.

[6] See Appendix I.

[7] Ἀνάσπαστος γέγονε καὶ . . . βασιλεὺς . . . ἀκούσεται.

[8] For the dating of Hermias, see Kahrstedt, op. cit., pp. 10 f. For discussion of the views of Sordi, art. cit., see Appendix II.

have been for the following year,[1] by which time the customary naval armament would be ready.[2]

The third and most important point is this. The Greeks in the royal army
amounted to ten thousand (Diod. 16. 44. 2-4). They played a decisive part
in the attack on Egypt and without them the attack could never have taken
place. In 344/3, just as in 401 and 380, Greeks were an indispensable part of
a Persian army fighting against Greek foot-soldiers[3] and Artaxerxes could not
contemplate an attack on Egypt until he was assured that he would have them
in sufficient numbers. Thus it is wholly credible that he should seek them
twelve months in advance (and Persian preparations were always lengthy),
while it is very unlikely that he would leave the first step in recruiting them
until within four months of the start of the march for Egypt. The events of 375
to 373 provide a parallel. The attack on Egypt began in winter 374/3, but the
Persian-dictated peace of 375 was due to the king's decision to attack Egypt
and to collect a suitable mercenary force for the purpose.[4] In 344 Ochus sought
to renew the φιλία and συμμαχία of his father and thus prepare for his new
attempt on Egypt. It is reasonable to suppose that like his father he took this
step in good time.[5] At least, it cannot be proved that he did not.

Thus the new dating for the Persian appeal for help does not involve the
rejection of the date 343/2 for the reconquest of Egypt.

(ii) *The embassy of Python.* There is ample evidence of Macedonian diplomatic
activity in 344/3. (*a*) The *hypothesis* of the Second *Philippic* speaks of an embassy
of Macedonians, Messenians, and Argives which was recorded in the Φιλιππικαὶ
ἱστορίαι, and relates the speech to it.

(*b*) Didymus (col. 8. 8)[6] speaks of an embassy from Philip περὶ εἰρήνης
in 344/3 which coincided with the Persian appeal recorded by Philochorus (in
his first entry for that year).

(*c*) There is ample evidence for the Macedonian embassy of Python of
Byzantium and representatives ἀπὸ τῆς συμμαχίας πάσης ([Dem.] 7. 20 f.,
12. 18; Dem. 18. 136). The Athenian response was to send an embassy to
Philip, which included Hegesippus, to whose part in it Demosthenes alluded
(19. 331) in the prosecution of Aeschines of 343. So, allowing time for the
Athenian embassy, one must put the embassy of Python back into 344/3 or
earlier, and in fact the Second *Philippic* shows that 344/3 is the right date. For
that speech, which is set by Dionysius of Halicarnassus[7] in 344/3, must either
have preceded the embassy of Python or have been actually delivered on the
very occasion of Python's attack on Athenian policy: whatever the business
of that speech, if there had been an earlier occasion when Python had made

---

[1] The Persians knew by experience the
danger of not starting the attack in good
time. Cf. Diod. 16. 43. 4 for the expedition
of 373, which was flooded out.

[2] In addition, the commissariat needed
careful long-term planning. The sort of preparations described in Theopompus F 263
could not be hurried. Cf. Diod. 16. 41. 5 for
the detail of fodder.

[3] Cf. Isoc. 5. 125 f., 4. 135; Xen. *Anab.*
2. 1. 14, 5. 13.

[4] Diod. 15. 38. 1. For the correct date of
the Peace of 375 see my article 'Notes on the
Peace of 375/4' in *Historia* xii (1963), 88 f.

[5] It is to be noted that Diodorus breaks
his narrative after the capture of Sidon and
resumes under a new archon. The general
impression his account makes, however, is
of one campaign. The truth is that his habits
in chronology are such that any precise inferences are dangerous. After all, the only
indication of interval between the expedition
of 351/0 and that of 343/2 is μετὰ δὲ ταῦτα
(16. 43. 1 under 351).

[6] Quoted by Jacoby with Philochorus
F. 157. Notice συμπροσήκαντο.

[7] *Ad Amm.* 10, p. 737.

his complaints and protested Philip's good faith, Demosthenes must have dealt with the matter in his speech. So the embassy of Python cannot have preceded the Second *Philippic* and must have fallen in 344/3.

How are the three related? Those who have dated the Persian appeal early in 343 have been content to identify the embassy in Didymus with that of Python, the embassy of the Second *Philippic* being set in autumn 344.[1] On the other hand, those who have put the Persian appeal in 344 have hardly troubled themselves with what the embassy in Didymus was about and have continued to assign the embassy of the Second *Philippic* to 344 and the embassy of Python to early 343.[2] I wish to propose that all three embassies should be identified, i.e. that Python's embassy happened to coincide with the Persian appeal in early 344/3 and Demosthenes delivered his Second *Philippic* in answer to Python's complaints about unfair attacks on Philip at Athens.

Although our picture of the fullness and range of interest of Philochorus is far from clear, it seems reasonably sure that the Macedonian embassy which prompted the Second *Philippic*[3] would have been recorded in the Atthis, from which indeed it is to be presumed that the dating for the speech given by Dionysius of Halicarnassus was derived. Since the Persian appeal for help was recorded by Philochorus before anything else in 344/3, the Macedonian embassy did not precede that appeal. Since this is so, why does the Second *Philippic* contain no reference to the Macedonian embassy alluded to by Didymus? Jacoby[4] has sought to deny that this embassy of Didymus did literally coincide with the Persian appeal, and has attributed the synchronism to Anaximenes to whom Didymus refers. 'It is obvious that Anaximenes, according to a well-known scheme, combines events not connected as to time nor (at least immediately) as to matter.' This will not do. Didymus refers to Androtion as well as Anaximenes and there is no justification for assuming that what he found in Anaximenes was not also in Androtion and, for that matter, Philochorus: Didymus was commenting on the Persian embassy alluded to in the Fourth *Philippic*, § 34, and there was no need whatsoever to drag in this Macedonian embassy, unless it was synchronized with the Persian appeal in the Atthides. He cites only the part of Philochorus necessary to fix the reference of Demosthenes, but presumably Philochorus proceeded directly to record the Macedonian embassy which coincided in time but merely by chance. So the absence of any reference in the Second *Philippic* to the Macedonian embassy mentioned by Didymus needs explanation. Commonly it is said that, because the Second *Philippic* does not allude to the Persian appeal,[5] the speech cannot be concerned with the Macedonian embassy which happened to coincide with that appeal. This is not cogent. If the Persian appeal had no connexion whatsoever with the Macedonian embassy, there was no reason why Demosthenes could not answer the charges of the latter without alluding to the former. Of course he might well have mentioned the reply made to the Great King and argued that the rebuff to Persia was no reason for not distrusting Philip, but if he chose to confine his speech to answering Macedonian complaints, it need hardly surprise us greatly. Rather, the reverse of this common view is true.

[1] e.g. Kahrstedt, op. cit., p. 15; Pickard-Cambridge, *Demosthenes and the Last Days of Greek Freedom*, p. 315; Wüst, op. cit., p. 65.

[2] e.g. Beloch, *G.G.* iii². 2, p. 290.

[3] G. M. Calhoun, *T.A.P.A.* lxiv (1933),

1 f., rejected the evidence of the Hypothesis to the speech, but has found few supporters. Cf. Wüst, op. cit., p. 57, n. 1.

[4] *Commentary* (on Philochorus F 157), p. 532.   [5] Cf. Beloch, loc. cit.

It is the absence from the speech of any reference to a recent Macedonian embassy περὶ εἰρήνης that is startling. Demosthenes was exposing the sham of Philip's words at the very moment when his troops were said to be going to the Peloponnese. What was more germane to his theme than an embassy that very summer περὶ εἰρήνης? I suggest that the right explanation of Demosthenes' silence about the Macedonian embassy recorded by Philochorus at the start of his account of 344/3 is that the whole speech was Demosthenes' answer to that embassy περὶ εἰρήνης. He did not allude to it as past, for he was answering it in its presence.

Now for Python. There are three important points of similarity. First, he denounced those at Athens who were attacking Philip, as is clear from Demosthenes (18. 136): ὅτε γὰρ Πύθωνα Φίλιππος ἔπεμψε τὸν Βυζάντιον καὶ παρὰ τῶν αὐτοῦ συμμάχων πάντων συνέπεμψε πρέσβεις, ὡς ἐν αἰσχύνῃ ποιήσων τὴν πόλιν καὶ δείξων ἀδικοῦσαν, τότ᾽ ἐγὼ μὲν τῷ Πύθωνι θρασυνομένῳ καὶ πολλῷ ῥέοντι καθ᾽ ὑμῶν οὐχ ὑπεχώρησα, ἀλλ᾽ ἀναστὰς ἀντεῖπον καὶ τὰ τῆς πόλεως δίκαι᾽ οὐχὶ προύδωκα, ἀλλ᾽ ἀδικοῦντα Φίλιππον ἐξήλεγξα φανερῶς οὕτως ὥστε τοὺς ἐκείνου συμμάχους αὐτοὺς ἀνισταμένους ὁμολογεῖν. Similarly the embassy which provoked the Second Philippic, as the Hypothesis (§ 2) says, accused the Athenians ὅτι διαβάλλουσιν αὐτὸν (i.e. Philip) μάτην πρὸς τοὺς Ἕλληνας ὡς ἐπαγγειλάμενον αὐτοῖς πολλὰ καὶ μεγάλα, ψευσάμενον δέ. So in this respect the description of the speech in the Hypothesis fits the account of Python. Secondly, Python came with a proposal for the amendment or extension of the Peace of Philocrates, and this matter of ἐπανόρθωσις was discussed at length by Hegesippus in 342 ([Dem.] 7. 18–32). (This proposal has been interpreted, and probably rightly, by Wüst[1] as being an offer to establish a Common Peace for all the Greeks.) Suggestively, Didymus' embassy of early 344/3 was said to have come περὶ εἰρήνης and the Second Philippic speaks (§ 34) of τοῖς ἐπανορθοῦν τι πειρωμένοις and says (§ 5) εἰ δ᾽ ὅπως τὰ παρόντ᾽ ἐπανορθωθήσεται δεῖ σκοπεῖν . . ., i.e. Demosthenes is dealing with the matter of ἐπανόρθωσις after his own fashion. Thirdly, Python came with ambassadors 'from all of Philip's allies' (Dem. 18. 136), ἀπὸ τῆς συμμαχίας πάσης ([Dem.] 12. 18). From the Hypothesis of the Second Philippic it is clear that Messenian and Argive embassies were present when the speech was made.[2] It is not sure that the Messenians and Argives were allies of Philip by 344, but the speeches which Demosthenes made on his Peloponnesian embassy of 344 and of which he gave the substance in the Second Philippic (§§ 19–26) sought to detach the Messenians and Argives from the φιλία of Philip (§ 26), and make better sense if these peoples had put themselves in the position of the Olynthians (§ 20) and the Thessalians (§ 22) earlier, viz. alliance. Even if these Peloponnesian peoples were not yet allies of Philip, their presence at the right moment shows that other peoples knew that the Macedonians were sending an embassy to Athens to complain. So if Philip took the trouble to summon his Peloponnesian friends, he may well have summoned ἀπὸ τῆς συμμαχίας πάσης.

On these grounds, though certainty is not possible, I dare to conclude that it was Python's embassy to which Didymus referred and which the Second Philippic answered. There are two supporting considerations. First, the speech is general in tone, rather than an answer to the Messenians and Argives. One may notice

---

[1] Op. cit, pp. 69 f.
[2] Dion. Hal. Ad Amm. 10, p. 737, said the speech was delivered πρὸς τὰς ἐκ Πελοπον-νήσου πρεσβείας.

its beginning: ὅταν, ὦ ἄνδρες Ἀθηναῖοι, λόγοι γίγνωνται περὶ ὧν Φίλιππος πράττει καὶ βιάζεται παρὰ τὴν εἰρήνην . . . . The Messenians and Argives play a role as examples; the speech does not seem directed at them particularly. In § 27, just before he gives his suggested response, his plea is to the Athenians not to be duped, and all this is very suitable to a speech concerned with the major issues raised by Python.[1] Secondly, it is wholly credible that Philip did not merely register complaints in 344: the constructive suggestion of the ἐπανόρθωσις is characteristic. Perhaps he had little taste for mere slanging matches.[2]

Some may dispute the identification on the ground that it presupposes too long an interval between the failure of Hegesippus' embassy, which was sent to Pella in answer to Python's appeal, and the prosecutions of Philocrates and Aeschines. But there is little in this. The embassy of Hegesippus presumably took about six or eight weeks and Philip's rejection of the Athenian proposal may not have been known in Athens until mid-344/3. If the result was a reaction against Philocrates which led to his prosecution by Hyperides, it does not follow that Demosthenes immediately attacked Proxenus and then Aeschines.[3] His reference in 343/2 (19. 116 f.) to the trial as recent (πρώην) is fairly vague. The interval between the two trials could be six weeks or six months.[4]

In short, the consequences of Jacoby's fixing the date of the Persian appeal as early as 344/3 are to extend the Persian operations in preparation for the attack on Egypt—not a matter of crucial importance—and to advance the date of Python's embassy to 344. One corollary of this latter point is that the date of Isocrates' *Second Letter to Philip* will need to be moved back to 345. It has been commonly dated[5] to the second half of 344 but Isocrates' remarks (§§ 14 f.) about the attitude of people at Athens to Demosthenes would be inappropriate after the crisis of public opinion occasioned by Python's embassy. The wounding of Philip alluded to in § 11 is shown by the scholiast to Demosthenes 18. 67 and by Didymus col. 12. 63 f. to belong to Philip's Illyrian campaign, but there is no cogent evidence for its date. Diodorus (16. 69. 7) recorded

[1] Wüst, op. cit., p. 65, argued that the Second *Philippic* cannot be Demosthenes' answer to Python because it did not discuss Python's proposals about peace. This is wrong. The whole speech seeks to show the hollowness of the proposals.

[2] Philip preferred charm to abuse. Cf. Cloché, *Un Fondateur d'empire*, pp. 24 f.

[3] One may note the distinctions made by Demosthenes in the Second *Philippic* (§§ 29 and 30). For the attack on Proxenus see Dem. 19. 280 with scholiast, and Din. 1. 63.

[4] One consequence of identifying the embassy of Python with that recorded by Philochorus early in 344/3 is that the period during which Philip's proposal for the amendment of the Peace of Philocrates was under consideration is extended from about twelve to eighteen months: for it was still open when Hegesippus dealt with further offers from Philip in early 342 ([Dem.] 7). Some may find this interval long, but in truth whether it was a matter of my eighteen or the usual twelve months the interval needs

explanation. Although the only evidence, that of the speeches, is not very satisfactory, the position seems to be that, although there was a lapse after the return of Hegesippus' embassy in the course of 344/3 (cf. Dem. 19. 331), the proposal which had been accepted by Athens ([Dem.] 7. 30) might still have been carried out (cf. Dem. 19. 204 and *vide infra*) and was definitely put forward again by Philip in early 342 in the letter (ἐν τῇ νῦν ἐπιστολῇ [Dem.] 7. 34) brought by the Macedonian embassy (ibid., § 1), whose formal business was perhaps the negotiation of σύμβολα (ibid., § 9). After Hegesippus' speech no more is heard of the matter. The negotiations were long and came to nothing because politicians like Demosthenes and Hegesippus kept using them for their own ends, but in itself the long interval of eighteen months is not impossible.

[5] Since Meyer, 'Isokrates' zweiter Brief an Philipp und Demosthenes' zweite Philippika', *S.B. Preuss. Akad.* (phil.-hist. Classe), 1909, pp. 760 f.

it under 344/3, but this is certainly too late just as his notice of the Thracian campaign under 343/2 (16. 71) is too early. So there is no objection to putting the campaign back in 345 where Schaefer put it;[1] there is nothing else known to us that demands the summer of 345.[2] Isocrates' letter can be safely assigned to 345, before either Python's complaints or indeed Demosthenes' spirited attacks on Philip in the Peloponnese—a rather flat epistle in fact, occasioned by news of the wound in war against barbarians of no interest rather than against τὸν βασιλέα τὸν νῦν μέγαν προσαγορευόμενον (§ 11). After 346, 345 was a disappointing year for the old man.

2. THE POWER AND INFLUENCE OF DEMOSTHENES IN 344/3 AND 343/2

It is commonly held that by the time of the trial[3] of Aeschines in 343 Demosthenes and his so-called 'anti-Macedonian party' were in a position of dominance, having routed their opponents of the 'pro-Macedonian party'. This needs modification.[4] Let us consider the position of Demosthenes at particular moments.

(a) *The answer given to Persia in 344.* What was the state of Athenian public opinion early in 344/3 when the city was confronted with appeals from Persia and from Macedon, and what part did Demosthenes play in the formulation of the answers? To answer this it is worth considering the likely attitude of Philip to the Athenian rebuff to Persia.

In his letter to Alexander (Arr. *Anab.* 2. 14. 2) Darius alluded to the φιλία καὶ συμμαχία of his father and Philip. That is the only evidence for it.[5] Some have placed this alliance in the late 350's,[6] but most[7] have supposed that it was part of the Great King's preparations for the attack on Egypt and was accepted by Philip as a safeguard which the Persians were silly enough to afford, thus allowing him a free hand in the Hellespont, and which he could very easily throw aside. It is useless to speculate about what Philip thought, but there is

[1] *Dem. u. s. Z.* ii². 345.

[2] It is common to assign to 345 the foundation of colonies (cf. Wüst, op. cit., p. 54, and Schaefer, op. cit., p. 344, and note Justin 8. 5. 7–6. 1), but these would not have required Philip's presence or the use of his whole military power. On the other hand, on the common hypothesis that he campaigned against the Illyrians in the first half of 344 and intervened in Thessaly in the second, there is barely room for his campaign. Isoc. 5. 21 says that by 346 Philip had mastered the mass of the Illyrians πλὴν τῶν παρὰ τὸν Ἀδρίαν οἰκούντων, and, as Meyer, op. cit., p. 761, remarked, the Pleuratus who wounded Philip on this campaign (Didymus, col. 12, 1. 65) probably dwelt right over near Scodra (cf. Polyb. 2. 2. 4). So a full campaigning season would have been necessary, and this, as well as the argument adduced in the text, argues for 345 as the date of his campaign and the letter of Isocrates.

[3] The date is provided by Dion. Hal. *Ad Amm.* 10, p. 737. Cf. § 11 of the second hypothesis to Dem. 19.

[4] Both in substance and in language. The 'pro' and 'anti' titles recur *ad nauseam* in even the best books, e.g. Wüst; they are useful only when not taken literally. Yet it is easy to slip into the habit of taking them literally, and in general Greek history is bedevilled by the practice, not just with regard to Philip, but almost universally— tyrants, Persia, Sparta, Thebes. A supreme instance is Kahrstedt's view of Demosthenes as the servant of Persian interests. Such crudities are only too frequent. It is best to avoid the 'pro' and 'anti' language which expresses them.

[5] If the story in Plutarch (*Mor.* 342 b, c) about Alexander's dealing with a Persian embassy in Philip's absence is true, it probably belongs to 341 or after. Cf. Wüst, op. cit., p. 89 n. 2. But it is perhaps fictitious.

[6] e.g. Schaefer, op. cit. ii. 33; Pickard-Cambridge, op. cit., p. 191 n. 1.

[7] Cf. Kahrstedt, op. cit., p. 139; Momigliano, *Filippo il Macedone*, p. 139 n. 1; Wüst, op. cit., pp. 89 f. Beloch, op. cit. iii². 1, p. 538 n. 1, puts the alliance after the conquest of Egypt.

one consideration which renders it unlikely that he made any such treaty in
343. The Panhellenist views of Isocrates brought to Philip's attention by the
letter of 346 were probably widely shared. In the course of the century, both at
at Athens and elsewhere there had been many who dreamed of a national
crusade against Persia, and this fact Alexander recognized and suitably exploited.[1] Certainly there was a real fear of Persia at Athens as the speeches of
Demosthenes show. In 354/3 he prefaced his speech against war with Persia
with a concession to popular sentiment—ἐγὼ νομίζω κοινὸν ἐχθρὸν ἀπάντων τῶν
Ἑλλήνων εἶναι βασιλέα (14. 3)[2]—and in 341 he has to urge the city τὴν ἀβελ-
τερίαν ἀποθέσθαι, δι' ἣν πολλάκις ἠλαττώθητε, "ὁ δὴ βάρβαρος, καὶ ὁ κοινὸς ἅπασιν
ἐχθρός," καὶ πάντα τὰ τοιαῦτα (10. 33). Since those who shared this sentiment
were Philip's strongest asset in the Greek cities, it is unlikely that after 346
when he emerged as the leader of Greece he would risk losing their sympathies
by making a treaty with Persia. Not even a secret treaty would have been
safe. Rumours got about, like the rumour of Macedonian negotiations with
Persia in 351 (Dem. 4. 48). Of course, states are prepared to risk alienating
sympathies, as the modern world well knows, if vital interests demand it. But
what had Philip really to gain by making such a treaty in the 340's? Persia was
occupied with Egypt and Philip had no need of the Great King's friendship,
let alone help in war, except in the sense that, by accepting it himself, he might
deny his enemies in Greece the use of it; and in view of the course of events
after 387/6 he had no reason to fear that Persia would physically intervene in
Greece itself. So Philip had no need of the treaty, which in fact proved valueless
in 340. On the other hand, in the late 350's a treaty was of advantage to both
sides. Philip was harbouring dangerous exiles (Diod. 16. 52. 3) and the Great
King had every reason to ensure that Macedonian troops would not assist
any attempts to return while he attacked Egypt in the winter of 351/0. Philip
was not yet strong enough to despise such a treaty, and since Persia had recently[3]
threatened to act against Philip's chief enemy, Athens, φιλία καὶ συμμαχία
was attractive. So it is likely enough that the rumour that circulated at the
time of the First *Philippic* was not without foundation and that the treaty alluded
to by Darius should be set in, or shortly before, 351. But in any case there is
little to be said for placing it in 344/3 or for imagining that when Athens rejected the Persian appeal her Panhellenists had been, or were shortly to be,
disillusioned about Philip as a leader. In fact, according to Philip ([Dem.] 12. 6)
the Athenian answer threatened to summon Philip to the defence of any Greek
city attacked by Persia. We cannot be sure that he had yet formed the plan of
invading Asia; certainly, if he had, the Greek world did not know it, as Isocrates'
letters of 346 and 345 show, together with the fact that Artaxerxes had to torture Hermias of Atarneus to confirm his suspicions;[4] but by 344/3 Philip had

[1] Cf. Arrian, *Anab.* 1. 11. 5–8, 1. 16. 6 f.,
2. 14. 4; Plut. *Alex.* 34.

[2] Cf. Dem. 15. 24.

[3] i.e. at the end of the Social War.

[4] There is no precise evidence about the
development of Philip's plans. There was no
point in warning the Persians. Some have
thought that it was not until he had
triumphed over Greece and founded the
League of Corinth that he turned his
thoughts to Persia: that is why he was not
appointed leader of the war until 336 (Justin
9. 5. 2 ff.). But the story of the torturing of
Hermias (Didymus col. 5, 1. 64 f., *F.G.H.*
124 F 2 and 3) shows both that the Persians
were suspicious and that Hermias probably knew something of the preparations
to which Demosthenes in 341 alluded (10.
32). Indeed the Persians aided Perinthus in
341/0 as a means of checking these preparations (Diod. 16. 75. 1). Some may doubt
whether Philip, despite Isocrates' letters,
had any serious idea earlier than 341 of
attacking Persia, but his very refusal to follow

put himself forward as the defender of Greece and the Athenian decree of that year recognized it.

It is worth remarking that the favourable reception of the Persian appeal by the Thebans and Argives (Diod. 16. 44. 2) does not contradict this conclusion. Thebes could have derived little satisfaction from the fact that Philip's settlement of the Sacred War had established him as the master of Central Greece, a mastery ensured by his control of the Gates (Dem. 5. 20), and it is not surprising that the party led by Timolaos who was blacklisted by Demosthenes (18. 295) for φιλιππισμός was gradually superseded in influence by their opponents, until in 340[1] during Philip's absence on the Scythian campaign the Macedonian garrison was thrown out of Nicaea (Philoch. F 56 B), a very serious matter for Philip. The limited evidence suggests that this was perhaps no sudden change. In 344 there were rumours that there was trouble between Thebes and Philip and that he intended to rebuild the walls of Elatea[2] —mere rumour, of course, but due perhaps to a deterioration in the relations of Philip with Thebes. Shortly after, the position of Phocis appears to have been considerably improved,[3] hardly a matter that could afford much pleasure in Thebes. The truth was that the Persian*occupation of Nicaea was a constant source of suspicion ([Dem.] 11. 4), and by 341 the disagreement was coming into the open.[4] So the right explanation of the Theban response to the Persian appeal may well be that Thebes was prepared as early as 344 to act openly in a way displeasing to Philip. Of course the Thebans may not have perceived so clearly that help to Persia, their ally since 367, was not consistent with alliance with Macedon; but, whatever the explanation of their action in 344, it is not legitimate to argue that their response to Persia shows that Philip was prepared to come to terms with Persia in this period or that Athens rejected Persia because Philip did not.

Similarly with Argos. There was constant stasis (Isoc. 5. 52) and Nicostratus, whom the Great King especially asked for to command the Argive contingent and whom Theopompus (F 124) described as προστάτης τῆς Ἀργείων πόλεως, was not included in Demosthenes' black list (18. 295).[5] So he may have been one of the opponents of Philip who in 343/2 got their city into alliance with

up the victory of 346 was, as the source of Diod. 16. 60. 5 saw, a sign that he was aiming at the domination of more than Greece. Perhaps the vague promises which he was said to have made in proposing the extension of the Peace of Philocrates reflect his plans. Both in the letter he sent with Python and in the letter of early 342 he indicated that he intended to do great things for Athens if she would only work with him ([Dem.] 7. 33–35). I suspect that he was alluding darkly to plans for colonization. Note especially § 35 οὔτ' ἐν τῇ οἰκουμένῃ αἱ δωρειαὶ ἔσονται, ἵνα μὴ διαβληθῇ πρὸς τοὺς Ἕλληνας, ἀλλ' ἄλλη τις χώρα καὶ ἄλλος, ὡς ἔοικε, τόπος φανήσεται, οὗ ὑμῖν αἱ δωρεαὶ δοθήσονται. Readers of Isocrates understood.

[1] Or earlier. See p. 135 n. 1.
[2] Dem. 6. 14.
[3] The cities of Phocis, with the exception of Abae, had been destroyed in 346 (Paus.

10. 3. 1; Dem. 19. 325), but their condition must have changed by 343 when ἀπὸ τῶν ἐν Φωκεῦσι πόλεων πρέσβεις came to support Aeschines (Aesch. 2. 142). Of course, this may be a misleading description, but the cities were rebuilt and, to judge by Demosthenes' allusion to Elatea (6. 14), not long after the peace. By 342/1 there was an archon for Phocis (S.I.G.[3] 231) and there was no Macedonian garrison in the state in 339/8. (Cf. R.-E. xx. 1, col. 490.)
[4] Cf. Dem. 9. 34 for the seizure of Echinus. Also it is to be noted that despite the vague phrase of 8. 63 (Θηβαίους νῦν ὑπάγει), repeated in the Fourth Philippic (§ 64), at 9. 27 Demosthenes speaks as if Thebes as well as Athens was menaced by the 'tyrannies' in Euboea.
[5] He was certainly alive after Chaeronea (Plut. Mor. 760 A and B).
* Read Macedonian in the present reprint. Ed.

Athens (Schol. Aesch. 3. 83) and thus rendered the Greek cause in 338 the negative service of not actively fighting for Philip despite the close ties contracted in 344.[1] If this be the right interpretation, the Argive participation in the embassies of protest to Athens organized by Philip in 344 will have been followed by a change of opinion in Argos so that by the time the Persian ambassadors arrived on their round of Greece Nicostratus was in control.[2] But all this is perhaps to make too much of the Argive action. Argos was Persia's ancient and constant 'friend and ally', and the sending of soldiers to help Artaxerxes may have been felt to be neither contrary nor even relevant to their new alliance with Philip. The city had nothing to gain from Persia save employment for an army no longer needed in the Peloponnese, while from the ancient sterile association Philip had nothing to fear. But whatever the explanation of the aid sent to Persia, there is no justification for arguing that it shows that Athens refused to help because Philip was allied with the Great King. Philip was too good a politician for that.

It is easy to exaggerate the significance of Athens's refusal to help. Certainly Isocrates and his sort must have been greatly relieved by the result; but on the other hand it would be absurd to represent it as a triumph for Philip. Many who had little interest in a Macedonian-led crusade must have shared Isocrates' opinion (12. 159) that to help Persia against Egypt was to enable Persia to act against Greece: this is the opinion expressed in Aristotle's *Rhetoric* (1393[a]) and may well have been that of a majority of Athenians. Nor is there reason to suppose that in 344 Demosthenes wanted to send help to Persia and looked to Persia for help in the future. By 341 the situation had entirely changed. Artaxerxes had at last succeeded in Egypt; in 344 there was little reason to think he would be any more successful than in 351. He had, too, by 341 begun to fear Philip and resorted to the torture of Hermias to find out Philip's plans; the more attention Philip paid to the Hellespontine area, the more Artaxerxes needed to deny his enemy the advantage of the Athenian fleet. So the proposal made in the Fourth *Philippic* (§ 33) developed a passing suggestion of the Third (§ 71), not heard before, and an embassy actually went to seek a defensive alliance ([Dem.] 12. 6).[3] That was the obvious step, once Demosthenes had, as it were, begun hostilities by preventing the recall of Diopeithes. But in 344 there is neither evidence nor probability that he sought actively to court Persian favour. There were two reasons for not doing so. First, even if Persia were successful against Egypt, there was little ground for hope that she would be prepared to help any Greek state with more than a subvention of money.'Although Athens would need money, she would need military aid more. Secondly, if any state did receive help, it was likely to be Thebes which had been the recipient of Persian favours since 367, whereas Athens had been on bad terms with Ochus himself. All in all, it does not seem likely that Demosthenes proposed help for Persia in Egypt.[4]

---

[1] Dem. 18. 64 for Argive neutrality.

[2] By the date of the trial of Aeschines, with Nicostratus and 3,000 hoplites in Egypt (Diod. 16. 44. 1), the position had changed somewhat (Dem. 19. 261), but early in 342 it changed again and the Athenian alliance, then formed, endured (Schol. Aesch. 3. 83).

[3] This embassy of 340 (note the tense of διαλέγεσθε in the *Letter* of Philip) was not successful, for there are no signs in 339/8 that Persia was obliged by ἐπιμαχία to help Athens. No doubt, after the rebuff of 344/3 the Great King was in the mood which he subsequently displayed in the letter to the δῆμος alluded to in Aesch. 3. 238.

[4] Wüst, op. cit., p. 67, professed to discern a change in Demosthenes' attitude towards the Great King between the Second *Philippic*

Conversely, although the evidence is not such as to allow a definite answer, it would appear that the response made to Persia was not proposed by Demosthenes nor made with his active support.[1] In his letter of 340 ([Dem.] 12. 6) Philip declared that on this occasion the Athenians had in their decree threatened, ἂν ἐκεῖνός τι νεωτερίζῃ, παρακαλεῖν ὁμοίως ἐμὲ καὶ τοὺς ἄλλους Ἕλληνας ἅπαντας ἐπ' αὐτόν. The similarity of this decree with the proposal made to the assembly in 354/3 in answer to rumours of Persian military preparations[2] suggests that Philip was giving the substance of the Athenian answer to Persia. Two points suggest that Demosthenes was not behind it. First, it seems unlikely that Demosthenes would have contemplated any sort of military action in co-operation with Macedon. He hated and distrusted Philip too much. Of course, the Athenian reply may not have specifically mentioned Philip; a vague reference to 'allies' need be all that is behind Philip's ἐμέ. But whether Philip was named or not, it would seem unlikely that Demosthenes would have made Philip's co-operation either welcome or possible. Secondly, the decree is so similar to the proposal of Eubulus and Aeschines in 347/6[3] that it is likely that the decree was the work of his opponents. That is, when Python came before the people, Demosthenes had receded from the power and influence indicated by his embassy to the Peloponnese not long before. That it was he who went to plead with Argos and Messene against inviting Philip to intervene in Peloponnesian affairs implies a period of popular favour, but by the date of the Second *Philippic* this was over. His fierce predictions had proved false. He could still repeat them, but instead of arms there was an embassy περὶ εἰρήνης. Philip sent no troops into the Peloponnese before he marched there himself after Chaeronea, and the confident assertions of 344[4] came to nothing if we may judge by the subsequent silence of Demosthenes on this subject. In short, by early 344/3 the prophecies of doom had not materialized and his opponents were again in favour.

(b) *The reception of Python.* The evidence concerning Python's embassy is hardly such as to encourage speculation about Athenian politics in 344, but, since its outcome was of considerable importance in the development of relations between Philip and Athens, some speculation is inevitable. The course

(§ 11) and the speech *On the Embassy* (§ 253), and, since he put the Persian appeal in 343, took this change as a sign that Demosthenes wished to accept the proposed alliance. Since, however, the Persian appeal came in early 344/3, the manner in which he referred to the Great King in the Second *Philippic* (§ 11) supports the view taken in the text. In any case it is doubtful whether Wüst is right to contrast the two passages in the way he does.

[1] The practically universal opinion is that it was Androtion who moved the response to Persia. Cf. Wüst, op. cit., pp. 66 f., and Jacoby's commentary on Philoch. F. 157. The opinion is based on Diels's supplement of Didymus, col. 8, 1. 15 (... ἀφηγοῦν]ται τ[αὖτ]α Ἀνδρο|τίων, ὃς καὶ τ[ότ' εἶπε, καὶ Ἀνα]ξιμένης). Jacoby in the Introduction to his Commentary on Androtion (p. 90, ll. 22 f.) has a great deal to say about the

Panhellenism of Androtion, all resting on this supplement. Is it the right one? εἶπε is hardly the word one would expect to find in a literary source: for δημηγορία it is inept; for mere proposal ἔγραψε would be the historian's word. The supplement has in fact found favour for want of a better. I suggest as no worse at any rate ὃς καὶ τ[ότε παρῆν...] or ὃς καὶ τ[ότ' ἔφυγε...], the former being two letters longer, the latter one, than the supplement of Diels which is itself one letter short of the possible (to judge by the copy of the papyrus on p. 34 of Diels–Schubart, *Didymus*). In any case, there is no need to seek for an explanation of why Didymus quoted Philochorus rather than Androtion or Anaximenes: Philochorus was here suitably brief, and Didymus constantly preferred him.

[2] Dem. 14. 12.   [3] Dem. 19. 10, etc.

[4] Dem. 6. 15 (ξένους εἰσέπεμπει, χρήματ' ἀποστέλλει).

of the decisive assembly is clear enough.[1] Python of Byzantium on behalf of the embassy made a speech in which he presented Philip's complaints and proposals. This was well received by the people (ηὐδοκίμησεν ὁ Π. παρ' ὑμῖν ἐν τῇ δημηγορίᾳ) and probably not just because Python (who had studied under Isocrates[2]) was an able orator. The complaints of Philip about the unjust slanders of Demosthenes and his supporters presumably arose from the recent embassy to the Peloponnese: Philip could claim that he had done no more than promise to give aid to Argos and Messene if they were attacked by Sparta and that this was no more than Athens had promised Messene ten years before.[3] His proposal followed from this: if Athens was unable to see Philip guarantee the peace of the Peloponnese without suspecting that this was a veiled form of conquest, let Athens and Philip agree on the establishment of some sort of system whereby the peace of states like Argos and Messene could be guaranteed without disturbance of the peaceful relations of Athens and Philip. The details of this proposal are somewhat obscure. To judge by what Hegesippus said of it ([Dem.] 7. 30), the idea was, clearly enough, to convert the Peace of Philocrates into a sort of Common Peace, but the form that this was to take is unclear. Yet there is no reason to suppose that Philip was thinking of something like the League of Corinth rather than the sort of peace envisaged by the δόγμα of the Allied Synedrion in 346, whereby it was to be possible for all the Hellenes who wished to be enrolled as participating in the agreement between Athens and Philip.[4] That is, Python proposed amending the Peace in a way worthy of serious consideration. Demosthenes responded, as I have above suggested, with the Second *Philippic* in which he sought to justify his distrust of Philip. Then came a decree which provided for an embassy to go to Philip to discuss his proposal. It gave the embassy two main tasks: the first was to accept the amendment Philip proposed guaranteeing the freedom, autonomy, and peace of all the Hellenes;[5] the second was to demand ἑκατέρους ἔχειν τὰ ἑαυτῶν, i.e. an amendment of the clause whereby Amphipolis had been conceded to Philip. The decree was passed and read out to the ambassadors who received it in silence.

This was a surprising result. Shortly before, perhaps on that very day, the Persian appeal had been rejected in accordance with advice that came from Demosthenes' opponents. Now an embassy, that had come to protest about Demosthenes and whose spokesman had been well received by the people, had been rudely handled. Despite the efforts of Hegesippus to suggest otherwise, neither Philip nor any embassy of his could conceivably have suggested that Amphipolis should return to Athens: the place was essential to the Macedonian empire and any offer to return it would have been so patently insincere that the result would have been to increase the ἀπιστία which Philip was trying to lessen. What emerges from Hegesippus' account is that a general offer to amend the Peace of Philocrates so as to remove the grounds for suspicion was turned into an occasion for demanding the reversal of the result of the twenty-two-year war for Amphipolis so that Athens might recover by treaty what had been irrecoverable by war. Hegesippus could not have hoped for more than a deterioration of Athens's relations with Philip.

[1] [Dem.] 7. 19 ff.
[2] Zosimus, *Vita Isocratis*, p. 256, 91 W., quoted by Jacoby in *F.G.H.* 324 T 2 B.
[3] Paus. 4. 28. 2.
[4] Aesch. 3. 70.

[5] [Dem.] 7. 30 περὶ δὲ τοῦ ἑτέρου ἐπανορθώματος, ὃ ὑμεῖς ἐν τῇ εἰρήνῃ ἐπανορθοῦσθε.... Hegesippus spoke here as if it was Athens who had proposed it, but see §§ 18 and 26.

The question naturally arises whether the decree was in accordance with the προβούλευμα of the council. One detail suggests that it was not. According to Hegesippus ([Dem.] 7. 19) 'in the same assembly Philip's ambassadors addressed the Athenians and τὸ ψήφισμα ἐγράφη'. If it is correct to take this as meaning that the decree was actually drafted in the assembly, it must have differed from the προβούλευμα. A similar situation occurs in Xenophon (*Hell.* 1. 7. 34) where Euryptolemus after a speech to the assembly ἔγραψε γνώμην which he put forward as an alternative to the council's προβούλευμα. Of course, one cannot be sure. Hegesippus may have spoken loosely or deliberately sought to mislead. But if, from the floor as it were, the party attacked by Python were able to carry an important amendment by working on the people's ancient senseless desire for Amphipolis, the sudden change in the influence of the Demosthenes group is explained. One fact supports this suggestion. The Aeschines group were in favour of Python's proposals: Demosthenes said (18. 136) that Aeschines συνηγωνίζετο with Python, and Hegesippus said ([Dem.] 7. 23) that Python spoke ὑπὸ τῶν ἐνθάδε διδασκάλων προδεδιδαγμένος. So those whose advice had prevailed over Persia thought to carry the day in support of Python. Oratory and prejudice defeated them.

It has been assumed earlier in this article that the Persian and Macedonian embassies only chanced to coincide, that the Persians came about Egypt and the Macedonian embassy about Demosthenes' slandering of Philip in the Peloponnese, and that the Athenians only συμπροσήκαντο, as Didymus (col. 8, 1. 10) says, by accident. Yet it is worth pointing out that, if the business of the two embassies was different, the reply made to the Persians perhaps pre-supposed that Python's proposals were to be accepted. That is, the decree to which Philip referred ([Dem.] 12. 6)—ἂν ἐκεῖνός τι νεωτερίζῃ, παρακαλεῖν ὁμοίως ἐμὲ καὶ τοὺς ἄλλους Ἕλληνας ἅπαντας ἐπ᾽ αὐτόν—was made in the belief that the Peace of Philocrates was to be developed into a system of guaranteeing the peace and freedom of all Greek cities. That is why part of the reply to Persia was διαμε[νεῖν] βασιλε[ῖ τὴν φιλ]ίαν, ἐὰν μὴ βασιλεὺς ἐπ[ὶ τὰς] Ἑλληνίδας ἴηι πόλεις—not an allusion, as some have fancied, to the danger threatening Hermias of Atarneus, but rather to the Common Peace proposed by Python and known to the council when it drew up its reply to Persia. Thanks to Demosthenes and Hegesippus, the Common Peace encountered delays. Demos-thenes concentrated on denouncing Philip as wholly untrustworthy, merely alluding (§§ 5 and 34) to the proposal to amend the Peace of Philocrates and turn it into a Common Peace. Hegesippus sought to ensure that nothing could come of the amendment.

(c) *The embassy of Hegesippus.* Demosthenes in his speech *On the Embassy* (§ 331) alluded to the abrupt treatment accorded to Hegesippus: Philip, as might have been expected, would have nothing to do with discussions about Amphipolis. But what became of Philip's proposed ἐπανόρθωσις to which the people had given its approval? There is nothing explicit on the subject, but another passage in the same speech of Demosthenes (§ 204) suggests that when Philip rebuffed Hegesippus he did not simply drop his own proposal. 'Aeschines cannot say that it is to the city's advantage that the Phocians are ruined, that Philip controls the Gates, that the Thebans are powerful, that there are soldiers in Euboea, that Philip is plotting against Megara and that the peace is unsworn (ἀνώμοτον εἶναι τὴν εἰρήνην).' Demosthenes seems to be referring to the situation in 343 and it is most unlikely that he added an allusion to the delay in swearing the peace of 346.[1] So the result of Hegesippus' embassy was that the possibility of ἐπανόρθωσις remained open[2] and if Athens was seriously interested she could recommence negotiations. In early 342 Philip himself sent an embassy to Athens with the same offer, Hegesippus' speech *Concerning Halonnesus* was delivered on that occasion, and as far as we know there were no further efforts by either party to create a system guaranteeing the peace and independence of the minor city-states of Greece.

It has already been noticed that there is no compulsive reason for dating the prosecution of Philocrates very shortly before the prosecutions of Proxenus and Aeschines. The distinction made by Demosthenes, when at the end of the Second *Philippic* (§§ 28 and 29) he demanded the prosecution of his opponents, between the originators of the peace and the Aeschines group shows that not all supporters of the Peace of Philocrates were equally in danger, and the rise of the prosecuting faction was perhaps neither sudden nor wholly due to the rebuff of Hegesippus at Pella. The Common Peace remained possible, and, although the condemnation of Philocrates showed the mood of the people, the acquittal of Aeschines by a narrow margin showed that Demosthenes was not yet supreme. Like Callistratus in 366, Aeschines was discredited, but the power and influence of his opponents was not yet sufficient to achieve all they might wish. The Common Peace remained possible and the people had not yet accepted that a new war was inevitable. Yet the tide was turning.

For the rise of Demosthenes to power in 343 it is necessary to look at events later than the embassy of Hegesippus. The Megarian crisis of that year was perhaps of special importance. At some moment Phocion hastily took an Athenian force to the help of the Megarians (Plut. *Phoc.* 15) and this was probably on the occasion of the crisis several times alluded to by Demosthenes in his attack on Aeschines.[3] Megara was too close for such an event not to be most seriously regarded in Athens, and it seems likely enough that, just as Philip's promises to Messene and Argos in 344 gave Demosthenes the chance to attack the Peace of Philocrates, so too the Megarian crisis gave him the confidence to prosecute Aeschines who had championed the policy of ἐπανόρθωσις.

In short, the failure of the embassy of Hegesippus left Philip free to intervene in Greek affairs, and the more he could be represented as doing so the less hope there was that Athens could create a system to prevent him. In this way the role played by Hegesippus in 344/3 had a decisive effect.

Appendix I

The Date of the Fourth *Philippic*

The Dionysian date[4] for the Fourth *Philippic*, 341/0, was rejected by Körte, *Rh. Mus.* vi (1905), 389 f., on the ground that the speech was prior to the expedition to Oreus (§ 9), which Didymus' commentary showed belonged to Scirophorion 342/1 (col. 1, ll. 13 f.). Cf. Sealey, *R.É.G.* lxviii (1950), 109 f. But this argument is not adequate to discredit Dionysius. In §§ 7–10 of the speech Demosthenes merely reviewed Philip's progress in wrong-doing, a list

---

[1] *Pace* Kennedy, who understood Demosthenes to refer to 'the dilatoriness of the ambassadors' in 346 (*The Orations of Demosthenes*, ii. 180).

[2] This is clear in any case from [Dem.] 7. 30.

[3] §§ 87, 204, 295, 326.

[4] *Ad Amm.* 10, p. 738.

very similar to that which he was later to give in the speech on the Crown § 71 : it is no more inconsistent with Athens having actually intervened in Euboea than, for instance, is the remark about Athens's lack of allies (§ 53) inconsistent with the alliances known to us from the scholiast on Aesch. 3. 83 and elsewhere.

The fact remains that Didymus (col. 1, ll. 29 f.) by using Philochorus appears to have dated the speech in the same year as Dionysius. Presumably he based himself on other internal evidence, notably the proposal to negotiate with Persia (§§ 31–34), which Demosthenes dealt with at some length, having merely touched on it in the Third *Philippic* (§ 71, if indeed he did so at all in the version he delivered—cf. Treves, *R.É.A.* xlii [1940], 354 f., and Sealey, art. cit., pp. 102 f.). Of course, Didymus and Dionysius may have been deceived. The embassy to Persia may belong to 341/0, but not necessarily the mere proposal of such a step. But it is noteworthy that in the Fourth *Philippic*'s advocacy of appeal to Persia there is an element not to be discerned in the Third, viz. the allusion in § 31—οἷς βασιλεὺς πιστεύει καὶ εὐεργέτας ὑπείληφεν ἑαυτοῦ, οὗτοι μισοῦσι καὶ πολεμοῦσι Φίλιππον—and this may well have furnished an argument for dating the speech in 341/0. It is most mysterious to us : Mr. G. T. Griffith has suggested (by letter) that the reference is to Memnon and Mentor of Rhodes and that the explanation of the word πολεμοῦσι may lie in the allusion made by Alexander in his letter to Darius (Arrian, *Anab.* 2. 14. 5) to a Persian force sent to help the Thracians against Philip. Whether this suggestion is the right one or not,[1] we have no means of knowing, but probably the κοιναὶ ἱστορίαι would have made the matter plain.

Another point worth considering is the contrast between the remarks Demosthenes made in the spring of 341 (8. 52 f.) about finance and his discussion of the Theoric distributions in the Fourth *Philippic* (§§ 35–45) : in the former Demosthenes is still adopting the tone of his earlier speeches (cf. § 66 f.), in the latter finance has ceased to be a problem. I suggest that the solution is that in 341/0 the Demosthenes group gained control of the financial administration. As I have argued elsewhere,[2] re-election to the Theoric Commission was perhaps permitted and customary before the law of Hegemon, and Demosthenes' supporters may have been in control of the Commission from the start of 341/0 to 337/6, the year in which Demosthenes himself is known to have been a Commissioner (Aesch. 3. 24). The law of Hegemon perhaps belongs to 337/6 :[3] it certainly lessened the importance of the Commission (ibid., § 25) and Mr. D. M. Lewis[4] has made the splendid conjecture that the law recorded

[1] Both Memnon and Mentor were probably 'enrolled as benefactors' of the king (cf. *R.-E.* xv, cols. 652 and 964) and Demosthenes' words in 10. 31 are perhaps best applied to individuals. Further, as Mr. Griffith has pointed out, the Persian help to Thrace, mentioned in Alexander's letter, probably preceded the attack on Perinthus, by which time Philip had completed the conquest of Thrace (Diod. 16. 71 and 74) ; so 341 is a suitable date for the Persian help. The only other serious possibility seems to me to be the Thebans, who had rendered the king such signal service in the recovery of Egypt, and whom he had favoured

amongst the Greeks since 367. But other references to Thebes in the speech (§§ 64 and 67) do not support this, and, although Theban relations with Philip were no doubt deteriorating, πολεμοῦσι would be far too strong a word. So I much prefer Mr. Griffith's suggestion, which goes beyond the similar explanation of the passage by Croiset (in the Budé edition, *Harangues* ii. 128).
[2] In a forthcoming article on Eubulus in *J.H.S.* lxxxiii (1963).
[3] It is prior to 335/4 (Bus.-Swob. *G.S.*, p. 1043 n. 1).
[4] In a paper not yet published.

M [161]

in Plut. *Mor.* 841 b (μὴ πλείω πέντε ἐτῶν διέπειν τὸν χειροτονηθέντα ἐπὶ τὰ δημόσια χρήματα) is none other than the law of Hegemon itself. Whether this is correct or not, Hegemon, who was an opponent of Demosthenes (Dem. 18. 285), may have aimed, in part, at breaking the hold of Demosthenes over the financial system, which had begun in 341/0 and which accounts for the change of heart shown in the Fourth *Philippic*. For us this must remain unverifiable conjecture, but the careful student of the speech in antiquity may not have been so limited.

It is to be noted that Didymus' discussion of the date of the speech is very fragmentarily preserved and breaks off in tantalizing fashion at the head of column 2 with the remark that 'some' say that the speech was composed in 342/1.[1] What the reasons for this divergence were we cannot know: perhaps there was no more to it than the fact that large parts of the speech are identical with parts of orations 8 and 9. Anyhow Didymus knew what 'some' said and rejected it. He may have erred.[2] Dionysius may have erred. But Körte's inference from § 9 hardly suffices to prove it.

APPENDIX II

SORDI'S REDATING OF THE PERSIAN CONQUEST OF EGYPT

The latest discussion of the chronology of the Persian reconquest of Egypt is that of M. Sordi in Κώκαλος v (1959), 107. Since her results are wholly rejected in the text of the present article, it is perhaps proper to explain why.

The central point in her discussion is that the Babylonian tablet which is no. 28 in Strassmaier, *Actes du 8ème Congrès des Orientalistes* (translated by Sidney Smith, *Babylonian Historical Texts*, pp. 148 f.)[3], and which speaks of the arrival in Babylon in October 345 of prisoners 'whom the King carried away from Sidon' is accepted as proof that Sidon was captured in 345 and indicating that Egypt was conquered in winter 345/4. In consequence Sordi dissociates the Persian appeal to Greece for help recorded by Diodorus (16. 44. 1) from both the embassy of 344/3 of Philochorus F 157 and the Panhellenist decree of [Dem.] 12. 6,[4] and sets it in 345. In support of all this, she revives the view that Hermias of Atarneus, who was certainly enough arrested by the Persians after the conquest of Egypt (Diod. 16. 52. 5), was arrested in 345/4. This view is based on a combination of Strabo 13, p. 610, who says that Aristotle left Atarneus when Hermias was arrested, and of Dionysius of Halicarnassus, *Ad Amm.* 5, who dates Aristotle's departure to 345/4.

This arrangement seems unsatisfactory for the following reasons:

(i) The Fourth *Philippic*, § 32, shows that at the date of that speech Demosthenes did not know that Hermias had been put to death, but merely that

---

[1] How far into columns 2 and 3 of the papyrus the discussion of dating extended we cannot know. The reference to Byzantium in line 23 of column 2 and to the Great King in line 28 may belong to it: certainly there is nothing in the early part of the speech which elucidates the remains of the summary of the contents of the column given at the top, and so the contents of the column may well be part of the introductory remarks.

[2] As he would appear to have done in the dating of Dem. 13 (cf. col. 13 of the papyrus).

[3] There is another translation in Olmstead, op. cit., p. 437.

[4] Sordi contends that this decree was not passed in answer to a Persian appeal, but in the Panhellenist high spirits of the δῆμος in late 347/6. If this were right, Artaxerxes need not have subsequently asked whether Athens kept her φιλία.

he had been taken up to Susa—βασιλεύς ... ἀκούσεται. So 345/4 is much too early for his arrest.[1]

(ii) Nektanebo may still have been regarded as king after the conquest, but this observation does not render the Dream pointless. What is surprising in this document is not so much that it represents Nektanebo as king in mid-343 as that it represents him as king in Memphis (dreaming of τὰ ἐνεστηκότα). The man who wrote this story either knew or pretended that in mid-343 Nektanebo was still ruling in Lower Egypt. One may disbelieve it but it is not irrelevant.

(iii) If Egypt was reconquered in 345/4, the consequent shortage of papyrus to which Speusippus alluded in March 342 was curiously delayed, or rather Speusippus chose a curiously gauche way of ending his letter!

(iv) If Egypt was reconquered in winter 345/4, since Hermias was arrested by Mentor, who had been the successful general in Egypt (Diod. 16. 51. 1 and 5), it is most unlikely that he was free from his command in Egypt in time to deal with Hermias within the same archon year.

(v) If Artaxerxes had appealed to Athens for help in 345/4, his asking in 344/3 (Philoch. F 157) whether Athens was prepared to be friendly with him as she had been with his father (ἀξιοῦντος τὴν [φι]λίαν [διαμενεῖ]ν ἑαυτῶι τὴν πατρώιαν) would have been very odd. According to Sordi, he had already received an affirmative reply to this question (Diod. 16. 44. 1). What was the point of asking the question in 344/3 in this way, viz. about τὴν φιλίαν τὴν πατρώιαν? What was the purpose of asking a second time? 'That he did desire something we may assume without hesitation : one does not send an embassy merely to ask whether "the friendship still continued" unless the factual political situation makes such a question necessary or desirable' (Jacoby ad Philoch. F 157). On the orthodox view, Artaxerxes in 344/3 asked the question for the first time and because he sought help for Egypt. On Sordi's view, the question is otiose and gratuitous.

There remains the problem of the Babylonian tablet, which for seventy years has been not so much disregarded (cf. Beloch, G.G. iii. 2, p. 286 n. 1) as discounted by reason of the weight of other evidence. Sordi's article has not disturbed the balance and, if the date of this tablet has been rightly read, either the tablet must be related to preliminary operations or the narrative of Diodorus must be wrong in setting the Persian appeal to Athens before the fall of Sidon. The tablet is odd in certain respects[2] and perhaps it is better not to interfere with Diodorus. But there is a serious question about the reading of this tablet. Mr. E. Sollberger of the British Museum has kindly inspected the tablet for me and reported about the reading of the numerals as follows : 'The only thing that is beyond any doubt is the numeral "4". What precedes it could be the numeral 10, thus making 14, but I am not at all sure that it is, in fact, 10. It rather looks to me as if it were the end of the sign Mu which is the logogram for "year". The tablet would thus be dated to the fourth year of the king. . . . I think this is the most likely reading.' If this is correct, our problem is to relate

---

[1] So either Strabo is wrong in saying that Aristotle left when Hermias was arrested or Dionysius has the wrong date.

[2] Mr. E. Sollberger points out that the king is referred to as 'Ochus, who is called Artaxerxes' whereas one would have expected the Babylonian scribe to give the Greek name as the alternative one. Again, as Mr. P. A. Hulin has pointed out to me, in mat Si-da-nu first the determinative mat indicating 'country' or 'district' as opposed to 'town' is rare, and secondly the usual spelling is Si-dun-nu.

the tablet to events in 355, and lies outside the scope of the present article. Yet it may be worth noticing one piece of evidence which shows that the Persians intervened in Sidon more often than Diodorus tells. Hieronymus *ad Jovinianum* 1. 45, in describing the death of Strato of Sidon, says: 'Strato regulus Sidonis manu propria se volens confodere, ne imminentibus Persis ludibrio foret, quorum foedus Aegyptii regis societate neglexerat, retrahebatur formidine . . .', etc. This connexion between Strato and the king of Egypt is supported by the fact that in 360 Tachos fled first to Sidon (Xen. *Ages.* 2. 3).[1] Furthermore, the discussion of R. P. Austin in *J.H.S.* lxiv (1944), 98 f., shows that the nearer to 355 we set the decree honouring Strato (*I.G.* ii.[2] 141) the better, epigraphically speaking. Therefore it may be suggested that these Sidonian captives of the Babylonian tablet were taken during the Persian intervention in Sidon to deal with Strato's disloyalty. Of course, the tablet says that it was Artaxerxes who sent the captives and we do not know that he was in Phoenicia in 355 or earlier.[2] Yet we do not know that he was not. His order to the satraps of Asia Minor to dismiss their forces was shortly before 355 and was, surprisingly, obeyed (Schol. Dem. 4. 19). Perhaps he was close at hand dealing with Phoenicia.

This is mere hypothesis. The important point is that the Babylonian tablet on which Sordi relies for her theory is far from plain in its bearing, and I reject her theory utterly.

University College, Oxford   G. L. CAWKWELL

(To be concluded)

[1] For the chronology of Tachos see Kienitz, *Die politische Geschichte Ägyptens*, pp. 175 f.

[2] Babelon, *Traité des monnaies*, ii. 2, p. 582, assigned the coins of Mazaeus bearing the number 1 to 4 to the first years of Artaxerxes Ochus. Leuze, *Die Satrapieneinteilung*, pp. 236 f., argued strongly that these coins relate to the reigns of Arses and Darius. If

perchance Babelon were right, the series would end in the year of our tablet, and it might be that the intervention of the Great King in Phoenicia in 355 led to the confinement of Mazaeus to Cilicia and the appointment of Belesys to Syria (for whom see Leuze, op. cit., pp. 350 f.). However, Leuze is probably correct about the dating of these coins.

DEMOSTHENES' POLICY AFTER THE PEACE OF PHILOCRATES. II

The Intervention of Philip in the Affairs of Greek Cities

It is perhaps worth briefly discussing a subject on which Demosthenes has so much to say and on which there is so little satisfactory evidence. In every speech which he delivered after 346 he referred, in greater or less detail, to breaches of the Peace of Philocrates, and this insistence on Philip's ἀδικία may mislead us. The case of Cardia is suggestive. In 341, in the speech *On the Chersonese*, he sought to create the impression that Philip was acting in breach of the peace by sending troops to help defend Cardia against Diopeithes: ἐγὼ δ᾽ οἶδ᾽ ἀκριβῶς ὅτι οὐ γράψαντος Ἀθηναίων οὐδενός πω πόλεμον, καὶ ἄλλα πολλὰ Φίλιππος ἔχει τῶν τῆς πόλεως καὶ νῦν εἰς Καρδίαν πέπομφε βοήθειαν (§ 58).[1] In the Third *Philippic* the climax of the list of Philip's acts of ὕβρις (§§ 32 f.) is his possession of Cardia: οὐχ ἡμῶν, ἐῶ τἆλλα, ἀλλὰ Χερρονήσου τὴν μεγίστην ἔχει πόλιν Καρδίαν; In § 16 Philip is said to be committing a breach of the peace ἡνίκ᾽ εἰς Χερρόνησον, ἣν βασιλεὺς καὶ πάντες οἱ Ἕλληνες ὑμετέραν ἐγνώκασιν εἶναι, ξένους εἰσπέμπει καὶ βοηθεῖν ὁμολογεῖ καὶ ἐπιστέλλει ταῦτα. Demosthenes was not alone in such a view, as the remarks of Hegesippus ([Dem.] 7. 41–44) show, and presumably the people were only too ready to accept it, but the truth is clearly otherwise. Cardia had been an ally of Philip before the Peace of Philocrates, as he remarked in his letter of 340 (§ 11), and the city had been explicitly listed as an ally of Philip in the Peace as Demosthenes himself had earlier acknowledged (5. 25). Nor was this a novelty, for in 353/2, when Cersobleptes handed over the Chersonese, Cardia was excepted (Diod. 16. 34. 4). The truth is that the Cardians claimed their territory for themselves, refused to allow the restoration of the fifth-century cleruchy within it, and were by reason of their geographical position able to maintain their independence. The Peace of Philocrates simply forced Athens to recognize what had long been the case.[2] But if Demosthenes could speak as he did about Cardia, his statements about cases where we are less informed should be treated with great caution.

Further it is to be noted that he could confidently assert what was probably at best mere rumour. For instance, in the Second *Philippic* (§ 15) he said τοῖς Μεσσηνίοις καὶ τοῖς Ἀργείοις ἐπὶ τοὺς Λακεδαιμονίους συλλαμβάνειν οὐ μέλλει, ἀλλὰ καὶ ξένους εἰσπέμπει καὶ χρήματ᾽ ἀποστέλλει καὶ δύναμιν μεγάλην ἔχων αὐτός ἐστι προσδόκιμος, but in subsequent speeches nothing is ever heard of these mercenaries or this money—not a word in the speech *On the Embassy*, where one would most expect it. It seems safe to conclude that in 344 Demosthenes went beyond the facts. Similarly, the assertion that Philip Γεραιστῷ ἐπιβουλεύων διατελεῖ (19. 326) is probably a mere guess. In an age when communications were slow, even disinterested persons were at the mercy of rumour, as Demosthenes himself noted (4. 47 f.), and since it was Demosthenes' aim to incite the people against Philip he had no reason to be cautious or moderate in what he said. He may have been right to pay little regard to the details of the truth in

---

[1] Cf. § 64.   [2] Cf. Dem. 23. 169 for Cardian hostility to Athens at an earlier date.

serving a good cause, but it is perhaps worth one's while to estimate the extent of his misrepresentations.

First, the matter of the Thracian fortresses, not mentioned in the Second *Philippic*, but constantly from 343 onwards.[1] After that year he confined himself to Serrium and Doriscus and gave no indication of when they were captured, but from the speech *On the Embassy* (§ 156) it would appear that it was during the Thracian campaign of 346. Philip left on this campaign immediately after his discussions with the First Embassy, having entered into an agreement that he would not touch the Chersonese, ἕως ἂν ὑμεῖς περὶ τῆς εἰρήνης βουλεύσησθε (Aeschin. 2. 82). So the Athenians knew well that he was attacking Cersobleptes' kingdom, which included Doriscus and Serrium.[2] There may have been in some of the fortresses mercenary forces under Athenians which might by a stretch of imagination have been regarded as Athenian forces,[3] but since Philip had not agreed to more than μὴ ἐπιβήσεσθαι μεθ' ὅπλων Χερρονήσου, and since he was still at war with Athens, he was free to conduct operations against any allegedly Athenian forces outside the Chersonese. The only possible ground for debate concerned the date of capture, and it would appear that it was precisely on this issue that the embassy of Euclides was sent to Philip (Dem. 18. 70). It was easy for Philip to answer. By the 24th of Elaphebolion Cersobleptes had lost his kingdom and the Sacred Mount had been captured, as the Athenians well knew from Chares' letter (Aeschin. 2. 90), and although the peace was voted on the 19th the Athenians did not swear until the 25th (Aeschin. 3. 73). Even if some of these places had been taken after that date, until Philip had himself sworn he was probably not bound by the Peace of Philocrates. This was in fact part of his reply to Euclides (Schol. Dem. 19. 162), and Philip had no reason to fear the results of arbitration, to which he professed himself ready to submit ([Dem.] 7. 36 f.). But his case did not rest solely on calculation of dates. These forts were not, as far as we know, in any way Athenian possessions, and the Peace concerned only the members of the Second Athenian Confederacy, not such allies as Cersobleptes, whom Demosthenes took care to have excluded from the oath-swearing (Aeschin. 2. 83–85, 3. 73 f.). Nor was the subsequent claim that Cersobleptes had been given Athenian citizenship of any value;[4] it required considerable effrontery to interpret honorific grants in this way, but in any case the reply which Philip gave in his *Letter* of 340 (§ 8 f.) shows just how weak the case of Hegesippus and Demosthenes was. The plain truth is that the capture of Serrium, Doriscus, and the other forts was in no sense a breach of the Peace of Philocrates. Demosthenes is just not truthful. It is noteworthy that these allegations are not made in the Second *Philippic* of 344. Only when the tide of popular favour had turned to his advantage did he begin to urge such an empty claim.

Euboea was a different matter. According to Demosthenes (9. 33 and 58), Philip sent Hipponicus at the head of one thousand mercenaries, who destroyed

---

[1] Save in the Third *Philippic*. Aeschines (3. 82) mocked Demosthenes for his obsession with these forts, so important to Athens that no one had ever heard their names before.

[2] Note ἐν εἰρήνῃ καὶ σπονδαῖς (Dem. 19. 156).

[3] Schaefer, op. cit. ii. 246, presumed there were Athenian forces in these forts. There is no evidence that this was so. If the forces were

mercenary and paid by Cersobleptes, it would have needed a Demosthenes to pronounce them Athenian.

[4] According to Philip ([Dem.] 12. 8) this claim was actually stated in decrees of the δῆμος. In 341 Cersobleptes was still no more than 'your ally' (Dem. 10. 8). The more secure Demosthenes' power became, the less did he need to regard the truth.

the walls of Porthmus, the port where the pro-Athenian party of Eretria had taken refuge; other mercenaries took Oreus and established Philistides in power, and prevented the return of the Eretrian exiles (9. 33, 59–62). A fragment of Carystius[1] in part confirms this, and the precise detail of Demosthenes shows that Athens was faced with a most serious situation in Euboea. So it is important to determine as far as possible what happened.

In March 342 Callias of Chalcis with the co-operation of Demosthenes attempted to include Oreus and Eretria in a Euboean League and at the same time to ally the League with Athens.[2] Since Aeschines could later accuse Demosthenes of taking bribes from the three states to secure this end,[3] presumably the movement was for the moment successful. By the date of the Third *Philippic* relations with Callias, the champion of Euboean independence, and Eretria and Oreus had gone sadly wrong, and Macedonian troops had established the opponents of Callias in power (§§ 57–62). Now if we compare what Demosthenes had to say in 341 with what he had said two years previously at the trial of Aeschines it is clear that the nature of the Macedonian threat in Euboea had changed a good deal in the interval. His charges in 343 were very general: the Euboeans were an 'accursed lot', Philip was securing bases, troops were in the island, and there were frequent rumours that Porthmus was to be attacked;[4] but nothing of the precise details of 341. So there is a strong case for putting the actual intervention later than the trial of Aeschines. Indeed, the speech of Hegesippus *On Halonnesus*, which belongs in early 342, at much the same time as Callias and Demosthenes were busy with the promotion of the Euboean League, suggests that none of the acts of violence that Demosthenes described a year later had yet occurred.[5] In § 32 Hegesippus could muster only a poor array of Macedonian abuses of autonomy. If anything so precise as a military intervention had happened in Euboea, surely he would have mentioned it. The likely interpretation of the evidence is this: in 343 Euboeans generally looked to Philip for the maintenance of their independence; early in 342 they all turned to Athens as guarantor of a Euboean League;[6] in the course of 342 the League either could not or would not cure the stasis in Oreus and Eretria, and Philip took his opportunity. What is notable is that he did not take it earlier. The speech of Hegesippus was aimed at rejecting a further appeal for the amendment of the Peace of Philocrates in the manner proposed by Python; before that Philip abstained from Euboea.

The suspicions aroused by Demosthenes' statements in 343 about Euboea affect us elsewhere. He implied that troops in Euboea were from Macedon

---

[1] In Athenaeus 508 e.

[2] Aesch. 3. 91–104. See Appendix III.

[3] Aesch. 3. 103.

[4] Dem. 19. 75, 204, 219, 326. , 8 ?

[5] So Wüst, op. cit., p. 110, in answer to Kahrstedt, op. cit., p. 72. The only real difficulty arises out of Demosthenes' account of Philip's acts of ἀδικία in 10. 8 and 9. He seems there to be following chronological order and he puts the destruction of Porthmus before the Megarian affair of summer 343 (*vide supra*). Yet in a similar review in 18. 71 he puts the destruction of Porthmus not only after the Megarian affair, but also after the Macedonian occupation of Oreus.

Comparison of the two passages suggests that in 10. 8 and 9 he compressed a whole series of events concerning Eretria and misdated it. If this were not so and the destruction of Porthmus by Macedonian troops belonged to 343, both the silence of Hegesippus and Athens' negotiations with Clitarchus would be hard to explain.

[6] Aeschines' statement (3. 90) that Callias turned to Athens παραγγελλομένης ἐπ᾽ αὐτὸν ἤδη στρατείας need not be taken seriously. If there were anything much in it, one would have expected more about it from Demosthenes.

(19. 204), but nothing happened until 342, and probably he was merely referring to mercenary troops kept by certain cities that had been friendly to Macedon since the Athenian expedition of 348. Similarly one might question whether the mercenaries used by Perillus in his attempt on Megara really were from Macedon, as Demosthenes asserted (19. 295). The silence of Hegesippus is again suggestive, and the account in Plutarch (*Phoc.* 15) commonly referred to the expedition of 343 makes no mention of Philip or Macedon. The popular agitation reflected in the speech *On the Embassy* may have gone far beyond the facts. Elis is another case. In 343 Demosthenes attributed the recent bloody revolution to the Philippizers (19. 260 and 294). In 341 he alluded to it as a recognized act of Philip (10. 10). In short, Demosthenes was not constrained by a strict regard for truth.

The result of this consideration of the allegations of Macedonian interference in Greek affairs is that Philip did not transgress the Peace of Philocrates as Demosthenes constantly alleged, nor did he physically intervene in the affairs of any Greek city before the collapse in early 342 of his proposals to amend the Peace. In truth, the situation was far more serious than that. In many states the sanction of independence or power was found in friendship with Philip, once he had broken through the natural defences of Greece. In 344 Argos and Messene sought his protection against Sparta; but the following year Elis and many of the Arcadians had come out in favour of Philip. The Euboean cities and Megara were also enmeshed. In 344/3 and 343/2 it was this spread of popularity that menaced Greece. Unless some system of κοινὴ εἰρήνη could be evolved that made Athens the guarantor of freedom, Philip was likely to be called on to act in her stead.

The causes of support for Philip were various. In the Peloponnese fear of Sparta played the major part, as the events of 344 showed. Elsewhere friendship with Macedon seemed the best guarantee of independence: this was probably the case with the Euboean cities before 342. Political parties too sought Philip's friendship in the struggle for power, as in Megara, and in Oreus and Eretria in 342. Wherever there was division, Macedonian diplomacy found its opportunity. But it would be false to posit that Philip was always the friend of the faction opposed to the δῆμος. Things were not as simple as that. In Oreus Philistides was the popular leader (Dem. 9. 61) and Euphraeus, whom Demosthenes lauds, had fought a lone battle against Macedonian influence after he had himself lived in Macedon and returned disillusioned and out of favour (Athenaeus 506 e). The use of the word τύραννος should not mislead us. It was a term of abuse for political leaders who pursued distasteful policies. Callias of Chalcis was said by Aeschines (3. 89) to have aimed at a tyranny; his brother, Taurosthenes, is said by Dinarchus (1. 44) to have enslaved Euboea. This was abuse of Demosthenes by way of abuse of his friends: it had nothing to do with the political divisions of Chalcis. To judge by the terms used by Demosthenes in the Second *Philippic* in his report of his speech to the Messenians (especially §§ 21 and 24) Messene was a democracy in 344, and as far as we know there was no revolution there before the League of Corinth was formed; but the speaker of [Dem.] 17 called the sons of Philiades 'tyrants' (§§ 4 and 7).[1] In short the use of the word by Demosthenes means very little: the same state is said at one moment to be under one tyrant, at

[1] The sons of Philiades were the only Messenians named by Demosthenes in his black list of guilty men (18. 295).

another to have five.[1] The sweeping statement made by Demosthenes in the Fourth *Philippic* (§ 4) is no more than a crude assumption that all who oppose his particular policies do so for corrupt reasons. Elsewhere (19. 259) he has to complain that the friends of Philip in the cities have popular support.[2]

For the success of Philip in winning supporters in Greece Demosthenes found a simple explanation in bribery. Generally the accusation is unsupported by evidence[3] but in the case of Athens he is specific. The origin of all his complaints would seem to lie in the events of Scirophorion 346: he held that Athens should have voted on the sixteenth of that month for an expedition to help Phocis and that, since Aeschines played a leading part in the decision to abandon Phocis, he must have acted from corrupt motives; since, too, the net result of the Peace was that Philip entered Greece unopposed, Philocrates as its author must also have been in Philip's pay.[4] This view was not confined to Demosthenes. In 342 Hegesippus ([Dem.] 7. 23) asserted that Philip spent large sums of money in 346 to get the terms he wanted, and Hyperides (4. 29 f.) emphasized the charge of bribery in his attack on Philocrates. Presumably it was the explanation of Philip's success current among the supporters of Demosthenes. Likewise it was the view of the author of the *Philippica* which was the source of Diodorus 16. 54. 3 f., and, whatever sober contemporaries thought, Philip became by repute *maiore ex parte mercator Graeciae quam victor* (Val. Max. 7. 2. 10).[5]

Bribery and corruption were common enough in Greece, if one is to judge by the frequency of the accusation,[6] and no doubt Philip, like the Great King, made gifts to ambassadors.[7] He may, for all we know, have gone further than this.[8] But it is highly doubtful whether bribery was of especial importance in the extension of his power. Demosthenes could hardly allude to his opponents without adding an allusion to their alleged treachery, but there is no reason to believe that Aeschines' policy in 346 was in any way due to corruption. The development of his policy in 346 is wholly explicable without the hypothesis of bribery, and in particular the charge that he used his influence to prevent the salvation of Phocis in Scirophorion is groundless, as a study of Demosthenes himself shows.[9] Nor are the accusations that Philocrates and Aeschines acquired land in Olynthian territory,[10] or Aeschines in Boeotia, as the rewards of treachery, of any value.[11] They may contain no truth whatsoever,[12] but, even if individuals did acquire land in these areas, there is no proof that they were given in return for political services. Philocrates is a shadowy figure, but we know enough about Aeschines to see that there was nothing whatsoever in Demosthenes' charges, certainly nothing which a court would accept as evidence, for he continued in public life long after his opponents gained the

---

[1] Oreus. Cf. Dem. 9. 59 and, for example, 8. 36.   [2] Cf. 18. 46.
[3] 9. 37; 18. 61, 247; 19. 259, 300.
[4] There are literally dozens of references bearing on these accusations.
[5] Cf. Horace, *Odes* 3. 16. 13 f.; Plut. *Aem. Paul.* 12; Cic. *ad Att.* 1. 16. 7.
[6] Cf. Dem. 19. 294, where it is said that there was bound to be corrupt practice in Megara. Aeschines accused Demosthenes of taking bribes (3. 103)—a foretaste of accusations to come.

[7] Dem. 19. 139; Theopompus F 162 μᾶλλον ἐν ταῖς συνουσίαις ἢ ταῖς δωρεαῖς.
[8] Cf. Cloché, op. cit., p. 26.
[9] See my article, 'Aeschines and the ruin of Phocis in 346', in *R.É.G.* lxxv (1962), 453.
[10] 19. 145.
[11] 18. 41.
[12] The fact that Demosthenes called Olynthians to bear witness to his statements about Philocrates (19. 146) is not very impressive; Demosthenes was suspected of fabricating evidence (Aeschin. 2. 154 f.).

favour of the people. If, then, Demosthenes was so wrong about Athens, is he to be taken seriously in his general charges? Polybius (18. 14) vigorously dissented from the Demosthenic view. The causes of Philip's success were more serious than mere corruption, and Demosthenes in his charges exhibited no more than a readiness to attribute moral turpitude to those who disagreed with him and, possibly, a serious failure to understand what was afoot in Greece.

In short, the sum total of Philip's actual interventions in the affairs of Greek cities in 344 to 342 was very slight. In support of this conclusion, one may cite the policy of Philip with regard to the activities of Diopeithes in the Chersonese. In the summer of 342[1] he was sent out as general to supervise the establishment of new cleruchs[2] to replace those who had gone home to Athens in the years before the Peace.[3] The exact date of his departure is not known, but perhaps he was sent partly as a precaution against Philip, who in the later months of 343/2 began his Thracian campaign.[4] Before that year ended, if we may trust the Scholiast on Aeschin. 3. 83, Diopeithes became involved in hostilities with the Cardians, who had been named in the Peace of Philocrates as allies of Philip.[5] Of course, these hostilities may not have been such as to require Philip's assistance, but it is notable that Philip does not appear to have intervened in Cardia or indeed to have taken any action in the matter until Diopeithes attacked Thracian towns outside the Chersonese.[6] In answer to this aggression, Philip sent a letter of protest to Athens and threatened to intervene,[7] but apart from perhaps sending a garrison to Cardia he did not carry out his threatened reprisal even though Diopeithes was not recalled.[8] For whatever reason, Philip did not seek a conflict with Athens. The opinion so constantly asserted by Demosthenes in 341 that Philip was virtually already at war with Athens was nothing else than an estimate of Philip's intentions. As yet, Philip had done nothing hostile.[9]

[1] The archon date is furnished by Philochorus F 158 and it seems fair to infer from Hegesippus' remarks in [Dem.] 7. 41 f. that the Cardians were not yet directly menaced by Diopeithes. Presumably cleruchs were normally established early enough in the summer to enable them to prepare the ground for sowing. For a conspectus of views see Wüst, op. cit., p. 114 n. 5.

[2] Dem. 8. 6 and Hypothesis § 1; Dem. 9. 15.

[3] Aeschin. 2. 72.

[4] Dem. 8. 2, 35.   [5] Dem. 5. 25.

[6] Dem. 8. 8 and Hypothesis § 3; [Dem.] 12. 3.

[7] Dem. 8. 16, 62 (ἀπειλεῖν ἤδη) and Hypothesis § 3. Demosthenes asserted (8. 58 and 9. 35) that Philip had actually sent forces into Cardia but this presumably was exaggeration, for Philip's letter merely threatened intervention.

[8] This seems a reasonable inference from the fact that Artaxerxes sent a gift to Diopeithes which did not reach him until after his death (Arist. Rhet. 1386ᵃ14). Pohlenz, Hermes lxiv (1929), 46, inferred from I.G. ii.² 228 (a decree of early 340) that he was

replaced by Chares, but there is no indication of when Chares was sent out to the Chersonese.

[9] In this section I have confined myself to the matters which Demosthenes regarded as showing Philip's aggressive intentions towards Athens. Perhaps something should be added about north-west Greece. Certainly Philip's activities in southern Epirus ([Dem.] 7. 32) must have disquieted Corinth, but they came to nothing: Philip did not attack Ambracia (Dem. 9. 72). Demosthenes claimed the credit for this (cf. 18. 244) but it is unlikely that Philip was deterred either by Demosthenes' diplomatic activity or by the Athenian expedition to Acarnania (Dem. 48. 24 and 26). Demosthenes probably exaggerated his own importance. It is to be noted that Corinth, which would have been especially concerned with the safety of Ambracia, did not enter into alliance with Athens in 342 (see W st, op. cit., p. 94 n. 1). Doubtless Demosthenes and Callias had much to say about the dangers of the situation in their embassies of early 342 (cf. Aeschin. 3. 94 f. and see Appendix III for the date), and they returned to Athens in

DEMOSTHENES' POLICY DURING THE YEARS OF PEACE

The debate about Philip's letter of complaint against Diopeithes in early 341[1] evoked from Demosthenes the frankest statement of his policy. It is unclear how closely Diopeithes acted in concert with the orator,[2] and Demosthenes may have been forced to make the best of what he himself would not have chosen, but he made it quite clear in the debate that a war in the north was the best possible thing for Athens. Not only did Demosthenes defend Diopeithes when he had broken the Peace of Philocrates by his operations in Thrace, and refuse to countenance the replacement of the offending general, but also he declared that, since Philip was virtually at war with Athens, anything that kept him out of Attica was justified: πότερον κρεῖττον ἐνθάδ' αὐτὸν ἀμύνεσθαι καὶ προσελθεῖν τὸν πόλεμον πρὸς τὴν Ἀττικὴν ἐᾶσαι, ἢ κατασκευάζειν ἐκεῖ τιν' ἀσχολίαν αὐτῷ; (8. 18). This was the logical consequence of everything that Demosthenes had said and done since the Peace. He made it his business συμβουλεύειν δι' ὧν καὶ τὰ παρόντ' ἔσται βελτίω καὶ τὰ προειμένα σωθήσεται (5. 3), and he deemed that this could only be achieved by war. From 344 on his speeches show his constant efforts to discredit Philip. All that Philip did was represented as in breach of either the letter or the spirit of the Peace. With Hegesippus he sought the rejection of the proposals to amend the Peace: Hegesippus was responsible for the amendment about Amphipolis, which virtually brought, as he must have known it would bring, the negotiations with Philip to a stalemate, but Demosthenes in the Second *Philippic* had played his part in the same affair by urging his countrymen not to trust Philip.[3] The aim of all this διαβολή[4] was to break up the Peace and resume the war, and Demosthenes was the leader of what was freely called the war-party, οἱ ποιοῦντες τὸν πόλεμον (Dem. 9. 6).[5] Was he right in this policy?

high hopes of creating a union of Peloponnesian states. But it is clear from Aeschines (cf. § 99 ἃ εὖ οἶδεν οὐδέποτε ἐσόμενα, § 100 ψήφισμα . . . μεστὸν ἐλπίδων οὐκ ἐσομένων καὶ στρατοπέδων οὐδέποτε συλλεγησομένων) that nothing came of it all. (The syntaxis of 15,000 hoplites and 2,000 cavalry of Plut. *Dem.* 17 is not the force proposed in 342, for which Aeschines gives different totals, but the force of Dem. 18. 237, which fought at Chaeronea.) The sum total of alliances for 343/2 is listed by the Scholiast on Aeschin. 3. 83, and of these the Achaeans alone appear to have fought at Chaeronea (Paus. 7. 6. 5). Their fear was that Philip would favour the claim of the Aetolians to Naupactus (Dem. 9. 34), as indeed he subsequently did (cf. *R.-E.* xvi. 2, col. 1990), and no doubt they were ready to respond to the appeal of Demosthenes and Callias. Corinth and Megara, however, did not stir. The meeting of the Synedrion, promised for 16th Anthesterion (Aeschin. 3. 98), did not happen. In the last prytany of the year Messene entered into alliance (*I.G.* ii.² 225), probably out of fear of Sparta, not of Philip, and the adhesion of other allies listed by the Scholiast was probably for the same reason. There are no

good grounds for asserting that Greece in general felt itself menaced by Philip in early 342 and that Demosthenes' analysis of the situation was widely shared.

[1] The date of Dem. 8 and 9 is derived from Dionysius of Halicarnassus *Ad Amm.* 10 and the allusions in 8. 14 and 18. Only Pohlenz, loc. cit., p. 46 n. 2, has wanted to reject this and put the speeches in early 342 on the strength of the Scholiast to Aeschin. 3. 83. But Philip's protest was occasioned by Diopeithes' invasion of Thrace, and there is no reason to think that this happened in the same year as the fighting over Cardian land began.

[2] *Pace* Beloch, *Att. Pol.*, pp. 216 f. However, Pohlenz's reasons (loc. cit., p. 45) for rejecting Beloch are unsound. The connexion between Hegesippus and Diopeithes is clear enough (Aeschin. 1. 63).

[3] There is no evidence that Demosthenes was in any way or on any ocasion after 346 opposed to Hegesippus.

[4] Cf. Isoc. *First Epistle to Philip* § 15.

[5] The occasion of Hegesippus' frank declaration that he was bent on war (Plut. *Mor.* 187 e) is not known. πόλεμον εἰσηγῇ shows that it was after 346.

Certainly, if the Macedonians were to be excluded from Greece, at some moment the settlement of 346 would have to be superseded, but the real difficulty for Athens lay in the fact that Philip physically controlled the Gates, and, until the Macedonians had been thrown out of Nicaea as they were in 339,[1] Philip was free to return to the invasion that Attica had been spared in 346. Unless Demosthenes had some political or strategic means to prevent this, his policy of war was likely to end in nothing but disaster for Athens. Did he have any such measures in mind?

It is sometimes suggested[2] that Demosthenes' real aim all along was to involve Thebes in the Hellenic resistance to Macedon, and to compensate for the loss of the Gates by Theban military power. The evidence for this appears to be very slight. First, in 343 Aeschines (2. 106) flung at Demosthenes the charge of being sympathetic to Thebes (καὶ γὰρ πρὸς τοῖς ἄλλοις κακοῖς βοιωτιάζει). This was based on the fact that during the second embassy to Pella in 346 Demosthenes, who was Theban proxenos,[3] had resisted Aeschines' proposal to try to influence Philip against Thebes. But there was no necessary connexion between προξενία and policy,[4] and the context of Aeschines' charge suggests the grounds of Demosthenes' opposition to Aeschines in this matter. Demosthenes refused to recognize that Philip would intervene in Greece: the aim of Athens should be to prevent that, not to accord Philip a tacit approval by advising him how to deal with outstanding disputes.[5] Aeschines skilfully turned this into a slanderous accusation—βοιωτιάζει. Secondly, in 330 Demosthenes claimed (18. 161) that he had continually looked for an alliance with Boeotia as a means of opposing Philip.[6] This, however, has to be considered in relation to what Aeschines had said on the subject. Aeschines had claimed (3. 137 f.) that the alliance did not come about διὰ τὰς Δημοσθένους δημηγορίας, but because the Thebans were obliged by the fear of the moment. Demosthenes replied by describing in detail his part in the making of the alliance (18. 160 f.), but, although he said that he had constantly sought to prevent trouble between Athens and Thebes, he adduced no evidence that this was so. One suspects that he was pretending to a policy which he had not had, simply to answer Aeschines; for inspection of his speeches of 344, 343, and 341 fails to reveal any trace whatsoever of a desire to establish a concert with Boeotia.[7] Indeed

---

[1] Philoch. F 56 B. It was after Philip declared war in 340 ([Dem.] 11. 4).

[2] e.g. by Beloch, *G.G.* iii.[2] 1, p. 507, and Jaeger, *Demosthenes*, pp. 161 and 178.

[3] Aeschin. 2. 141 and 143.

[4] For the position of πρόξενος see Busolt–Swoboda, *G.St.*, pp. 1246 f. Pericles had been ξένος of the Spartan King, Archidamus, in the years before 431 (Thuc. 2. 13. 1), but his policy was hardly λακωνισμός. Alcibiades was able to resume his family's Spartan προξενία during the Archidamian War (Thuc. 6. 89. 2). If προξενία had implied anything about a statesman's policy, Aeschines would have had a great deal more to say in 343 and 330 about Demosthenes' relation to Thebes.

[5] This is to be inferred from the words which Aeschines (2. 106 f.) imputed to Demosthenes, but which Demosthenes cannot actually have uttered.

[6] It is not clear to what Demosthenes referred in his statement that Eubulus 'constantly wanted to make this treaty of friendship' (18. 162).

[7] Jaeger, op. cit., pp. 161 and 251 n. 20, claimed that Dem. 5. 15, 18, and 24 showed that Demosthenes wanted a concert with Thebes. Of these passages Jaeger appears to mistranslate § 24 (Demosthenes was not proposing that Thebes should be allowed to keep Oropus); § 15 merely contains the suggestion that Thebes would not want to join Philip in a war against Athens, where only he could profit (for they would certainly suffer). § 18 does appear to protest against Athenian bitterness against Thebes, as might be expected from a proxenus, but this is very far from proposing that Athens should ally with Thebes.

in the Second *Philippic* (§ 14 f.) he belittled the possibility of any disagreement between Philip and Thebes and in 341 in the speech *On the Chersonese* (§ 63) he remarked quite flatly Θηβαίους νῦν ὑπάγει, as if there was no question of its being otherwise. In the Third *Philippic* he braved the ire of the Panhellenists by proposing (§ 71) an embassy to Persia, but there was not a word about Thebes, and similarly in the Fourth *Philippic*, when he discussed more fully his hopes of Persia (§ 31 f.), he had nothing whatsoever to propose about Thebes. In short, as far as we know, before 339/8 there was never any suggestion of attempting to secure Theban alliance. It may be thought that, though he wanted alliance, he dared not say so—a curious hope for the salvation of Athens— but, if there were anything in his claim in 330 of being always on the watch for an opportunity to improve relations with Thebes, we should certainly find that he at least made some move when opportunity offered. Now, if ever opportunity offered, it was when Thebes took the extremely serious step of expelling the Macedonian garrison from Nicaea in 339.[1] The politicians who did that would need friends. But Athens did nothing and Demosthenes proposed nothing. Those, therefore, who accept Demosthenes' claim and attribute to him the intention of combining with Thebes in the liberation of Greece, are confronted by a dilemma. Either Demosthenes rested his hopes on a policy which was so little likely to be adopted that in the speeches of 341, when he was advocating war, he did not feel it expedient to advocate it, and of so little practical use that only in the direst emergency and the stupefaction of Greece could it be put into effect, or he had no such policy. Certainly at the time of the debates of 344 and 343 he could have had practically no hope of aid from Thebes.

Nor does it appear that Demosthenes had anything to offer in the realm of strategy. Again we search in vain for any sign that Demosthenes had any more idea in 341 of how to fight Philip than during the Olynthian war. His language was extraordinarily vague—κατασκευάζειν ἐκεῖ τιν' ἀσχολίαν αὐτῷ (8. 18)! Athens had to have a suitable force ready and compel Philip μένειν ἐπὶ τῆς αὑτοῦ (8. 47). But what was the force to do? ὑπάρχει, ἄν περ, ὦ ἄνδρες Ἀθηναῖοι, ποιεῖν ἐθέλωμεν ἃ δεῖ, ἡ φύσις τῆς ἐκείνου χώρας, ἧς ἄγειν καὶ φέρειν ἔστι πολλὴν καὶ κακῶς ποιεῖν, ἄλλα μυρία (9. 52). An away match with Macedonian cavalry, and ἄλλα μυρία! The truth is that Demosthenes had no idea how Philip was to be contained in the north. In fact he confessed as much when he said (8. 69) that he 'chose the sort of policy in which πλειόνων ἡ τύχη κυρία γίγνεται ἢ οἱ λογισμοί'.

In the last resort, to prefer τύχη, to trust to luck, was not to be despised, and if all rational calculations counselled acceptance of Macedonian domination it was better to follow Demosthenes and the war-party than to submit. Before 346 there had been for Athens a serious alternative to fighting the war on her own in the north at the full stretch of her communications, viz. the alternative of uniting the Hellenes in the defence of Greece at the Gates, and, as I have argued elsewhere,[2] this was in fact the strategically sounder plan. But what alternative to Demosthenes' plan of renewing the war could be found after 346? Something had to be done to keep Philip out of Greece and Demosthenes' plan of trusting to τύχη did not turn out all that badly. There was a formidable array in the field at Chaeronea and Attica was not invaded. It should be added in defence of Demosthenes that if Philip had laid siege to Athens, he might well have damaged his own cause more than the city.

---

[1] See p. 167 n. 1.   [2] *C.Q.* N.S. xii (1962), 134 f.

The alternative to seeking to exclude Philip from Greece by war was to amend the Peace of Philocrates as Python's embassy in 344 proposed. The offer remained open until 342, when it was contemptuously rejected by Hegesippus in the speech *Concerning Halonnesus*, after which, as far as we know, Philip ceased his efforts to overcome Athenian distrust and began effectively to interfere in the affairs of Euboea. Was Demosthenes right to seek the rejection of this proposal?[1] The answer to this largely depends on the form of amendment that was proposed. If Philip was proposing that there should be some form of Common Peace like the League of Corinth, Demosthenes was rightly suspicious. To install Philip with hegemonic powers and control of a league army while he remained in control of the Gates would have established him more firmly as master of Greece. If, on the other hand, Philip was proposing that the Peace of Philocrates should be extended to take the form proposed by Aeschines and the allies in 346 whereby any Greek state could share with Athens in the peace, the proposal was not to be rejected out of hand. Much would depend on how the sanctions clause was drafted. If by negotiation Athens could secure the προστασία of the peace such as Sparta had had under the King's Peace, Philip might have been kept out of Greece and Athens have secured the position to guarantee the peace. Philip was certainly proposing some means of avoiding the sort of situation that had arisen in 344 when Peloponnesian states sought his protection and perhaps negotiation might have shown that Philip was not intent on intervening in Greek affairs.

There is reason for thinking that it was this second form of ἐπανόρθωσις that Philip offered. First, Philip was proposing amendment, and the creation of something like the League of Corinth could hardly have been so described. Secondly, the position and powers of Philip in the League of Corinth reflected the change in the balance of power due to his victory in 338 and it is unlikely that Philip thought of such an arrangement before that date. Thirdly, Aeschines, who opposed the war party, was most likely to accept an amendment of the peace in the way he had himself advocated in 346. Finally, Hegesippus would have attacked any radically new proposals, but in his speech of 342 he had no serious criticisms to make of the amendment envisaged (§ 30 f.). For these reasons it would seem that the Macedonian proposal was not necessarily aimed at strengthening Philip's hold on Greece.

The truth is that the only way to discover Philip's intentions was to negotiate seriously. If his aim in 344 had been merely to deceive, negotiation would have proved it. If, on the other hand, he had no desire to intervene in Greece, but had already formed the intention to attack Persia, Athens might have installed herself in the position in which her refusal seriously to negotiate placed Philip—the ἡγεμονία of Greece. For if Athens would not negotiate, there was only one end—a final conflict which would either utterly expel Philip from Greece or subject the country to Macedonian domination. By insisting that Philip was wholly untrustworthy, Demosthenes and the war-party involved their country in a war which ended in disaster. The policy of his opponents might have both avoided that war and left Philip free to go against the Great King.

---

[1] It is not clear that Demosthenes' view of the situation in 344 was not clouded by the hope of somehow recovering Amphipolis. In 5. 14 he spoke of war being renewed with Philip δι' Ἀμφίπολιν ἤ τι τοιοῦτον ἔγκλημ' ἴδιον. He must have realized that Philip would never yield by negotiation to Hegesippus' demand for Amphipolis, but he may still have dreamed of recovering it in the war he was so anxious to bring about.

4599.2

APPENDIX III

EUBOEAN AFFAIRS 343–340

The conventional picture of events[1] in Euboea in the late 340's is as follows:
(i) late in 342/1, shortly before the joint expedition of Chalcis and Athens to
liberate Oreus from Philistides, Athens made an alliance with Chalcis (Philoch.
F 159)[2] and this is the alliance proposed by Demosthenes and discussed by
Aeschines (3. 91 f.).
(ii) in 341/0, after the liberation of Oreus and the restoration of democracy
(δημοκρατουμένων τῶν Ὠρειτῶν, Aeschin. 3. 103) and before the suppression of
Clitarchus, Demosthenes proposed and carried a decree which exempted
Eretria and Oreus from paying συντάξεις to Athens, so that they could pay
them to Chalcis for the Euboean League. The Athenians were persuaded to
accept the loss of these payments by Callias of Chalcis and Demosthenes;
Callias said that he had arranged a Hellenic σύνταγμα in which a large part
would be played by the cities of Euboea, and Demosthenes reported on his
embassy to the Peloponnese, saying that he had organized a combined Greek
army and that the states were sending representatives to Athens by the next
full moon, on the 16th of Anthesterion (Feb./Mar.). In this interpretation of
Aeschin. 3. 89–105 the Euboean League was formed by Callias in spring 340
and was part of Demosthenes' preparations for the war.

To ruin this, one might simply point out that, as the notice in Philochorus
concerning the suppression of Clitarchus (F 160) is one that begins ἐπὶ τούτου
and is therefore the first entry for 341/0, Philochorus probably recorded it well
before events of Anthesterion. So the League must have been founded in an
earlier year while Clitarchus was in power in Eretria. But, since the account of
Aeschines has been commonly used to date the suppression of Clitarchus late
in 341/0,[3] this account might also be used to impugn the value of inferences
about the dates of ἐπὶ τούτου entries. In what follows an attempt is made to
date the foundation of the Euboean League to spring 342 without assuming
that Clitarchus was suppressed early in 341/0.

The main point to notice is that there is no justification for supposing that
Demosthenes' decree concerning Oreus and Eretria came between the liberation
of the former and the expulsion of Clitarchus from the latter. Aeschines alleged
(3. 103) that Demosthenes was bribed into proposing his decree, τάλαντον μὲν
ἐκ Χαλκίδος παρὰ Καλλίου, τάλαντον δ' ἐξ Ἐρετρίας παρὰ Κλειτάρχου τοῦ τυράννου,
τάλαντον δ' ἐξ Ὠρεοῦ, δι' ὃ καὶ καταφανὴς ἐγένετο, δημοκρατουμένων τῶν
Ὠρειτῶν καὶ πάντα πραττόντων μετὰ ψηφίσματος—ἐξανηλωμένοι γὰρ ἐν τῷ
πολέμῳ καὶ παντελῶς ἀπόρως διακείμενοι, πέμπουσι πρὸς αὐτὸν (i.e. Demosthenes) Γνωσίδημον . . . δεησόμενον τὸ μὲν τάλαντον ἀφεῖναι τῇ πόλει κτλ. and
Aeschines goes on to cite a decree of Oreus as evidence for his statements. What
exactly the circumstances were in which Oreus owed Demosthenes a talent it
is impossible for us to discover, but, whatever the debt was, there is no reason
to suppose that, if the Oreitans contracted it at the date when the Euboean
League was being formed, their appeal for relief did not follow at an interval,
possibly a large one. So by the time the decree was passed, δημοκρατουμένων

---

[1] See Wüst, op. cit., pp. 110 f., and Cloché,
op. cit., p. 238.
[2] Cf. Charax (F. Gr. Hist. 103) F 19.
[3] Cf. Beloch, op. cit. iii. 2, p. 292. Jacoby's
answer in his commentary on Philoch. F. 160
is not entirely clear.

τῶν Ὠρειτῶν Clitarchus may have been expelled from Eretria. Nor is there any inference to be drawn about the state of affairs in Oreus when the League was formed from the fact that Aeschines says τάλαντον ἐξ 'Ερετρίας παρὰ Κλειτάρχου τοῦ τυράννου but simply τάλαντον ἐξ 'Ωρεοῦ with no allusion to Philistides. Aeschines was on friendly terms with people at Oreus (Aeschin. 2. 89, Dem. 18. 82)[1] and may have taken a less unfavourable view of Philistides who had, after all, had the support of the populace (Dem. 9. 61). So Aeschines' omission of the name Philistides does not show that he had already been deposed. In short, Aeschines' account does not force us to conclude that the Euboean League was founded after the liberation of Oreus.

On the other hand there are reasons for putting Demosthenes' decree concerning Oreus and Eretria earlier than 341/0. First, the decree proposed an embassy to Euboea, and when Demosthenes in 330 listed in seemingly chronological order the measures for which he, as proposer, was strictly responsible (Dem. 18. 79) he put an embassy to Euboea before the expedition to Oreus. So unless he omitted a later embassy or Aeschines said that Demosthenes proposed what in fact he only supported, it would appear that the decree concerning Oreus and Eretria preceded the expedition of July 341. Secondly, the speech *On the Chersonese* and the Third *Philippic* indicate that by spring 341 both Philistides and Clitarchus had gone too far in their association with Philip for Demosthenes to contemplate negotiation with either.[2] In particular Parmenio had appeared in the island[3] and in despair at his presence Euphraeus of Oreus had committed suicide,[4] while once again Macedonian mercenaries had frustrated the Eretrian democrats in their plans to regain the city.[5] Is it likely that Demosthenes thought that such a man as Clitarchus could be counted on in the defence of Greece after the events of 341? Surely with Callias he saw that such men must be removed. The league to which Clitarchus was admitted must be set before 341.

This leaves only Anthesterion 343/2. Early 343 is ruled out because there is no hint of these developments in the speech against Aeschines, and early 342 is in fact strongly supported by Aeschines' own account (3. 97 f.). The very date of 16th Anthesterion was named as part of Demosthenes' report on his embassy to the Peloponnese and Acarnania and this embassy is securely dated by the allusion in the Third *Philippic* (§ 72) to αἱ πέρυσιν πρεσβεῖαι περὶ τὴν Πελοπόννησον and by the Scholiast on Aeschines 3. 83, who supplies the archon date 343/2.[6]

If the co-operation of Callias and Demosthenes in the establishment of the Euboean League is set in early 342, the sequence of events is intelligible. The Euboean cities made peace with Athens at the end of the Tamynae campaign in mid-348 (Aeschin. 2. 12) and shortly afterwards Callias began to promote the Εὐβοϊκὸν συνέδριον (Aeschin. 3. 89).[7] For a period he courted the friendship

---

[1] Dem. 18. 82 alleged that Aeschines had the representatives of both Philistides and Clitarchus staying in his house when the δῆμος rejected their claims (presumably vis-à-vis Callias and his League). Even if true, this would not prove Aeschines was necessarily closely linked with Clitarchus.

[2] 8. 18, 36, 59; 9. 12, 33, 57 f.

[3] Dem. 9. 58 and Carystius *ap.* Ath. 508 e.

[4] Dem. 9. 62. [5] Dem. 9. 58.

[6] Cf. Jacoby's commentary on Philoch. F 158. The fact that the Scholiast does not mention the Euboean cities in his list of alliances does not prove that Callias' negotiations do not fall in 343/2. The Scholiast confined himself to elucidating Aeschin. 3. 83. By the time he came to § 95, where he could have helped us about the Euboean League, his comments had become very sketchy.

[7] The history of this movement is obscure,

of Macedon and then of Thebes,[1] and in the prosecution of Aeschines Demosthenes let out a snarl against τοὺς καταράτους Εὐβοέας τουτουσί (§ 75), but in early 342 the tide had turned. Callias saw that the only way to unite Euboea under his leadership and keep out the Macedonians who had turned against him (Aeschin. 3. 90) was to unite with Athens. Hence the embassies and negotiations of early 342. Presumably Oreus and Eretria welcomed the decree of Demosthenes (otherwise Aeschines could hardly have accused Demosthenes of taking bribes from them to propose it). But in 342/1 local rivalries proved too strong and Philistides and Clitarchus brought the Macedonians into the island. Demosthenes denounced them in his speeches of spring 341. In July Philistides was killed and shortly afterwards Clitarchus was expelled.[2] The economic difficulties of Oreus to which Aeschines (3. 103) alluded would have been due to the disruption of life caused first by the Macedonian visit κατ᾿ εὔνοιαν[3]

but the coinage of Eretria shows that the resistance to Athenian imperialism in the fifth century in Euboea as elsewhere, e.g. in Chalcidice, Rhodes, and Boeotia, took the form of a movement for federal unity. Cf. Head, *H.N.*², p. 362, for coins with inscription **EYB** or **EYBOI**. Thucydides affords supporting evidence. He was careful in his use of names (cf. Clement and Robinson, *Excavations at Olynthus*, ix. 122 n. 55, for his careful use of Χαλκιδῆς rather than ᾿Ολύνθιοι), and, except at 1. 98. 3, he reserves the term Εὐβοεῖς for the peoples of Euboea when they were in opposition to the Athenians. The history of this movement in the fourth century is less clear, because neither Xenophon nor Demosthenes can be relied on for exact usage, but inscriptions (e.g. *I.G.* ii.² 16, 43, and 44) suggest that Athens continued to support the anti-federalists. This may lie behind Xenophon's use of Εὐβοεῖς at *Hellenica* 6. 5. 23, or Demosthenes' at 8. 74 (of Athenian help in 357/6 to Euboea before the cities returned to the Second Athenian Confederacy, which they rejoined in fact separately—as *I.G.* ii.² 124 shows) and at 4. 37 (of Philip's letter in the late 350's). The only evidence which might be opposed to this has, I believe, been wrongly dated. *I.G.* ii.² 149, which is concerned with an alliance between Athens and οἱ Εὐβοεῖς was assigned by Koehler to the 350's by reason of the style of lettering and confidently related by Woodward in *J.H.S.* xxviii (1908), 307, to the settlement of Euboea in 357, despite the fact that *I.G.* ii.² 124 showed that the Euboean cities made separate alliances. I suggest that the inscription in fact records the alliance between Athens and the Euboean League in 342 (*vide infra*). (In passing it may be noted that there is no necessity to read τοὺς 'Εστιαιᾶς in line 8, or 'Εστιαιεῦσιν in line 24. Woodward's suggestions in *J.H.S.* xxx (1910), 266, of τοὺς Εὐβοεῖς and

Εὐβοιεῦσιν have the merit of reducing line 24 to its proper length and eliminate a name alien to 342, for by then Histiaea was known as Oreus; cf. Aristotle, *Politics* 1303ᵃ for an allusion to the grandfather (probably) of the 'Ηρακλειόδωρος in line 7.) Conversely, *I.G.* ii.² 230 should be connected with the settlement of 357, when Eretria rejoined the Athenian alliance (cf. lines 12 to 16 with lines 4 to 7 of *I.G.* ii.² 124).

[1] Aeschin. 3. 89 f.
[2] In a separate expedition. Cf. διέβησαν εἰς 'Ερετρίαν in Philoch. F 160. The use of this phrase in contrast to the plain ἠλευθέρωσαν of F 159 suggests a different explanation of the fact that two separate generals were involved in the operations in Euboea from that of Beloch, op. cit. iii.² 293, who took it as evidence that the two expeditions were separated by a long interval of time. At some time Cephisophon of Aphidna was general on Sciathus. Pace Kroll in *R.-E.* xi. 1, col. 240, and Kirchner, *Pros. Att.* 8410, there is no reason to assign his period as general on Sciathus to 340; neither *I.G.* ii.² 1623. 35 (of 333/2) nor *I.G.* ii.² 1629. 484 (of 325/4) furnish any date (and it may be remarked in passing that *I.G.* ii.² 1622. 213 is not evidence that he was trierarch in the year he led the attack on Oreus). I suggest that he was on Sciathus in 342/1 and conducted the operation from there. After all, if Philip was sending forces into Euboea (Dem. 9. 57 f.), the island of Sciathus was an important position, and one would expect it to be occupied in 342/1, and if it was occupied it was the right base for assaulting Oreus. For Eretria it was better to send another force across under Phocion, who knew the terrain by bitter experience. Cf. Dem. 8. 36, where he says that Philip established two tyrants in Euboea, τὸν μὲν ἀπαντικρὺ τῆς 'Αττικῆς ἐπιτειχίσας, τὸν δ᾿ ἐπὶ Σκίαθον.
[3] Dem. 9. 12, and 33.

followed by the Athenian expedition with the violent expropriations which it no doubt brought.[1]

A major difficulty confronts us in all this. According to Philochorus (F 159) it was in 342/1, either in the last month or shortly before, that συμμαχίαν Ἀθηναῖοι πρὸς Χαλκιδεῖς ἐποι[ήσαντο, καὶ] ἠλευθέρωσαν Ὠρ[ί]τας μετὰ Χαλκιδέων κτλ., and since Aeschines discusses an alliance with Chalcis as part of the preparation of the Euboean League[2] it is hard to explain Philochorus' notice if there had been an alliance of the sort described by Aeschines fourteen months earlier. This needs an answer indeed. Yet it is only part of the difficulty. In reality we are on the horns of a dilemma. Not only is it hard to see why there should be two alliances with Chalcis within fourteen months but also it is hard to identify the alliance of Philochorus with that described by Aeschines. The alliance of Philochorus was made on the eve of the attack on the Philippizers in Euboea. At that late date, as I have already remarked, there could have been no thought of alliance with either of the 'tyrants'. Yet in Aeschines' account the alliance was made on such terms as to enable the establishment of the Εὐβοϊκὸν συνέδριον (3. 91 f.). To the period between the speeches of spring 341 and the liberation of Oreus it seems more appropriate to assign the Athenian rebuff to the ambassadors of Philistides and Clitarchus (Dem. 18. 82) than the comparatively friendly diplomatic exchanges presupposed by Demosthenes' decree. So there is a dilemma to solve.

The solution I propose is that the alliance discussed by Aeschines was part of a larger agreement whereby Athens made an alliance with the Euboean League. Aeschines is here most concerned to mislead : the plain fact which he sought to obscure was that the adhesion of Chalcis under Callias was an immense gain to Athens and greatly to Demosthenes' credit. So we can expect misrepresentation. What appears in Aeschines as a simple alliance must have been a complex arrangement whereby some were to be released from certain of the obligations imposed by membership of the Second Athenian Confederacy and others obliged to military aid from which they had previously been exempt at least since the peace made in 348. So Chalcis could well be represented as making an alliance, just as Oreus was to be asked to do, but, conversely, Chalcis and Eretria were to be exempted explicitly from συντάξεις and participation in the Synedrion at Athens. Obscure as it all is, the alliance of Chalcis may be conjectured to have been involved with the functioning of the Εὐβοϊκὸν συνέδριον.[3] Now there is no reason to think that this Euboean League survived the crisis of 341.[4] Callias could not have consented to the reception of Parmenio and his mercenaries, and one may conjecture that the fine political structure of 342 collapsed and was replaced by a plain old-fashioned alliance in virtue of which the dissident states were dealt with.

University College, Oxford   G. L. CAWKWELL

[1] Since Philistides had popular support (Dem. 9. 61), there were many who could be treated as Philippizers.   [2] 3. 91 f.
[3] See p. 211 n. 7 for the suggestion that *I.G.* ii.[2] 149, an alliance between Athens and

'the Euboeans', is the fruit of these negotiations.
[4] *Pace* the comment on *I.G.* xii (9), 207, a document of the early third century.

XI

U. Wilcken

Philip II von Makedonien und die
panhellenische Idee

Philipp II. von Makedonien und die panhellenische Idee.

Von ULRICH WILCKEN.

(Vorgetragen am 18. April 1929 [s. oben S. 213].)

Nach dem Vortrag, den RUDOLF v. SCALA 1891 auf dem Münchener Philologentag über »Isokrates und die Geschichtsschreibung« gehalten hat, wird heute wohl von den meisten Forschern mit Recht angenommen, daß der $\Phi i\lambda\iota\pi\pi os$ des Isokrates, in dem er im Jahre 346 König Philipp aufforderte, die Griechen miteinander zu versöhnen und zum panhellenischen Nationalkrieg gegen Persien zu führen, nicht ohne Einfluß auf die Maßregeln geblieben ist, die der König als Sieger von Chaeronea 338/7 in Korinth getroffen hat[1]. Aber über die Art und das Maß der Beeinflussung gehen die Ansichten sehr auseinander. Am weitesten in der Bejahung geht wohl BELOCH (Griech. Gesch. III 1² 525 A. 1) — dem sich MÜNSCHER (RE IX 2214) in bezug auf Philipp wörtlich anschließt —, wenn er meint, daß Philipp und Alexander die Ideale des Isokrates »fast Punkt für Punkt verwirklicht« hätten. Das geht viel zu weit! In Wirklichkeit ist das Problem viel komplizierter. BELOCH konnte, von anderem abgesehen, nur deswegen zu dieser Ansicht kommen, weil er glaubte, daß Isokrates dem Philipp eine staatliche Einigung der Griechen empfohlen habe, die in dem korinthischen Bunde verwirklicht sei. Die Überzeugung, daß diese letztere, weitverbreitete Ansicht irrig ist, hat mich dazu geführt, Philipps Werk von Korinth einer genaueren Prüfung in bezug auf sein Verhältnis zum $\Phi i\lambda\iota\pi\pi os$ des Isokrates zu unterziehen[2]. Zugleich möchte ich auch zur Klärung der Frage beitragen, wie der korinthische Bund staatsrechtlich zu rubrizieren ist.

I. Zur Vorgeschichte des $\Phi i\lambda\iota\pi\pi os$.

Der Gedanke, daß die Griechen sich miteinander versöhnen sollten, um gemeinsam einen Nationalkrieg gegen Persien zu führen, ist allmählich lebendig geworden, nachdem die Perser als Verbündete der Spartaner, die ihnen dafür die kleinasiatischen Griechen preisgaben, in den peloponnesischen Krieg eingetreten waren. Dieses erneute Eingreifen des persischen Weltreiches in die

---

[1] Die Ansicht von ERNEST BARKER (Cambridge Ancient History VI 518), daß Isokrates' Pamphlete keine Wirkung (*effect*) ausgeübt hätten, dürfte ziemlich allein stehen. Isokrates gehört zu den erfolgreichsten Publizisten der alten Welt. Vgl. auch S. 294 über sein Verdienst um das Zustandekommen des II. attischen Seebundes.

[2] Die Hauptergebnisse dieser Untersuchung habe ich bereits im August 1928 auf dem Internationalen Historikertag in Oslo vorgetragen.

griechische Geschichte, das dann die Niederlage Athens herbeigeführt hat, erzeugte einen Druck, der als Gegendruck jene »panhellenische Idee« hervorgerufen hat. Wir würden die Genesis dieses Gedankens viel klarer erfassen können, wenn es authentisch feststünde, in welchem Jahre GORGIAS vor der olympischen Festversammlung als erster dieses Programm in seinem Olympikos verkündet hat. Die modernen Berechnungen gehen weit auseinander: die einen sind für 408, die anderen für 392. Ich halte dieses sehr verwickelte Problem noch nicht für definitiv gelöst. Jener persische Druck fand dann seine staatsrechtliche Fixierung in dem Königsfrieden von 386, der darauf ein halbes Jahrhundert lang auf Hellas gelastet hat. Da dieser Königsfriede, durch den der von Sparta aufgenommene Perserkrieg mitsamt dem sogenannten korinthischen Kriege, der sich aus ihm entwickelt hatte[1], sein Ende fand, für das Verständnis von Philipps Maßregeln in Korinth von Wichtigkeit ist, sei hier kurz an seine Hauptbestimmungen erinnert: § 1 besagte, daß die kleinasiatischen Griechen dem Großkönig gehören sollten, § 2, daß alle anderen griechischen Staaten, klein und groß, frei und autonom sein sollten[2]. Darauf

---

[1] Der Perserkrieg, den die Spartaner seit 400 führten, konnte nicht als Realisierung des panhellenischen Nationalkrieges betrachtet werden, so gern wie auch Agesilaos, wie seine Agamemnongeste zeigt, gesehen hätte, weil es doch zu offenkundig war, daß es hierbei wesentlich um das Sonderinteresse Spartas ging, die Machtstellung in Kleinasien zu wahren. So hat denn Isokrates später den Philipp den Agesilaos, weil dieser daneben auch Parteipolitik treiben wollte, als warnendes Beispiel dafür vorgehalten, wie man einen Perserkrieg nicht führen solle (Phil. § 86 ff. und dazu ED. MEYER, AG V S. 206). Wie wenig die anderen Mächte diesen Krieg für einen panhellenischen hielten, zeigt die Koalition gegen Sparta, die sogar mit dem Großkönig ging.

[2] Mit Recht hat R. v. SCALA, Die Staatsverträge des Altertums I (1898) S. 114, in seiner Rekonstruktion des Königsfriedens den Xenophontischen Text von § 2 mit U. KÖHLER ergänzt zu: τὰς δὲ ἄλλας Ἑλληνίδας πόλεις καὶ μικρὰς καὶ μεγάλας ⟨ἐλευθέρας [ἐλευθέρους ist ein S. 115 wiederholtes Versehen] καὶ⟩ αὐτονόμους ἀφεῖναι. Die Einwendungen, die FERDINAND NOLTE in seiner durch die Selbständigkeit des politischen Denkens anziehenden Frankfurter Dissertation »Die historisch-politischen Voraussetzungen des Königsfriedens von 386 v. Chr.« (1923) S. 10 f. gegen die Ergänzung von ἐλευθέρας καὶ erhoben hat, sind nicht stichhaltig. KÖHLER und v. SCALA stützten sich auf den athenischen Vertrag mit Chios (übrigens, wie AD. WILHELM inzwischen festgestellt hat, nicht vom J. 386, sondern 384/3, vgl. DITT., Syll. I3 142), in dem es Z. 19 ff. heißt: συμμάχος δὲ ποιεῖσ[θα]ι [Χί]ος ἐπ᾿ ἐλευθ[ε]ρίαι καὶ αὐτονομί[α]ι, μὴ παραβαίνοντας τῶν ἐν ταῖς στήλαις γεγραμμένων περὶ τῆς εἰρήνης μηδέν. Die damalige politische Situation macht es verständlich genug, daß die Athener unter dem Druck des Königsfriedens, auf den sie mit den letzten Worten ausdrücklich hinweisen (vgl. auch schon Z. 8 ff.), den Chiern die ἐλευθερία und αὐτονομία geben mußten (ebenso wie nachher den Bündnern den II. attischen Seebundes, s. unten), eben weil beides im Königsfrieden festgelegt war. Vergeblich sucht NOLTE dies Zeugnis zu eliminieren, indem er diesen Doppelbegriff nur für eine »verstärkte Ausdrucksweise« erklärt, die mit Rücksicht auf die früheren üblen Erfahrungen der Bündner gewählt sei! Aber die Inschrift von Chios und die Urkunde über den II. attischen Seebund sind nicht die einzigen Beweise für die Notwendigkeit jener Ergänzung. Auch Isokrates spricht im Paneg. 117, wo er vom Königsfrieden handelt, von τῆς ἐλευθερίας καὶ αὐτονομίας. Vor allem ist beweisend eine Polybiosstelle, auf die zur Widerlegung von NOLTE zuerst hingewiesen zu haben das Verdienst von Dr. MARIA BRITSCHKOFF (Sofia) ist. Vgl. ihre (ungedruckte) Berliner Dissertation »Über Freiheitserteilungen an die Griechen durch auswärtige Machthaber« (1925) S. 6 f. Polyb. IV 27, 5 sagt: (Λακεδαιμόνιοι) πάλιν ἐκήρυττον ἀφιέντες τὰς πόλεις ἐλευθέρας καὶ αὐτονόμους κατὰ τὴν ἐπ᾿ Ἀνταλκίδου γενομένην εἰρήνην! Damit dürfte NOLTES Einspruch erledigt sein. Damit ist aber auch den allgemeinen Ausführungen NOLTES über die Begriffe ἐλευθερος und αὐτονομος der Boden entzogen: ἐλεύθερος soll niemals als staatsrechtlicher Begriff empfunden sein, sondern nur ein propagandistisches Schlagwort oder Phrase sein (S. 11), und H. BERVE, Das Alexanderreich I 229 A. 2 hat dies bereits unter Hinweis auf NOLTE übernommen. NOLTES Ausführungen stehen um so mehr auf

folgte eine Sanktion, wonach der Großkönig gegen jeden, der diesen Frieden nicht annehme, zusammen mit den Friedenswilligen Krieg führen werde. Mit dem § 1 war definitiv alles preisgegeben, was im 5. Jahrhundert für die Freiheit der kleinasiatischen Brüder getan war; der § 2 bedeudete für den Großkönig die dauernde politische Zerstückelung Griechenlands, für die Spartaner die Aussicht auf eine ständige Vormachtstellung in Hellas, da hiernach nur der peloponnesische Bund durch die Autonomiebestimmung für seine Bündner zulässig war. Dieser Königsfriede, der — wie ich glauben möchte, nach den Grundsätzen des persischen Weltreiches[1] — auf ewige Zeiten geschlossen war, ist von vielen und nicht den Schlechtesten, namentlich wegen der Preisgabe der kleinasiatischen Griechen[2], aber auch wegen der demütigenden Formen, in denen er ihnen vom Großkönig mit dem Säbel in der Hand oktroyiert war, als eine nationale Schmach empfunden worden und wird daher jenen panhellenischen Gedanken gestärkt haben.

In dieser Stimmung trat sechs Jahre danach (380) Isokrates in seinem Panegyrikos, diesem gewaltigen Meisterwerk der epideiktischen Beredsamkeit, für eine schleunige Aufnahme des panhellenischen Nationalkrieges gegen Persien ein, um diesen Schmachfrieden, der kein »Vertrag« (συνθῆκαι), sondern ein »Diktat« sei (πρόσταγμα), zu beseitigen (§ 176). Seit Gorgias' Olympikos hatten schon mehrere Redner dies panhellenische Programm behandelt (§ 3), aber noch niemand hatte die Frage erörtert, wer denn führen solle (§ 15ff.). Isokrates spielt mit dem Gedanken einer Versöhnung von Athen und Sparta

schwankem Boden, als er nicht bedacht hat, daß die Schriftsteller vielfach aus Bequemlichkeit nur von αὐτονομία (vielleicht auch einmal nur von ἐλευθερία) reden, wo sie von ἐλευθερία καὶ αὐτονομία reden müßten. Dafür habe ich ein evidentes Beispiel bei Diod. XV 28, 4 gefunden, wo er bei Wiedergabe der Bestimmungen des II. attischen Seebundes sagt: πάσας (scil. πόλεις) δ' ὑπάρχειν αὐτονόμους. Hier haben wir einmal glücklicherweise den urkundlichen Beleg dafür, daß in dem Vertrage selbst vielmehr ἐλευθερ/α καὶ αὐτονομία zugesichert war. Vgl. DITT., Syll. I3 147, 10 und 20. Dasselbe gilt von Isokrates, Paneg. 115, wo er in bezug auf den Königsfrieden nur von der αὐτονομία spricht, während er gleich danach in § 117, wie oben bemerkt, korrekter von ἐλευθερία und αὐτονομία redet. Danach ist auch die Verkürzung im Xenophontischen Text zu verstehen. Somit hatte BRUNO KEIL, den NOLTE S. 11 bekämpft, doch recht, wenn er (GERCKE-NORDEN III²318) die ἐλευθερία als die Unabhängigkeit nach außen, die αὐτονομία als das Recht, ohne fremden Einfluß die Verfassungsform selbst zu bestimmen, definierte und in der Zusammenfassung der beiden Termini den Begriff der vollen Souveränität, der völkerrechtlichen wie der staatsrechtlichen sah. — Auch darin irrt NOLTE, daß er S. 6 die Griechen, mit denen Artaxerxes den Königsfrieden schloß, für seine »Untertanen« hält und daraus sich erklärt, daß der Großkönig den Frieden nicht »unterzeichnet« habe, was er mit dem universalen Charakter des Achämenidenreiches begründet. Beides ist irrig. »Untertanen« wurden durch diesen Frieden nur die kleinasiatischen Griechen (nebst Klazomenae und Cypern), indem sie dem οἶκος des βασιλεύς zugeteilt wurden (s. Philochoros bei Didy. 7, 22). Darin liegt schon, daß die andern Griechen, in Hellas und auf den Inseln, nicht seine Untertanen wurden. Das fand eben in der Anerkennung ihrer ἐλευθερία seinen Ausdruck. Andererseits ist durch der Vertrag mit Chios einwandfrei bezeugt, daß auch der Großkönig den Frieden beschworen hat (Syll. I 3 142, 7 ff.: τὴν ε[ἰρήνην καὶ τὴν φι]-λίαν καὶ τὸς ὅρκος καὶ [τὰς οὔσας συνθήκας], ἃς ὤμοσεν βασιλεὺ[ς] κα[ὶ Ἀθηναῖοι καὶ] Λακεδαιμόνιοι καὶ οἱ ἄλλο[ι Ἕλληνες]. Ebenso hat der Großkönig später den Frieden von 371 mitbeschworen. Vgl. Dion. Hal. de Lys. 12: τὴν εἰρήνην Ἀθηναῖοί τε καὶ Λακεδαιμόνιοι καὶ βασιλεὺς ὤμοσαν.

[1] Vgl. meine Griech. Geschichte² S. 239 zu S. 149.
[2] Platon, Menex. 17 sagt in bezug auf die am Widerspruch Athens gescheiterten Verhandlungen mit Antialkidas vom J. 392: ὅμως δ' οὖν ἐμονώθημεν πάλιν διὰ τὸ μὴ ἐθέλειν αἰσχρὸν καὶ ἀνόσιον ἔργον ἐργάσασθαι Ἕλληνας βαρβάροις ἐκδόντες. Der Tatbestand ist inzwischen durch Philochoros (Didy. 7, 19 ff.) bestätigt worden.

und einer gemeinsamen Führung durch die beiden (§ 16, 188)[1], sucht dann aber in einem großen Exkurs zu zeigen, daß Athen den höheren Anspruch erheben könne. Hierbei macht er, wie v. WILAMOWITZ erkannt hat[2], Propaganda für einen neuen attischen Seebund, der ja auch drei Jahre später (377), gewiß nicht ohne das publizistische Verdienst des Isokrates, begründet worden ist. Dann kehrt er zu seinem Hauptthema zurück (§ 133) und fordert unter Hinweis auf die momentane Schwäche des Perserreiches (§ 138 ff.) und auf die schmachvollen Wirkungen des Königsfriedens, der beseitigt werden müsse (§ 175 ff.), zum panhellenischen Nationalkrieg auf.

So wirksam Isokrates' Propaganda für einen neuen attischen Seebund war, so utopisch erwies sich, angesichts der wachsenden Streitigkeiten und Kämpfe der Griechen untereinander, seine Hoffnung, daß Athen und Sparta sich versöhnen, oder daß überhaupt von innen heraus die für den Nationalkrieg nötige Eintracht (ὁμόνοια) der Griechen hergestellt werden könnte. Enttäuscht von dieser Entwicklung und nicht unbeeinflußt von dem Erstarken des monarchischen Gedankens, der damals mehr und mehr diskutiert wurde — auch von ihm selbst, wenn auch nur im Hinblick auf ein Ausland wie Cypern —, ging er dazu über, an der Peripherie des Griechentums nach einem starken Manne zu suchen, der, nicht abhängig von einer Polis und ihren Gesetzen (Phil. 14), die Macht und den Willen hätte, das panhellenische Programm auszuführen. Er hielt nichts mehr davon, wie einst zu einer Festversammlung zu reden[3], denn wenn man sich »an alle« wende, so sei das so gut, als wenn man zu niemand spreche; wer praktisch etwas erreichen wolle, müsse sich an eine machtvolle Persönlichkeit wenden (Phil. 12 f.). So hat er nacheinander mehreren Potentaten sein Programm empfohlen, so dem Jason von Pherae, dem mächtigen Herrscher Thessaliens, von dem es hieß, daß er einen Perserzug plane, der aber bald darauf ermordet wurde (370), so dem Dionysios von Syrakus, der das Griechentum Siziliens gegen die Karthager gerettet hatte, der aber an anderes zu denken hatte und auch bald danach gestorben ist (367). Doch Isokrates verstand zu warten, und trotz aller Enttäuschungen, die ihm die weitere Entwicklung Griechenlands und im besondern auch Athens brachte, hielt er fest an der panhellenischen Idee, die allein nach seiner Ansicht einen dauernden Frieden für die Griechenwelt bringen konnte[4]. Als dann im Frühling 346 der philokratische Friede den langjährigen Kriegszustand zwischen seiner Vaterstadt und Philipp von Makedonien beendete, griff der neunzigjährige Greis, hoch beglückt durch diesen Frieden, zur Feder und unterbreitete dem König in einem offenen Sendschreiben, dem Φίλιππος, sein panhellenisches Programm.

---

[1] In § 16 ist überliefert: Ὅστις οὖν οἴεται τοὺς ἄλλους κοινῇ τι πράξειν ἀγαθὸν, πρὶν ἂν τοὺς προεστῶτας αὐτῶν διαλλάξῃ. Ich verstehe dies ἄλλους nicht. Sollte es nicht für Ἕλληνας verschrieben sein?

[2] Arist. u. Athen II 380 ff. Vgl. dazu ED. MEYER, AG V S. 372.

[3] Im Panegyrikos hatte er sich freilich nur formell an Olympia gewendet. In Wirklichkeit war die Rede nur als Broschüre erschienen.

[4] Aus Paneg. 173 scheint mir zu folgen, daß der Nationalkrieg an sich nicht das letzte Ziel des Isokrates war, sondern nur das Mittel, um zu einem Dauerfrieden in Griechenland zu kommen.

II. Der Eindruck des Φίλιππος auf den König.

Wie die Bedeutung des Isokrates als Publizist erst von der neueren Forschung — ich nenne nur J. Beloch und Ed. Meyer — erkannt worden ist, so ist man auch erst zu einer gerechten Würdigung Philipps gekommen, nachdem man aufgehört hat, ihn, wie in der klassizistischen Zeit, vom athenischen oder gar demosthenischen Standpunkt aus zu bewerten, und vielmehr den Maßstab seiner Verdienste um Makedonien an seine Taten anlegt. Tut man dies, so steht Philipp als einer der bedeutendsten und erfolgreichsten Herrscher, die die Geschichte kennt, vor uns, gleich groß als Staatsmann und Diplomat wie als Feldherr und Organisator der Wehrkraft seines Volkes zur ersten Armee seiner Zeit. Um sich vorzustellen, wie wohl der Φίλιππος auf ihn gewirkt hat, ist es nötig, sich die Ziele seiner makedonischen Politik klarzumachen.

Darüber herrscht heute wohl ziemlich Übereinstimmung, daß es zunächst sein Hauptziel war, das kleine makedonische Reich, das er übernommen hatte, womöglich über den ganzen Balkanrumpf auszudehnen. Durch unermüdliche Kämpfe gegen die Illyrier im Westen und die Thraker im Osten sowie die nördlichen Nachbarn hatte er dies Ziel am Ende seines Lebens auch in der Hauptsache erreicht, wo seine Macht oder doch sein Einfluß sich vom Adriatischen Meer bis zum Schwarzen Meer und hinauf bis zur Donau erstreckte. Strittig dagegen ist die Frage, ob er auch schon von früh her an eine Beherrschung Griechenlands gedacht hat. Ihre Beantwortung wird dadurch erschwert, daß dieser kluge Politiker wohlweislich seine letzten Pläne in seiner Brust verschloß, was seine monarchische Stellung ihm erlaubte[1]. Gleichwohl möchte ich es als mehr denn wahrscheinlich, ja als so gut wie sicher betrachten, daß auch die Gewinnung dieses griechischen Südens der Balkanhalbinsel von früh an — jedenfalls, worauf es mir hier ankommt, schon vor der Lektüre des Φίλιππος — zu seinen letzten Plänen gehört hat. Es wäre schwer begreiflich, wenn dieser große Imperialist an diese natürliche Abrundung seines Reiches nach Süden nicht gedacht hätte, und sein Vorgehen in Thessalien, sein Eingreifen in den »Heiligen« Krieg werden unter dieser Annahme besonders verständlich[2]. Freilich wird er sich von vornherein darüber klar gewesen sein, daß Hellas nicht wie die barbarischen Nachbarn des Nordens seinem Reiche einverleibt werden konnte. Schon seine Kulturpolitik, durch die er seinen Imperialismus geadelt hat, die darauf ausging, durch Einführung der griechischen Kultur sein makedonisches Reich zu einem großen Kulturstaat zu machen, mußte ihm das Problem nahelegen, für eine Beherrschung

---

[1] Letzteres erkennt auch Demosth. de coro. 235 als einen Vorzug der Monarchie an: ἔπραττεν ἃ δόξειεν αὐτῷ, οὐ προλέγων ἐν τοῖς ψηφίσμασιν οὐδ᾽ ἐν τῷ φανερῷ βουλευόμενος κτλ.
[2] Richtig Kärst, Hellenismus I3 273 A. 3, dem ich hierin durchaus zustimme. Dies hebe ich besonders hervor, da er ebendort S. 534 A. 2 meine frühere, allerdings sehr kurze Bemerkung in diesen Sitzungsberichten 1922 XVI S. 102f. mißverstanden hat. Eindeutig habe ich es schon in meiner Griech. Geschichte[2] S. 155 ausgedrückt. Im übrigen will ich hier auf seine kritischen Bemerkungen in dieser Beilage III über frühere Arbeiten von mir nicht eingehen. Die obige Abhandlung zeigt, daß ich an den früheren Ansichten festhalte. Aber ich freue mich, daß er in manchen Punkten mir entgegengekommen ist, wie auch, daß wir in mehreren wichtigen Fragen übereinstimmen.

Griechenlands möglichst schonende Formen zu suchen, um trotzdem die Sympathien der Griechen gewinnen zu können.

Aber auch die Notwendigkeit, schließlich einmal mit dem Perser die Schwerter zu kreuzen, wird ihm früh klar gewesen sein. Denn wenn seine thrakischen Pläne gelangen, und er die thrakischen Nordküsten der Propontis und des Bosporos gewann, so war ein Konflikt mit dem jenseitigen Perserreiche kaum zu vermeiden, wie es ja auch später gekommen ist. Auch mußte es für den Herrn jener nördlichen Küsten der so wichtigen Wasserstraße ein fast selbstverständlicher Wunsch sein, auch die gegenüberliegenden Küsten zu beherrschen, was nur durch Vorschiebung der makedonischen Grenzen nach Kleinasien hinein, also durch einen Perserkrieg, zu erreichen war. Dazu kam noch ein anderes Moment. Wenn er die Hegemonie über Hellas in irgendeiner Form gewann, so mußte auch dies ihn in Konflikt mit dem Großkönig bringen, denn nach dem Königsfrieden stand dem Perser die Oberkontrolle über Griechenland zu, die Philipp in irgendeiner Form für sich gewinnen wollte. Auch deswegen war mit einem Perserkrieg zu rechnen. So möchte ich glauben, daß für Philipp, als er die Denkschrift des Isokrates in die Hand nahm, bereits die Gewinnung der Hegemonie über Griechenland und schließlich ein Perserkrieg zu den letzten, wenn auch noch fernen Zielen seiner makedonischen Reichspolitik gehört haben.

Welchen Eindruck wird nun der *Φίλιππος* auf ihn gemacht haben? Es ist schon oft mit Recht gesagt worden, daß es eine große Freude und Genugtuung für ihn gewesen sein muß, daß dieser erste Publizist Griechenlands, der berühmte athenische Professor der Beredsamkeit, der die einflußreichsten Männer Griechenlands zu seinen Schülern zählte, ihn, den König Makedoniens, zur Führung des seit langem ersehnten panhellenischen Nationalkrieges aufforderte. Es mußte ihm dies um so wertvoller sein, als dies Schriftstück nicht für die geheimen Akten Philipps bestimmt war, sondern gleichzeitig als Broschüre in der griechischen Welt verbreitet wurde, wie Isokrates gleich zu Anfang andeutet[1].

Aber es finden sich in der Schrift auch gewisse Naivitäten, über die Philipp nur gelächelt haben kann. Schon PAUL WENDLAND hat in seiner trefflichen Abhandlung über »König Philippos und Isokrates« hervorgehoben, wie verständnislos Isokrates den makedonischen Interessen Philipps gegenüberstand[2]. In der Tat sind es rein griechische Interessen, für die Philipp sein makedonisches Schwert ziehen soll: die Griechen Kleinasiens sollen befreit werden; Kleinasien soll erobert werden, damit das auf den Landstraßen umherirrende griechische Proletariat (die *πλανώμενοι*) dort angesiedelt werde, um die wirtschaftliche und soziale Not Griechenlands zu lindern; durch die Stadtanlagen in Kleinasien soll Griechenland einen Schutzwall gegen den Orient erhalten; die Griechen sollen die Herren Asiens werden usw. Nur an einer einzigen Stelle (§ 133) deutet er einmal im Vorübergehen an, daß auch Philipp äußere Vorteile durch einen solchen Krieg haben werde,

---

[1] Phil. 1: *ἵνα δηλά̄-ω καὶ σοὶ καὶ τοῖς ἄλλοις.*
[2] P. WENDLAND , Beiträge zur athen. Politik und Publizistik des IV. Jahrhunderts I (Nachr. Gött. Ges. d. W. phil.-hist. Kl. 1910) S. 125, 135.

indem er sagt, er wolle den Krieg nicht wegen der Macht und des Reichtums, den er bringe, empfehlen, denn daran habe Philipp schon mehr als genug. Vielmehr empfehle er ihn wegen des höchsten Ruhmes, den er bringen werde. Überhaupt sind der Ruhm und das Wohlwollen (εὔνοια) der Griechen die Kampfziele für Philipp, die Isokrates ständig im Munde führt. Diese völlige Außerachtlassung der realen makedonischen Interessen erklärt sich vielleicht daraus, daß Philipp als Heraklide — im Gegensatz zu seinem Volk, das für Isokrates nicht ein ὁμόφυλον γένος war (§ 108) — für ihn ein Vollgrieche war, wie er ihm denn den Herakles als höchstes Muster aller Tugenden (§ 109 ff.), im besonderen der Menschenfreundlichkeit und des Wohlwollens gegenüber den Griechen (§ 114), vor Augen stellt. Über dieser starken Betonung des Heraklidentums, durch die er auch dem griechischen Leser die Pille versüßen wollte, scheint er mir ganz vergessen zu haben, daß er zu dem Herrscher eines fremden Staates redete. Er hat vielfach schablonenhaft die alten Gedanken aus dem Panegyrikos wiederholt, ohne daran zu denken, daß er sich jetzt nicht mehr an die Griechen, sondern an den König Makedoniens wendete. Wenn er aber glaubte, daß Philipp nur um der freundlichen Augen der Griechen willen den Perserkrieg führen werde, so hat er den Philipp freilich schlecht gekannt. Er hat offenbar diesen massiven Realpolitiker für einen ebensolchen Idealisten gehalten, wie er selber einer war.

Als eine Utopie mußte es dem Philipp auch sogleich erscheinen, daß Isokrates glaubte, daß es ihm als Herakliden ein leichtes sein werde, die Griechen miteinander zu versöhnen, was er mit Recht für die notwendige Voraussetzung des gemeinsamen Nationalkrieges hielt. Wenn Philipp zurückblickte auf die leidenschaftlichen Kämpfe der Griechen untereinander, die seit Jahrzehnten zur Selbstzerfleischung der Nation geführt hatten, so konnte er als Staatsmann sich keinen Augenblick darüber im unklaren sein, daß für ihn eine innerliche Aussöhnung durch freundliches Zureden (πείθειν) ein Ding der Unmöglichkeit war. Und lag eine solche innerliche Aussöhnung, die dem Griechentum eine ungeheure Kraft gegeben hätte, im Interesse seiner makedonischen Politik? Doch wohl nur, wenn er vorher Griechenland fest in seiner Faust hatte.

Aber trotz allem wird Philipp sogleich erkannt haben, daß ihm in dem Antrag des Isokrates, die Griechen gegen Persien zu führen, Gedanken nahegelegt wurden, die sich aufs engste mit seinen (oben erwähnten) intimsten Zukunftsplänen berührten — Gedanken, die er nur geschickt umzuwandeln brauchte, um seine makedonischen Ziele mit der panhellenischen Flagge zu verdecken. Und dies hat er in Korinth in meisterhafter Weise durchgeführt.

III. Philipps Werk von Korinth.

Über die nächsten Jahre bis Chaeronea möchte ich mit wenigen Worten hinweggehen. Für die Lebhaftigkeit, mit der in griechischen Kreisen über den Φίλιππος debattiert wurde, spricht der Brief des Speusippos an Philipp, dessen Echtheit kürzlich von E. BICKERMANN und JOH. SYKUTRIS erwiesen worden ist[1]. Isokrates, der vor 346 keine persönlichen Beziehungen zu Philipp gehabt hatte[2], hat von nun an mehrfach an ihn geschrieben[3]. Ungeduldig wartete er auf die Erfüllung seiner Wünsche, während Philipp, nachdem er den Heiligen Krieg durch die Kapitulation der Phoker beendet hatte und durch seine Aufnahme in die Amphiktionie einen großen Schritt vorwärts auf dem Wege zur Anerkennung in Hellas getan hatte, sich zunächst wieder in Kämpfen mit Dardanern und Illyriern dem Ausbau seines makedonischen Reiches hingab. Beunruhigt durch eine schwere Verwundung Philipps, hat Isokrates ihn 344 in Epist. 2 nochmals ermahnt, an dem großen Ziel des Nationalkrieges festzuhalten[4]. Selbst noch nachdem trotz des ernstlichen Strebens Philipps, ohne Kampf mit Athen auszukommen, schließlich doch die Feindseligkeiten mit seiner Vaterstadt ausgebrochen waren, hat Isokrates in seinem Panathenaikos (nach Wendlands Deutung) dem Philipp, wenn auch in versteckter Form, das Vorbild des Agamemnon vor Augen gehalten[5].

Und nun kam der große Tag von Chaeronea, der Philipps Hoffnung auf die Herrschaft über Griechenland erfüllte! Schon auf dem Schlachtfeld nach errungenem Siege zeigte er, daß er bereit war, die Hand zur Versöhnung auszustrecken. Denn während er in seinen früheren Schlachten im Norden als ein Vertreter der Niederwerfungsstrategie die geschlagenen Feinde möglichst bis zur Vernichtung verfolgt hatte, hat er hier, und nur hier, auf die Verfolgung verzichtet und ist nach alter griechischer Weise auf dem Schlachtfeld stehengeblieben, während er den geschlagenen Feind abziehen ließ. Das soll man nicht aus militärischen Motiven erklären[6], sondern das ist die

---

[1] Berichte ü. d. Verh. d. Sächs. Ak. d. Wiss. phil.-hist. Kl. 80 Bd. 1928, 3. Heft. Zur Datierung vgl. jetzt auch M. Pohlenz, Hermes 64, 55 A. 1. Durch seinen Nachweis, daß der im Demosthenischen Korpus erhaltene Brief Philipps an die Athener echt ist, gewinnt die Tatsache, daß Philipp hier (19) auf eine Stelle im *Φίλιππος* (73) anspielt, noch an Interesse. Vgl. Diod. 18, 10, 1. Dies zeigt, wie gut der König die Schrift kannte.

[2] Isokr. Ep. 3, 3: οὐ γὰρ συνγεγενῆσθαί σοι πρότερον. Zur Echtheit des Briefes vgl. Ed. Meyer, Sitz. Pr. Ak. 1909 XXXI S. 766 und besonders P. Wendland l. c. S. 177 ff. mit eingehender Begründung.

[3] Einem derselben (aber nicht Ep. 2) hat Isokrates den Brief an Alexander (Ep. 5) beigefügt. Vgl. Ed. Meyer l. c. 763 A. 3.

[4] Vgl. die überzeugenden Ausführungen von Ed. Meyer l. c.

[5] P. Wendland l. c. S. 137 ff. Die Gegenschrift von Rostagni, Isocrate e Filippo (Entaphie in memoria di Emilio Pozzi) Torino 1913, die in der Preuß. Staatsbibliothek nicht vorhanden ist, kenne ich nur aus dem Referat von Th. Lenschau in Bursians Jahresb. Bd. 180 (1919 III) S. 164.

[6] Joh. Kromayer, Antike Schlachtfelder I (1903) S. 169. Nur nebenbei erwähnt er eventuelle politische Überlegungen. Kromayer sagt dann: »Eine Verfolgung von der Energie, wie wir sie bei den Alexanderschlachten gewohnt sind, hat hier nicht stattgefunden« und so stehe Chaeronea auch in dieser Hinsicht erst an der Grenze der neuen Zeit. Aber vorher hat er selbst gesagt, daß wir von einer weitergehenden Verfolgung hier überhaupt nichts hören, und Philipp noch am folgenden Tage in der Gegend von Chaeronea stand. Von den früheren Verfolgungen des Philipp spricht Kromayer nicht. Er kannte damals noch nicht den Didymoskommentar (1904), der uns erst Zeugnisse hierfür gebracht hat. Nach 12, 65 wurde Philipp auf der Verfolgung des Illyriers Pleuratos verwundet, ebenso nach 13,3 ff. auf der Verfolgung der Triballer, denn daß Philipp hier nicht der Verfolgte war, wie Ed. Meyer l. c. S. 759 A. 1 (= Kl. Schr. II 104) annahm, sondern der Verfolger, haben schon Foucart, Étude sur Didymos (1906) S. 120 f. und W. Florian, Studia Didymea Historica (Diss. Lips. 1908) S. 38 f. gezeigt. Nur irrte Foucart, indem er den seinen König verwundenden σαρισσοφόρος für einen Phalangiten hielt, statt für einen reitenden Sarissophoren (Florian S. 39), und Florian, indem er die *praeda amissa* nicht

Geste eines Politikers, für den der Krieg, nach dem Wort des Generals
v. Clausewitz, nur eine Fortsetzung der Politik mit andern Mitteln war. Mit
größter Milde ist er dann den Athenern in den Separatverhandlungen entgegengekommen und hat φιλία und συμμαχία mit ihnen geschlossen (Diod.
16, 87, 3. Justin 9, 4, 5), hat aber auch schon von seinen weiteren großen
Organisationsplänen den Schleier ein wenig gelüftet, indem er ihnen nahelegte,
wenn sie wollten (Ps.-Dem. 17, 30), sollten sie der geplanten κοινὴ εἰρήνη und
dem συνέδριον beitreten (Plut. Phok. 16). Bald ließ Philipp, um sich die Sympathien
der Griechen zu gewinnen, auch schon das Gerücht verbreiten, daß er den
panhellenischen Nationalkrieg zu führen beabsichtige[1]. Um diese Zeit hat
Isokrates seinen letzten Brief an Philipp geschrieben (Ep. 3, über die Echtheit
s. oben S. 298 A. 2), in dem er ihn mit bewegten Worten ermahnte, den Plan
des Nationalkrieges auch wirklich zur Ausführung zu bringen. Danach ist er im
Alter von 98 Jahren gestorben.

Nachdem Philipp in den Peloponnes eingerückt war und Sparta, das
sich ihm nicht fügen wollte, unterstützt von den alten Feinden Spartas, auf
seine ursprünglichen Grenzen beschränkt hatte, ging er nun an die große
Aufgabe, seiner Herrschaft über Griechenland die rechtlichen Formen zu geben.

Ich bin vor mehreren Jahren im Anschluß an BELOCH dafür eingetreten[2],
daß zwischen der konstituierenden Versammlung zu Korinth. in der der sogenannte korinthische Bund[3] begründet wurde, und der späteren Sitzung, in
der der Perserkrieg beschlossen wurde, streng zu scheiden ist, denn in jener
verhandelte Philipp mit den Gesandten Griechenlands, in dieser mit dem
Synedrion des neuen Bundes. Die erstere möchte ich daher den Friedenskongreß nennen, die spätere die Kriegssitzung oder die erste Bundesratssitzung. Jene begann wohl ganz am Ende des Jahres 338 und erstreckte sich durch mehrere Wochen oder einige Monate ins Jahr 337 hinein,
diese, von kurzer Dauer, mag etwas vor Sommeranfang 337 begonnen haben[4].

A. Der Friedenskongreß.

Nachdem mit Ausnahme von Sparta, das trotz seiner Ohnmacht die
Beteiligung stolz abgelehnt hatte, die sämtlichen souveränen Staaten Griechenlands, die von Philipp geladen waren, ihre Gesandten geschickt hatten[5], er-
öffnete Philipp den Kongreß, indem er in einem διάγραμμα, einem königlichen

---

als die skythische Beute erkannte. Diese Schilderungen des Didymos, namentlich die zweite,
geben uns eine Vorstellung von dem turbulenten Ungestüm, mit dem Philipp und seine Mannen
die Verfolgungen betrieben. Diese neue Kriegsweise ist also nicht erst von Alexander (s. KRO-
MAYER l. c.), sondern schon von Philipp eingeführt. S. meine Griech. Geschichte[2] S. 156, auch
schon Sitz. Bayer. Ak. 1917 10. Abh. S. 24 A. 1.
[1] Vgl. meine Ausführungen in Sitz. Bayer. Ak. 1917 10. Abh. (Beiträge zur Geschichte des
korinthischen Bundes) S. 10 ff.
[2] Sitz. Bayer. Ak. l. c. S. 20 ff.
[3] Die Bezeichnung »korinthischer Bund« kommt, soweit ich sehe, im Altertum nicht vor.
[4] Sitz. Bayer. Ak. l. c. S. 21 ff.
[5] Daß die Ladungen nicht nur bis zu den Thermopylen, sondern bis zur makedonischen
Grenze gingen, hat die von AD. WILHELM meisterhaft zusammengefügte Inschrift Syll. I3 260
gelehrt. Vgl. Sitz. Bayer. Ak. l. c. S. 5 A. 2.

Erlaß — jedenfalls in den verbindlichsten Formen, da er ja um die Sympathien der Griechen warb —, seine Organisationspläne als Unterlage für die Verhandlungen darlegte[1]. Das Schlußergebnis der langwierigen Verhandlungen[2] war ein ewiger Vertrag (συνθῆκαι), den Philipp mit dem neu gebildeten Hellenenbund (genannt οἱ Ἕλληνες) schloß. Betreffs der Organisation des Bundes sei hier zunächst nur hervorgehoben, daß »die Hellenen« ein repräsentatives Organ in dem συνέδριον erhielten, in dem die einzelnen Städte oder Stämme bzw. κοινά oder die ad hoc zusammengelegten Gruppen kleinerer Bündner je nach ihrer Kriegstärke[3] in verschiedener Zahl durch Abgeordnete vertreten waren[4], während Philipp zum lebenslänglichen Bundesfeldherrn »zu Wasser und zu Lande« (Polyb. IX 33, 7) mit dem Titel ἡγεμών erwählt war. Ehe ich auf die Verteilung der Kompetenzen zwischen Synhedrion und Hegemon eingehe, möchte ich die noch nicht genügend geklärte Frage erörtern, wie dieser Hellenenbund staatsrechtlich zu deuten und zu rubrizieren ist.

Weit verbreitet ist die Annahme, daß der Bund auf der κοινὴ εἰρήνη, dem allgemeinen Landfrieden, aufgebaut sei, der auf diesem Kongreß für das ganze Bundesgebiet für ewige Zeiten vertraglich festgelegt worden ist.

Dieser Landfriede besagte einmal, daß die Bündnerstaaten untereinander keine Fehden führen durften, andererseits aber auch, daß innerhalb der einzelnen Bundesstadt alle gewaltsamen Umstürze verboten waren. Alle Revolutionen mit ihren verheerenden Begleiterscheinungen, wie sie damals an der Tagesordnung waren, wie die Konfiskationen, die Landaufteilungen (γῆς ἀναδασμοί), die Schuldentilgungen (χρεῶν ἀποκοπαί), sollten verhindert werden. Städte, die Verbannte aufnahmen und duldeten, daß diese mit Gewalt die Rückkehr in die Heimat erzwangen, sollten vom Vertrage ausgeschlossen werden (ἔκσπονδοι). Wie segensreich ein solcher Landfriede nach allen den inneren Stürmen wirken mußte, wenn er wirklich durchgeführt wurde, liegt auf der Hand. Man soll nicht sagen, daß Philipp durch solche Beschränkungen etwa das politische Leben erstickt habe, im besonderen auch durch die Bestimmung, daß die Verfassungen, wie sie zur Zeit der Eidesleistung bestanden, nicht verändert werden dürften, denn auch in diesem Paragraphen ist, wie

---

[1] Sitz. Bayer. Ak. l. c. S. 29 ff. Auf S. 34 bei der Parallelisierung dieses Vorganges mit den Verhandlungen in Sardes vom J. 386 hätte ich hervorheben sollen, daß trotz der ähnlichen Form doch sachlich ein großer Unterschied besteht: Artaxerxes oktroyierte seinen Ukas unter Kriegsandrohung, Philipp dagegen unterbreitete sein Exposé als Unterlage für die Verhandlungen, die viele Wochen gedauert haben. Immerhin ist es bemerkenswert, daß Philipp die ihm geläufige Form des διάγραμμα gewählt hat.

[2] Allein schon die Enquête über die Wehrkräfte der sämtlichen Bündner muß längere Zeit in Anspruch genommen haben.

[3] Die Kriegstärke als Maßstab für die Zahl der Abgeordneten zu nehmen, ist kürzlich von J. A. O. LARSEN vorgeschlagen worden in seiner interessanten Arbeit »*Representative government in the panhellenic leagues*« (*Classical Philology* XX Nr. 4, Oct. 1925) S. 319. Auch Hr. Dr.W. SCHWAHN (Berlin), mit dem ich das Vergnügen hatte, mich mehrfach über die Probleme des korinthischen Bundes zu unterhalten, ist unabhängig von LARSEN auf dieselbe Erklärung gekommen. Ich bemerke hierzu, daß es unter dieser Annahme sich von selbst versteht, daß die Kriegstärke schon auf dem Friedenskongreß festgestellt wurde, wie auch Justin berichtet (s. unten), und nicht etwa erst in der Kriegssitzung, denn die Normierung der Zahlen der Abgeordneten fand natürlich auf dem Friedenskongreß statt.

[4] Auch dies ist erst durch die von AD. WILHELM zusammengesetzte Eidesinschrift Syll.[3] 260 klar geworden.

überall, nur vom gewaltsamen Umsturz, vom καταλύειν, die Rede[1]. Also eine friedliche Weiterentwicklung und Ausgestaltung der Verfassung war durchaus nicht unter Strafe gestellt und war an sich zulässig[2]. Auch bei dem Verbot der Hinrichtungen und Verbannungen heißt es ausdrücklich, daß dies nur gilt, wenn sie gegen die bestehenden Gesetze der Stadt verstoßen (Ps.-Dem. 17, 15: παρὰ τοὺς κειμένους ταῖς πόλεσι νόμους). Damit ist also, entsprechend der gewährleisteten Autonomie (s. unten), die Gültigkeit der bestehenden Gesetze der Städte ausdrücklich sanktioniert, und die Städte konnten nach wie vor nach ihren Gesetzen sowohl hinrichten wie verbannen[3]. Nur die Revolutionen sollten aus der Welt geschafft werden.

Im Hinblick auf diesen Landfrieden hat RANKE den korinthischen Bund als »eine Art von Landfriedensbund« bezeichnet[4]. Diese Definition hat viel Anklang gefunden, nur daß manche die wohlbedachte Einschränkung, die in den Worten »eine Art von« liegt, außer acht lassen und geradezu von »Landfriedensbund« sprechen[5]. RANKE hat mit diesem Versuch, den Bund auf der κοινὴ εἰρήνη aufzubauen, darauf verzichtet, ihn aus staatsrechtlichen Begriffen der griechischen Geschichte abzuleiten — begreiflich genug, da es hierfür, soweit ich sehe, Parallelen in dieser kaum geben dürfte —, und hat vielmehr eine Analogie aus der deutschen mittelalterlichen Geschichte herangezogen. Soweit ich, der ich auf diesem Gebiet leider Laie bin, mir ein Urteil erlauben darf, scheint mir eine Analogie nur insofern vorzuliegen, als in beiden Fällen Landfrieden verkündet wird, im übrigen aber die Organisation zum Schutze des Landfriedens, und darauf kommt es hier an, verschieden zu sein. Jene Landfriedensbünde des 13. und 14. Jahrhunderts werden in der Regel von einzelnen Städten oder Fürsten ad hoc geschlossen, um den vom Kaiser verkündeten Landfrieden in ihrem Gebiet durchzuführen, und zwar war dieser Landfriede nur für bestimmte Jahre und meist auch für bestimmte Reichsteile gegeben. Dem steht der korinthische Bund gegenüber als ein für ewige Zeiten geschlossener Bund, dessen Landfriede alle »Hellenen« binden sollte, und der zudem doch auch noch andere Aufgaben gehabt hat, als nur den Landfrieden zu wahren, wie z. B. zunächst die Beteiligung am Perserkrieg. Wenn also zwischen Art und Zweck des korinthischen Bundes und jener Landfriedensbünde doch nur oberflächliche Beziehungen bestehen, scheint mir andererseits eine schlagende Parallele zu Philipps Landfrieden der allgemeine ewige Landfriede zu sein, den Kaiser Maximilian I. im Jahre 1495 auf dem Reichstag zu Worms verkündet hat. Hier aber ist von Landfriedensbünden nicht mehr die Rede, denn hier wurde das Reichskammergericht geschaffen, um den Landfriedensbruch zu ahnden. Sobald das Reich selbst die Durchführung des Landfriedens übernahm, war

---

[1] Syll. I3 260, 12 ff. = Ps.-Dem. 17, 10. Das Gewaltsame unterstreicht mit Recht auch KÄRST, Hellenismus I3 276. Vgl. dagegen z. B. KESSLER (s. S. 311 A. 6) S. 75.

[2] Richtig KÄRST, Hellenismus I3 276/7.

[3] Auch in Ps.-Dem. 15 möchte ich das ἐπὶ νεωτερισμῷ nicht nur auf das nächst vorhergehende Glied μηδὲ δούλων ἀπελευθερώσεις beziehen, sondern auch auf μηδὲ χρημάτων δημεύσεις μηδὲ γῆς ἀναδασμοὶ μηδὲ χρεῶν ἀποκοπαί. Das ist auch die Auffassung von BERVE, Das Alexanderreich I 229.

[4] Weltgeschichte I5 2 S. 151.

[5] So KÄRST, Hellenismus passim.

für Landfriedensbünde kein Platz mehr. Dies entspricht aber der Situation unter Philipp, wo der ganze Hellenenbund für den Landfrieden einzutreten hatte. Ja, wir können mit dem Reichskammergericht geradezu das Synhedrion in Parallele stellen, zu dessen Aufgaben, wie wir sehen werden, es gleichfalls gehörte, den Landfriedensbruch zu verhindern und zu bestrafen. Diese Parallele mit dem ewigen Landfrieden von 1495 lehrt uns aber nichts über die staatsrechtliche Bedeutung oder den Zweck des korinthischen Bundes, denn dieser Bund entspricht bei dieser Parallele dem Deutschen Reich, und ebensowenig wie dieses kann der korinthische Bund aus dem Landfrieden heraus erklärt werden. Wie das Reich, mußte auch dieser Bund erst da sein, damit der Landfriede verkündet werden konnte.

Wenn ich also RANKES Definition, selbst in seiner vorsichtigen Formulierung als »einer Art von Landfriedensbund«, ablehne, scheint es mir andererseits nicht zweifelhaft zu sein, wie ich schon in diesen Sitzungsberichten 1927, XXVI S.298/99 (vgl. 281) äußerte, daß wir den korinthischen Bund vielmehr auf der von RANKE und anderen übersehenen συμμαχία aufbauen müssen, jenem Schutz- und Trutzbündnis, das nicht nur Philipp mit den Hellenen, sondern, wie die Epidaurische Inschrift von 302 wahrscheinlich macht[1], gleichzeitig in demselben Vertrage auch die Hellenen untereinander geschlossen haben.

Freilich könnte man vielleicht auf den Gedanken kommen, daß in Philipps Schöpfung, anders als in jenem Vertrage des Antigonos und Demetrios, die Symmachie nicht die Grundlage des ewigen Bundesvertrages, sondern vielmehr nur ein vorübergehendes Kampfbündnis gegen Persien gewesen sei, das daher auch nicht auf diesem Friedenskongreß, sondern erst nachher in der Kriegssitzung begründet sei[2]. Aber dies wird durch den ausgezeichneten Bericht Justins IX 5, 4 ff. ausgeschlossen. Dort heißt es: *Auxilia deinde singularum civitatum describuntur, sive adiuvandus ea manu rex oppugnante aliquo foret seu duce illo bellum inferendum neque enim dubium erat imperium Persarum his apparatibus peti.* Es handelt sich hier um die Feststellung der griechischen Wehrmacht, aus der im Ernstfall der Hegemon die zu stellenden Kontingente zu bestimmen hatte. Ich habe schon früher[3] hervorgehoben, daß man hier den Eindruck hat, daß Trogus (bzw. seine Quelle) »geradezu auf den Wortlaut des Schutz- und Trutzbündnisses zurückgegriffen hat«, und daß die Alternative *sive adiuvandus* usw. »direkt an die Sprache der Verträge« erinnert[4]. Wenn nun zu dem zweiten Glied hinzugefügt wird *neque enim dubium erat imperium Persarum his apparatibus peti*, so wird damit ausgeschlossen, daß diese Bestimmung in der Kriegssitzung getroffen wäre, denn diese wurde ja mit der Proklamation des Perserkrieges eröffnet (s. unten), so daß die Bemerkung, daß niemand daran zweifelte, daß dies gegen Persien gerichtet war, unverständlich wäre. Diese Worte passen nur für den Friedenskongreß[5], während

---

[1] Sitz. Pr. Ak. 1927 XXVI 299.
[2] Dieser Einwand ist mir von geschätzter Seite gemacht worden.
[3] Sitz. Bayer. Ak. 1917 10, S. 16.
[4] Die erstere erinnert an eine Formel wie: Ἐὰν δέ τις ἴῃ ἐπὶ —, βοηθεῖν —.
[5] Siehe auch oben S. 300 A. 3.

dessen Philipp, wie ich früher dargelegt habe[1], aus politischen und militärischen Gründen offiziell noch nicht vom Perserkrieg gesprochen hat. Zu
dieser Situation, aber auch nur zu dieser, passen jene Worte ausgezeichnet.

Ist diese Symmachie aber auf dem Friedenskongreß beschlossen worden, dann
war sie nicht ein temporäres Waffenbündnis für den Perserkrieg[2], sondern,
ebenso wie die κοινὴ εἰρήνη, eine für ewige Zeiten vereinbarte Grundlage der
neuen Ordnung.

Hiernach dürfen wir der Symmachie Philipps dieselbe Bedeutung zu-
schreiben wie der des Antigonos und Demetrios. Wie diese war auch jene
ein Schutz- und Trutzbündnis, wie es ja auch Justin klar charakterisiert.
Ich möchte auch heute wie in diesen Sitzungsberichten 1927 XXVI S. 298
für wahrscheinlich halten, daß nicht erst Antigonos und Demetrios, sondern
schon Philipp jene einst schon von Aristides beim Abschluß des attisch-
delischen Bundes[3] gebrauchte Formel ὥστε τοῖς αὐτοῖς ἐχθροῖς καὶ φίλοις
χρῆσθαι angewendet hat, die das Offensivbündnis charakterisiert (l. c. S. 282),
wenn sie auch nur in den συνθῆκαι gestanden haben wird und in der uns
erhaltenen Eidesinschrift (DITT., Syll. I³ 260) nicht erscheint.

Nach der Epidaurischen Inschrift ist nun aber klar, daß der Bund der
Könige mit den Hellenen auf dieser Symmachie aufgebaut war. Abgesehen
von den zahlreichen Erwähnungen der συμμαχία und der σύμμαχοι in den
συνθῆκαι, beweist es der Anfang des Eides (V 24 ff.): Ἐμμε]νῶ ἐν τῆι συμ[μαχίαι
τῆι πρὸς τοὺς βασιλεῖς Ἀντίγονον καὶ Δημήτριον] καὶ τοὺς τού[των ἐκγόνους
καὶ τοὺς ἄλλους συμμάχους τοὺς μετέχον]τας τοῦ συν[εδρίου ὥστε καὶ(?) χρῆσθαι
ἐχθροῖς καὶ φίλοις τοῖς αὐ]τοῖς. Hier ist kein Zweifel, daß wir einen Symmachievertrag vor uns haben, und daß dieser Hellenenbund von 302 ein
Symmachiebund war. Was ich aber bei meiner letzten Behandlung dieser
Inschrift (1927) noch nicht erkannt hatte, ist dies, daß die darauffolgenden
Ausführungen καὶ οὐ[χ ὅπλα ἐποίσω ἐπὶ πημονῆι κτλ. den Inhalt der κοινὴ
εἰρήνη angeben. Dementsprechend heißt es auch vorher in den συνθῆκαι in
I 12: Πολεμίους δὲ εἶναι πᾶσι τοῖς τῆς] εἰρ[ή]νης [τῆς] πατρώιας μετέχου[σιν,
weil die folgenden Handlungen, die unter Strafe gestellt werden, gegen die
κοινὴ εἰρήνη verstoßen. Also sind hier die Landfriedensparagraphen
in den Symmachievertrag eingefügt worden. So heißt es denn auch
in der Eidesformel in dem letzten uns erhaltenen Satz (V 34 ff.): ἀλλὰ πο[λε-
μήσω τῶι τὴν κοινὴν εἰρήνην παραβαίνοντι κατὰ τὴν συμμα]χίαν. Also die
Symmachie verpflichtet hier zur Wahrung und zum Schutz des Landfriedens.
Die Symmachie ist also die Grundlage und der Landfriede nur ein Haupt-
und Kernstück des Symmachievertrages[4].

Hiernach ist nun auch der dem Philipp geleistete Eid (Syll. I³ 260) zu
deuten und zu ergänzen. Für den Anfang habe ich in diesen Sitzungsbe-

---

[1] Sitz. Bayer. Ak. l. c. S. 26 f.
[2] Dagegen spricht auch die erste Alternative bei Justin.
[3] Aristoteles, Ἀθ. πολ. 23, 5: ὥστε τὸν αὐτὸν ἐχθρὸν εἶναι καὶ φίλον. Zu dieser Formel vgl.
Sitz. Pr. Ak. 1927 XXVI S. 282.
[4] Bei den Verhandlungen mit Athen ergab es sich von selbst, daß zunächst die φιλία
und συμμαχία geschlossen wurde, und erst später die κοινὴ εἰρήνη hinzutrat.

richten 1927 XXVI S. 281 folgende Ergänzung vorgeschlagen (die Zeile zu 33 Buchstaben):

Ἐμμενῶ [ἐν τῆι][1]
[ι συμμαχίαι καὶ οὔτε τὰς σ]υνθήκας τὰ[ς πρ]
[ὸς Φίλιππον καταλύσω οὔτ]ε ὅπλ[α] ἐ[π]οί[σω ἐ] κτλ.

Nach den obigen Ausführungen habe ich hier mit Recht die συμμαχία an die Spitze gestellt, und nicht etwa die εἰρήνη. Aber an dem καταλύσω nehme ich jetzt Anstoß, da ich mich inzwischen überzeugt habe, daß in diesem Zusammenhang nur λύσω zu erwarten ist. Das erfordert, immer unter dem Zwang der στοιχηδόν-Schreibung, eine starke Umänderung. Ich möchte jetzt folgenden Text vorschlagen:

Ἐμμενῶ [τῆι σ]
[υμμαχίαι[2] καὶ οὐ λύσω τὰς σ]υνθήκας τὰ[ς πρ]
[ὸς Φίλιππον Μακεδόνα οὐδ]ὲ ὅπλ[α] ἐ[π]οί[σω ἐ] κτλ.

Das οὐδ]ὲ nötigt zu der Annahme, daß schon eine Negation vorhergegangen ist. Dies führt auf eine Zweiteilung des Gedankens nach der positiven und negativen Seite hin, wie ich sie hier mit ἐμμενῶ — καὶ οὐ λύσω vorschlage. Eine gewisse formale Parallele bietet z. B. der Eid des Vertrages von 420 bei Thuk. V 47, 9: Ἐμμενῶ τῇ ξυμμαχίᾳ κατὰ τὰ ξυγκείμενα δικαίως καὶ ἀβλαβῶς καὶ ἀδόλως καὶ οὐ παραβήσομαι τέχνῃ οὐδὲ μηχανῇ οὐδεμιᾷ. Auch bei dieser Ergänzung bleibt bestehen, daß Philipp nicht als βασιλεύς bezeichnet ist, denn βασιλέα würde einen Buchstaben zuwenig haben[3]. Auch Ἀμύντου wäre um einen Buchstaben zu kurz, auch wäre wohl τὸν Ἀ. zu erwarten. Mit οὐδ]ὲ ὅπλ[α] ἐ[π]οί[σω κτλ. beginnt dann auch hier, wie in der Inschrift von Epidauros, die Einarbeitung der Landfriedensparagraphen in den Symmachievertrag. Darum ist es durchaus korrekt, wenn es nachher in Z.13f. heißt: ὅτε τ[οὺς ὅρκους τοὺς περὶ τ]ῆς εἰρήνης ὤμνυον, denn diese Verpflichtung, nicht die Verfassungen gewaltsam umzustürzen (wie auch das Königtum des Philipp und seiner Nachkommen), gehört speziell zu den Bestimmungen des Landfriedens. Vgl. das oben S. 303 zu Epid. I 12 Bemerkte. Auch in der Epid.-Inschr. V 30 ist vielleicht besser τῶν μετεχόντων τῆς εἰρήνης zu ergänzen als τοῦ συνεδρίου. Im übrigen vgl. den Neudruck der Eidesinschrift im Anhang S. 316f.

Aus der großen Bedeutung, die der Landfriede für das politische Leben der Griechen hatte, erklärt sich wohl, daß in der Tradition mehr von der κοινὴ εἰρήνη als von der συμμαχία die Rede ist, wiewohl letztere die Voraussetzung für jene war, und dieser Umstand mag die Aufstellung der Theorie von dem Landfriedensbund mit begünstigt haben[4].

---

[1] Es war nur ein Versehen, wenn ich ἐ[ν druckte. Das ω steht unmittelbar vor dem Bruch.
[2] Nach der Buchstabenzahl könnte hier statt τῆι συμμαχίαι auch ἐν τῆι εἰρήνηι ergänzt werden, aber nach den obigen Darlegungen kommt das hier nicht in Betracht.
[3] Zu meinen Bemerkungen über den Verzicht auf den Königstitel in Sitz. Pr. Ak. 1927 XXVI S. 281 trage ich nach, daß Justin IX 4, 2 im Anschluß an die Schlacht von Chaeronea sagt: nec regem se Graeciae, sed ducem (= ἡγεμόνα) appellari iussit. Natürlich kommt in Wirklichkeit nur der βασιλεὺς Μακεδόνων in Betracht. Der Zusatz Graeciae mag erst von Justin stammen.
[4] Daß in Ps.-Dem. 17 durchweg von der κοινὴ εἰρήνη und nicht von der συμμαχία die Rede ist, erklärt sich dadurch, daß die Übertretungen, die der Redner dem Alexander vorwirft,

Nach den obigen Ausführungen kann es wohl nicht zweifelhaft sein, daß wir in dem korinthischen Bunde (wie in dem des Antigonos und Demetrios) nicht einen Landfriedensbund, sondern einen Symmachiebund zu sehen haben[1].

Dann aber brauchen wir nicht mehr im deutschen Mittelalter nach Parallelen zu suchen, sondern haben genügend Parallelen in der griechischen Geschichte selbst, um nur — trotz mancher Abweichungen — den peloponnesischen Bund und die attischen Seebünde zu nennen. Eigentümlich ist dem korinthischen Bunde die Verbindung mit dem Landfrieden. Aber auch hierfür gibt es ein Beispiel in der älteren griechischen Geschichte: ich meine die sogenannte Eidgenossenschaft, die 481 in Erwartung des Angriffs des Xerxes gebildet wurde. Damals haben ihre πρόβουλοι beschlossen, daß alle Feindschaften zwischen den Bündnern aufhören sollten. Auch für diese Symmachie wurde also ein Landfriede verkündet. Schon v. Wilamowitz hat einmal geäußert, daß Philipp seinen Bund »in Nachahmung der großen Zeit von 480« gestiftet habe[2], und wenn wir bei Besprechung der Kriegssitzung sehen werden, daß Philipp sein Unternehmen gegen Persien direkt mit dem großen Perserkrieg gegen Xerxes verknüpft hat, so darf vielleicht die Vermutung gewagt werden, daß ihm auch bei der Konstituierung seines Hellenenbundes der Gedanke an jene den Landfrieden einschließende Zusammenfassung der Hellenen gegen Xerxes lebendig gewesen ist.

Dieser auf der Symmachie aufgebaute Staatenbund[3] war also die staatsrechtliche Form, die Philipp für die schon seit langem erstrebte Beherrschung Griechenlands gefunden hat. Indem er für sich und seine Nachkommen inner-

---

sämtlich den Landfrieden betreffen. Wenn Alexander in dem Erlaß für Chios (Syll. I 3 283) von den Bundesstädten als τῶν πόλεων τῶν τῆς εἰρήνης κοινωνουσῶν spricht, so wird das damit zusammenhängen, daß diese Verräter, über deren Bestrafung er handelt, die Aristokraten waren, die die Demokratie gestürzt hatten, deren Wiedereinführung er in den Zeilen vorher angeordnet hat. In anderen Fällen ist kein spezieller Grund zu erkennen, so in dem Brief Alexanders an Darius (Arr. II 14, 6, vgl. Diod. 18, 56. 3). Anderseits wird die Symmachie hervorgehoben bei Diod. 17, 63, 1, wo mit τῶν συμμαχούντων Ἑλλήνων die durch die Symmachie dem Antipater zur Heeresfolge verpflichteten Hellenen bezeichnet werden, ferner bei Arr. II 1, 4. Beide Momente zusammen nennt Arr. III 24, 5: ὅσοι πρὸ τῆς εἰρήνης τε καὶ τῆς ξυμμαχίας τῆς πρὸς Μακεδόνας κτλ. Den Inhalt der Symmachie gibt (abgesehen von der Epidaurischen Inschrift) am genausten Justin an der oben S. 302 behandelten Stelle IX, 5, 4.

[1] Dieselbe Auffassung vertreten, wie ich nachträglich zu meiner Freude fand, Busolt-Swoboda, Griech. Staatskunde II (1926) S. 1389 ff. Auch für A. W. Pickard, Cambridge Anc. Hist. VI 267, ist der Bund eine *alliance, offensive and defensive*. Meine Darstellung in Sitz. Bayer. Ak. 1917 10. S. 5 ff. (Hellenenbund, mit dem die κοινὴ εἰρήνη und die συμμαχία geschlossen sei) war unbefriedigend, denn dabei blieb ungeklärt, was denn der Hellenenbund war.

[2] Staat u. Gesellsch. d. Griech. (1910) S. 141. Vgl. auch Kärst, Hellenismus I 3 275 f., auch J. A. O. Larsen l. c. XXI S. 59, der auch auf Thirlwall und Bury hinweist.

[3] Dieser Bund ist nicht ein Bundesstaat, sondern ein Staatenbund (so auch Busolt-Swoboda l. c.). Er ist auch kein κοινόν. Daß mit der Wendung τὸ κοινὸν τῶν Ἑλλήνων συνελθόντες — εἴλαντο in der Chronik von Oxyrhynchos (P. Oxy. I 12, III 9 ff.) offenbar das συνέδριον gemeint ist, habe ich schon in Sitz. Bayer. Ak. 1917 10. S. 6 A. 1 bemerkt. Busolt-Swoboda, die dies akzeptieren (l. c. S. 1390 A. 5), halten aber ebenso wie ich l. c. daran fest, daß Arr. III 24, 4 ὅτι Σινωπεῖς οὔτε τοῦ κοινοῦ τῶν Ἑλλήνων μετεῖχον mit diesem κοινὸν τῶν Ἑλλήνων den korinthischen Bund meint. Zumal in der Epidaurischen Inschrift die Formel μετέχειν τοῦ συνεδρίου ständig für die Bezeichnung der Bündner gebraucht wird, ist es mir inzwischen sehr wahrscheinlich geworden, daß auch bei Arrian unter dem κοινόν das κοινὸν συνέδριον zu verstehen ist, wie in jener Chronik. Dann haben wir überhaupt keinen Beleg mehr für die Bezeichnung des korinthischen Bundes als κοινόν. Tatsächlich entspricht er auch nicht den bekannten κοινά.

halb dieses Bundes die Stellung eines lebenslänglichen Bundesfeldherrn (ἡγεμών) sicherte, hat er diesen an sich freien und souveränen Hellenenbund durch Personalunion mit seinem makedonischen Reiche dauernd verbunden. Hatte er, wie ich oben S. 295f. annahm, wegen seiner kulturpolitischen Ziele von früh an den Wunsch gehabt, eine möglichst schonende Form für die erstrebte Herrschaft über Hellas zu finden, so muß man sagen, daß er dies ungemein schwierige Problem so geschickt gelöst hat, wie es überhaupt nur möglich war. Wenn das Ergebnis trotzdem in weiten Kreisen Griechenlands eine kühle Aufnahme fand und auf passive Resistenz stieß, so liegt das an geschichtlichen Tatsachen, für die er nicht verantwortlich war, und die er nicht aus der Welt schaffen konnte. Die Griechen in ihrem alten Freiheitsdrange fühlten trotz aller ihnen gewährten Rechte in dieser Neuordnung doch die tatsächliche Abhängigkeit von der Politik des Königs von Makedonien heraus und empfanden dies um so schwerer, als sie sein Volk, die Makedonen, für ein nichtgriechisches, für ein barbarisches Volk hielten, mochten sie ihn selbst vielleicht auch als Herakliden für einen Griechen ansehen. So sahen sie, wenn es auch nach den Paragraphen des Bundesvertrages nicht begründet war, in seiner Hegemonie doch eine tatsächliche Fremdherrschaft. Hierin liegt der Schlüssel für die Schwierigkeiten, denen Alexander in Hellas nach der baldigen Ermordung des Philipp gegenüberstand. Vielleicht wäre an einen gewissen Ausgleich zu denken gewesen, wenn Philipp noch dreißig Jahre regiert und im Geiste von Korinth die Bundesparagraphen durchgeführt hätte.

Jedenfalls hat Philipp sich bei der Konstituierung des Bundes die größte Mühe gegeben, die Sympathien der Griechen zu gewinnen, indem er durchaus liberal und weitherzig auf ihre freiheitlichen Aspirationen Rücksicht nahm, soweit es irgend mit seiner makedonischen Machtpolitik vereinbar war. So wurde gleich zu Anfang des Vertrages jedem Bündner ἐλευθερία und αὐτονομία zugesichert, vielleicht auch ἀφορολογησία und ἀφρουρησία[1]. Als Artaxerxes im Königsfrieden die ἐλευθερία und αὐτονομία für jede Polis, klein und groß, festsetzte, bedeutete dies eine Zerstückelung Griechenlands in eine Unsumme souveräner Staaten. Jetzt dagegen hatte diese Bestimmung eine ganz andere Bedeutung, wo Philipp einen nationalen Einheitsstaat in dem Hellenenbunde geschaffen hatte, und innerhalb dieses jeder Einzelstaat frei und autonom sein sollte. Während die Athener in ihrem Vertrag mit Chios (384/83) und dann bei der Begründung des II. attischen Seebundes mit ängstlicher Rücksichtnahme auf den Königsfrieden jedem Bündner Freiheit und Autonomie hatten versprechen müssen (s. oben S. 292 A. 2), hat Philipp jetzt im Kampf gegen den Königsfrieden diesen Paragraphen aus ihm entnommen, so daß er es jetzt war, der als Hegemon des Bundes anstatt des Großkönigs die Garantie für Freiheit und Autonomie der Hellenen übernahm, und damit hat er, gewiß mit voller Absicht, den § 2 des Königsfriedens zerrissen[2].

---

[1] Hierüber vgl. Sitz. Bayer. Ak. 1917 10 S. 7 A. 2.
[2] Vgl. zu dieser Tendenz Philipps meine Ausführungen in Sitz. Bayer. Ak. 1917 10 S. 34/5. Die Einwendungen, die F. NOLTE l. c. S. 5 hiergegen erhoben hat, beruhen auf Mißverständnis meiner Worte. Daß Philipps Rechtsstellung gegenüber den Hellenen als ἡγεμών eine völlig

Weitherzig hat Philipp aber auch die Stellung des Synhedrion ausgebaut. Über die Rechte dieses repräsentativen Organs der Hellenen und im besonderen über seine Rechte gegenüber dem Hegemon haben wir bisher nur geringe Nachrichten, während wir für die Geschäftsordnung des Synhedrion aus den sehr ausführlichen Angaben der Epidaurischen Inschrift von 302 manches auch für Philipps Ordnung haben entnehmen können. Allgemein anerkannt ist, daß das Synhedrion das Bundesgericht darstellte[1]. Überliefert ist auch, daß zur Verhütung von Revolutionen und ihren Begleiterscheinungen das Synhedrion mit den vom Hegemon in Hellas zum Schutz der Bundesverfassung eingesetzten Instanzen zusammen operieren sollte (Ps.-Dem. 17, 15). Einen bedeutsamen Schritt weiter führt uns eine neue Lesung, die ich für den dem Philipp geleisteten Eid vorzuschlagen habe. In Syll. I³ 260, 19 ff. heißt es nach Ad. Wilhelm, der um das Verständnis dieser Inschrift außerordentliche Verdienste hat:

$$\kappa\alpha\grave{\iota}\ \pi o\lambda\epsilon\mu\acute{\eta}\sigma\omega\ \tau\hat{\omega}\text{-}$$
$$[\iota\ \tau\grave{\eta}\nu\ \kappa o\iota\nu\grave{\eta}\nu\ \epsilon\grave{\iota}\rho\acute{\eta}\nu\eta\nu\ \pi\alpha\rho]\alpha\beta\alpha\acute{\iota}\nu o\nu\tau\iota\ \kappa\alpha\theta\acute{o}\tau\iota$$
20 $$[\ \grave{\alpha}\nu\ \hat{\eta}\iota\ \sigma\upsilon\nu\tau\epsilon\tau\alpha\gamma\mu\acute{\epsilon}\nu o\nu\ \grave{\epsilon}\mu\alpha\upsilon]\tau\hat{\omega}\iota\ \kappa\alpha\grave{\iota}\ \acute{o}\ \acute{\eta}\gamma\epsilon[\mu\acute{\omega}\text{-}$$
$$[\nu\ \kappa\epsilon\lambda\epsilon\acute{\upsilon}\eta\iota\ -\ \text{12 l.}\ -\ \kappa\alpha]\tau\alpha\lambda\epsilon\acute{\iota}\psi\omega.$$

Ich habe schon früher meine Bedenken gegen die Ergänzung καθότι [ἀν ἦι συντεταγμένον ἐμαυ]τῶι ausgesprochen[2]. Wie könnte denn hier ein Reflexivpronomen stehen? Auch wäre die Hauptsache gar nicht angegeben, von wem denn dieser Befehl gegeben wäre. Immer wieder habe ich vergeblich nach einer anderen Ergänzung von]τωι gesucht. Nun bin durch die ausgezeichnete Photographie des Steines, die mir Johannes Kirchner freundlichst geliehen hat, die mir schon in diesen Sitzungsberichten 1927 XXVI S. 281 zu einer neuen Lesung verholfen hatte, auch hier zu einer neuen Lesung gekommen. Auf den ersten Blick sieht es zwar fast so aus, als wenn T dastünde, nur fällt auf, daß der Querstrich schräg nach oben führt und links nicht über die Hasta hinwegführt. Mit der Lupe erkannte ich deutlich, daß dieser scheinbare Querstrich nur eine Verletzung des Steines darstellt, daß in Wirklichkeit also I, ein Iota dasteht. Sobald ich]ιωι hatte, schwebte mir natürlich συνεδρ]ίωι vor, und dies wurde mir dadurch bestätigt, daß vor dem Iota noch ein winziger Buchstabenrest steht, den ich zwar für sich nicht als P zu lesen wagen würde, der aber doch wohl zum Kopf eines P gehören könnte. Damit ergab sich von selbst die Ergänzung: καθότι [ἀν δοκῆι τῶι κοινῶι συνεδρ]ίωι. Das ergibt 34 Buchstaben für die Zeile statt der normalen 33. Aber in der vorhergehenden Zeile ist sogar zweimal ein Iota mit seinen Vordermännern

---

andere war als die des Artaxerxes, geht aus meiner Arbeit doch klar hervor. Wenn Nolte schreibt: »W. bezeichnet es geradezu als Ziel der Philippischen Politik, seinen Frieden an die Stelle des Königsfriedens zu setzen [das ist auch heute meine Ansicht], um so Rechtsnachfolger des persischen Königs zu werden«, so muß der Leser glauben, die von mir jetzt gesperrten Worte stammten von mir; sie stammen vielmehr von Nolte. Ich habe das nirgends gesagt. Ich sprach l. c. vielmehr von »einer bewußten gewaltsamen Beseitigung des Königsfriedens« und betonte Philipps Stellung als Hegemon.

[1] Dies hat Kärst, Rhein. Mus. LII 521ff. erwiesen. Es ist ein Rückschritt, wenn A. W. Pickard, Cambr. Anc. Hist. VI 267, statt dessen wieder für den Amphiktionenrat als Bundesgericht eintritt.

[2] Sitz. Bayer. Ak. 1917 10 S. 36 A. 1, auch Sitz. Pr. Ak. 1922 XVIII 132 zu 32—35.

zusammengerückt worden (in αι und τι in παραβαίνοντι), so daß diese Zeile sogar 35 Buchstaben zählt. So wird auch in unserm Fall eines der drei Iota adscripta in der Ergänzung an seinen Vordermann herangerückt sein. Als ich später die Originalpublikation Wilhelms in den Sitz. Wien. Akad. 1911, 165 Bd. 6 Abh. heranzog, las ich auf S. 7, daß er »seinerzeit mit ausdrücklichem Vorbehalt eingesetzt hatte«: καθότι [ἂν δοκῆι τῶι κοινῶι συνεδρί]ωι, was er nunmehr aber zugunsten des oben von mir bestrittenen Textes aufgab[1]. Wilhelm hatte also ursprünglich das Richtige vermutet. Den weiteren Text ergänzte ich schon früher: καὶ ὁ ἡγεμ[ὼν παραγγέλληι καὶ οὐκ ἐνκα]ταλείψω. Vgl. den Anhang S. 317.

Dieser neue Text scheint mir für die Stellung des Synhedrion gegenüber dem Hegemon von großer Bedeutung zu sein. Schon äußerlich fällt auf, daß der Hegemon hinter dem Synhedrion genannt wird. Das hat seinen guten Grund, denn den militärischen Befehlen des Hegemon muß hiernach vorangehen ein δόγμα des Synhedrion. Dabei handelt es sich um die außerordentlich wichtige Frage, ob im Falle eines Vertragsbruches ein Bundeskrieg stattfinden soll oder nicht. Diese gewichtige Entscheidung steht also dem Synhedrion zu, während der Hegemon im Falle, daß das Synhedrion den Krieg beschließt, die nötigen militärischen Befehle betreffs der Kontingente zu geben und den Krieg zu führen hat. Wir haben schon immer angenommen, daß der Hegemon die Exekutivgewalt hatte und dem Synhedrion nur Beratung und Beschlußfassung zustand. Ich gestehe, daß ich mir bei dieser Formel die Stellung des Synhedrion immer als eine dem Hegemon untergeordnete gedacht habe. Das vorliegende Beispiel aber zeigt uns, daß bei dieser prinzipiellen Machtverteilung unter Umständen dem Synhedrion die Entscheidung über die wichtigsten Fragen wie die über Krieg und Frieden zufallen konnte, während der Hegemon hierbei fast den Eindruck eines Werkzeuges zur Ausführung des Bundesbeschlusses macht. Hiernach wird man auch bei der oben S. 302 aus Justin zitierten Formel des Schutz- und Trutzbündnisses (*sive adiuvandus ea manu rex oppugnante aliquo foret seu duce illo bellum inferendum*) vielleicht geneigt sein, die Entscheidung darüber, ob der Bund überhaupt mobil machen soll, ob also der casus foederis vorliegt, dem Synhedrion zuzuschreiben. Danach würde also der Hegemon im Falle der Abwehr eines Angriffs nicht ohne weiteres die griechischen Kontingente aufrufen können, sondern es müßte vorher, wie in der Inschrift, ein Bundesbeschluß herbeigeführt werden, der ihn dazu ermächtigte. Jedenfalls, daß im Falle eines Offensivkrieges *duce illo* zuerst das Synhedrion den Krieg beschließen mußte[2], zeigt uns ja das Beispiel des Perserkrieges, der, wie wir

---

[1] In dem, was ich für den Kopf des P nehme, glaubte er jetzt einen Rest von Υ zu sehen, was ihn in der Ergänzung ἐμαν]τῶι bestärkte.

[2] Kärst, Hellenismus I³ 279 spricht in diesem Zusammenhange von einem »auswärtigen, von der Heeresversammlung beschlossenen Kriege«. Eine solche Heeresversammlung kennen wir nur in Makedonien. Liegt hier ein Druckfehler für Bundesversammlung vor? Das würde nach Obigem richtig sein. Jedenfalls konnte doch die Heeresversammlung der Makedonen, die gar nicht zum korinthischen Bunde gehörten (Sitz. Bayer. Ak. 1917 10 S. 5 A. 2), keinen diesen Bund bindenden Beschluß fassen. Im übrigen gehörte die Entscheidung über Krieg und Frieden nicht zu den normalen Privilegien der makedonischen Heeresversammlung.

sogleich sehen werden, von Philipp nur beantragt, vom Synhedrion aber beschlossen worden ist.

Dies Recht des Synhedrion ist um so höher einzuschätzen, als dieser Bundesrat, so bedeutend auch faktisch der persönliche Einfluß Philipps sein mochte, rechtlich nach dem Bundesvertrage durchaus unabhängig vom Hegemon war. Wenn ich früher geglaubt habe, daß Philipp und Alexander eventuell persönlich das Präsidium im Synhedrion geführt hätten[1], so war das, wie ich mich seit einiger Zeit überzeugt habe, ein großer Irrtum[2]. Das Präsidium wird immer bei einem der 5 Prohedroi gewesen sein, die aus sich den Epistates erlost haben werden. Der Hegemon dagegen stand ebenso außerhalb des Synhedrion, wie das athenische Volk im II. attischen Seebund außerhalb des συνέδριον τῶν συμμάχων gestanden hat. Er konnte wohl außerordentliche Bundesratssitzungen beantragen und auch berufen und konnte dann vor dem Synhedrion Anträge stellen -- beides hat Philipp, wie wir sehen werden, 337 getan —, aber an der Beratung und Beschlußfassung hatte er keinen Anteil. Dazu kommt, daß die Beschlüsse des Synhedrion absolut gültig waren, wie wir aus der Epidaurischen Inschrift III 18 auch für Philipps Bund entnehmen dürfen, das bedeutet in diesem Zusammenhange, daß der Hegemon kein Veto einlegen und sie nicht kassieren konnte[3]. Man muß nach alledem doch sagen, daß Philipp dem neuen Hellenenstaat große Rechte gegeben hat, so daß ein politisches Leben trotz der tatsächlichen Abhängigkeit von der makedonischen Vormacht durchaus möglich war. Philipps Schuld ist es nicht, wenn die Griechen nachher diese Rechte nicht ausgenutzt haben. Aber auch Alexander trägt nicht allein die Verantwortung für den allmählichen Niedergang des Prestiges des Synhedrion, wenn auch seine ungeheure innere Entwicklung bis zum Weltherrscher hin notwendig nach dieser Richtung wirken mußte und er zuletzt durch die Forderung der Apotheose die Basis verschoben hat. Schon in den ersten Jahren Alexanders hören wir nicht viel mehr vom Synhedrion, als daß es dem König zum Siege mit goldenem Kranz gratulierte. Ja, als im Jahre 331 dem Synhedrion vertragsmäßig eine wichtige Entscheidung zufiel, das Urteil über die von Antipater niedergekämpften Spartaner und ihre Bundesgenossen, da hat das Synhedrion sich selbst entmannt, indem es diese Entscheidung vielmehr dem König überließ. So tragen die Griechen selbst ein gut Teil der Schuld daran, daß Philipps Saat von Korinth nicht voll gereift ist.

B. Die Kriegssitzung.

Nach Schluß des Friedenskongresses, auf dem Philipp, wie unsere Quelle sagt, persönlich und amtlich allen mit größter Liebenswürdigkeit entgegengekommen war[4], ließ er den Städten durch ihre Gesandten mitteilen, daß er

---

[1] Sitz. Pr. Ak. 1922 XVIII (Über eine Inschrift aus dem Asklepieion von Epidauros) S. 136, 145. Ebenso spricht Kärst, Hellenismus I³ 280 von der »Leitung der Bundesversammlung« durch den Hegemon.
[2] Mit Recht hat I. A. O. Larsen l. c. XX S. 326 A. 4 widersprochen.
[3] Vgl. I. A. O. Larsen l. c. XXI S. 54.
[4] Auf diesem Kongreß, wo Philipp mit den Gesandten verhandelte, wird er den Vorsitz geführt haben.

in der ersten Bundesratssitzung einen Antrag περὶ τῶν συμφερόντων stellen wolle. Es war das die übliche allgemeine Formel für die Tagesordnungen, die dann erst bei der Eröffnung der betreffenden Versammlung durch das spezielle Thema ersetzt wurde[1]. So konnte Philipp auch jetzt noch seinen Plan des Perserkrieges offiziell geheimhalten. Nachdem überall in Griechenland der in Korinth ausgearbeitete Vertrag akzeptiert und beschworen war — auch Philipp hat ihn beschworen — und darauf die Abgeordneten gewählt waren, kam es etwas vor Anfang Sommers 337 in Korinth zur ersten Sitzung des Synhedrion[2]. Hier stellte Philipp den Antrag, daß er mit dem Hellenenbunde zusammen mit seiner makedonischen Kriegsmacht einen Feldzug gegen Persien führen wolle, um Rache zu nehmen für die Frevel, die einst Xerxes an den Tempeln der Götter begangen habe. Das Synhedrion beschloß hierauf den Krieg und übertrug dem Philipp speziell zu diesem Perserkrieg, wohl in Anbetracht der großen Bedeutung dieses Krieges, der über eine Bundesexekution weit hinausging, noch ein außerordentliches Spezialoberkommando für den Perserkrieg mit dem Titel eines στρατηγὸς αὐτοκράτωρ[3].

Im nächsten Frühling, 336, schickte Philipp eine Avantgarde von 10000 Mann unter Parmenion und Attalos nach Kleinasien hinüber, um zunächst die Befreiung der Griechen Kleinasiens von der Perserherrschaft in Angriff zu nehmen (Diod. 16, 91, 2). So sollte auch der § 1 des Königsfriedens beseitigt werden.

IV. Philipps Werk von Korinth und Isokrates.

Jetzt komme ich zu meinem Hauptthema, zu der Frage, inwieweit und in welcher Weise Philipp bei seinem in Korinth geschaffenen Werk auf die Anregungen des Φίλιππος eingegangen ist.

Mehrfach ist die Ansicht geäußert worden, daß Isokrates dem König eine staatliche Einigung der Nation, sei es in einem Bundesstaat oder einem Staatenbunde, anempfohlen habe[4]. Demnach wird dann die Schöpfung des korinthischen Bundes als eine Erfüllung dieser Anregung betrachtet. Ich halte diese Auffassung für durchaus irrig. Durch genaueste Prüfung des Wortlautes hat sich mir ergeben, daß sich in der ganzen Schrift auch nicht die leiseste Spur davon findet, daß Isokrates an einen politischen Einheitsstaat gedacht hätte. Es ist ausschließlich die innerliche Einigung der Griechen, die er Philipp zu vermitteln auffordert, die Eintracht (ὁμόνοια) unter den πόλεις[5], die durch die Versöhnung der bestehenden Gegensätze

---

[1] Sitz. Bayer. Ak. 1917 10. S. 13/4.
[2] Sitz. Bayer. Ak. 1917 10. S. 21.
[3] Sitz. Bayer. Ak. 1917 10. S. 27. Ich glaube jetzt (anders als l. c. S. 25), daß der Beschluß, daß kein Hellene beim Perser Solddienste nehmen dürfe, auch erst in dieser Kriegssitzung gefaßt ist.
[4] Wo nur von einer »Einigung« gesprochen wird, ist nach dem Wortlaut nicht erkennbar, ob an einen Einheitsstaat oder nur an eine innerliche Einigung gedacht ist, doch scheint nach dem Zusammenhang meist an ersteres gedacht zu sein. KÄRST, Hell. I³ 143 hat die Idee »einer gemeinsamen politischen Verfassung (von K. gesperrt), welche die nationale Zusammengehörigkeit der Hellenen zu einer dauernden staatlichen Verkörperung bringen sollte«, mit Recht abgelehnt, aber doch nicht scharf genug, wenn er sagt, daß sie bei Isokrates »wohl kaum« zu finden sei. Vgl. auch seine weiteren Betrachtungen auf S. 144.
[5] Vgl. Phil. 16, 30, 40, 83, 141. Vgl. auch Ep. 3, 2.

(διάλυσις)¹ auf dem Wege der Überredung² herbeigeführt werden soll³. Da
Isokrates ein Publizist war, der sich auch darüber den Kopf zerbrach, wie
man die von ihm empfohlenen politischen Gedanken in der Praxis durch-
führen könne⁴, so hat er auch hier sich bemüht, dem Philipp einen prakti-
schen Rat an die Hand zu geben: er meinte, der König brauche nur die
vier Großmächte (Athen, Sparta, Argos, Theben) miteinander zu versöhnen,
dann würden auch die kleineren Staaten ihrem Beispiel folgen⁵.

Für die irrige Vorstellung, daß Isokrates einen Einheitsstaat beabsich-
tigt habe, hat man sich namentlich auf § 69f. berufen, wo er dem König aus-
malt, wie glücklich dieser sich preisen würde, wenn er seinen Rat (die
Griechen zu versöhnen) ausführe: τίς γὰρ ἂν ὑπερβολὴ γένοιτο τῆς τοιαύτης
εὐδαιμονίας, ὅταν πρέσβεις μὲν ἥκωσιν ἐκ τῶν μεγίστων πόλεων (das sind
wieder die vier Großmächte) οἱ μάλιστ᾽ εὐδοκιμοῦντες εἰς τὴν σὴν δυναστείαν,
μετὰ δὲ τούτων βουλεύῃ περὶ τῆς κοινῆς σωτηρίας, περὶ ἧς οὐδεὶς ἄλλος φανήσεται τοιαύτην πρόνοιαν πεποιημένος, αἰσθάνῃ δὲ τὴν Ἑλλάδα πᾶσαν ὀρθὴν
οὖσαν ἐφ᾽ οἷς σὺ τυγχάνεις εἰσηγούμενος, μηδεὶς δ᾽ ὀλιγώρως ἔχῃ τῶν παρὰ σοὶ
βραβευομένων κτλ. Aus diesen Worten hat PAUL WENDLAND l. c. I 134 gefolgert,
es solle ein Bundesstaat begründet werden, an dessen Spitze Philipp stehe.
Ebenso AD. WILHELM l. c. S. 44. Ich suche vergeblich in dem Text nach einer
Andeutung eines Bundesstaates⁶. In Wirklichkeit wird hier nur ausgeführt, wie
die Versöhnung der Griechen praktisch durchgeführt werden könne. Zu diesem
Zweck sollen die vier Großmächte ihre Gesandten nach Pella schicken, um ihre
Streitigkeiten vor Philipp beizulegen, damit die für den Nationalkrieg nötige
Eintracht — um nichts anderes handelt es sich hier — hergestellt werde. Dort
soll Philipp mit ihnen beraten über das gemeinsame Heil (eben die allgemeine
Aussöhnung). Philipp wird dabei wohl Vorschläge machen (εἰσηγούμενος),
und schiedsrichterliche Entscheidungen werden bei ihm⁷ getroffen werden
(βραβευομένων), aber diese vier Großmächte stellt Isokrates sich durchaus als
selbständige Staaten vor, die nebeneinander oder miteinander dort unter Philipps Vermittlung verhandeln werden. Irgendein Bundesverhältnis ist in keiner
Weise angedeutet. Das Neue an diesem Phantasiebild ist, daß die Griechen

---

¹ Vgl. Phil. 9, 50, 52, 88. Vgl. 45 (διαλλαγαί), 83 (διαλλάττειν), auch Ep. 3, 2 (διαλλάξαντα).
² Phil. 16.
³ So auch in den mythischen Beispielen von Herakles (Phil. 111 διαλλάξας) und Agamemnon
(Panath. 77 ὁμόνοια).
⁴ Am berühmtesten ist sein Vorschlag betreffs der Kolonisation Kleinasiens (Phil. 120ff.).
Bemerkenswert ist aber auch der Gedanke, Philipp solle in Kleinasien mit dem Ruf der Freiheit
auftreten, dann würden die Satrapen zu ihm übergehen (Phil. 104, nicht die kleinasiatischen
Griechen, wie v. SCALA S. 113 es interpretiert). Dieser Gedanke war bei den damaligen Zu-
ständen im Perserreich gar nicht dumm und wird dadurch nicht ad absurdum geführt, daß zu
Alexanders Zeit die Satrapen treu zum Großkönig gehalten haben. Dazwischen lag die Kon-
solidierung des Reiches durch Ochos.
⁵ Phil. 30, 31. Es ist im Grunde derselbe Gedanke, der jetzt auch beim Kellogg-Pakt für
praktisch befunden wurde.
⁶ Ebensowenig ist von einem Staatenbund die Rede, an den Jos. KESSLER denkt: Isokrates
und die panhellenische Idee (Studien z. Gesch. u Kultur d. Alt. IV 3. Heft, Paderborn 1910)
S. 54/55. Vgl. S. 80.
⁷ Man beachte παρὰ σοί, nicht ὑπὸ σοῦ.

jetzt, wo es sich um den Krieg gegen Persien handelt, ihre Streitigkeiten nicht mehr wie früher in Susa, sondern in Pella vorbringen und ausgleichen sollen[1]. Mit dem Bundesstaat fällt zugleich WENDLANDS Vorstellung, daß Isokrates sich den Philipp als die amtliche Spitze desselben — wie es nachher heißt, als Hegemon — gedacht habe[2]. Der Titel ἡγεμών wird in dieser Schrift überhaupt nicht angewendet auf Philipp. Isokrates nennt ihn den ἐπιστατοῦντα ταῖς διαλλαγαῖς (§ 45) oder τῆς εἰρήνης (§ 50) oder den ἐπιστάτην τηλικούτων πραγμάτων (§ 71, vgl. 151) oder spricht von προστῆναι τῆς τῶν Ἑλλήνων ὁμονοίας (§ 16) oder von seiner ἐπιμέλεια τῶν Ἑλλήνων (§ 128). Offenbar vermeidet er jeden amtlichen Titel, da ihm ja eine staatliche Einigung gar nicht vorschwebt. Natürlich soll Philipp nachher im Perserkrieg der gemeinsame Führer sein. So sagt er § 97: σέ τε τὸν νῦν ἡγησόμενον τῆς στρατείας καὶ βουλευσόμενον περὶ ἁπάντων[3]. Bezeichnend für Isokrates' Auffassung ist, daß er den König hier mit dem Kondottiere Klearchos in Parallele stellt, der einst die Zehntausend gegen Artaxerxes geführt hat.

Andererseits hat R. v. SCALA l. c. S. 113 A. 7, aus jenen Worten in § 69 f. herausgelesen, daß dem Isokrates »ein κοινὸν συνέδριον, durch den König berufen«, vorgeschwebt habe, und unter Hinweis hierauf hat dann B. v. HAGEN gemeint, daß Philipp durch die Gründung des κοινὸν συνέδριον die »dringende Forderung« des Isokrates in § 69 erfüllt habe[4]. Vgl. auch BELOCH, Gr. Gesch. III 1² S. 575 A. 2: »Eine Einrichtung dieser Art [wie das κοινὸν συνέδριον] hatte bereits Isokrates Phil. 69 ff. gefordert«. Ja, MÜNSCHER, RE IX 2215, sagt sogar: »Der Bund[!] von 338 entsprach genau dem von I(sokrates) 69 empfohlenen συνέδριον«, was in mehrfacher Hinsicht schief ist. Aber nach den obigen Ausführungen über Philipps Synhedrion (S. 307 ff.) braucht kaum gesagt zu werden, daß dies Synhedrion mit jenen Verhandlungen Philipps mit den Gesandten der vier Großmächte in Pella auch nicht die geringste Ähnlichkeit hat, zumal Philipp, wie wir sahen, ganz außerhalb des Synhedrion stand.

Ich muß also feststellen, daß der König durch § 69 ff. ebensowenig zur Schöpfung des Synhedrion wie zur Bildung eines Einheitsstaates angeregt werden konnte. Dagegen möchte ich es nicht für unmöglich halten, daß diese Darstellung des Isokrates in § 69 ff. auf Philipp eingewirkt hat, als er 338 die Staaten Griechenlands aufforderte, ihre Gesandten zu ihm nach Korinth zu schicken. Das steht jedenfalls in einer gewissen Parallele zu jenem Vorschlag des Isokrates. Also der Kongreßgedanke könnte von Isokrates beeinflußt sein. Freilich war die Ausführung — entsprechend der nicht vorauszusehenden Situation nach Chaeronea — doch auch wieder völlig anders, denn nach Pella gingen die Gesandten nach Isokrates freiwillig, nach Korinth aber sind sie auf Ladung bzw. Befehl Philipps gegangen.

---

[1] So richtig KÄRST, Hell. I³ 143 A. 3 Schluß.

[2] Vgl. WENDLAND l. c. 134, 181; KESSLER l. c. S. 48, 54. Vgl. auch KÄRST I³ 144 (»des zur Hegemonie über Hellas Berufenen«).

[3] Bemerkenswert ist auch dies βουλευσόμενον: nur Ratschläge soll Philipp geben. Ihm fehlt eben jede amtliche Qualität, durch die er außer dem Militärischen hätte Verordnungen treffen können.

[4] B. v. HAGEN, Isokrates und Alexander (Philol. LXVII [N. F. XXI]) S. 125. Vgl. auch KESSLER l. c. S. 54. 76.

Ebensowenig wie im *Φίλιππος* finde ich nun aber auch im Panegyrikos irgendeinen Hinweis auf eine Forderung des politischen Einheitsstaates[1]. Auch hier handelt es sich nur um die Herstellung der Eintracht (ὁμόνοια) unter den Griechen als Vorbedingung für den Nationalkrieg. Gleich in § 3, wo er sein Programm klar kundgibt, rät er zum πόλεμος πρὸς τοὺς βαρβάρους und zur ὁμόνοια πρὸς ἡμᾶς αὐτούς (vgl. auch § 173f.), und mehrfach bezeichnet er es daher als das Haupterfordernis, die Griechen miteinander zu versöhnen (διαλύειν, διαλλάττειν, vgl. § 15, 16, 129, 131, 188). Gehen wir aber über die vielen Vorgänger, von denen Isokrates in § 3 spricht, bis zum ersten, bis zu Gorgias hinauf, so sehen wir, daß schon er das Stichwort der ὁμόνοια ausgegeben hat. Nennt doch Plutarch seinen Olympikos geradezu den λόγος τῆς ὁμονοίας[2].

Ich komme somit zu dem Ergebnis, daß nicht nur dem Isokrates, sondern überhaupt dem panhellenischen Programm von vornherein und durchweg die Idee einer staatlichen Einigung der Nation völlig ferngelegen hat. Darin unterscheidet sich diese neue Bewegung aber nicht von der älteren Zeit, denn wenn man etwa von Alkibiades letzten Plänen absieht, wird man nicht sagen können, daß der Gedanke des nationalen Einheitsstaates jemals vorher in der griechischen Geschichte lebendig gewesen wäre[3]. Darin hat sich auch jetzt in den Kreisen der Panhellenisten nichts geändert. Es beruht daher auf einer irrigen Auffassung des Isokrates und der panhellenischen Idee, wenn man neuerdings von der Sehnsucht der Besten »nach einer politischen Einigung der Nation«[4] oder von dem »Traum der griechischen Einheit« spricht[5], oder den Isokrates mit den Männern von 1848 vergleicht, die der deutschen Einheit den Boden bereitet hätten[6], oder den Philipp als den »so oft und so heiß ersehnten Mittler und Einiger der sich zerfleischenden Städte« bezeichnet, ohne zu bemerken, daß die von Philipp gebrachte Einigung niemals ersehnt worden war[7]. In Wahrheit hat Isokrates trotz seiner panhellenischen Hoffnungen über die nebeneinander stehenden πόλεις nicht hinaus gedacht[8]. Das Ideal des nationalen Einheitsstaates war ihm ebenso fremd wie den früheren Generationen.

So ist denn die staatliche Einigung, die Philipp vollzogen hat, sowohl in dem Gedanken an sich wie in der Ausführung im einzelnen, Philipps

---

[1] Nach Kessler l. c. S. 8ff. hätte Isokrates auch im Panegyrikos, wie nach seiner Annahme im Philippos, einen Staatenbund (συμμαχία) angeraten. Er verkennt durchweg, daß, wo von ἡγεμονία die Rede ist, die Führerschaft im Perserkrieg oder aber die Hegemonie Athens in einem attischen Seebund gemeint ist, nicht aber die Hegemonie Athens über ganz Griechenland gemeint ist.

[2] H. Diels, Fragmente der Vorsokratiker II³ 249, vgl. 235.

[3] Vgl. hierzu Matthias Gelzer, Hist. Z. (118. Bd.) 3. Folge 22. Bd. S. 489f.

[4] M. Pohlenz, Staatsgedanke u. Staatslehre d. Griech. 146, vgl. auch 63.

[5] W. Kolbe, Partikularismus und Einheit (Greifswalder Universitätsreden 4, 1921) S. 9.

[6] J. Beloch, Gr. G. III 1. 525.   Hiergegen schon R. v. Pöhlmann, Gr. Gesch.⁵ S. 274.

[7] W. Weber, Zur Geschichte der Monarchie 1919 S. 15. Auch R. Laqueur, Hellenismus (Schriften d. Hess. Hochsch., Gießen 1924 Heft 1) S. 13 hat offenbar nicht bemerkt, daß die von Philipp erzwungene Einigung etwas völlig anderes war als die von Gorgias und Isokrates gepredigte Eintracht.

[8] Diesen Gedanken fand ich jetzt gut formuliert von Ernest Barker, Cambr. Anc. Hist. VI 519: The symmachy of his (Isokr.) dream would thus have been a military *entente* of autonomous cities under a generalissimo who might be king in his own country, but among his allies was simply a chosen commander.

314 Gesamtsitzung vom 13. Juni 1929. — Mitteilung vom 18. April

eigenstes Werk und steht in bewußtem Gegensatz zu den Vorschlägen des Isokrates. Die Einigung der Griechen im korinthischen Bunde ist also nicht aus der panhellenischen Idee abzuleiten, sondern ist ein Produkt der makedonischen Machtpolitik Philipps. Diese Einigung war für ihn notwendig als Voraussetzung für die Hegemonie über Hellas, die für ihn die Hauptsache war. Diese Erkenntnis ist neben anderen schon oben S. 306 erwähnten Momenten wichtig zum Verständnis der kühlen und ablehnenden Haltung, die viele der Griechen diesem Einheitsstaat gegenüber eingenommen haben.

Dagegen wird man annehmen dürfen, daß der von Isokrates so warm vertretene Versöhnungsgedanke nicht ohne Einfluß auf die Verkündigung des Landfriedens gewesen ist. Freilich ist dieser Gedanke in völlig andern Formen durchgeführt worden, als Isokrates es sich gedacht hatte. Daß seine naive Vorstellung, Philipp könne die Griechen durch freundliches πείθειν zur Versöhnung und zur ὁμόνοια bringen, vom König sofort als Utopie erkannt sein muß, wurde schon oben S. 297 gesagt. Gewiß wäre eine wahrhaftige innerliche Eintracht mehr gewesen, aber wer auf die Selbstzerfleischung der griechischen Kleinstaaterei zurückblickt, wird zugeben, daß das von Philipp erdachte Surrogat des erzwungenen Friedens das praktisch allein mögliche war, das aber auch ein Aufatmen der Nation verhieß, wenn es nur weiter im Geiste von Korinth gepflegt wurde. So hat Philipp in das Schutz- und Trutzbündnis, das ihm die Hegemonie sicherte, die Paragraphen über den Landfrieden eingefügt, durch die der äußere und innere Friede unter den Bündnern mit harten Sanktionen garantiert war.

Den Gedanken des panhellenischen Nationalkrieges endlich hat Philipp zweifellos von Isokrates übernommen. Wie fein er es jedoch verstanden hat, mit dieser nationalgriechischen Flagge seine makedonischen Kriegsziele gegenüber Persien, von denen ich oben S. 296 sprach, zu verhüllen und zugleich seine Herrschaft über Griechenland moralisch zu legitimieren, wird doch erst klar, wenn man sich überzeugt, daß nur der Grundgedanke des panhellenischen Nationalkrieges ihm von Isokrates suggeriert worden ist, nicht aber die packende Motivierung als Rachekrieg für die Gottesfrevel des Xerxes. Gleichwohl sprechen wohl die meisten Forscher von dem von Isokrates gepredigten Rachekrieg[1], und nirgends, soweit ich sehe, ist dieser Gedanke ausdrücklich zurückgewiesen. Auch ich selbst muß bekennen, bis vor kurzem an ihn geglaubt zu haben[2]. Erst als ich mir die Belege für den Rachekrieg aus dem Φίλιππος ausziehen wollte, bemerkte ich zu meiner Überraschung, daß es solche gar nicht gibt. Tatsächlich findet sich in der ganzen Schrift keine Spur von diesem Rachekrieg. Der Nationalkrieg erscheint hier vielmehr durchaus als ein Eroberungskrieg, durch den vor allem die wirtschaftliche und soziale Not Griechenlands behoben werden soll. Kleinasien soll erobert werden, nicht nur um die dortigen Griechen zu befreien,

---

[1] R. v. Scala l. c. 111 ff. R. v. Pöhlmann, Gr. Gesch.[5] S. 273, 284 A. 3. Kärst, Forschungen z. Gesch. Alex. (1887) S. 33. P. Wendland l. c. 133, 148/49. M. Pohlenz l. c. 147. Fr. Geyer, Alex. d. Gr. u. d. Diadochen (1925) S. 11. W. W. Tarn, Cambr. Anc. Hist. VI 357.
[2] Sitz. Bayer. Ak. 1917 10 S. 28. Griech. Gesch.[2] S. 159.

sondern auch um es mit dem überschüssigen Proletariat zu besiedeln (120ff.), und der Reichtum Asiens soll den Griechen zufließen (130, 132). Um πλεονεξίαι und ὠφέλειαι geht es (9, 131), nicht um Rache für Xerxes¹.

Als ich dann voll Erwartung den Panegyrikos auf diese Frage hin untersuchte, ergab sich, daß auch dieser Schrift jener Rachegedanke fremd ist. R. v. SCALA, l. c. S. 112 A. 7, beruft sich zwar auf Paneg. 155ff. (im Φίλιππος scheint also auch er keinen Beleg gefunden zu haben), um diesen Gedanken als Isokratisch zu erweisen. Dort wird allerdings auf die Zerstörung der Tempel durch Xerxes hingewiesen, aber nur, um den Haß zwischen Hellenen und Persern zu begründen, von Rache ist keine Rede. Wenn irgendwo, so hätte aber hier von ihr gesprochen werden müssen, wenn wirklich der Nationalkrieg für Isokrates ein Rachekrieg gewesen wäre. So beweist die Stelle eher das Gegenteil von dem, was v. SCALA mit ihr beweisen wollte. Wohl begegnet im Panegyrikos zum Schluß ein Rachemotiv für den Nationalkrieg (181f.), aber das ist nicht die Rache für die Frevel des Xerxes, sondern die Rache für den schmachvollen Königsfrieden, dessen unheilvolle Wirkungen vorher von 175—180 dargestellt sind². Nur leise streift er dann in § 183 einmal auch die Leiden der früheren Zeit, wobei er an die Perserkriege gedacht haben wird (οὐ πρὸς τοὺς καὶ πρότερον κακῶς τὴν Ἑλλάδα ποιήσαντας), aber sogleich folgt der Hinweis auf die jetzige Bedrängung durch die Perser (καὶ νῦν ἐπιβουλεύοντας), und ganz allgemein schließt er καὶ πάντα τὸν χρόνον οὕτω πρὸς ἡμᾶς διακειμένους. Jedenfalls wird man aus dieser Stelle nicht folgern können, daß dem Isokrates ein Rachezug für die Gottesfrevel des Xerxes vorgeschwebt hätte. Vielmehr erscheint auch im Panegyrikos — abgesehen von der damals zeitgemäßen Rache für den Königsfrieden — der Nationalkrieg durchaus als ein Eroberungskrieg mit denselben Kriegszielen wie im Φίλιππος, in dem er sich eben nur wiederholt hat: der Reichtum der Asiaten soll die griechische Armut beseitigen (182, 189), Asien soll von den Griechen ausgenutzt werden (τὴν Ἀσίαν καρπούσθαι 133, 166). Auch hier geht es um πλεονεξίαι (17, 183) und ὠφέλειαι (15, 173).

Befragen wir endlich den Olympikos des Gorgias, von dem wir freilich nur dürftige Nachrichten haben, so ergibt sich, daß auch schon für ihn der Nationalkrieg nicht ein Rachekrieg, sondern ein Eroberungskrieg gewesen ist. Nach Philostrat hat er als ἄθλα τῶν ὅπλων bezeichnet: μὴ τὰς ἀλλήλων πόλεις, ἀλλὰ τὴν τῶν βαρβάρων χώραν³. Das ist in Kürze ganz der Grundgedanke des Isokrates. Vgl. z. B. seine programmatische Formulierung im Phil. 9: τὰς πλεονεξίας, ἃς νῦν παρὰ τῶν Ἑλλήνων ἀξιοῦσιν αὐταῖς γίγνεσθαι, ταύτας εἰ παρὰ τῶν βαρβάρων ποιήσασθαι βουληθεῖεν. Hätten wir mehr von Gorgias' Rede, würde wahrscheinlich Isokrates' Abhängigkeit sich sehr stark hervortreten.

---

¹ In § 125 stellt er den Barbaren, die sogar gewagt haben, mit Feindseligkeiten gegen Griechenland zu beginnen, die Hellenen gegenüber, die nicht einmal wagen, wegen erlittener Unbilden Rache zu nehmen (ἡμεῖς δ᾽ οὐδ᾽ ὑπὲρ ὧν κακῶς ἐπάθομεν ἀμύνεσθαι τολμῶμεν αὐτούς). Das ist eine geschichtliche Feststellung, nicht eine Motivierung des Nationalkrieges. Im übrigen fehlt der Hinweis auf Xerxes' Frevel.
² Im Φίλιππος (346) fehlt diese Rache für den Königsfrieden.
³ H. DIELS, Fragmente d. Vorsokratiker II³ 235.

Wenn sich somit ergibt, daß der Gedanke des Rachekrieges für die Frevel des Xerxes dem Isokrates wie überhaupt dem panhellenischen Programm fremd ist, anderseits aber feststeht, daß Philipp ihn in der Bundesratssitzung 3ᵤ7 proklamiert hat[1], so werden wir zu dem Schluß berechtigt sein, daß Philipp selbst es gewesen ist, der diese Motivierung gefunden hat. Dann aber stehen wir von neuem bewundernd vor der Klugheit und der Feinfühligkeit dieses großen Staatsmannes. Da er die rein philhellenischen Kriegsziele des Isokrates (s. oben S. 296) natürlich nicht aufnehmen konnte, weil er seiner makedonischen Politik damit unerträgliche Fesseln angelegt hätte, seine wirklichen makedonischen machtpolitischen Ziele (s. oben S. 295 f.) aber nicht enthüllen wollte, so ist er auf den genialen Gedanken verfallen, den Krieg zu einem heiligen Kreuzzug zur Rache für die Frevel des Xerxes zu stempeln. Er spielte damit die Rolle weiter, die er schon zweimal im Auftrage der Amphiktionen als Schützer und Rächer des Apollon erfolgreich durchgeführt hatte[2]. Es war darauf berechnet, durch Eintreten für dieses hellenische Interesse die Sympathien der Griechen zu gewinnen und seine makedonischen Ziele mit dieser ehrwürdigen panhellenischen Flagge zu verdecken. Zugleich knüpfte er damit ein geistiges Band zwischen seinem Unternehmen und der großen Zeit der Perserkriege. Ich wies schon oben, S. 305, darauf hin, daß bei der Organisation des korinthischen Bundes ihm wahrscheinlich das Vorbild dieser Zeit vorgeschwebt hat. Bund und Perserkrieg, beide aufs engste zusammengehörig, waren nun beide mit diesen den Griechen heiligen Erinnerungen verknüpft und sollten ihnen damit nahegebracht werden.

So bin ich durch diese Untersuchungen ungefähr zu derselben Anschauung gekommen, der Polybios III 6, 12 f. Ausdruck gegeben hat, wenn er von Philipp sagt: *ἔτι δὲ καὶ τὸ μέγεθος καὶ τὸ κάλλος τῶν ἐσομένων ἄθλων ἐκ τοῦ πολέμου[3] πρὸ ὀφθαλμῶν θέμενος, ἅμα τῷ περιποιήσασθαι τὴν ἐκ τῶν Ἑλλήνων εὔνοιαν ὁμολογουμένην, εὐθέως προφάσει χρώμενος ὅτι σπεύδει μετελθεῖν τὴν Περσῶν παρανομίαν εἰς τοὺς Ἕλληνας, ὁρμὴν ἔσχε καὶ προέθετο πολεμεῖν κτλ.*

Alles in allem hat sich Philipps Werk von Korinth als ein sehr kompliziertes Kompromiß zwischen seiner makedonischen Machtpolitik und dem panhellenischen Programm herausgestellt, bei dem die makedonischen Interessen die ausschlaggebende Rolle gespielt haben.

Anhang: Syll. I³ 260.

Bei der großen Wichtigkeit, die diese Inschrift für das Verständnis des korinthischen Bundes hat, möchte ich hier den Text des Hauptstückes abdrucken, so wie er sich mir jetzt nach den an verschiedenen Orten von mir

---

[1] Diod. 16, 89, 2 : *διαδοὺς δὲ λόγον ὅτι βούλεται πρὸς Πέρσας ὑπὲρ τῶν Ἑλλήνων πόλεμον ἄρασθαι καὶ λαβεῖν παρ' αὐτῶν δίκας ὑπὲρ τῆς εἰς τὰ ἱερὰ γενομένης παρανομίας.* Diodor gibt diesen Inhalt schon beim Ausstreuen des Gerüchtes vom Perserkrieg an (s. oben S. 299).

[2] Hieran erinnert auch KÄRST, Hell. I³ 272. Den Gedanken des Rachekrieges für die Zerstörung der Tempel bringt Herod. VIII 144. Vgl. auch Thuk. I 96, 1.

[3] Damit meint er die makedonischen Eroberungspläne.

XII

C. Roebuck

The Settlements of Philip II in 338 B.C.

MEGARA AND THE STATES OF THE
NORTHERN PELOPONNESUS

Megara, Corinth, the Achaean League,
and the towns on Akte had been members
of the Athenian coalition. None, however,
had been a particularly formidable ad-
versary against which Philip needed to
take severe action. Yet Corinth had considerable strategic value as the gate-keep-
er of the Peloponnesus.[68] Thus in the settlements it is singled out to house a Macedonian garrison, as Ambracia and Thebes
had been. Although the terms of the settlements are almost completely lost, Hyperides' speech against Athenogenes
throws a flash of light on the events in
Troezen immediately after the battle of
Chaeronea. They are probably typical of
the sudden reversals of government which
occurred in many of the anti-Macedonian
states. Athens, in the flush of excitement
following the battle, called on its near-by
allies for aid, among which were Troezen
and Epidaurus.[69] Although the Troezenians passed a decree voting aid, they
would scarcely have had time to send
their troops across the gulf. In the meantime, a Macedonian partisan, Athenogenes by name, who had come from
Athens in the course of the war (with
malice aforethought?), called upon Mnasias of Argos for aid and brought about a
change of government. Like the other
refugees, the exiled Troezenians fled to
Athens and were made citizens.[70] Philip
must have made his settlement with the
new pro-Macedonian government,[71] which
was apparently sufficient guaranty of the

city's loyalty to keep it independent of
Argos, for it continued to send its own
delegates to the meetings of the naopoioi
in Delphi.[72]

In Megara there was probably a change
of government similar to that in Troezen,
followed by the surrender of the state to
Philip.[73] None of the terms of settlement
are known; but Megara, which had not
sent delegates to the meeting of the naopoioi in 339 B.C., did so again in the autumn of 338 B.C.[74]

Corinth, like Athens, at first made
ready for a siege[75] but on Philip's approach, or possibly after an internal revolution, gave up the idea of resistance and
surrendered.[76] Philip garrisoned Acrocor-
inth[77] and, when the time was ready,
called the first meeting of the delegates to
the new league in Corinth. No other penalties are known to have been imposed,
although, if Corcyra and Ambracia were
regarded as Corinthian colonies, they
would presumably be freed from any juris-
diction which the city had exercised over
them.[78]

The Achaean League surrendered[79] and
seems to have been generously treated.
Its extra-territorial possession, Naupac-

[68] Plut. Apophthegmata Laconica 221 F; when a Spartan saw the camp of Philip near Corinth, he re-proached the Corinthians for being bad gate-keepers of the Peloponnesus.

[69] Lycurg. Leoc. 42.

[70] Hyperides Athenogenes 29–35.

[71] Aelian op. cit. vi. 1. Philip made his settlements in the Peloponnesus after his arrival there (Arrian op. cit. vii. 9. 5), probably in November, 338 B.C. (above, n. 19).

[72] Troezen sent a delegate in autumn, 339 B.C. (Cloché, BCH, XL [1916], 117; Bourguet, op. cit., p. 169, No. 47, l. 76), but not to the meeting held in the autumn of 338 B.C. Probably, then, the revolution in Troezen is to be dated in September–October, 338 B.C. A Troezenian delegate was present again in 335 B.C. (BCH, XL [1916], 128).

[73] Aelian op. cit. vi. 1.

[74] Cloché, BCH, XL (1916), 117, 123–24; Bourguet, op. cit., p. 176, No. 48, l. 21.

[75] Lucian On the Writing of History 3.

[76] Aelian op. cit. vi. 1. Corinth, with strong econom-ic interests at Delphi, sent its delegates to the meet-ings of the naopoioi in both 339 and 338 B.C. (Bour-guet, op. cit., p. 169, No. 47, ll. 74–75; p. 175, No. 48, ll. 17–18).

[77] Plut. Aratus 23; Pol. xxxviii. 3. 3.

[78] Wüst, op. cit., p. 94, n. 1. Demosthenes' refer-ence (ix. 34) to Ambracia as "Corinthian" is probably to be interpreted as indicating its traditional affiliation only.

[79] Aelian op. cit. vi. 1; above, n. 1.

P

tus, was lost to Aetolia,[80] but the League itself was not dissolved.[81] Further, its government seems to have been more stable than those of many other of the Greek states, as there is an indication that no revolutions took place.[82]

Elis, although it had sent no aid to Philip at Chaeronea, had been allied to him since 343 B.C. as the result of an oligarchical revolution in the state.[83] The policy of the oligarchs had been maintained with difficulty against democratic opposition,[84] so that, when Philip entered the Peloponnesus, the Eleans, apparently to allay suspicions as well as to satisfy a desire for revenge, joined him in the invasion of Laconia.[85] There is no indication that Elis received any direct reward for this aid, but the sanctuary at Olympia was later enhanced by the erection of the Philippeion,[86] and the Eleans themselves set up an equestrian statue to Philip.[87]

[80] This would probably be one of the terms of settlement which would thus legally confirm its reversion to Aetolia (see above, p. 77).

[81] Polybius (ii. 40. 5, 41. 9) remarks that the League was dissolved by the early Macedonian leaders, but it was in existence in 324 B.C. (Hyperides i. 18).

[82] In Pellene a tyrant, Chairon, came into power with the support, or the acquiescence, of Alexander (Ps.-Dem. xvii. 10; Athen. xi. 509b; Paus. vii. 27. 7). It was charged by the writer of Ps.-Dem. xvii that this was a breach of the regulation of the Corinthian League which guaranteed the governments existing at the time of its foundation. It is probable, then, that there was no disturbance before Pellene's entrance into the Corinthian League, or that would have provided additional material to the pamphleteer. Also, Pellene was the only Achaean state not to co-operate with Agis in 331 B.C., which may be explained by the presence of this tyrant and the continuance of anti-Macedonian governments in the other cities of the Achaean League (Aesch. iii. 165; Ernst Meyer, P.-W., XIX, 362–63).

[83] Paus. v. 4. 9; above, n. 18; for discussion and further evidence see Beloch, op. cit., III, 1, 541.

[84] Plut. De ira cohib. 457 f.; Apophth. reg. 179a; Glotz-Cohen, op. cit., III, 332.

[85] Paus. v. 4. 9. According to Aelian (op. cit. vi. 1) the Eleans surrendered to Philip after Chaeronea. This is a mistake, possibly originating in a reminiscence of the hostility noticed in the preceding note.

[86] Paus. v. 20. 10.

[87] Ibid. vi. 11. 1.

SPARTA, ARGOS, ARCADIA, AND MESSENE

It remains to discuss the adjustment made by Philip in the relations between Sparta and his allies, Argos, Arcadia, and Messene. This problem was of a different nature from that of the other settlements. Naupactus could have been given to Aetolia, Nicaea restored to Locris, and Oropus given to Athens without difficulty, since they had all been in enemy possession and Philip, as victor, had them at his disposal. Sparta, however, was not a member of the Athenian coalition and had not taken any action hostile to Macedonia. Yet the relations of Sparta and its neighbors constituted the "Peloponnesian problem" of the fourth century, so that some settlement was necessary in the interests of a quiet Greece.

The ownership of the border districts of Thyrea and Cynuria had been a point of contention between Argos and Sparta for generations, with both sides developing, in the course of time, a claim by appeal to the traditional division of the Peloponnesus by the Heraclidae.[88] Sparta, however, had usually been able to make good its claim by force of arms. Sparta had also had a long dispute with Megalopolis over the Belbinatis and with Tegea over the Skiritis and Karyae.[89] After the establishment of Messene as an independent power in 369 B.C., its Laconian frontier became a subject of dispute, for Sparta retained territory to the west of Taygetus—the Ager Denthaliatis, the coastal territory in southeastern Messenia, and some of the perioecic towns farther to the west along the coast of the gulf.[90] This dispute would merge into the same general issue as a result of Epaminondas' policy in supporting Argos, Arcadia, and Messene

[88] Ibid. ii. 20. 1, 38. 5, vii. 11. 1–2; Isoc. Panath. 91.

[89] Paus. viii. 35. 4; Livy xxxviii. 34. 8; Pol. ix. 28. 7; Theopompus, Frag. 238 (Jacoby, op. cit.); Beloch, op. cit., III, 1, 575, n. 1.

[90] Roebuck, op. cit., pp. 38–39, 56–57.

as a bloc against Sparta. Thus Messene, too, developed a claim based on its version of the traditional division of the Peloponnesus by the Heraclidae.[91] This contention would, of course, fit neatly into Philip's propaganda and plans, for he claimed to be a Heraclid and had adopted Epaminondas' solution of the Peloponnesian problem. Not only was the issue one of traditional prestige and even of economic advantage in the possession of additional territory, but the passes by which Sparta had access to the fertile plains of its neighbors and thence to the outside world lay through these border areas. Sparta had never recognized the establishment of Messene[92] and had shown little disposition to acquiesce in its own diminished power, for southern Arcadia had been invaded in 352 B.C.[93] and further aggressive action had been planned in 344 B.C.[94] The armed intervention of Thebes

had saved Megalopolis in 352, and the strong diplomatic *démarche* of Philip in 344; but, before Chaeronea, no change had been made in the control of the border territory. Although Philip had no grievance to find in Spartan action after 344 B.C.,[95] what guaranty was there that they would remain quiescent? It remained to complete the work already begun.

After Philip had received the surrender of Megara, Corinth, the towns on Akte, and Achaea, he proceeded to Argos, the traditional homeland of his ancestor Heracles. The Argive political leader, Mnasias, had already shown his zeal by assisting the pro-Macedonian party in Troezen, and Philip was warmly welcomed in Argos.[96] Thence he proceeded to Arcadia, where he may have taken steps to mend the rift in the Arcadian League,[97] as well as to sponsor the terri-

[91] *Ibid.*, p. 44; see Isoc. *Archidamus* 17 ff. for the Spartan claims. Treves (*op. cit.*, pp. 103–4) has cogently argued that a national Messenian tradition must have been developed in the century preceding the refounding of the city and received renewed impetus, reflected by Alcidamas' *Messeniakos logos* and Isocrates' *Archidamus*, upon the refounding. Certainly, there are traces of it in the sources before 369 B.C. For example, to the passages noticed by Treves might be added some of the fragments of Hellanicus, which show a tendency to connect Attic and Messenian history (L. Pearson, *Early Ionian Historians* [Oxford, 1939], p. 213) and the evidence of a treaty(?) between Athens and the Messenians in the middle of the fifth century B.C. (*IG*, I², 37; Merritt, *Hesperia*, XIII [1944], 224–29). How much of this tradition was truly Messenian, however, and how much Athenian fabrication, inspired by political opportunism to take advantage of the sporadic outbreaks of a serf population, would be a very difficult problem to resolve. In any case it seems probable that only when there was some actual hope of establishing Messenian ownership to land within their natural boundary, Taygetus, with the help of Thebes or Macedonia, would the Messenians make full use of the opportunity to utilize and embellish their national traditions. This legendary material would provide the sources on which Aristotle based his *dikaiomata* (see appendix); for, as Nissen pointed out (*op. cit.*, pp. 168–70), mythological tradition had as much validity as legal decisions to the Greek mind of that period.

[92] Roebuck, *op. cit.*, pp. 44–47.

[93] Diod. xvi. 39; Glotz-Cohen, *op. cit.*, III, 256–57.

[94] Roebuck, *op. cit.*, pp. 49–50.

[95] The Spartans had remained aloof from the diplomatic entanglements and intrigues of the years immediately preceding the war. They had, however, continued to take a part in Delphic affairs, except for the meeting of the *naopoioi* in autumn, 339 B.C. Cloché has explained this abstention as caused by resentment at the creation of the board of *tamiai* (*BCH*, XL [1916], 122–23; XLIV [1920], 318–19). The Spartans also sent four delegates to the meeting held in the autumn of 338 B.C., some two months after Chaeronea, which, then, took place before the invasion of Sparta by Philip and, presumably, before his intentions were known (Cloché, *BCH*, XL [1916], 127–28; Bourguet, *op. cit.*, p. 176, No. 48, ll. 20–22).

[96] Plut. *Erot.* 760a–b. Argos sent delegates to the meetings of the *naopoioi* in both 339 and 338 B.C. (Cloché, *BCH*, XL [1916], 121–25; Bourguet, *op. cit.*, p. 169, No. 47, ll. 72–74; pp. 175–76, No. 48, ll. 17, 19).

[97] On the reconstitution of the League see Beloch, *op. cit.*, III, 1, 574; 2, 173–77. Beloch's attribution to Philip of the reorganization of the Arcadian League rests mainly on the dating of the inscription (Ditt. *Syll.*², No. 183) to the period after Chaeronea. It is an honorary decree for an Athenian, Phylarchus, voted by the Council and the *myrioi* of the Arcadians. The decree contains a list of 50 *damiourgoi* from 10 member-states, including Megalopolis, the Maenalians, and the Cynourians. The two last-mentioned became members of the city-organization of Megalopolis in 369 and 361 B.C. (Paus. viii. 27. 3–4; Hiller von Gaertringen, *Ath. Mitt.*, XXXVI [1911], 355–58). The decree omits, however, most of the towns of northern Arcadia, including Stymphalus, one of whose citizens served as general for the Arcadian League in 366 B.C. (Xen. *Hell.* vii. 3. 1). Thus the decree would seem to

torial claims of Megalopolis and Tegea. From Arcadia he invaded Laconia in the late autumn of 338 B.C. and laid it waste.[98]

There is a certain amount of fragmentary information in the sources concerning the invasion and the subsequent territorial adjustments; but it represents two conflicting traditions, derived from the claims of the two parties to the dispute. Thus it has led to different interpretations in the modern treatments. There are three main literary sources: passages in Polybius, particularly the debate of Chlaineas, the Aetolian, and Lyciscus, the Acarnanian, before the Spartan assembly in 210 B.C.;[99] a poem of Isyllos, the Epidaurian

poet,[100] who wrote paeans celebrating the "miracles" of Asclepius in the early third century B.C.; some of the *Apophthegmata Laconica* of Plutarch.[101] It has been stated that Polybius' evidence is valuable for the "conflicting political ideologies prevailing in the age of Philip V ... but almost valueless as evidence for *our* reconstruction of the history of the age of Demosthenes." That is true of the manner and spirit in which the passages are written and of the judgments expressed on Philip in them; but is the factual material, some of it attested from other sources, false and to be ignored?[102] Isyllos' poem and the *Apophthegmata* might seem in themselves to be worthy of little credence; but Isyllos lived only two generations after Philip's invasion of Laconia, and, since his poem was set up in the sanctuary of Epidaurus, it should represent a popular tradition of so recent an event. The *Apophthegmata*, for their part, apparently depict successive steps in the negotiations between Philip and the Spartans.

It seems clear from Polybius that Argos, Arcadia, and Messene invited Philip to support their claims to the disputed territories at the opportune moment after the battle of Chaeronea, probably when he had arrived at the Isthmus or at Argos.[103] As pointed out above, Philip would

---

represent the condition of the League at a period before the Maenalians and Cynourians were completely absorbed by Megalopolis, before Stymphalus joined the League, and when Mantinea and Megalopolis were not at odds—that is, before 366 B.C. The period is difficult to fix, however, because of the internal dissensions which rent the League in its formative stage and which, presumably, are not all mentioned in the sources. Beloch's view that such a period is best found at the time of the settlements after Chaeronea involves rejecting Pausanias' evidence as mistaken and placing the final absorption of the Maenalians and Cynourians into Megalopolis at some unknown date after 338 B.C. Cary, on the other hand, has argued that the document belongs to the year 369, 368, or 367 B.C., before northern Arcadia was drawn into the League (*JHS*, XLII [1922], 188–90). Yet, if Stymphalus provided a general in 366 B.C., it seems likely that the city was a League member of tried loyalty and several years' standing, so that the period 369–367 B.C. seems very brief in which to fit the decree. Cary's view is probably to be preferred as doing no violence to the existing evidence, although that of Beloch has usually been followed and rests on historically sound considerations (Hiller von Gaertringen, *Klio*, XXI [1927], 10, who has withdrawn his former dating of the decree in 361 B.C.; Momigliano, *Filippo*, p. 162; Wüst, *op. cit.*, p. 173; none of these scholars refers to the argument of Cary). Whatever Philip's action with respect to the League may have been, he was regarded by the Megalopolitans as a great benefactor of their state (Pol. xviii. 14; a stoa bordering on the agora was erected in Philip's honor, Paus. viii. 30. 6, 31. 9). It is possible, of course, that such an honor was only in gratitude for the territorial adjustments made in favor of Megalopolis.

[98] See below, n. 107.

[99] Pol. xviii. 14; ix. 28–31, 32–39. "The speeches of Chlaeneas and Lyciscus of Acarnania are to be regarded as essentially based on a genuine record" (F. W. Walbank, *Philip V of Macedon* [Oxford, 1940], p. 87, n. 1).

[100] *IG*, IV, 950; Wilamowitz, "Isyllos von Epidauros," *Philologische Untersuchungen*, Vol. IX (1886), poem E. It is usually accepted that the Philip mentioned is Philip II, not Philip V, and that Isyllos' *floruit* is to be placed *ca.* 280 B.C. (R. Herzog, *Die Wunderheilungen von Epidaurus, Philologus*, Supplementband XXII, Heft 3 [1931], 41 ff.).

[101] They are collected by Schaefer, *op. cit.*, III[2], 44–46. References to the *Apophthegmata* are to the edition of the *Moralia* by W. Nachstädt, W. Sieveking, and J. Titchener (Leipzig, 1935).

[102] See appendix.

[103] Roebuck, *op. cit.*, p. 54, n. 19; as indicated above (n. 95), the Spartans attended the meeting of the *naopoioi* in 338 B.C., which would have taken place in October. Philip, then, would have had no dealings with them up to this point, and he apparently made no attempt to deal with Peloponnesian affairs until his arrival there (Arrian *op. cit.* vii. 9. 5). Thus the negotiations with Sparta would not have started until he was at Corinth or on his way to Arcadia.

desire a settlement in their favor to complete the policy embarked upon in 344 B.C. Accordingly, he would make his wishes known to the Spartans, hoping that he could intimidate them into acquiescence. Some of the *Apophthegmata* mention an exchange of letters between Philip and the Spartans, in which he made certain requests which were refused.[104] The nature of the requests is not specified, but it is reasonable to suppose that they

were the territorial adjustments, since another apophthegm quotes an observation to the effect that Philip would make Greece inaccessible to the Lacedaemonians.[105] If the nature of the replies has been correctly stated by Plutarch, they were scarcely likely to appease Philip. Others of the *Apophthegmata* indicate that the requests of Philip were debated and refused, a vote taken for war by the Spartan assembly, and discussions held on the proper military policy, the decision being in favor of fighting in Laconia.[106] Thus, if the *Apophthegmata* may be taken as really indicating the course of events, they show that Philip made an attempt to come to a settlement with the Spartans by negotiation, which was refused. There was, then, nothing wilful in the invasion save in the nature of the demands themselves, which, it seems, were the demands for cession of the border areas. Philip, as we know, did invade Laconia and lay it waste;[107] but he does not seem to have made a serious effort to destroy the state and its institutions. It was sufficient for the moment to weaken the Spartans and give his allies an opportunity to occupy the disputed territory.[108]

Isyllos, however, presents us with another tradition. Philip is said to have invaded Laconia with the purpose of destroying the royal house and the Lycurgan institutions. He failed in this, so that the Spartans, who had invoked the aid of

[104] Archidamus, No. 1 (*Apophth. Lac.* 218 E): Philip wrote a rather stern letter to Archidamus, to which the latter replied impertinently (since Archidamus is reported to have died in Italy on the day on which the battle of Chaeronea was fought, the attribution to him of certain of the *Apophthegmata* is incorrect [see Schaefer, *op. cit.*, III², 44, n. 5]). *Incert.*, No. 28 (*Apophth. Lac.* 233 E): Philip wrote, upon arriving in Laconia, "Whether they wish him to come as friend or foe"; they replied, "Neither." This is couched in the normal language of a request for passage through the territory of another state (cf. Agesilaus, Nos. 42–43 [*Apophth. Lac.* 211 C–D]). *Incert.*, No. 53 (*Apophth. Lac.* 235 A): Philip made a request by letter, to which they replied, "No." Agis, No. 16 (*Apophth. Lac.* 216 A–B): Agis went alone as an envoy to Philip. The anecdote retailed by Stobaeus would fit here (*Flor.* vii. 59): Philip came to Laconia, encamped, and threatened stern measures unless the Spartans carried out his orders; one of the Spartans, hearing the threats, said that he was very glad that nothing prevented warriors from dying (this same story is told by Cicero *Tusc. disp.* v. 14. 42; Frontinus *Strategemata* iv. 5. 12; Valerius Maximus vi. 4. E 4). Another apophthegm may refer to a moment when Philip's requests had been presented but not officially answered—Damindas (*Apophth. Lac.* 219 E): it was observed that the Lacedaemonians would suffer terribly unless they came to terms with Philip (εἰ μὴ τὰς πρὸς αὐτὸν διαλλαγὰς ποιήσονται). Schaefer has arranged these and some of the other *Apophthegmata* in a different order to fit his reconstruction of events (*op. cit.*, III², 44–46). Archidamus, No. 4, and Agis, No. 14, are placed before the battle of Chaeronea; but, as has been noticed, the attendance of the Spartans at the meeting of the *naopoioi* in 338 B.C. seems to indicate that no contention had taken place publicly between them and Philip until after that date. Then, Archidamus, No. 1, and *Incert.*, No. 28, are placed after Chaeronea, but the nature of the demands is not explained by Schaefer. He considers that Philip invaded Laconia and forced the Laconians to ask for peace (there is no evidence of this) but that the terms offered were so harsh that the Spartans preferred death (hence Damindas, *Incert.*, No. 53, and the anecdote of Stobaeus). It is suggested that the terms were that Sparta should enter the League and serve against Persia; but so obdurate was the Spartan attitude that Philip yielded to it and, instead, deprived the Spartans of their border territories by a judicial decision binding on both parties to the dispute.

[105] Agis, No. 14 (*Apophth. Lac.* 216 A).

[106] Archidamus, No. 4 (*Apophth. Lac.* 218 F): in the war against Philip, some advised that battle should be joined far from their homeland, but Archidamus replied that winning was sufficient (the same story is told of Phocion, Plut. *Phocion* 16). Eudamidas, No. 4 (*Apophth. Lac.* 220 E): the citizens chose war against the Macedonians.

[107] Paus. iii. 24. 6, v. 4. 9, vii. 10. 3; Pol. ix. 28. 6–7, 33. 8–12; *Incert.*, No. 53 A (*Apophth. Lac.* 235 A–B); Orosius (iii. 14) linked Thebes and Sparta as suffering the penalties of executions, banishments, and confiscations at the hands of Philip. There is no other evidence of this, so that it is apparently only a perverted condensation.

[108] See appendix.

Asclepius, saw the god's hand in the matter and instituted a festival of Asclepius Soter.[109] The account must represent some Spartan popular tradition, such as Isyllos, a follower of the archaic Doric tradition, would be predisposed to fasten upon. It is another question, however, how truly it represents Philip's intentions. Wilamowitz, following the view that Philip's aim was to establish friendly governments in the Greek states, considered that Sparta was the only stumbling block to such a scheme. Philip tried to carry out his aim but failed because the bitter Spartan resistance would have made it too costly. In reprisal, the land was laid waste, and the Spartans were deprived of their border territory.[110] The requests and the negotiations of the *Apophthegmata* would, then, refer to a demand by Philip that the Spartans depose their king and reform their political institutions. It seems a better explanation, however, that the devastation of their land and the loss of territory would, in the Spartan mind, be confounded with a blow at the very existence of their state. Isocrates' *Archidamus* reveals how the Spartans had identified the loss of Messene in 369 B.C. with the feeling that their traditional prestige and way of life were lost;[111] the adjustment of Philip was but a corollary to the policy of Epaminondas. Further, an attack on the hoary traditions of Sparta would make a much better literary theme[112] than would a boundary adjustment. Therefore, no

precise significance need be attached to Isyllos' words. If the question is considered in the light of Philip's other settlements, there seems no reason to believe that he envisaged the destruction of the Spartan institutions.[113] He would, of course, desire friendly governments; but only in the case of Thebes is there evidence that Philip interfered personally to insure that result. Elsewhere the reversals seem to have taken place by the spontaneous action of his partisans. Thus the restored exiles and his own followers held magistracies and conducted internal purges. Similarly, where political and territorial changes had been deemed necessary, Philip had sought to give them as valid a legal sanction as possible. The Amphictyonic Council had been used to restore Phocis and grant Nicaea to Locris; the territorial transfers of Naupactus to Aetolia and of Oropus to Athens were made from enemy states which he had defeated.

Sparta, however, was not one of the enemy states opposed to Philip at Chaeronea; nor were Argos, Arcadia, and Messene among the allies who had aided him there. Since the procedure used in the other cases would not apply, a new one was devised. The changes which Philip had made *de facto* were made *de iure* by an arbitration process of the League after it was established, and the title of Philip's

---

[109] *IG*, IV, 950. 57–79; Wilamowitz, *op. cit.*, pp. 24, 31–35.

[110] Wilamowitz, *op. cit.*, pp. 31–35.

[111] Roebuck, *op. cit.*, p. 44. Some notion of the Spartan reaction to the loss of their territory in 338/7 B.C. may be seen in *Apophth. Lac.* 192 B: when Antiochus, serving as ephor, heard that Philip had given the land to the Messenians, he asked whether he had also given them the military power to hold it. In the *Archidamus* see, in particular, secs. 8, 12, 16, 21, 25, 48, 89, 98, and 110.

[112] Isyllos thought of states in such terms—see his poem A.

[113] Beloch (*op. cit.*, III, 1, 574, n. 3) interprets Isyllos in a general sense only, arguing that Philip's policy was to preserve existing governments as a principle in founding the League of Corinth. That was true after the League had been founded and has some justification in the cases of Athens and the Achaean League. In many states, however, there is evidence of a change in the personnel of the government to Philip's own partisans and, since it is well known that they were wealthy oligarchs, presumably in most cases a change from democracy to oligarchy. Beloch (*ibid.*, pp. 574–75) also suggests that Sparta was not destroyed in order that its neighbors should be kept dependent on Macedonia. That, too, would be only partially true, for, in the Peloponnesus, as in central Greece, the result of Philip's changes was to establish a balance of power among small, weak states.

allies to the territories was confirmed. Philip's wishes would be known to the arbitrators and hardly disregarded. It is scarcely an objection that Sparta was not a member of the League. If the Spartans refused to sign a treaty relinquishing the territory, the only course left was to take it from them by force and then to give the transaction a legal basis through the League of Corinth.[114] After the revolt of Agis, too, when Sparta was not a member of the League, the settlement was turned over to the *synedrion* by Antipater. This reconstruction of the settlement also accounts for the divergent tradition in our sources. The anti-Macedonian tradition, put forward by Sparta when the issue was raised on later occasions, as before Tiberius, represented it as a personal, violent act of Philip, which it was *de facto*.[115] The pro-Macedonian tradition represented it as a legal settlement of the respective claims of the contestants, made by the League, which it was *de iure*.[116] Tiberius, incidentally, decided the claim in favor of Messene.

If our reconstruction of this adjustment is correct, Philip then attempted to give it as valid a legal sanction as he was able, while still putting his policy, conceived in 344 B.C., into effect. The result was similar to that achieved in central Greece—a balance of power among small, weak states, with the potentially dangerous one held in check by the obligations of the others to Philip.

CONCLUSIONS

What answers may be made, from this examination of the settlements and the circumstances surrounding them, to the questions raised in the introduction? In the first place, it is to be noted that Philip

made formal treaties of settlement with the members of the anti-Macedonian coalition. It is stated only in the case of Athens that an alliance was also made; but, as has been noticed, the known terms of the treaty do not seem to indicate this. Philip apparently planned to insure alliances with both former friends and enemies by the organization of the League of Corinth as a symmachy, which would place all the Greek states on a similar footing. Then there is no hint in the treaty terms, so far as they are known, that changes of government, either in personnel or in form, were arranged by them. It is likely that, when such changes occurred, they would, as in the case of Troezen, be spontaneous acts of Philip's partisans on receipt of the news of his victory. In some states, as in Athens and the Achaean League, there seems to have been no change. The treaties were made, then, in some cases with previously anti-Macedonian governments, which, as in the case of Achaea, later led to trouble. There seems to be no reason to connect territorial changes with action by the League, save in the important and exceptional case of Sparta. The separate treaties or, as in the case of Nicaea, the Amphictyonic Council would have arranged the revisions.

The more general problem of whether Philip used the settlements to correct some of the political ills of Greece must be taken into account with his policy before Chaeronea and with the purpose of the new league. It is apparent that the settlements put the crowning touch on a policy which had been formulated well in advance of the opportunity to make them. Philip had endeavored to seize Ambracia in 342 B.C. and had supported the anti-Spartan bloc in the Peloponnesus in 344 B.C. Evidence appears, however, of a reasoned solution for the key problems of the various areas of Greece. The former

114 See appendix.
115 Pol. ix. 28. 7; Tac. *Ann.* iv. 43. 1.
116 Pol. ix. 33. 11–12; Tac. *op. cit.* iv. 43. 3.

90   CARL ROEBUCK

systems of political control were destroyed—those of Thebes in central Greece, of Athens in the Aegean, of Sparta in the Peloponnesus. To replace them Philip initiated a subtle balance by building up the power of the weaker states, but none unduly. In central Greece, Phocis was restored and the influence of the Amphictyonic Council increased; in the Aegean, some of the islands were freed, some left under Athenian control; in the Peloponnesus, Argos, Arcadia, and Messene were strengthened. Thus better balances of power were set up which were not entirely sterile. They did not prevent the revolt of Thebes in 335 B.C. or the war of Agis of Sparta in 331 B.C., but they may have done something to prevent them from spreading. To create this balance, certain changes had been necessary; but Philip had been adept in finding traditional precedents for them and had sought to give them as much validity as possible by the use of treaty forms, decrees of the Amphictyonic Council, and the arbitration of the new league.[117] Philip may be more justly criticized for displaying his military control in the garrisons of Ambracia, Thebes, Corinth, and probably Chalcis. These had, however, all been enemy states, and such a precaution should not appear unreasonable for the initial stages of a new order.[118] Certainly, the Greeks could not complain that it was an innovation.

Philip planned that all the sovereign political organizations of Greece were to be members of the League of Corinth. The settlements show a disposition to favor federal organizations. Of the hostile states, the Achaean, Boeotian, and Euboean leagues were apparently allowed to survive. Among his allies, Philip had mended the rift in the Arcadian League, restored the Phocian League, and added Naupactus to Aetolia and Nicaea to Locris. While this may in part be ascribed to the practical convenience of dealing with relatively few large units rather than a host of separate cities,[119] Philip must also have hoped for a solution of political difficulties in general by federations, as, of course, his own scheme of a panhellenic league and the measures taken to form artificial combinations of states for the purpose of representation in it would indicate.

These various political remedies were not, it may be supposed, entirely altruistic. They were designed to organize Greece in Philip's interest as a quiet and co-operative ally, which would enable him to turn his attention to the projected war against Persia. But his conquest was not essentially military, and he attempted to deal with the psychological problems which arose. Care was taken to avoid personal antagonism, for only in Thebes did Philip interfere personally as a military victor in the political organization of the city. Elsewhere his partisans made the changes. Naturally, Philip allowed such reversals of government, but he may have hoped that the bitterness following upon them would be directed primarily upon their fellow-citizens by the sufferers. The League, of course, attempted to insure that no counterrevolution would take place. It was not a healthy state of affairs, but Philip tried not to leave time for antagonism and resentment to grow. As

[117] Wüst (op. cit., p. 174) has emphasized the view that Philip's territorial changes were designed to restore the "Old Order" in Greece as it was before Thebes, Athens, and Sparta had enlarged their territory at the expense of their neighbors. Emphasis on the "Old Order" was, of course, a part of his propaganda but scarcely a serious political aim. It was designed to facilitate the imposition of the Macedonian hegemony.

[118] See above, n. 44.

[119] This is not to suggest that the separate settlements arranged the political units which were to be represented in the League. Various combinations based on military strength were made for that purpose (for a recent study see Raue, op. cit., pp. 43–66).

[216]

soon.as possible, he turned the attention of the Greeks to the formation of the League and to the war on Persia, rumors of which were set in motion very soon after Chaeronea.[120] Philip failed in this reorientation of Greek political thought, as the events after his death showed. The failure was not caused merely by lack of time for his policies to work themselves out but by the inability of Greek political thought to reconcile local "nationalism" with a true national unity.

APPENDIX

THE ARBITRATION OF THE CORINTHIAN LEAGUE FOR ARCADIA, ARGOS, MESSENE, AND SPARTA

Dr. Treves has observed (op. cit., pp. 105–6) in the course of his criticism of the view of the Spartan settlement which I had previously sketched (op. cit., pp. 53–57): "At the utmost, all that one can surmise is that the territories which Sparta was compelled to surrender in the autumn of 338 B.C. were then merely 'occupied' by hostile troops, and that the annexation took place, legally and formally, only after the work of the League began." This is, I think, substantially correct, except for the term "annexation" and the view of the League's activity which it implies, stated elsewhere as a "task of demarcation and guarantee" and a legalization of the status quo. His criticism is based primarily on the objection to accepting Polybius' tradition, favorable to Philip, as evidence for the period of Chaeronea. One should perhaps distinguish between Polybius' judgment (v. 10. 1; xviii. 14—his own views; ix. 33 —the view put in Lyciscus' mouth) and the factual content of the material. The judgment on Philip is favorable, but the factual basis should be either disproved or established independently. Treves considers that Pol. ix. 33. 11–12 means that "the Spartans agreed, though under compulsion, to become a party to the agreement and to submit their disputes with their neighbors to the arbitration of the

League." It is objected that this procedure can scarcely be correct, for Sparta did not adhere to the symmachy until forced to do so after its defeat at Megalopolis in 331 B.C., and that the Spartans were not therefore bound by its decisions; also, that Justin (ix. 5. 1–3) states that the representatives of the member-states of the League were summoned to the constituent meeting, only after the territorial claims had been settled by the king to their satisfaction. First of all, is there any evidence besides that of Polybius for a settlement through arbitration? An inscription (Ditt., Syll.[3], No. 665. 19–20) refers to a settlement by judicial procedure ([κ]ρ[ί] σεις). The literary tradition, too, has preserved a somewhat confused record of a settlement by judicial process. Strabo mentions a Messenian-Lacedaemonian dispute in the time of Philip (viii. 4. 6), while Tacitus refers to it as decided ex vero by Philip (op. cit. iv. 43. 3). Pausanias records that Philip acted as arbitrator between the Argives and the Lacedaemonians (vii. 11. 2). In the case of the Arcadian-Lacedaemonian dispute, Livy has a reference to its settlement by an old decree of the "Achaeans" (xxxviii. 34. 8; is "Achaeans" written by mistake for "Hellenes," since the Achaeans are mentioned so frequently in this chapter?). Thus, this evidence taken as a whole would seem to amplify and confirm that of Polybius for an arbitrated settlement by the League. As we have noticed, Treves states that the League's activity was one of demarcation and legalization of the status quo (the state resulting from the forcible occupation of the territories); but Polybius' evidence is readmitted so far as to be interpreted that the demarcation and the guaranty are alluded to by κριτήριον (ix. 33. 12); so, too, the [κ]ρ[ί]σεις of the inscription. Polybius, however, uses κριτήριον as object of καθίσας; κριτήριον might, in itself, be used to mean a "judgment"; but, when used with καθίσας, it can scarcely mean anything else than "tribunal" (see Liddell-Scott-Jones, Greek Lexicon, κριτήριον, 2). Thus Polybius' phrase will mean "setting up a tribunal," not "making a decision." What, then, was the function of this tribunal—demarcation and ratification of a boundary already established or determination of the ownership of the terri-

[120] According to Wilcken, Philip began to circulate rumors of a Persian war shortly after the separate peace with Athens (Sitzungsber. München, 1917, p. 13).

tory? Treves has pointed out that Aristotle drew, at Philip's request, the *dikaiomata* of the Greek states to this end of demarcation and guaranty of boundary lines. A fragment (No. 276) from the Marcian *Vita* of Aristotle indicates the purpose of the *dikaiomata: καὶ τὰ γεγραμμένα αὐτῷ δικαιώματα Ἑλληνίδων πόλεων ἐξ ὧν Φίλιππος τὰς φιλονεικίας τῶν Ἑλλήνων διέλυσεν, ὡς μεγαλυρρημον⟨ήσαντά π⟩οτε καὶ εἰπεῖν· ὥρισα γῆν Πέλοπος.* Thus they are specifically connected with the Peloponnesian adjustments. One of the surviving fragments, however (No. 571, *Opera Aristotelis*, ed. Acad. Boruss., V, 1572) refers to the expedition of Alexander of Epirus to aid the Tarentines, which was made *ca.* 333 B.C. (Hackforth, *CAH*, VI, 300–301). Schaefer has suggested (*op. cit.*, III², 55, n. 1) that the *dikaiomata* were not published (according to Diog. Laert. v. 26, in one book) until the time of Alexander and were designed to counteract the rising tide of discontent against the settlements made by Philip. Nissen (*op. cit.*, pp. 168–71) resolved the difficulty by assuming that the *dikaiomata* were compiled for Philip's use but not published until later, and then in an expanded form to include "Rectifications" for the western Greek states. There is, then, some difficulty in accepting the statement in the *Vita* literally. In any case it throws no light on the action of the League but tells us only that Philip's adjustments, or his opinions on them, were based on Aristotle's researches. The procedure by which Philip made them is not mentioned. Should we not, then, accept the evidence of Polybius literally—that a tribunal was set up under the auspices of the League to act in this case and, as the evidence for *judicial* action indicates, that it decided *ownership* in favor of Philip's allies? If the League was founded to preserve the peace of Greece and organized as a symmachy, its guaranty of the decision would be automatic. Further, the scope of its activity would extend to nonmembers, should the latter menace that peace; for, after the war of Agis in 331 B.C., Antipater referred the settlement to the *synedrion* of the League (Diod.

xvii. 73. 5; Q. Curtius vi. 1. 19). Sparta may have gone so far as not to send a representative to defend its case before the tribunal; but would that prevent a decision's being taken? That Sparta would not consider itself bound by the decision goes without saying. It had never recognized the establishment of Messene and had withdrawn from the peace conference of 362 B.C. on that account (Roebuck, *op. cit.*, p. 46). So far as the objection raised on the evidence of Justin is concerned, I think Treves has suggested the correct solution: the territories were occupied before the first meeting of the League, so that the question was settled *de facto.* Justin would scarcely notice the arbitration which confirmed it *de iure*, in such a condensed account as he gives. This distinction between the ratification of an occupation and a determination of ownership by the League might seem to be trivial. So far as the practical result was concerned, it made no difference; but the procedure was important. It was in accordance with Philip's usual gilding of the bitter pill, as, for example, in his use of the Amphictyonic Council both in 346 and in 338 B.C.; and it would establish a precedent for what, in the course of time, might prove to be an equitable method of procedure in territorial disputes. The League did make use of such procedure by arbitration in the subsequent case between Cimolus and Melos, which was referred to Argos (Ditt., *Syll.*³, No. 261; Larsen, *CP*, XXI [1926], 55). The case of Sparta was of more importance and thus needed a larger tribunal picked from the League members; possibly the *synedrion* acted as a committee for the purpose. Other territorial adjustments were, of course, made after Chaeronea, but, as we have noticed, they were a part of the separate treaties made with enemy states or handled through the Amphictyonic Council. Accordingly, there seems to be no reason to suppose that territorial adjustments were a regular part of the League's work at the time of its foundation.

DALHOUSIE UNIVERSITY
HALIFAX, CANADA

Select Bibliography

1 HISTORY OF MACEDON TO THE ACCESSION OF PHILIP II

S. Casson, *Macedonia, Thrace and Illyria*, Oxford, 1906.
F. Geyer, 'Makedonien bis zur Thronbesteigung Philipps II' (*Historische Zeitschrift*, Beiheft 19), München und Berlin, 1930.
C. F. Edson, 'Early Macedonia', in B. Laourdas, Ch. Makaronas ed., *Ancient Macedonia*, Institute for Balkan Studies, Thessaloniki, 1970, 17–44.
R. Paribeni, *La Macedonia sino ad Alessandro Magno*, Milano, 1947.
J. N. Kalléris, *Les anciens Macédoniens, Athènes*, 1954.
D. Raymond, *Macedonian Regal Coinage to 413 B.C.* (Numismatic Notes and Monographs, no. 126), New York, 1953.
P. Cloché, *Histoire de la Macédoine jusqu'à l'avènement d'Alexandre le Grand*, Paris, 1960.
A. Dascalis, *The Hellenism of the Ancient Macedonians*, Thessalonike, 1965.
A. Toynbee, 'What was the ancestral language of the Makedones?', *Some problems of Greek history*, Oxford, 1969, 64–79.
A. Rosenberg, 'Amyntas, der Vater Philipps', *Hermes* 51 (1916) 499–509.
J. Kaerst, *Geschichte des Hellenismus*[3], i, Leipzig, 1927.

2 MACEDONIAN CONSTITUTION

F. Granier, 'Die makedonische Heeresversammlung', *Münchener Beiträge zur Papyrusforschung und antiken Rechtsgeschichte*, Heft 13, München, 1931.
V. Costanzi, 'Sulla costituzione macedonica', *Athenaeum* 8 (1930) 157–67.
F. Hampl, 'Der König der Makedonen', Diss. Weida in Thür., 1934.
A. Momigliano, 'Re e popolo in Macedonia prima di Alessandro', *Athenaeum*, 13 (1935) 3–21.
A. Aymard, '*ΒΑΣΙΛΕΥΣ ΜΑΚΕΔΟΝΩΝ*', *Études d'histoire ancienne*, Paris, 1967, 100–22.
A. Aymard, 'Sur l'Assemblée Macédonienne', *Études d'histoire ancienne*, Paris, 1967, 143–63.

3 INTERNATIONAL RELATIONS; KOINE EIRENE

P. Cloché, *La politique étrangère d'Athènes de 404 à 338 avant Jésus-Christ*, Paris, 1934.
A. Momigliano, 'La κοινὴ εἰρήνη dal 386 al 338 A.C.', *Rivista di filologia e di istruzione classica* n.s. 12 (1934) 482–514 (= *Terzo contributo alla storia degli studi classici e del mondo antico*, tomo primo, Roma, 1966, 393–419).
F. Hampl, *Die griechischen Staatsverträge des vierten Jahrhunderts v. Chr.*, Leipzig, 1938.
I. Calabi, *Ricerche sui rapporti fra le poleis*, Firenze, 1953.

4 PHILIP II

R. Schubert, *Untersuchungen über die Quellen zur Geschichte Philipps II von Makedonien*, Königsberg, 1904.
E. Pokorny, 'Studien zur griechischen Geschichte im sechsten und fünften Jahrzehnt des vierten Jahrhunderts v. Chr.', Diss. Greifswald, 1913.
A. Momigliano, *Filippo il Macedone*, Firenze, 1934.

SELECT BIBLIOGRAPHY

F. R. Wüst, *Philipp II von Makedonien und Griechenland in den Jahren 346 bis 338* (Münchener historische Abhandlungen, erste Reihe, Heft 14), München, 1938.

V. Chapot, *Philippe II de Macédoine*, Paris, 1936.

F. Carrata, *Cultura greca e unità Macedone nella politica di Filippo II* (Pubblicazioni della Facoltà di lettere e filosofia, Università di Torino, vol. 1, fasc. III, 1949).

P. Cloché, *Un fondateur d'empire, Philippe II, roi de Macédoine*, Paris, 1955.

5 ISOCRATES

G. Mathieu, *Les idées politiques d'Isocrate*, Paris, 1925.

E. Mikkola, *Isokrates, seine Anschauungen im Lichte seiner Schriften*, Helsinki, 1954.

M. A. Levi, *Isocrate, saggio critico*, Milano, 1959.

P. Cloché, *Isocrate et son temps*, Paris, 1963.

K. Bringmann, 'Studien zu den politischen Ideen des Isokrates' (*Hypomnemata*, Heft 14), Göttingen, 1965.

E. Meyer, 'Isokrates' zweiter Brief und Demosthenes' zweite Philippika', *Sitzungsberichte der Preussischen Akademie der Wissenschaften* 31 (1909) 758–79.

P. Wendland, 'Beiträge zu athenischer Politik und Publizistik des vierten Jahrhunderts' (I. 'König Philippos und Isokrates'; II. 'Isokrates und Demosthenes)', *Nachrichten von der Königlichen Gesellschaft der Wissenschaften zu Göttingen, philologisch-historische Klasse*, 1910, 123–82, 282–323.

E. Bickermann and J. Sykutris, *Speusipps Brief an König Philipp* (Berichte über die Verhandlungen der Sächsischen Akademie der Wissenschaften zu Leipzig, philologisch-historische Klasse, 80 (1928) Heft 3.

F. Taeger, 'Isokrates und die Anfänge des hellenistischen Herrscherkultes', *Hermes* 72 (1937) 355–60.

J. de Romilly, 'Eunoia in Isocrates', *Journal of Hellenic Studies* 78 (1958) 92–101.

E. Buchner, *Der Panegyrikos des Isokrates* (*Historia*, Einzelschriften 2, 1958).

S. Perlman, 'Isokrates' Advice on Philip's Attitude towards Barbarians (V, 154)', *Historia* 16 (1967) 338–43.

G. Dobesch, *Der panhellenische Gedanke im Jh. v. Chr. und der 'Philippos' des Isoburates*, Wein, 1968.

H. Kelsen, 'The Philosophy of Aristotle and the Hellenic Macedonian Policy', *International Journal of Ethics* 48 (1937), 1–64.

6 DEMOSTHENES. THE END OF ATHENIAN DEMOCRACY

A. Schäfer, *Demosthenes und seine Zeit*, Leipzig, 1885 (reprint 1966).

E. Drerup, *Aus einer Advokatenrepublik* (Demosthenes und seine Zeit) (Studien zur Geschichte und Kultur des Altertums, 8/3–4), Parderborn, 1916 (reprint 1967).

A. Momigliano, 'Contributi alla caratteristica di Demostene', *Civiltà Moderna*, 3 (1931) 711–44.

G. Mathieu, *Démosthène, l'homme et l'œuvre*, Paris, 1948.

SELECT BIBLIOGRAPHY

A. W. Pickard-Cambridge, *Demosthenes and the Last Days of Greek Freedom*, London, 1914.
P. Treves, *Demostene e la liberta greca*, Bari, 1933.
P. Cloché, *Démosthène et la fin de la démocratie athénienne*, Paris, 1957.
J. Luccioni, *Démosthène et le Panhellenisme*, Paris, 1961.
C. Mosse, *La fin de la démocratie athénienne*, Paris, 1962.
A. H. M. Jones, *The Athens of Demosthenes*, Cambridge, 1952 (= *Athenian Democracy*, Oxford, 1957, 23–38).
M. I. Finley, 'Athenian Demagogues', *Past and Present* 21 (1962) 3–24.
S. Perlman, 'Political Leadership in Athens in the Fourth Century B.C.', *La Parola del Passato*, 114 (1967) 161–76.
L. Pearson, 'The Development of Demosthenes as a Political Orator', *Phoenix*, 18 (1964) 95–109.
H. J. Wolff, *Demosthenes als Advokat*, Berlin, 1968.

7 THE FIRST YEARS OF THE REIGN OF PHILIP II. THE BEGINNING OF THE THIRD SACRED WAR

A. Aymard, 'Philippe de Macédoine otage à Thebes', *Revue des études anciennes* 56 (1954) 15–36.
J. R. Ellis, 'The security of the Macedonian throne under Philip II', in B. Laourdas, Ch. Makaronas ed., *Ancient Macedonia*, Institute for Balkan Studies, Thessaloniki, 1970, 68–75.
P. Cloché, 'Philippe, roi de Macédoine, de 359 à 351 avant J.-C.', *Les études classiques* 18 (1950) 385–416; 19 (1951) 17–46.
P. Cloché, 'Athènes et Kersobleptes de 357/6 à 353/2', *Mélanges G. Glotz* I, Paris, 1932, 216–26.
A. B. West, 'The Early Diplomacy of Philip II of Macedon Illustrated by His Coins', *Numismatic Chronicle*, 5th series, 3 (1923) 169–210.
P. Cloché, 'La traité Athéno-Thrace de 357', *Revue de philologie* 46 (1922) 1–13.
D. M. Robinson, 'Inscriptions from Olynthus 1934: 1. Treaty between Philip and the Chalcidians, 356 B.C.', *Transactions of the American Philological Association* 65 (1934) 103–22.
P. Cloché, *Étude chronologique sur la troisième guerre sacrée*, Paris, 1915.
N. G. L. Hammond, 'Diodorus' Narrative of the Sacred War and Chronological Problems of 357–352 B.C.', *Journal of Hellenic Studies* 57 (1937) 44–78.
M. Sordi, 'La terza guerra sacra', *Rivista di filologia e di istruzione classica* 86 (1958) 134–66.

8 THE SOCIAL WAR. THE PEACE OF PHILOCRATES. PHILIP AND GREECE TO THE BATTLE OF CHAERONEA

G. L. Cawkwell, 'Notes on the Social War', *Classica et Mediaevalia* 23 (1962) 34–49.
G. L. Cawkwell, 'Eubulus', *Journal of Hellenic Studies* 83 (1963) 47–67.
R. Sealey, 'Athens after the Social War', *Journal of Hellenic Studies* 75 (1955) 74–81 (= *Essays in Greek Politics*, New York, 1968, 164–82).

SELECT BIBLIOGRAPHY

P. Cloché, 'La politique de Démosthène de 354 à 346 av. J.-C.', *Bulletin de correspondance hellénique* 47 (1923) 97–162.

H. W. Parke, 'Athens and Euboea 349–348 B.C.', *Journal of Hellenic Studies* 49 (1929) 246–52.

G. L. Cawkwell, 'Aeschines and the Ruin of Phocis in 346', *Revue des études grecques* 75 (1962) 453–59.

F. Hampl, 'Zur angeblichen κοινὴ εἰρήνη des Jahres 346 und zum philokrateischen Frieden', *Klio* 31 (1938) 371–88.

R. Sealey, 'Proxenos and the Peace of Philocrates', *Wiener Studien* 68 (1955) 371–88.

P. Cloché, 'La Grèce de 346 à 339 av. J.-C.', *Bulletin de correspondance hellénique* 44 (1920) 108–59.

P. A. Brunt, 'Euboea in the Time of Philip II', *Classical Quarterly* 19 (1969) 245–65.

G. Glotz, 'Démosthène et les finances athéniennes de 343 à 339', *Revue historique* 170 (1932) 385–97.

G. L. Cawkwell, 'Demosthenes and the Stratiotic Fund', *Mnemosyne*, ser. 4, 15 (1962) 377–83.

G. Glotz, 'Philippe et la surprise d'Élatée', *Bulletin de correspondance hellénique* 33 (1909) 526–46.

9   THE LEAGUE OF CORINTH

U. Wilcken, *Beiträge zur Geschichte des korinthischen Bundes* (Sitzungsberichte der Königlich Bayerischen Akademie der Wissenschaften, philosophisch-philologische Klasse, 10, 1917).

W. Schwahn, 'Zu I G II 160 (Philipps Landfriede)', *Rheinisches Museum* 78 (1929) 188–98.

W. Schwahn, 'Heeresmatrikel und Landfriede Philipps von Makedonien' (*Klio*, Beiheft 21, 1930).

E. Schehl, 'Zum korinthischen Bunde vom Jahre 338/7 v. Chr.', *Jahreshefte des österreichischen archäologischen Institutes* 27 (1932) 115–45.

H. Raue, 'Untersuchungen zur Geschichte des korinthischen Bundes', Diss. Marburg, 1937.

I. Calabi, 'Il sinedrio della Lega di Corinto e le sue attribuzioni giuris-dizionali', *Rivista di filologia e di istruzione classica* 78 (1950) 63–9.

K. Dienelt, 'Der korinthische Bund', *Jahreshefte des österreichischen archäologischen Institutes* 43 (1958) 247–74.

10   THE MURDER OF PHILIP

H. Willrich, 'Wer liess König Philipp von Makedonien ermorden?' *Hermes* 34 (1899) 174–82.

E. Badian, 'The Death of Philip II', *Phoenix* 17 (1963) 244–50.

J. R. Ellis, 'Amyntas Perdikka, Philip II and Alexander the Great', *Journal of Hellenic Studies*, 91 (1971) 15–24.

[222]